# The Atlantic in Global History

# The Atlantic in Global History

## 1500–2000

*Edited by*

## Jorge Cañizares-Esguerra

*and*

## Erik R. Seeman

PEARSON

Prentice
Hall

Upper Saddle River, New Jersey 07458

Library of Congress Cataloging-in-Publication Data

The Atlantic in global history, 1500–2000/eds., Jorge Cañizares-Esguerra and Erik R. Seeman.
   p. cm.
  Includes bibliographical references and index.
  ISBN-13: 978-0-13-192714-8
  ISBN-10: 0-13-192714-0
  1. History, Modern. 2. Atlantic Ocean. I. Cañizares-Esguerra, Jorge. II. Seeman, Erik R.
  D208.A76 2006
  909'.09821—dc22

2006005784

**Executive Editor:** *Charles Cavaliere*
**Editorial Director:** *Charles Jones Owen*
**Editorial Assistant:** *Maria Guarascio*
**Marketing Manager:** *Emily Cleary*
**Marketing Assistant:** *Jennifer Lang*
**Managing Editor:** *Joanne Riker*
**Production Liaison:** *Fran Russello*
**Manufacturing Buyer:** *Ben Smith*
**Cover Design:** *Bruce Kenselaar*
**Cover Illustration/Photo:** *Courtesy Library of Congress*
**Photo Researcher:** *Elaine Soares*
**Image Permission Coordinator:** *Robert Farrell*
**Composition/Full-Service Project Management:** *Karpagam Jagadeesan/GGS Book Services*
**Printer/Binder:** *RR Donnelley & Sons Company*

Credits and acknowledgments borrowed from other sources and reproduced, with permission, in this book appear on appropriate page within text.

---

"Empires in Their Global Context, ca. 1500–1800" © 2007 by Felipe Fernández-Armesto.

Pearson Education LTD., London
Pearson Education Singapore, Pte. Ltd
Pearson Education, Canada, Ltd
Pearson Education–Japan
Pearson Education Australia PTY, Limited

Pearson Education North Asia Ltd
Pearson Educación de Mexico, S.A. de C.V.
Pearson Education Malaysia, Pte. Ltd
Pearson Education, Upper Saddle River, New Jersey

10 9 8 7 6 5 4 3 2 1
ISBN 0-13-192714-0

# CONTENTS

## Part I  Comparing Atlantics                                                    *1*

## Part II  Beyond the Atlantic                                                   *91*

## Part III  The Evolving Atlantic                                                *177*

# LIST OF FIGURES

# LIST OF MAPS

*All maps use today's national boundaries for orientation purposes. Maps drawn by Bill Jurgelski.*

# PREFACE

This volume emerges from "Beyond the Line: The North and South Atlantics and Global History, 1500–2000," a conference hosted by the State University of New York at Buffalo in October 2004. We organized this event to mark the creation of a new Ph.D. field in SUNY-Buffalo's Department of History, a field in North and South Atlantic history. Along with several of our colleagues, we had inaugurated a field that went beyond the Atlantic paradigm that currently dominates the English-speaking academy, in which the early modern North Atlantic is the focus. We had created a program that reflects our interests in the South Atlantic, the modern Atlantic, and even areas beyond the Atlantic.

All this crossing of intellectual boundaries hints at why we chose the title "Beyond the Line" for the conference. The original meaning of the phrase, at least regarding the Atlantic, goes back to sixteenth-century international relations. In 1559, French and Spanish diplomats worked out a policy whereby they could remain allies even as they fought over possessions in the Caribbean. A person who sailed beyond the "line of amity," west of the mid-Atlantic and south of the Tropic of Cancer, was on his own, outside the territorial limits of European treaties. Conflicts "beyond the line" would not endanger peace in Europe.

In time, this legal usage came to have more broadly metaphorical meanings. To sail "beyond the line" to the Caribbean meant, according to Richard S. Dunn, "a general flouting of European social conventions."[1] The conference didn't flout any social conventions, but it did flout some intellectual ones: the conventional boundaries that have been drawn between nation-based Atlantics like the French Atlantic and Spanish Atlantic, between the modern and early modern, between North and South, and between the Atlantic and other regions of the globe.

But we also consider the "Atlantic" to be a concept to interrogate rather than as a given or natural unit of analysis. Again, a history of the word is useful. We have reproduced a 1562 map of what today would be called "The Atlantic" (fig. 1). Yet the cartographer conformed to standard sixteenth-century usage and divided this body of water into three parts: he referred to the North Atlantic as "Oceanus Septentrionalis," the Equatorial Atlantic as "Oceanus Occidentalis," and the South Atlantic as "Oceanus Australis." Likewise, in the seventeenth and eighteenth centuries, the concept of a single Atlantic remained far in the future: mapmakers usually called the North Atlantic the Mar del Norte (the Northern Sea) and the South Atlantic the Ethiopian Ocean. It was not until the nineteenth century that the expanse of water between the Americas and Europe and Africa came to be known by the single term: "The Atlantic Ocean."

This is why geographers assert that the modern concept of the Atlantic Ocean is no more natural or "correct" than earlier naming systems.[2] To get a sense of whether the Atlantic is a natural category, try to answer these questions: What are its northern and southern boundaries? Where does the Atlantic end?

Thus, another goal of this collection is to draw attention to the constructedness of the Atlantic as a unit of analysis. Some of the authors in this volume find the Atlantic to be a

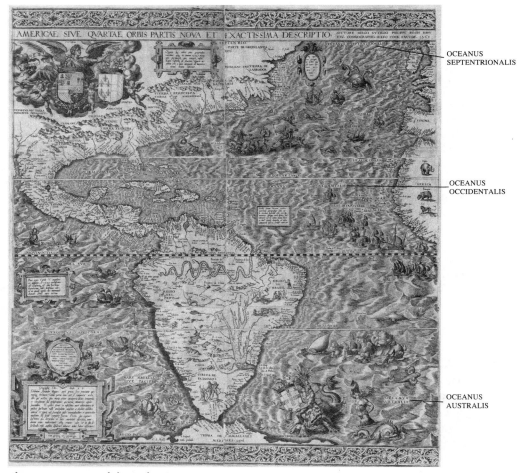

OCEANUS
SEPTENTRIONALIS

OCEANUS
OCCIDENTALIS

OCEANUS
AUSTRALIS

**Figure 1**  Map of the Atlantic, 1562

valuable unit of analysis for the questions they are trying to answer. Others, especially the authors in part II, "Beyond the Atlantic," see the Atlantic as a partial or limiting unit of analysis. But all of us are united in interrogating the concept and working to understand its strengths and limitations.

For helping us in this endeavor, our first thanks must be to the authors of the chapters in this volume. It is no coincidence that the best work in Atlantic and global studies is in the form of collections of essays; intellectual tasks this ambitious must be collective efforts. We are grateful for the skill and expertise of our collaborators. Moreover, this volume represents a collaboration between ourselves and our students. We sincerely thank the graduate students in SUNY-Buffalo's "North and South Atlantic Core," fall 2004, who read a draft of this volume and offered valuable suggestions about how to improve it for use in the classroom. In addition, we are grateful to the commentators at the conference who helped bring our themes into clearer focus: Michael Frisch,

Michael Jarvis, and Carl Nightingale. And we must thank those outside evaluators of our book proposal and draft manuscript whose comments helped improve the collection: Thomas Bender, New York University; Troy Bickham, Texas A&M University; Ignacio Gallup-Diaz, Bryn Mawr College; Eliga Gould, University of New Hampshire; Michael Guasco, Davidson College; Rebecca Hartkopf Schloss, Texas A&M University; Adam McKeown, Columbia University; Matthew Restall, Pennsylvania State University; and James H. Williams, Middle Tennessee State University.

We wish to thank those whose financial assistance helped make the conference a reality. At SUNY-Buffalo, this includes the Center for the Americas, Dennis Tedlock's McNulty Chair in the Department of English, the Canadian-American Studies Committee, the College of Arts and Sciences, and especially the Department of History and its chair, Tamara Thornton. Prentice Hall and our editor Charles Cavaliere also deserve thanks for providing generous support. Finally, we gratefully acknowledge the grant we received from the Publication Subvention Fund of SUNY-Buffalo's College of Arts and Sciences.

## Notes

1  Richard S. Dunn, *Sugar and Slaves: The Rise of the Planter Class in the English West Indies, 1624–1713* (Chapel Hill, N.C., 1972), 12.
2  Martin W. Lewis, "Dividing the Ocean Sea," *Geographical Review* 89 (April 1999): 188–214.

# CONTRIBUTORS

**Jorge Cañizares-Esguerra** is Professor of History at the University of Texas at Austin. He is the author of the prize-winning *How to Write the History of the New World: History, Epistemology, and Identities in the Eighteenth-Century Atlantic World* (2001) and has two forthcoming books: *Puritan Conquistadors: Iberianizing the Atlantic, 1550–1700* and *Nature, Empire, and Nation: Explorations of the History of Science in the Iberian World.*

**Erik R. Seeman** is Associate Professor of History at the State University of New York at Buffalo and is the author of *Pious Persuasions: Laity and Clergy in Eighteenth-Century New England* (1999) and "Reading Indians' Deathbed Scenes: Ethnohistorical and Representational Approaches" (*Journal of American History*, 2001). He has received National Endowment for the Humanities and Fulbright fellowships to work on his current project, "Final Frontiers: Cross-Cultural Encounters with Death in the New World."

**Thomas Bender** is University Professor of the Humanities and Professor of History at New York University. He is the author and editor of numerous books, including *Community and Social Change in America* (1978), *New York Intellect: A History of Intellectual Life in New York City, from 1750 to the Beginnings of Our Own Time* (1987), *Intellect and Public Life: Essays on the Social History of Academic Intellectuals in the United States* (1993), and *Rethinking American History in a Global Age* (2002).

**Peter A. Coclanis** is Albert R. Newsome Professor of History and Associate Provost for International Affairs at the University of North Carolina at Chapel Hill. He is the author of *The Shadow of a Dream: Economic Life and Death in the South Carolina Low Country, 1670–1920* (1989), which won the Allan Nevins Prize of the Society of American Historians; *The South, the Nation, and the World: Perspectives on Southern Economic Development* (2003); and about ninety articles. His current project is a history of the world rice trade between about 1600 and 1940.

**Felipe Fernández-Armesto** is the Principe of Asturias Chair at Tufts University. His numerous books, which have been translated into twenty-two languages, include *Before Columbus: Exploration and Colonization from the Mediterranean to the Atlantic, 1229–1492* (1987), *Columbus* (1991), and *Millennium: A History of the Last Thousand Years* (1995).

**Allan Greer** is Professor of History at the University of Toronto, specializing in colonial history. His books include *Peasant, Lord, and Merchant: Rural Society in Three Quebec Parishes, 1740–1840* (1985), *The Jesuit Relations: Natives and Missionaries in*

*Seventeenth-Century North America* (2000), *Mohawk Saint: Catherine Tekakwitha and the Jesuits* (2004), and, with Jodi Bilinkoff, *Colonial Saints: Discovering the Holy in the Americas, 1500–1800* (2003). These works have merited several prizes, including the John A. MacDonald Prize, the Allan Sharlin Prize, and the Prix Lionel-Groulx. His current research focuses on the emergence of property regimes in colonial North America through the interplay of European and indigenous forms of possession.

**Pier M. Larson** is Associate Professor of History at The Johns Hopkins University. He is author of *History and Memory in the Age of Enslavement: Becoming Merina in Highland Madagascar, 1770–1822* (2000). His research continues along two tracks: collecting personal narratives of enslavement and servitude in Africa as an entry to the continent's diverse experiences of slavery, and preparing a book on the translation of the Bible into Malagasy during the early nineteenth century.

**Patrick F. McDevitt** is Assistant Professor of History at the State University of New York at Buffalo. He is the author of *May the Best Man Win: Sport, Masculinity and Nationalism in Great Britain and the Empire, 1880–1935* (2004). He is currently working on a history of progressive Catholicism in Ireland and the Atlantic World.

**Kenneth Mills** is Professor of History at the University of Toronto. His books include *Idolatry and Its Enemies: Colonial Andean Religion and Extirpation, 1640–1750* (1997) and, with William B. Taylor and Sandra Lauderdale Graham, *Colonial Latin America: A Documentary History* (2002).

**José C. Moya** is Associate Professor of History and Director of the Latin American Studies Program at the University of California, Los Angeles. His book *Cousins and Strangers: Spanish Immigrants in Buenos Aires, 1850–1930* (1998) received five awards, including the Bolton Prize for best book in Latin American history from the American Historical Association. Recent publications include "Immigrants and Associations: A Global and Historical Perspective" (*Journal of Ethnic and Migration Studies*, 2004) and "The Positive Side of Stereotypes: Jewish Anarchists in Early-Twentieth-Century Buenos Aires" (*Jewish History*, 2003). He is currently working on an intellectual, social, and cultural history of the anarchist movement in Buenos Aires during the belle epoque, a project that has received support from the American Council of Learned Societies Burkhardt Fellowship, the University of California President's Research Fellowship in the Humanities, the National Endowment for the Humanities, and the Fulbright Fellowship.

**Claudio Saunt** is Associate Professor of History at the University of Georgia. His book *A New Order of Things: Property, Power, and the Transformation of the Creek Indians, 1733–1816* (1999) won prizes from the Southern Historical Association and the American Society for Ethnohistory. He is also author of *Black, White, and Indian: Race and the Unmaking of an American Family* (2005).

**Claire S. Schen** is Associate Professor of History at the State University of New York at Buffalo. She is the author of *Charity and Lay Piety in Reformation London, 1500–1620* (2002); "Greeks and 'Grecians' in London: The 'Other' Strangers," in Randolph Vigne and Charles Littleton, eds., *From Strangers to Citizens: The Integration of Immigrant Communities in Britain, Ireland, and Colonial America, 1550–1750* (2001); and essays on women and piety. She is currently working on a project about piracy and captivity in early modern Britain and North Africa and British relations with the Ottoman Turks in the seventeenth century.

**Christopher Schmidt-Nowara** is Associate Professor of History at Fordham University and Director of the Latin American and Latino Studies Institute. He is the author of *Empire and Antislavery: Spain, Cuba, and Puerto Rico, 1833–1874* (1999) and is currently working on a monograph titled "The Conquest of History: Spanish Colonialism and National Histories in the Nineteenth Century."

**Patricia Seed** is Professor of History at the University of California, Irvine. She is the author of three books, including *American Pentimento: The Invention of Indians and the Pursuit of Riches* (2001). She has received five prizes for historical writing on a variety of different subjects and is currently writing "The Navigation and Cartography of the Atlantic from A.D. 800 to 1600."

**Reed Ueda** is Professor of History at Tufts University and is on the Steering Group of the Inter-University Committee on International Migration at the MIT Center for International Studies. He is an associate of the New Global History Initiative directed by Akira Iriye of Harvard and Bruce Mazlish of MIT. He has authored *Avenues to Adulthood* (1987) and *Post-War Immigrant America* (1994) and has edited books and written many articles on U.S. social history and global migration.

**Jason Young** is Assistant Professor of History at the State University of New York at Buffalo. His book manuscript, "Rituals of Resistance: The Making of an African Atlantic Religious Complex in Kongo and the Lowcountry in the Era of Slavery," explores the cultural connections between Africans captured in west-central Africa and their progeny enslaved in South Carolina and Georgia.

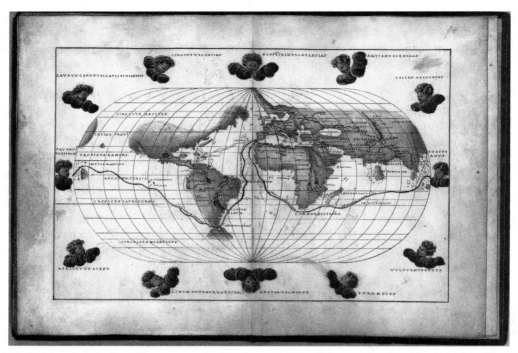

World Map by Battista Agnese, ca. 1540. Agnese traced the route of Ferdinand Magellan's historic circumnavigation of the globe, 1519–1522. Magellan, born in Portugal but sailing for the Spanish crown, laid the foundation for Spain's extensive trade networks in the Pacific and Indian Oceans. Agnese's map demonstrates the global nature of Iberian expansion in the sixteenth century.

# FOREWORD

*Thomas Bender*

This book contributes to one of the most important historiographical developments in the discipline today: opening the nation as the container that has framed historical analysis since the nineteenth century. The professional practice of history grew up with the making of modern nation-states. The profession was supported by and supported the developing nation-states in Europe and the Americas. Whether an individual historian was an apologist or a critic of a given state, history as a discipline sustained the national state by effectively designating it the natural carrier of history. The combination of multiculturalism and a new awareness of global connections and interconnections as elements of national histories has led to a fundamental reconceptualization of the nature of history, and that historiographical work is reflected and advanced in this volume. The authors of these quite original chapters have stretched themselves beyond their specializations to produce these pathbreaking analyses that offer exciting points of departure for class discussions and future research.

Those historians who first began moving away from the national framing of history were early modern historians, particularly those examining the European empires in the Americas. Europe, Africa, and the Americas were linked as a single field of inquiry. The idea of the Atlantic World as a possible domain for historical inquiry dates back to the 1950s, but it was defined and partly sponsored by the establishment of the North Atlantic Treaty Organization. It was assumed that the South Atlantic (Africa, the Caribbean, and South America) was at best a junior partner in Atlantic history as well as in the alliance. The current rendition, which has been remarkably quickly institutionalized, is more comprehensive. Still, most of the work has been within given empires, and very rarely has the history of the South Atlantic and the North Atlantic been brought together for a truly Atlantic World history. Precisely that bringing together is one of the accomplishments of this volume. But that is only the first of its innovations.

The second innovation is more radical. In chapter after chapter, the end game is revealed as the globe itself. Again and again, we see that if one is willing to cross inherited historiographical boundaries, one's topic often extends beyond them. The point is not to begin with the global; it is only to allow it. Here the rule is—or ought to be—follow the people, the money, the things, and the knowledges wherever they go. Not every historical phenomenon is global, but one must keep open the possibility that it might be. If so, one can best explain a given local historical development by following the line of inquiry to this end point.

The resulting history is not a global history; it remains local, regional, thematic, or even national. But it is a history that recognizes a global context, and at one level and in various degrees all histories share in a global history after 1500. That context invites two kinds of inquiry that are distinct but are likely to be blended in different degrees. First there is a relational history that inquires into the interconnections and interactions that make every history a part of every other history—a point made long ago in 1891 by Frederick Jackson Turner in his essay "The Significance of History," which preceded his famous frontier essay. "In history," Turner wrote, "there are only artificial divisions," for "not only is it true that no country can be understood without taking account of all the past; it is also true that we cannot select a stretch of land and say we will limit our study to this land; for local history can only be understood in the light of the history of the world. . . . Ideas, commodities even, refuse the bounds of a nation. All are inextricably connected, so that each is needed to explain the others. This is true especially in the modern world with its complex commerce and means of intellectual communication."[1] Second, by pursuing those connections, one is almost naturally invited to speculate on comparisons, on local variations of more general developments.

One must take care—as these chapters do—not to claim too much for the unity of the world or of a common history. Even today, globalization talk notwithstanding, there is neither an integrated culture nor a unified economy that encompasses the world. Historically, there have been different levels and kinds of common institutions and histories. There are—in order of increasing density and commonness—levels of interconnection, interaction, and interdependence. But all these different degrees of integration fall short of a monolithic or universal history; even today the current worry about global homogenization is much overstated. So the challenge is not that of writing a global history but rather that of being ready to move out from the local, the particular, to find translocal, even global, contexts, connections, interactions, and interdependencies that have explanatory value rather than offering a mere decorative show of erudition. In these chapters, reaching out has produced important explanatory and interpretive gains.

What do we learn from this approach? More than I have space to address, and readers will soon enough be able to discover for themselves the contributions these chapters make. But let me highlight those themes that particularly strike me as important not only for their intrinsic interest but also for what they may contribute to a rather large reshaping of the historiography. Not surprisingly, these themes are mostly sustained by more than one of the chapters.

Adam Smith declared in *The Wealth of Nations* (1776) that the most important event in human history was the establishment of sea routes to Asia and the Americas. One might insist that the invention of agriculture and cities may have been at least as important. Still, we should recall his declaration, for we have not sufficiently recognized how profoundly important was the shift of the center of the world from the Mediterranean Sea to the oceans. The Oceanic Revolution is the fundamental geography for understanding the history of the Americas and, for that matter, Asia, Africa, and Europe as well.

This is a shared history; by connecting all continents, the Oceanic Revolution made the world and the globe one and the same, thus initiating a global history that no people or place could escape. And this circumstance opens up both explanations and comparisons—the role of the East in the economic development of the West and, more specifically, the Americas; the differences in slavery under Mediterranean Islam and the plantation systems of the Atlantic World; and the continuing role of the Muslim Mediterranean in American histories during the whole of the period up to the end of the first age of European empires, noting that the first foreign war of the United States was in the eastern Mediterranean, while Muslim religious traditions were vital among Africans in the Americas well into the nineteenth century.

We see here the importance of a renewed, even militant, Christianity with global ambitions. Adam Smith may have been right about the results, but the impulse that impelled Europeans onto the seas included more than truck, barter, and trade. They were also embarked on a grand Christianizing project. The thrust toward Christianization and the campaign against Satan was global in scope. In the era of the Protestant Reformation and of Catholic renewal, which was also the age of empire making, Christianity, both Catholic and Protestant, sought to extend its domain, partly by focusing new energy on the eradication of witchcraft and Satanic dangers, whether in the New World or the Old. Parallel efforts to Christianize indigenous peoples were made not only in the Western Hemisphere and Europe itself but also in Asia. A stunning example of this global reach is an early seventeenth-century painting celebrating St. Francis Xavier's work in Asia that hung in a Cusco church.

The narrative structure central to the story of religion is more general; one finds it in different ways in each of the chapters of this volume. The stories are local variations of larger histories, some of which are global in scope, within and beyond empires. This pattern of the general with local variation characterizes empires in general—as opposed to the later nation-state, which sought uniformity. By opening up the frame, we realize that the early modern period was organized by empires, not only in the Atlantic World but globally as well. How much can we generalize about the structure of empires, compared to each other and to nation-states, something of increasing historiographical importance in studies of indigenous peoples in the Americas? How is a world of empires different from a world of nation-states? If it was a world of empires, these chapters make clear that they contained many kinds of diversity. The approach of this volume invites questions about different kinds of empires: Catholic and Protestant; European, Ottoman, African, and Asian; land and maritime; and settler and trading.

That said, one must inquire into the political and coercive capacity of empire and the ways in which it did or did not limit agency of the colonized or ruled. Recently, historians have been anxious to emphasize the agency of groups previously marginalized in historiography—especially slaves, indigenous peoples, and women. These studies have made their point, but there is always the danger that too tight a focus on and commitment to agency may erase important structures of power. The variegated but related histories of the Atlantic World—and Asia—offer illuminating comparisons that should enrich analysis of this fundamental issue. In the end, we may be brought back to the famous comment of Marx that individuals have agency, but they cannot determine the conditions under which they exercise it. Tocqueville made the same point, referring to the sailor's capacity to tack against the wind but not control the wind. To what extent is empire that kind of limiting condition? And were there significant differences among empires or even within empires over time and space?

A conventional focus on the settlement of the Americas makes settlement seem natural. The English, worried about overpopulation at home, were the most aggressive settlers, but other empires took large territories in the Americas and proposed to settle them. Taking territory and settling it was not the practice of these early empires in other parts of the world. Why? Again, the wider view raises questions that had not seemed to require asking.

The European category of "civilization" is also illuminated by examining the reactions to the different peoples encountered. The peoples of the Americas were categorized as not civilized. Muslims, however, mostly were (because they were monotheistic? literate?). So were Asians, but what were the criteria? Was it their historical cultures, older than Europe? Or was it their commercial cities? But to the Chinese, who had their own sense of civilization, it was the Europeans who seemed to lack the qualities of civilization.

By expanding the geography of historical inquiry to the Atlantic and beyond, various peoples in motion and in networks outside of nations or imperial projects—and the ocean itself—are given greater historical presence. The focus on nation or singular empires overlooks the great Atlantic diasporas or at least distorts them, obscuring the geographical extent of their dispersion. An exclusive focus on the importation of African slaves into British mainland colonies, for example, suggests a more central role for those colonies in the making of the Black Atlantic than is warranted, and it implies that the Chesapeake was a more significant site for the "plantation complex" than was the case. The Atlantic perspective offers a fuller account of the African diaspora, including the complex identities formed in the diasporic experience. It also invites notice of smaller ones: Jews, Huguenots, and Quakers.

Commodities, things as well as people, money, and ideas, began moving around the world. Sugar and spices have been studied, and now others are being examined. Rice is one of the most important commodities in the world, but one understands the American place in the production and consumption of rice only by way of obtaining a sense of the larger geography of production, marketing, and consumption of rice. Other commodities are now being examined in an Atlantic and increasingly global framework: cotton, coffee, cocoa/chocolate, mahogany, and even Madeira wine.

For most students of the Atlantic World, the so-called Age of Democratic Revolutions marks the chronological end point for Atlantic World studies. Surely it was a major turning point, when the empires were challenged and independent republics came to distinguish the western Atlantic from its eastern shore. This era offers a good example of a well-integrated Atlantic World that was marked by the general circulation of political ideas and sympathies not only among elites but also among ordinary sailors and enslaved Africans. The revolutionary age was, like much of this story, a general phenomenon but one also marked by imperial and national differences. It is important to recognize that what happened in one place was typically a part of the history of another. Historians of the French and American revolutions are quick to point out the precedence and thus importance of these revolutions for the Atlantic World, and that is correct. Yet more comparison is wanted. Only now are historians granting the Haitian Revolution its place and emphasizing how widely knowledge of it was circulated. It directly and powerfully raised the question of whether the Enlightenment principles of the French Revolution would be extended to nonwhites. Its impact on the early United States was enormous, and it was on the mind of Francisco de Miranda and other South American revolutionaries as well. It made the white elites of North and South America more cautious about revolution and the risk of slave uprisings.

If most of those scholars who sail under the flag of the Atlantic World do not carry their inquiries beyond the age of revolution, the topic remains, and this volume is unusual in acknowledging that by including chapters on the nineteenth and twentieth centuries. The Atlantic and global connections and comparisons that have been so illuminating from the sixteenth, seventeenth, and eighteenth centuries need to be carried forward into the nineteenth and twentieth centuries, where they promise to be just as fruitful. One hopes that the impact of this volume will not only extend the geography of inquiry for the early modern period, which it will surely do, but also stimulate a temporal extension of the study of the Atlantic World in a global framework.

## Notes

1   Frederick Jackson Turner, "The Significance of History" [1891], in Frederick Jackson Turner, *Frontier and Section: Selected Essays* (Englewood Cliffs, N.J., 1961), 20–21.

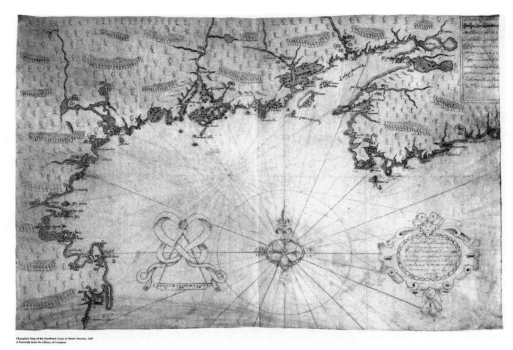

Northeastern Coast of North America, Samuel de Champlain, 1607. European territorial ambitions helped fuel the integration of the Atlantic World. Maps charted and whetted these desires.

# Introduction: Beyond the Line: Nations, Oceans, Hemispheres

## Jorge Cañizares-Esguerra and Erik R. Seeman

In recent years, historians—especially of the early modern period—have become increasingly attracted to the Atlantic paradigm, which focuses on exchanges of peoples, commodities, and ideas among the four continents bordering the Atlantic. With a backdrop formed by current forces of globalization—from jet travel to the Internet, from the International Monetary Fund to Coca-Cola—historians have been eager to apply today's transnational insights to the past. The Atlantic paradigm is a way to transcend the historiographical fixation on the nation-state. Or is it?

The nation, as Thomas Bender shows in this volume's foreword, lies at the very core of how modern historiography originated. Calls to break the shackles that national narratives have put on the historian's imagination are on the rise today. Global, regional, comparative, and transnational narratives are increasingly popular. Globalization, we have been told, is making the nation obsolete as the dominant form of political community and the dominant organizational paradigm in historical studies. This volume participates in this process at the same time that its contributors are aware of the enormity of the task. Even as capacious an organizing principle as the Atlantic can remain captive to national narratives if scholars are not careful.

The genesis and evolution of the spatial category of the Atlantic is very telling. Its popularity in the Anglophone academy is the result of the external and internal needs of the United States beginning in the 1950s. In the wake of World War II and within the geopolitical realities of the Cold War, the North Atlantic Treaty Organization was created as both a military and an ideological alliance against the "Oriental despotism" of Stalinism and the Soviet Union. This alliance inspired, in turn, new Atlantic sensibilities among U.S. historians, who set out to find traces of a common Atlantic (actually North Atlantic) civilization in the past.[1]

The colonial period of North America was ripe for this new Atlantic approach, particularly the narrative of the American Revolution. The wars of independence now came to be understood as part of larger political transformations in the Atlantic World, including the French Revolution. The first histories of the "Age of Revolutions," however, did not include the Haitian Revolution, one of the most influential struggles for democracy and equality ever fought on either side of the Atlantic.[2] Black intellectuals had long been imagining African American history in Atlantic, transnational terms. Yet this

Black Atlantic had to wait for the aftermath of the Civil Rights Movement to become mainstream.

Inspired by the Civil Rights Movement, a generation of scholarship on slavery and New World plantations turned the history of British North America on its head. For over a century, the history of New England or, more precisely, of the Puritans had dominated interpretations of the colonial period. By the 1980s, however, historians began to realize that rather than being typical of the colonial experience, New England was atypical. The middle colonies, the South, and the Caribbean—societies of planters and slaves—had in fact been the norm.[3] This realization coincided with the turn to the Atlantic. The thirteen mainland colonies came to be understood as part of the much larger British Empire in the New World, with plantations and settlers spanning from Nova Scotia to South America and the Caribbean. Greater attention to the British Empire begged the comparative question of what other empires were doing in the New World. Historians therefore brought Spain, France, and Holland back into the picture. Colonial North American history is now conceived of largely as the competition among several European empires and the colonists who came to the New World in the name of those empires. In the wake of the Civil Rights Movement, the American Indian Movement, and the general turn toward multicultural awareness in the 1980s, scholars of colonial North America also pay increasing attention to interactions among Indians, Africans, and Europeans—that is, among the peoples of the four continents surrounding the Atlantic Ocean.

Suddenly, it seems, colonial North American history has become transnational—but only to a degree, for colonial North American history with an Atlantic twist is still dominated by the pedagogical and ideological needs of the nation. For all its newfound cosmopolitanism, colonial American history is still organized around the needs of a national narrative that privileges the teleology of the ultimate creation of the United States. For example, the teaching of the colonial period in the U.S. history survey at American universities continues to be dominated by the looming formation of the United States—even when taught from an Atlantic perspective. Non-British areas that eventually became part of the United States, such as Florida and New Mexico, typically garner more attention than far less marginal parts of the Spanish Empire, such as Peru and even Mexico. And when areas that never became part of the United States—such as Quebec—are in fact taught during the colonial period of the U.S. survey, they are almost never discussed after the national period begins in 1789.

But how are we to cut loose from these narrative restrictions? This volume seeks to do so by building on and expanding the current Atlantic paradigm. The chapters in this volume pay more attention to non–North American topics than is typical in Anglophone Atlantic scholarship. The chapters bring the transnational story of Atlantic exchange into the nineteenth and twentieth centuries. And they point to areas where a global perspective may help enrich topics of interest to Atlanticists. In all these ways, the authors in this volume avoid the teleology of the creation of the United States.

Most studies of the early modern Atlantic are organized along national lines. Thus, there are as many narratives of the Atlantic as there were empires: British, Spanish, Portuguese, French, Dutch, and so on. This volume seeks to complicate these nation-driven narratives. Part I, "Comparing Atlantics," includes five chapters that compare the experiences of different European empires in the New World. Allan Greer and Kenneth Mills, for example, set out to find a common "Catholic Atlantic," bringing Europe and the New World into a single narrative of shared historical processes. Greer and Mills suggest that the historiographies of early modern European Catholicism and colonial New France and Spanish America have oddly gone their own separate ways, as if the confessional age (of building both Catholic and Protestant churches and national states) and the age of overseas missions were two different processes. Greer and Mills demonstrate that this was not the case, that there was little that distinguished the spread of Catholicism in the metropolis and the colonial peripheries in the early modern period. Seen through the lens of religion, the French and Iberian colonial expansions do not look that different from one another.

Jorge Cañizares-Esguerra goes a step further. Whereas Greer and Mills postulate a common Catholic Atlantic distinct from a Protestant one, Cañizares-Esguerra argues for a common Christian Atlantic. The notion that British America and Spanish America had very different ways of using religion to approach colonization does not withstand close scrutiny. Cañizares-Esguerra uses demonology to show that two very different communities, namely, Puritans and Catholic Iberians, thought that colonization was about ending the absolute sovereignty that Satan had enjoyed for centuries over the New World. Puritan and Iberian clerics understood the conquest to be an epic struggle that pitted Christian heroes against Satan, bent on destroying the local polities by all means possible: storms, earthquakes, epidemics, pirates, foreign enemies, tyrannous crown officials, and Indians.

Erik R. Seeman also goes against the grain of nationally driven narratives of the Atlantic by focusing on one religious community: the Jews. By looking at the deathways of the Jews in the Caribbean islands held by the British and the Dutch, Seeman argues that variations in Jewish religious identities cannot be explained by any essentialist argument that posits national differences between the Dutch and British Atlantics. Where the Jews owned plantations and large numbers of slaves (particularly in Dutch Surinam), their deathways evolved in a manner distinct from elsewhere. Like Greer and Mills, Seeman suggests that all across the Atlantic, local forms of religion sprang up and that similarities and differences were greatly influenced by local conditions. Local conditions, not essentialist arguments about the national character of each Atlantic empire, should be the focus of analysis.

Claudio Saunt likewise calls attention to the importance of local conditions to any transnational Atlantic narrative. All over the New World, European powers sought to expand by pitting indigenous groups against one another and by recruiting Indians as proxy armies. "Borderlands" and "middle grounds" are two of the conceptual categories historians have devised to describe these spaces where struggles over imperial control took place. Using these categories, historians have sought to portray these Indians as cunning actors who played European empires against one another. Saunt maintains, instead, that outcomes in these hemisphere-wide struggles were the result of the local transformations brought about by the militarization of indigenous societies. His focus is on the Choctaws caught in between French and English imperial rivalries over the control of what is today the southeastern United States.

Finally, Patricia Seed shows that the local always has the potential of transforming the global. Her chapter studies the ways sailors in the mid-fifteenth century took advantage of the uniquely hybrid intellectual culture of Portugal, where Arab and Jewish scholars devised mathematical and astronomical tools that allowed sailors to develop new forms of scientific navigation and thus to break the lock that winds and ocean currents had long had over navigating the Atlantic. Portuguese sailors managed for the first time to move in the Atlantic at will and thus to bring the Atlantic and the Indian Oceans together, transforming global history.

If the nation has offered us a narrow and ideologically suspect definition of space, the concept of the Atlantic is likewise not without its blind spots. Seed reminds us of the global context in which Atlantic history unfolded. This is the focus of Part II, "Beyond the Atlantic." Even Atlantic perspectives can, on occasion, be distorting, for most of the early modern European empires were in fact global ones. As Felipe Fernández-Armesto demonstrates, European empires are best understood in a global context. It is only in light of other, contemporary empires, such as indigenous ones in the Americas or Russian and Chinese models on the Eurasian landmass, that the distinctive aspects of European empires may be seen.

Peter A. Coclanis has a similar agenda. The Atlantic paradigm has prevented historians from seeing the global dimensions of certain processes, including the production of staples, such as rice. Coclanis demonstrates that since the eighteenth century, parts of Asia and the various locations of rice production in the West have been locked into a well-integrated process of global supply and demand that cannot be separated analytically without doing violence to the larger picture. It is clear that we need to interrogate the power of geographical enclosures, be it the nation or the Atlantic. This volume is an invitation for historians to imagine social worlds that unfold and interact in different geographical spaces (local, national, regional, and global) at once.

A global perspective can enrich much that is otherwise familiar. There is indeed little reason to avoid including, for example, the Pacific in the geographies of the Spanish Atlantic since the colonization of the Philippines was directed from and through Mexico, not Madrid. The Portuguese and Dutch empires are also a case in point; their colonization of the Americas was marginal and subordinate to their adventures in South and East Asia. It was only after their displacement by Ottoman, Mogul, Japanese, and Dutch traders in Asia that the Portuguese merchants and bureaucrats turned to Brazil in the late seventeenth century, particularly after the discovery of gold in Minas Gerais.

Pier M. Larson contributes to this globalization of familiar topics. He makes evident the perils of reducing the African diaspora solely to its Atlantic dimensions, for the history of African slavery is a global one. Larson describes how millions of African slaves moved across the Sahara and the Indian Ocean. Just as important, millions of slaves remained in Africa and circulated through local kingdoms and polities. Larson shows that sex ratios and demographic patterns of Atlantic slavery, for example, cannot be explained without first understanding the dynamics and history of slavery in these other destinations. Moreover, it is only by looking at slavery in this global context that the uniqueness (or lack thereof) of Atlantic slavery can be understood.

Claire S. Schen also demonstrates the value of moving beyond the Atlantic to follow topics that did not adhere to oceanic boundaries. She shows that the history of the English Atlantic cannot and should not be severed from the history of English interactions with the Ottomans in the Mediterranean. The history of English imperial expansion takes on a new richness when the familiar Atlantic story is compared with the less familiar history of English interactions with North Africans. Whereas English expansion in the Atlantic can seem almost inevitable, the English were chastened in their dealings with the sophisticated states of North Africa.

Part II closes where it began—with an analysis of the fundamental connections between the Atlantic and the Pacific. Reed Ueda uses Hawaii as a case study of the profound linkages between the two largest oceans. When the United States expanded westward to the Pacific shore in the nineteenth century, it linked the Atlantic and Pacific in new ways. Hawaii's population became increasingly heterogeneous as indigenous Hawaiians were joined by individuals from around the Atlantic (New England, the Azores, and Puerto Rico) and the Pacific (Japan, China, and Korea). Today, Hawaii's unique culture represents its dual Atlantic and Pacific heritages.

Just as Ueda's chapter shows how expanding the Atlantic paradigm into the Pacific can pay intellectual dividends, the next part of the volume aims to expand the Atlantic paradigm chronologically. But it must be noted that the chapters in Part III, "The Evolving Atlantic," do not employ the global perspective advocated by the authors in Part II. José C. Moya and Christopher Schmidt-Nowara, in particular, offer powerful defenses of the appropriateness of an Atlantic perspective. They regard the Atlantic as a more useful analytical category for understanding their nineteenth-century topics. This tension between global and Atlantic perspectives is, we believe, a productive tension. Atlanticists must be willing to expand their field of vision when doing so generates important insights, but not all analyses will be improved by a global perspective.

Thus, the four authors in Part III help bring the Atlantic paradigm into the national period. They apply to the nineteenth and twentieth centuries the insights and methodologies honed by historians of the early modern Atlantic. Historians of the United States and Latin America have been reluctant to think outside the boundaries of the nation when crafting narratives of the nineteenth and twentieth centuries. Yet Part III demonstrates that the Atlantic is a valuable spatial category for understanding not only colonial but also nineteenth- and twentieth-century historical phenomena. Moya powerfully makes the case that the Atlantic became especially well-integrated in the nineteenth century. Global migrations, it is true, carried cheap labor across the Pacific, Indian, and Atlantic oceans in the nineteenth century. But the Atlantic nineteenth-century migrations, Moya argues, were of a special kind. Migrants wove a dense fabric of shared everyday experiences linking large cities and small villages across the ocean, from Chicago to São Paulo to Buenos Aires to Sicily to Krakow. Never before and never again has the local been so enmeshed with the global as in the nineteenth-century Atlantic World.

That the North and South Atlantics are powerful analytical categories for understanding not only colonial but also nineteenth-century historical phenomena likewise lies at the heart of Schmidt-Nowara's chapter. Schmidt-Nowara deftly borrows the category of Atlantic Age of Revolution to describe an Atlantic Age of Emancipation. Emancipation, Schmidt-Nowara reminds us, cannot be explained solely within narratives that privilege the nation (e.g., British abolitionism or the U.S. Civil War). Emancipation was a complex pan-Atlantic phenomenon experienced differently in each corner of the Atlantic. The various timings of emancipation make sense only when local, national, and Atlantic events are taken into account, including the degree of slave resistance, rivalries among European powers, the nature of the violence that shattered the European empires in the New World, the impact of the Haitian Revolution, and the pace of the nineteenth-century global industrialization. All these factors combined help explain why societies like Cuba and the U.S. South first witnessed an expansion of slavery before they experienced emancipation.

Jason Young is also concerned with the members of the African diaspora. He shows how a black "double consciousness," originally hammered out in the crucible of eighteenth-century Atlantic slavery and abolitionism, has continued into the twenty-first century. The phenomenon of an Atlantic black double consciousness—that is, the experience of belonging both to "Africa" and the "West," drawing on both European and African inheritances—lies as much at the heart of eighteenth-century Black Atlantic sources as it does in those of the late twentieth century.

But if the category of the Black Atlantic remains central to U.S. African American identities today, the category of a "Green" Atlantic is no less vital. The Irish are quintessentially Atlantic. Irish migrations were central both to the making of the colonial British Atlantic and to the industrialization of the United States in the nineteenth century. Yet the Green Atlantic, Patrick F. McDevitt argues, has as much to do with the South Atlantic as it does with the North. McDevitt demonstrates the connections linking the Irish with Latin American Catholics in the twentieth century. According to McDevitt, liberation theology (which, along with dependency theory and magical realism, was a characteristically Latin American twentieth-century global export) helped shape reforms in the Irish Catholic Church from the 1960s through the 1980s.

Thus do the chapters of Part III bring the historiography of the national period into contact with the Atlantic paradigm. But there is always the danger that by breaking the self-contained and self-referential nature of the national period's narratives, we might again be surrendering to the ideological needs of the nation, for the United States is today the only standing global empire, an empire whose corporations have declared everyone else's national boundaries outmoded. Is the new corporate cult of globalization seeping into the historical profession's calls to globalize the historical imagination?[4] We invite readers to explore the following fourteen chapters and begin to decide for themselves.

## Notes

1 Bernard Bailyn, "The Idea of Atlantic History," *Itinerario* 20 (1996): 19–44.

2 R. R. Palmer, *The Age of Democratic Revolution: A Political History of Europe and America, 1760–1800*, 2 vols. (Princeton, N.J., 1959–1964); Jacques Léon Godechot, *France and the Atlantic Revolution of the Eighteenth Century, 1770–1799* (New York, 1965).

3 Jack P. Greene, *Pursuits of Happiness: The Social Development of Early Modern British Colonies and the Formation of American Culture* (Chapel Hill, N.C., 1988).

4 Louis A. Pérez Jr., "We Are the World: Internationalizing the National, Nationalizing the International," *Journal of American History* 89 (2002): 558–67.

# Part I

# *Comparing Atlantics*

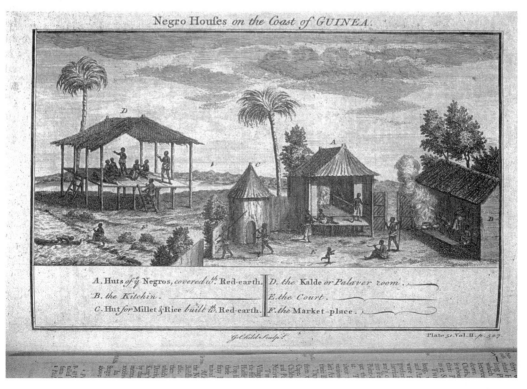

Negro Houses on the Coast of Guinea. Thomas Astley, *A New General Collection of Voyages and Travels* (London, 1745). From the West Coast of Africa came slaves—nearly 50,000 a year at the time this engraving was published—to work the plantations and mines of the New World. Slavery paid no heed to imperial boundaries.

*The authors in part 1, "Comparing Atlantics," question the ways historians have used the "Atlantic" as a category of analysis. Most studies of the early modern Atlantic World offer narratives along strict national lines, with as many Atlantics as there were European empires: Portuguese, Dutch, British, Spanish, French, and so on. This emphasis on the national not only has obscured similarities and shared experiences but has also projected our notions of essential national differences back onto the past. The chapters in part 1 go out of their way to demonstrate that we should do away with these nationally inspired categories of historical analysis or at least move beyond them where appropriate.*

*Allan Greer and Kenneth Mills, for example, question how the European Reformation and the Christianization of the New World, which happened at about the same time, have been studied by historians as two distinct events. Rather, they offer a common transatlantic narrative. State authorities, the Catholic Church, and local peasant communities behaved in similar ways on both sides of the Atlantic. The state sought to expand its authority over recalcitrant agrarian communities in similar ways. Seeking to respond to the challenge of the Protestant Reformation, the Catholic Church, on the other hand, pursued its own policies of purging "pagan" and "superstitious" behaviors typical of peasant communities on both sides of the Atlantic. At the receiving end of these disciplining efforts stood either European peasants or Indians. Greer and Mills suggest that historians are wrong to assume that the local religious worlds that emerged out of these encounters of the state, the church, and the peasantries were simply a thin veneer of Catholic rituals disguising an authentic core of pagan and indigenous beliefs. Early modern "Christendom" was in fact a world teeming with local forms of Catholic religion on both sides of the Atlantic. Given that the European state and the Catholic Church also reached Africa and Asia, the question thus remains, Can Greer and Mill's model of New World–European Christendom be applied to Africa and Asia as well?*

# A Catholic Atlantic

## Allan Greer and Kenneth Mills

The "Atlantic World" paradigm, pioneered by economic historians, has had its greatest successes in the area of trade and migration studies. Studies of the African slave trade and of points within a broad African diaspora stand out in particular, as do investigations of heartlands and frontiers.[1] The religious and cultural history of an early modern Atlantic, in contrast, remains uneven and fragmentary, with research still conducted largely in isolated silos divided by language, nationality, and region.[2] The example of Charles Boxer's transoceanic work across various zones of Iberian domination or influence in Africa, the Americas, and Asia stands almost alone and ought to both inspire and challenge current Atlanticist projects.[3] Studies that focus on "missionaries" and a variety of religious transformations in the Americas connect quite imperfectly with abundant research on earlier and contemporaneous Christian cultures of western and northern Europe and the circum-Mediterranean region. The gap between Atlantic promise and reality may yawn widest in discussion of the expansion and trajectories of Roman Catholicism in the sixteenth and seventeenth centuries. Our aim in this chapter is thus twofold: to survey the Atlantic dimensions of early modern Catholic Christianity in light of recent developments on a number of largely separate scholarly fronts and to explore a few of the most promising lines along which investigations might proceed. We believe that a reconsideration of Catholic Christianities in the colonial Americas can lead historical interpreters away from artificial fragmentation and toward some illuminating connections and reverberations. As will become clear, we regard the Atlantic World as an organizing frame and set of principles in a discussion that is still very much being determined. Certainly, we are not the first to attempt an integrative move in religious terms.[4]

## CATHOLIC REFORMATION: EUROPEAN CONTEXTS

The multiform transformations of Catholic Christianity in the sixteenth and seventeenth centuries have been the subject of a rich and voluminous historiography. Much discussion has focused on the deceptively simple question of labeling.[5] At one time, the favored term was "Counter-Reformation," suggesting a belligerent reaction—one best apprehended at the level of doctrinal debate, politics, and war—to the challenges posed by Luther and Calvin. In recent decades, however, the scholarly consensus has shifted. There is a growing appreciation of the "constructive" rather than purely reactive side of Catholicism; in its cultural program, its institutional restructuring, and its ambitious attempts to reengineer society, the Church was, to put it crudely, on the side of modernity. Consciously combating what Simon Ditchfield calls "the curse of Max Weber,"[6] many specialists today explore parallels between Protestant and Catholic Christianity of the period and prefer to characterize their subject in terms not only of "Catholic Reformation" or "early modern Catholicism" but also of "Catholic renewal" and "revitalization."[7]

In a similar spirit, some scholars have stressed the need for a more continuous story, particularly with regard to the attitudes of Catholic religious authorities to local religion.[8] That said, no amount of study of the antecedents of the Reformations displaces the Council of Trent (1545–1563) as the pivot point where questions of doctrine and ecclesiastical governance were hammered out by leading figures in the Church. Other scholars have charted the rise of new religious orders that emerged from the cloisters to engage with secular society, such as the Ursulines and the Jesuits (discussed later in this chapter); they have also studied the reform and reinvigoration of older orders. The papacy and the world of diplomacy, art, and war are other subjects capturing the attention of historians. In the works of investigators such as Louis Châtellier, Brian Pullan, John Henderson, and Maureen Flynn, among many others, the study of new styles of lay piety, lay organizations, and confraternities pick up and reexplore some of the more intricate threads in medieval European social and religious historiography.[9]

In this chapter, we highlight connections that develop from one central dimension of the Catholic Reformation, that is, the program of renewing the Christian faith and correcting the behavior of the lay population of Europe. Given the social structures of the time, this amounted, in effect, to an intense engagement between the clergy and a broad peasantry, though townspeople were certainly often involved as well. Jean Delumeau, a pioneer of the new approach to the so-called Counter-Reformation, characterized the Protestant and Catholic Reformations as "convergent processes of Christianization of the masses."[10] In the wake of pre-reform efforts and especially of Trent, there was more emphasis on making the parish clergy, now morally upright and properly trained in newly established seminaries, effective agents in this struggle. Bishops, following the example of Carlo Borromeo, were to be more attentive managers of diocesan affairs, even taking on the semi-independent religious orders when needed. Preaching would be used more fully to animate the faith of the people, and catechistic instruction would inculcate proper principles in the young. Male and female religious orders contributed their energies to focused efforts wherever needed, with a new order such as the Jesuits founding numerous colleges between the 1550s and the 1620s and mixing their educational and missionary labors.

Along with encouragement and improved examples, however, it was widely believed by Catholic churchmen that the people at large were in need of stern and careful correction. As important as standardized learning of catechisms and the principal articles of the faith became, reform was always about far more than reciting the Paternoster without mistakes. The Protestant schism had only intensified longstanding clerical fears about the far graver threat of heresy; the assumption was that lay folk, especially those in the lower orders of a society still often understood in medieval terms, were in grave danger because of their ignorance and vulnerability. It was thought that, like children, they would inevitably go further astray in the absence of firm supervision. Periodic outbreaks of witchcraft were only the most dramatic signs of a deep and vibrant popular culture that included beliefs and gestures considered "superstitious" and opposed to Christianity. Church authorities increasingly turned their regulatory attention to the amulets, magic potions, and curative springs by which rural folk tried to ward off illness, stimulate love, or find lost objects. What was of course forgotten by Catholic gatekeepers in such times was just how much related "magic" had been brought inside the sanctioned realm of Catholic Christian ritual.[11] The attempt fully to Christianize a benighted peasantry has become a major theme in current views on the Catholic Reformation.[12] The Inquisition played a part in stamping out superstition in some jurisdictions, but so too did Marian congregations, lay associations, and a number of other more mundane institutions of parochial and diocesan administration.

Christianization efforts among a vast peasantry coincided with efforts to purify what was seen in some jurisdictions as a far more variously contaminated religion. The problems that Jesuit correspondents reported in a variety of local settings—in the sixteenth-century Spanish kingdoms, in southern Italy, and in the interior of Brittany—capture the connections vividly. Such regions were commonly dubbed "these Indies" or the "other Indies" by itinerant Jesuits wishing to point out everything from the extent of popular ignorance and Christian errors to the abysmal guidance offered by resident secular clergy.[13] The substantial wrinkles of the regulatory and redemptive challenges posed to the Catholic Christian body social by new converts from Judaism and, more particularly, from Islam in the case of Iberian regions have become familiar, albeit still protean and artificially disconnected, realms of transatlantic investigation.

Church efforts to remedy such pollution and to discipline the laity meshed almost seamlessly with similar programs on the part of the emergent national monarchies of the period. Along with the state, the Church played its part in the "civilizing process." In the seventeenth and eighteenth centuries, for example, many bishops took steps to reduce the number of annual holidays, moving some to the nearest Sunday and eliminating others entirely, all in the interests of limiting village festivities, so often attended with drunkenness and disorder.

Viewed from the top down, the Catholic Reformation was a constituent element of the general program of disciplining society that ushered in the modern age. Inseparably linked with state building, it reinforced regulatory institutions, made efforts to suppress the exuberant cultures of the lower classes, contributed to the emergence of new models of the self (individually responsible and sober), promoted obedience to authority, regulated sexuality, and so on.

Social historians of the past century who attempted to examine these phenomena have, however, generally tried to explore them "from the bottom up," often employing the paradigm of "popular culture" as a means of linking religious conflict with class conflict. Work in the Annales School tradition brought to light an array of village festivities, games, folk medicine, and so on, contributing richly to our sense of the vitality and diversity of plebian cultures in the early modern countryside.[14] Most noted the coexistence of Christian and non-Christian elements in rural folklore—peasants conscientiously attending mass on Sunday, concocting love potions on Monday, organizing ribald dances to celebrate the local patron saint on Saturday—but the prevailing tendency was to treat these as indications of tension and contradiction. Historians argued that the Catholic dimension of popular culture was often a thin veneer, even a disguise to fool the authorities, and that the other elements came from a deeper, more fundamental stratum, one deriving from "pagan survivals" rooted in an ancient pre-Christian past.[15] Thus, an underlying sense of basic conflict between peasant atavism and urban modernization structured these interpretations, with orthodox Catholicism and pagan superstition at opposite poles of the encounter. A corollary seemed to be the presentation of "paganism" as more authentically an expression of the peasantry and Christianity something imposed from the outside.

Superseding this interpretation, heavily influenced by both Marxism and modernization theory, has been a view of lay Catholicism as "local religion," an authentic set of Christian forms rooted in particular societies, featuring individuals who worshiped at local shrines, venerated their religious heroes and saints (whether canonized by the Vatican or not), and "living" a religion that coincided significantly but imperfectly with the "universal religion" of the clergy. William A. Christian Jr.'s work has proved seminal in its reluctance to identify local versions of early modern Catholicism with any one social class and in its insistence on a Christianity in which orthodox and unorthodox dimensions are not more or less authentic but rather vital and emerging religious forms.[16] Catholicism, according to this view, is not simply imposed from without; it is "lived" and thus actively shaped by the communities in which it flourishes.

For those of us looking for transatlantic connections and comparisons, a few points of special interest emerge from even so rapid a survey of scholarship on early modern Catholicism in its European settings:

1. Catholicism was, from one point of view, a diverse, locally rooted, popular set of beliefs and gestures, constantly evolving and adapting.

2. At the same time and from a different perspective, it was a dynamic program of discipline and regulation intruding into local societies with the aim of reshaping the outlook and behavior of peasants and others in the laity.

3. As a form of rule, the Church worked hand in glove with the emergent monarchies of early modern Europe. It was indeed an integral aspect of the state-building process characteristic of the period even as it invited and/or could not stem its local developments.

Historiographically, the thrusts of research and interpretation in the European theaters of Catholic Reform mirror work on the contemporaneous efforts to Christianize the indigenous peoples of the Americas, as will soon become apparent. On both sides of the Atlantic, historians chronicled the campaigns to convert unbelievers, investigate the suspect beliefs and practices of the "ignorant" and error prone, and regulate villagers' habits of life. Over time, historiographic attention has shifted, in both European and American studies, from one of principal interest in the outlooks and projects of the "Christianizers" to the points of view and religious creativity of the "Christianized"— or, more accurately in some cases, the "Christianizing"—whether native Andean or Calabrian peasant. A few recent works have made a point of charting particular aspects of the Catholic Reformation's transatlantic reach: Dominique Deslandres, for one, has looked at French mission campaigns targeting the peasants of Brittany and native peoples in Canada.[17]

# CATHOLIC *IMPERIUM*

Not only was the extension of Christianity and the conversion of the heathen an indispensable project and ideological justification favored by all the European empires grasping for territories beyond the Atlantic, but the very concept of "empire" itself conveyed religious overtones inherited from Roman times:

> To claim to be an *imperator* was to claim a degree, and eventually a kind of power, denied to mere kings. And the theocratic dimension which *imperium* acquired during the reign of Augustus, and which was reinforced by the Christian emperors and their apologists, widened still further the distinction between imperial and royal authority.[18]

Likewise, the aspiration to universal empire, traceable itself to classical origins, embodied religious ideals; the empire, *imperium*, was God's instrument to allow humanity to flourish.[19]

Protestant powers engaged in the early modern scramble for the Americas were by no means immune to the Christian overtones in the language of empire. The 1606 Charter of Virginia spoke of the projected colony as "so noble a Work, which may, by the Providence of Almighty God, hereafter tend to the Glory of his Divine Majesty, in propagating of Christian Religion to such People, as yet live in Darkness and miserable Ignorance of the true Knowledge and Worship of God and may in time bring the Infidels and Savages, living in those parts, to human Civility, and to a settled and quiet Government."[20] Most other British colonial charters of the seventeenth century, however, make no mention of the "noble work" of Christianizing. Moreover, other terms seem notable, such as those in Virginia's charter emphasizing "civility" rather than salvation as the ideal product of empire. Surveying the promotional writings of Richard Hakluyt and Samuel Purchas, David Armitage concludes that, pious formulas notwithstanding, British imperial ideology of the period was fundamentally secular.[21]

Christian or not, empires are by definition multicultural; *imperium* implies the subjection of more than one nation to a single ruler. At home, in Europe, as John Elliott and others have established, the typical nation-state of the period was a "composite monarchy," and abroad the indigenous peoples of the New World were to be incorporated under the king's benevolent reign.[22] The Catholic monarchs of Spain, heirs to the crusading traditions of the Middle Ages and to their own kingdom's intermittent struggles for territorial dominion in the Iberian Peninsula, sometimes had recourse to the language of "conquest" to characterize the process by which independent Indian nations were brought into the colonial orbit.[23] In the case of the Portuguese, the notion of Catholic crusades, missionary élan, and military conquests abroad found a notable rebirth under the personal rule of the youthful crusader-king Dom Sebastião in the sixteenth century.[24] But early modern Portuguese policymakers were more generally swayed by expansionist arguments about the consolidation of trading alliances and defensive arrangements than by those stressing crusading glory. Only with the arrival of Jesuit missionaries in Brazil from the mid-sixteenth century was substance put to the ardent strain of Portuguese claims that the Tupí-Guaraní were also souls who required direction and nurturing as well as protection from the rapacious European colonists.[25] In the French Empire, where there had never been anything resembling the conquests of Mexico and Peru or the crusading fervor of a Dom Sebastião, ramifying networks of native alliance were always the chosen instrument for establishing and expanding colonial rule.[26] Here, too, colonial discourse revolved around the attachment of distinct Indian nations to the French polity.

Following their break with Rome, the English, by contrast, seem to have been more inclined to speak of their empire as a collection of "plantations" or, in classical terms, *colonia*, which is to say "a settlement from a metropole in a foreign territory."[27] Thus, the expansion of Christendom appeared in this Protestant context to be primarily a matter of the export of Christians to overseas settlements. In contrast to the Catholic conception of empire, the Protestant English tended to regard Native Americans as an external factor, a help or a hindrance to colonization, rather than a central object of Christian rule.[28]

Paralleling the religious coloration of theories of empire in the Catholic Atlantic were the concrete contributions of the Church and clergy to the institutions and practices of colonial rule. Bishops and other ecclesiastical dignitaries were often integrated into the highest councils presiding over the Spanish viceroyalties, New France, Brazil, and other American jurisdictions. In 1516–1517, with the death of Fernando of Aragón and the minority of the future Charles V (who was being raised in Flanders), the Spanish regent Cardinal Francisco Jiménez de Cisneros engineered an attempt to halt exploitative colonial policies on the island of Hispaniola that he and Dominican campaigner-informants believed had brought disorder and the devastation of the island's indigenous peoples.[29] At the other end of the scale of government, parishes often functioned as a basic unit of local administration. Monarchs depended on the prelates and clergy to use their literacy to report on problems and to describe the Americas. Secular governors counted on priests to encourage the people in time of war, to police morals, and to care for the sick and destitute. Above all, they relied on agencies of the Church to act as intermediaries between indigenous peoples and the imperial state.

The Church's role as sometime partner to the secular states it accompanied was rarely free of tensions and contradictions. While the Catholic empires were plural and in competition with one another, the Church was theoretically singular and universal. Yet to a striking extent, the Church was actually organized on a "national" scale. The Gallican monarchs of France maintained tight control over the bishop of Quebec as well as the religious orders of New France. Even the supposedly cosmopolitan Jesuits remained almost entirely French in recruitment; they reported to superiors in France and wrote only rarely to Rome. Jesuits in Spanish America, as well as members of other religious orders, included large numbers of foreigners and Creoles in their numbers, but they too generally maintained a sense of identity with the Spanish colonial enterprise.

Drawing strength from their own sources of legitimacy and prestige, members of the regular and secular clergy could nevertheless voice opposition to the secular authorities and to the elite of colonial society. Bartolomé de Las Casas is the obvious case in point, but we might also mention the Brazilian Jesuits who courted murder in their courageous denunciation of the enslavement of Indians, or Bishop Laval of Quebec, who fulminated against the governor of New France for permitting the sale of liquor to the natives. The Church's missionary responsibilities, of course, made conflict with Creole societies, as well as with diocesan and secular authority, inevitable across the Catholic Atlantic.

While the notion that the Church in its diverse elements played an essential though occasionally critical role in the administration of Catholic empires is a common observation, as is the proposition that Christianity was integral to imperial ideology (with this, rather more so in Catholic than in Protestant empires), the ideal of Christendom has been less fully explored as an aspect of the emergence of the early modern Atlantic World. We wish to suggest that, as an animating concept, Christendom had a life of its own, arching over (or underpinning, if you prefer) the Catholic ideology of a Portuguese or a Spanish or a French empire.

Aspirations to worldwide expansion were, of course, built into the "catholic" idea of the Christian Church. That universalism, like the universalism of empire in its more secular form, dates back to the time of Rome:

> The Christian world order whose origins could not be separated from those of the Roman *Imperium* had always, like the empire itself, been thought of as identical *de iure* with the world—the *orbis terrarum*—and thus potentially as a cultural, moral and finally political order with no natural frontiers.[30]

Over the centuries, the universal ideal found expression in various forms and at different levels. Imperfect insofar as it was not coterminous with humanity, Christendom existed as a gathering of believers or as a collection of nations. It could be conceived in spatial terms as the territory subject to God's rule or combatively as the force opposing false religions and the necessarily oppressive regimes that protected them. The Christendom ideal came to the fore particularly during the Crusades of the Middle Ages and then again in the conflict with the Ottomans in the early modern period.

In the centuries that concern us, while Muslim incursions in eastern Europe and the Protestant schism threatened the integrity and extension of Christendom, discoveries abroad stimulated the expansionist tendencies inherent in the ideal. Iberian conquests in America, themselves often trumpeted in terms derived from medieval crusading traditions, helped give shape in turn to a newly militant view of Christendom. Some Spanish missionaries were inclined to favor the language of "conquest" over another favorite idiom, that of the fragile vineyard, to describe their efforts to bring the natives into God's empire. One of the early apostles to the Guaraní, Antonio Ruiz de Montoya, gave his cross-genre chronicle-memoir of 1639 the revealing title of *The Spiritual Conquest*,[31] while other Spaniards deployed similar militaristic language in their accounts. Christendom's boundaries were being pushed forward, they suggested, through the progressive defeat of a diabolic darkness, the annexation of territories, and the incorporation of peoples into the true and universal Church.

Interestingly, similar language occurs in missionary writings emanating from New France, where literal conquests, not to mention the theory of empire resting on the legitimate triumph of arms, were largely absent. French Jesuits among the Indians of seventeenth-century Canada rejoiced in their successes, modest as they were, as triumphs for Christendom and defeats for Satan. They explained their setbacks as due partly to the weakness of the European presence. Wrote Father Jérôme Lalement of the Huron mission,

> Finally, we cannot here have force at hand, and the support of that sharp sword which serves the Church in so holy a manner to give authority to her Decrees, to maintain Justice, and curb the insolence of those who trample under foot the holiness of her Mysteries.[32]

The wistful note of envy here probably refers to the Iberian-American missions of South and Mesoamerica, of which the French Jesuits were fully aware. Although the latter worked within a different kind of European empire, their norms and expectations were nevertheless shaped by the ideal of spiritual conquest.

In many areas of Latin America and North America evangelized by Catholic missionaries, the "*reducción*" (as idea and as practice) was a favored instrument of conversion. The discourse surrounding this important ideal and institution is also revealing on the concept of Catholic *imperium*. The purpose of *reducción*—in Jesuit-missionized Brazil, the *aldeia*—was to relocate indigenous people away from their usual habitat and often sacred topographies to specially designed villages of perfect godliness. Such attempts were sometimes nothing more than brutal resettlements for European convenience, but others were closer to utopian experiments, and both varieties were found in Brazil, New Spain, Peru, and Paraguay as well as New France. Implicit in the scheme was an assumption that space could be highly charged with positive or negative value. Places, like peoples, could be "wild" or "civil." A *reducción* at its most theoretical level represented newly hallowed ground carved out of the wilderness, but unlike the vaguely similar notion of redeemed space that prevailed on the Anglo-Protestant frontier of North America, this "clearing in the forest" was for Indians rather than settlers. What made the *reducción* a special place was the fact that it was sanctioned by and subject to God's law. The Indians living there, previously "proud" and independent, had now been "reduced" to obedience and to the experience of regular teaching through sermons, catechization, music, ceremony, religious theater, and new understandings of illness and forms of healing. That they obeyed the rules of the king and the directives of the missionaries was of secondary importance: above all, the converts were obedient to God. This was, of course, a utopian vision, obliquely related, at best, to the actual experience of Lupaqas, Guaraní, or Iroquois, but it conveys something of the day's current and vital sense of Christendom as *imperium:* in these sanctified enclaves, more perfectly than elsewhere, the universal Church claimed its new territories and new peoples.

Christendom, in the sixteenth and seventeenth centuries, was an expansive ideal striving in the direction of global unity, with lands and nations flourishing together in common subjection to the rule of God. Its rhetoric, replete with references to "conquest" and "obedience," has an unmistakably aggressive edge at times, mirroring the founding and recurring belligerence of its secular counterpart. Yet it is essential to note that the impulse to incorporate lands and peoples leaves room for a multiplicity of cultures and identities. Much more than in Protestant ideologies of empire, where the non-Christian peoples across the sea were subject to drives that would assimilate them completely or brush them aside,[33] the Catholic visions of Christendom sought to incorporate (albeit sometimes forcibly) existing American peoples, along with a number of their languages and significant portions of their cultures.

The newer historians of (secular) empire have taught students of the early modern world to see that, notwithstanding European pretensions to regulate and control, subject peoples were never passive. In one way or another, they played roles as dynamic and active agents, shaping the terms of imperial rule.[34] So it was with the European ideal of an expanded Atlantic Christendom: priests sought to reengineer native life to conform with the law of God as they understood it, but Indians fashioned their own versions of Christianity, and, in so doing, they had a hand in creating the multiple realities of overseas Christendom.

## CHRISTIANIZING THE NEW WORLD

Catholicism looms large in the historiography of the early modern Americas, though traditionally the subject has been treated in ways that minimize the opportunities for fruitful dialogue with scholarship on the European Catholic Reformation. Scholars tended to assume that religion was significant insofar as the confrontation between Christianity and indigenous systems of belief and practice formed part of a greater and broader encounter of European and American cultures. If Christianization represents the cultural dimension of colonization and if its interest resides in the world-historical dynamics by which Europe subordinated the peoples and cultures of the New World, then the history of Catholicism in the Americas does seem to belong to a different narrative framework than the one in which the history of European Catholicism is usually recounted.

Through much of the twentieth century, historians of colonial religion did indeed concentrate on themes that implicitly emphasized the peculiarities of the New World.[35] Catholic apologetic works overlapped with nonsectarian studies, all tending, when they did not actually lionize the European missionaries, to at least place them, their heroism and limitations, their successes and failures, at the center of the story. The French historian Robert Ricard's 1933 monograph *La conquête spirituelle du Mexique* might be taken as paradigmatic, its title assuming the sixteenth-century metaphor of his sources and forcefully linking conversion to Christianity with colonial conquest. Easily and frequently caricatured by revisionists, Ricard's interpretation actually contained a richness and subtlety, not to mention suggestive hints leading in the direction of an alternative interpretation; yet his work did focus attention on the thoughts and deeds of the evangelists from Europe. As to the natives of central Mexico, the Sorbonne professor asked loftily, "Who can flatter himself that he knows what takes place in the dark minds of the natives?"[36]

A later work in the same tradition, James Axtell's *The Invasion Within*, proves that it is possible to be much more attentive to and respectful of Amerindian viewpoints while maintaining a primary focus on the European pole of the "Contest of Cultures in Colonial North America," Axtell's subtitle and his theme.[37] Informed by ethnohistorical research on native cultures, *The Invasion Within* nevertheless treats Christianization as part of a strictly European agenda of change; conversion therefore appears as a kind of cultural surrender to the colonizing power. Whereas Axtell is open in his admiration of the French Jesuits who labored in northeastern North America, some other researchers tend to be critical of them, stressing their interference with native customs or their attempts to subordinate women to the authority of their husbands.[38] Whether pro- or anti-Jesuit, however, North American historians of the second half of the twentieth century tended to treat missionaries as the main agents of religious change, while Indians in these accounts displayed either resistance or compliance.

Somewhat similar approaches, in which religion appeared as the battleground for the contending cultures of colonizers and colonized, can be found in Latin American scholarship of the same period—thus the division of Inga Clendinnen's *Ambivalent Conquests*(1989) into a section on "Spaniards" followed by another on "Indians" and the memorably dichotomous images of Spanish Catholicism's "tempered steel" and native Andeans' "closely woven cloak" in a glorious chapter by Karen Spalding titled

"Belief and Resistance." The oppositional predication and choice of terms defined the historiographical moment well beyond the Andes: "European Catholicism" and indigenous "traditions" face off in "a battle" that Europeans and their indigenous "accomplices" waged in a singular effort "to replace one set of beliefs by another."[39]

More recent work in the field, some of it influenced by developments in modern African history (Robin Horton, Terence Ranger, and John and Jean Comaroff), has moved away from the assimilation/resistance paradigm in the direction of a more complex take on the religious interchange characteristic of colonial societies. Colonial Catholicism was made, it is increasingly being argued, by Indians—not to mention Mestizos and other mixed-race persons—as well as by Europeans and white Creoles. The so-called "dark minds of the natives" have turned out to be the site of religious creativity where indigenous traditions and Christian influences did not so much merge as combine and collide to produce a variety of shifting local variants.[40] The parallels are not perfect (in part because "race" looms so large in the New World setting), but a certain transposition can be performed that brings out the parallel tendencies of scholarship on the two sides of the Atlantic. Historians are increasingly inclined to shine the spotlight on the various Catholicisms of the laity and of the unprivileged portions of society; moreover, they are discovering in both cases that change, impelled by forces emanating from "above" and "below," was multidirectional.

The African and Afro-American dimensions of the Catholic Atlantic are only beginning to receive the attention they deserve, but here too scholars are reaching broadly similar conclusions about missionaries and "missionized." In coastal regions of the seventeenth-century kingdom of Kongo, Richard Gray observes, the Christianity preached by Italian Capuchins was taken over by Soyo elites for their own purposes, purposes inseparable from indigenous concerns about ancestors, magic, and self-discipline.[41] Across the sea in the colonies of Spain, Portugal, and France, millions of Africans and people of African descent, both enslaved and free, were exposed to Catholicism and made it their own. By 1600, in places as different as the sugar-producing Bahian coast of Brazil and Lima, the capital of the Peruvian viceroyalty, people of African descent outnumbered all other groups, posing significant new challenges and emergent identities that are only beginning to be faced.[42] In the circum-Caribbean region, as in much of Portuguese Brazil, an expanding enslavement of Africans drove entire economies and underpinned societies in such a way as to challenge the evangelizers who accompanied empire to turn their attention away from native peoples and toward the slaves' suffering and their position as new Christians.[43] Scholars in these different settings in the Catholic Atlantic World share several features, not least a growing curiosity about both the fundamental relationship between European and American theaters of Christianization and correction and what the entwined processes of evangelization, response, and emergence might contain. What appears particularly to be needed are ways of thinking further about the extraordinary mobility and proliferation that coexists with early modern Catholic attempts to define, reform, and fix its doctrines as much as its locations. A plurality of local religious realities emerges and comes fitfully and incompletely into "fruition,"[44] from Brittany to Kahnawake, from Valencia to Valparaiso. Appreciating them fully, that is, understanding their simultaneous connectedness and autonomy, requires giving up on reigning notions of Roman Catholicism as a singular entity or "teaching" that moves the whole, or even the larger part, of itself as its most willful agents wish.

Twisting and redeploying the historian of late antiquity Peter Brown's idea of "micro-Christendoms,"[45] recent work on the Spanish world insists on local people's particular, small-scale cultic priorities, their plural and variant Christian enthusiasms and forms—the *micro*—while also capturing their persistent and largely self-defined membership in and relationship to larger collections of people, beliefs, rules, and practices—the *Christendoms* of a given context.[46] Accordingly, a student of any part of the Catholic or Catholicizing world would be repaid for an alertness to the unevenness and incompleteness of religious and cultural transformation, to the diffusion of Christianities as much through unsanctioned processes of reinvention as through the sanctioned channels of evangelization and response. The dialectical relationship between the official purveyors and promoters of certain aspects of Catholic Christianity, on the one hand, and the reconfiguring recipients, some of whom fast became new owners and promoters, on the other, is essential. Subordinating pressures and constraints are omnipresent, and resistance is sometimes possible, but gone are the clearly polarized assumptions about who imposes and just what ends up being received.

## OTHER SEAS?

Do our efforts to emphasize the continuous relationships among metropolitan European and colonial American Catholic and Catholicizing settings generate an artificially Atlantic unit of analysis when our historical subjects thought and acted in terms of a more expansive whole—a global whole in which the key processes we have set out in a Catholic Atlantic also cohere?

Our answer leaves the Catholic Atlantic not only standing but also vital as a unit of study, even as it recognizes wider resonances with Asian settings, among others. Fundamentally, the effective control that Spanish, Portuguese, and French invaders were able to claim and exercise on many American lands and peoples was sufficiently profound to mark a difference from the situations in most of Asia, thus significantly affecting what could be (and what was) attempted in terms of the cultural and religious transformation of originally non-Christian "others." Of course, in more particular terms, effective rule in the Americas varied greatly both between their respective regions and within them. In some of the colonial American hinterlands, European rule was little more than an administrator's distant notion, and actual interactions between native peoples and missionaries were rather more akin to those in an Asian enclave, such as the port city of Melaka on the Malay Peninsula, stations in the Spice Islands (Moluccas), or the Chinese court: missionaries were effectively dependent on local whim and mercy.

With such important qualifications acknowledged, however, Europeans' broad claims to territorial dominion and authority in the Americas mattered greatly in many areas. These claims were judgments handed down by rulers whose decisions, as we have seen, were underpinned by Catholic Christianity. Their very building blocks were massive presumptions about the spiritual state and prospects of respective autochthonous peoples, many only dimly known, from Hudson Bay to Tierra del Fuego. Even in American regions far from the heartlands of colonial control or where a cluster of missionaries were the sole markers of Europeanness and acted accordingly, a powerful series of pretenses could still be drawn on and fed: a French, Portuguese, or Spanish crown laid claim to these lands and souls; with these claims came the opportunity and obligation granted by God to evangelize and reform places in which the Devil had not only been confirmed present but also proven himself to be vicious and unchecked; and finally, because of the broad claim to rule, there was a belief that difficult situations would only improve, that severe isolation, reverses, and sticky predicaments would fall away once a tighter control could be exercised and consolidated. With a few notable exceptions (such as the Philippines archipelago), nothing quite like this presumption and pretense could be exercised by Catholic churchmen in Asia.

The relationship between much of Asia and the Americas in terms of Catholic Christianization was perhaps more mental than practical. Take the familiar example of Jesuit endeavor and diffusion as an illustrative point of entry (fig. 1). Francis Xavier was one of two from the newly minted Society of Jesus who accepted the invitation of King João III of Portugal in 1541 to carry the Catholic faith to the East Indies and the trading empire he hoped to consolidate and expand there. Because of the vivid letters Xavier composed and saw circulated about his adventures throughout the Portuguese possessions in the Far East, about his beginnings in Japan, and his experience of the Chinese and dreams for China, he fast became exemplary. Xavier was the forerunner, a new apostle whose life Jesuit novices would learn about and follow for generations. He offered integration and unity of purpose when Protestantism loomed in Europe and invitation toward what must have seemed a much wider and possibly Christianizable world that was enlarging dramatically with every year. Xavier moved so fully and powerfully across what might be called the base of the early modern Catholic world in part, of course, because he wrote. His letters and their intimate portrayals of mission experience, of new converts, of his doubts, became edifying archetypes. He became generalizable, applicable, like the best of early modern saints. The power of his words potentially reached any reader or hearer, lay or clerical, and Xavierian words and the episodes they conveyed fast became "the man" and soon "the saint" for people whose briefs were enacted far from Japan or the Fishery Coast.

Yet Xavier, the man and composer of edifying words, was also advanced on high by others. Precisely as in the Catholic Atlantic, official personages and channels of promotion were fundamental parts of the story of Catholic Christian trajectories and their transformations. Over the course of the late sixteenth and early seventeenth centuries, Portuguese Jesuits worked up miracles, prophecies, and renewed notions of providence to fashion what amounted to a simultaneously Portuguese, Asian, and Jesuit saint out of a Spanish (Basque, in fact) missionary. The spread of Xavierian devotions, miracle narratives, and paintings that depicted moments in his life often surpassed those of the founder, his one-time spiritual and intellectual companion Ignatius. It is the dialectical relationship between promotions and devotions, between the universalizing Catholic Christendom and its particularizing micro-Christendoms, that marks out a story and style so common to the early modern period. Long before his canonization by Rome, devotees could find in the figure of Xavier whatever they needed. His circle of promoters were transoceanic colonial players par excellence, beating a calculated drum for Portuguese and Jesuit destinies in Asia even as, from another angle, they glorified a Spaniard and legitimized Spanish and Jesuit efforts.[47]

A massive oil painting of a Xavierian miracle in the East that was hung just inside the main door of a church in the center of the former Inka capital of Cusco, Peru, offers one way of thinking about Asia and the Catholic Atlantic. Xavier's stories and his

**Figure 1** Allegory of the Jesuits and their missions in the four continents. Anonymous painter (eighteenth century). Courtesy José Luís Fernández-Castañeda, S.J., parish priest of the Church of San Pedro, Lima, and Administrator of the Jesuit Order in Peru. St. Ignatius is flanked on his right by Francis Xavier, sporting a chasuble with Asian motifs. In the background, Jesuits living all over the world and occupying a variety of hierarchies within the Church, including those wearing Chinese costumes and prelate robes, preside over the conversion of the faithful in India, China, Africa, and the Americas. Like Atlas, the Jesuits carry the globe on their shoulders.

promoters' converting influence included but also stretched well beyond the cluster of post-Tridentine politicoreligious lobbyists shuttling tirelessly between Lisbon, Madrid, and Rome in the interest of his and Ignatius's sanctification cases. The Cusco canvas is not alone and attests to the fact that Xavier and Asia were otherwise important and that they became part of lived religion in the Catholic Atlantic.

## Notes

1   But two examples in these burgeoning subfields would be John Thornton, *Africa and Africans in the Making of the Atlantic World, 1400–1680* (Cambridge, 1992), and Christine Daniels and Michael V. Kennedy, eds., *Negotiated Empires: Centers and Peripheries in the Americas, 1500–1820* (New York, 2002).

2   Compounding the challenges posed by this fragmentation of knowledge in accordance with perceived geographic and cultural boundaries is an important subject that should not be forgotten, even if it must remain beyond the purview of this brief chapter: what Talal Asad and others have noted to be a peculiarly stubborn Western and modern inclination to conceive of "religion" as a separate subject rather than as one that was integral to most realms of human thought, experience, and action in an early modern period, not to mention others; see Talal Asad, *Genealogies of Religion: Discipline and Reasons of Power in Christianity and Islam* (Baltimore, 1994), esp. chap. 1.

3   See especially *The Church Militant and Iberian Expansion, 1440–1770* (Baltimore, 1978).

4   See especially selected proceedings from the international "Conference on the History of Religion in the New World during Colonial Times" (December 17 and 18, 1957) published in *The Americas* 14, no. 4 (1958) and featuring summaries that attempt more integration than most of the contributors; a separatist, three-voice overview by Charles H. Lippy, Robert Choquette, and Stafford Poole, *Christianity Comes to the Americas, 1492–1776* (New York, 1992); and a more creative pass by Dominique Deslandres, "Dans les Amériques," in *Histoire du Christianisme des origines à nos jours*, gen. eds. Jean-Marie Mayeur et al., *Vol. 9: L'Âge de Raison (1620/30–1750)*, ed. Marc Venard (Paris, 1997), Troisième partie, "Le christianisme dans le monde," chap. 1, 615–736. While conforming, on the whole, to the inherited pattern of moving through each of the colonial American lands established by language and phases of imperial enterprise, Deslandres does ingeniously imagine, in a section on African Christianity (706–27), a history across an Atlantic American whole, with some shared phenomena but also contrasting experiences. Two recent collections of essays also deserve mention, though their isolated contributors largely suggest broader relationships rather than explore them: Nicholas Griffiths and Fernando Cervantes, eds., *Spiritual Encounters: Interactions between Christianity and Native Religions in Colonial America* (Lincoln, Nebr., 1999), and Allan Greer and Jodi Bilinkoff, eds., *Colonial Saints: Discovering the Holy in the Americas, 1500–1800* (New York, 2003).

5   John W. O'Malley, *Trent and All That: Renaming Catholicism in the Early Modern Era* (Cambridge, Mass., 2000).

6   Simon Ditchfield, "Of Dancing Cardinals and *Mestizo* Madonnas: Reconfiguring the History of Roman Catholicism in the Early Modern Period," *Journal of Early Modern History* 8, nos. 3–4 (2004): 386–408.

7   For example, R. Po-chia Hsia, *The World of Catholic Renewal, 1540–1770* (Cambridge, 1998).

8   To offer the Spanish kingdoms as only one example, on the Catholic attempts at "pre-reform" in the Castilian diocese of Cuenca, see Sara T. Nalle, *God in La Mancha: Religious Reform and the People of Cuenca, 1500–1650* (Baltimore, 1992), 23–31, within 3–31; while

surveying matters over a broader set of prelates and places, see A. D. Wright, *Catholicism and Spanish Society under the Reign of Philip II, 1555–1598, and Philip III, 1598–1621* (Lewiston, Me., 1991).

9  Louis Châtellier, *L'Europe des dévots* (Paris, 1987), published in an English translation by Jean Birrell as *The Europe of the Devout: The Catholic Reformation and the Formation of a New Society* (Cambridge, 1989); John Henderson, *Piety and Charity in Late Medieval Florence* (Oxford, 1994); Brian S. Pullan, *Poverty and Charity: Europe, Italy, Venice, 1400–1700* (Aldershot, 1994); A. N. Galpern, *The Religions of the People in Sixteenth-Century Champagne* (Cambridge, Mass., 1976); Maureen Flynn, *Sacred Charity: Confraternities and Social Welfare in Zamora, 1400–1700* (Ithaca, N.Y., 1988).

10  *Catholicism between Luther and Voltaire: A New View of the Catholic Reform* (London, 1977), 237.

11  Valerie I. J. Flint, *The Rise of Magic in Early Medieval Europe* (Princeton, N.J., 1991).

12  See, for example, A. D. Wright, *The Counter Reformation: Catholic Europe and the Non Christian World* (New York, 1982), 267.

13  Nigel Griffin, "'Un muro invisible': Moriscos and Cristianos Viejos in Granada," in *Medieval and Renaissance Studies in Honour of P. E. Russell*, ed. F. W. Hodcroft et al. (Oxford, 1981), 135; Adriano Prosperi, "'Otras Indias': Missionari della Controriforma tra Contadini e Selvaggi," in *Scienze credenze occulte livelli di cultura*, ed. Eugenio Garin et al. (Florence, 1982), 205–34; Jennifer D. Selwyn, *A Paradise Inhabited by Devils: The Jesuits' Civilizing Mission in Early Modern Naples* (Burlington, Vt., 2004); Dominique Deslandres, *Croire et faire croire: Les missions française au XVIIe siècle* (Paris, 2003).

14  See, for example, Robert Mandrou, *Introduction to Modern France, 1500–1640: An Essay in Historical Psychology* (New York, 1977); Robert Muchembled, *Société et mentalités dans la France moderne, XVIe-XVIIIe siècle* (Paris, 1990).

15  The "pagan survival" interpretation is most fully articulated in the work of Carlo Ginzburg in *The Cheese and the Worms: The Cosmos of a Sixteenth-Century Miller*, trans. Tedeschi (Harmondsworth, 1982) and *The Night Battles: Witchcraft and Agrarian Cults in the Sixteenth and Seventeenth Centuries* (Baltimore, 1992).

16  See especially William A. Christian Jr., "De los santos a María: Panorama de las devociones a santuarios españoles desde el principio de la Edad Media hasta nuestros días," in *Temas de antropología española*, ed. C. Lison Tolosana (Madrid, 1976), 49–105; *Local Religion in Sixteenth-Century Spain* (Princeton, N.J., 1981); *Apparitions in Late Medieval and Renaissance Spain* (Princeton, N.J., 1981); and *Person and God in a Spanish Valley* (1972; rev. ed., Princeton, N.J., 1989).

17  Deslandres, *Croire et faire croire.*

18  Anthony Pagden, *Lords of All the World: Ideologies of Empire in Spain, Britain and France c. 1500–c. 1800* (New Haven, Conn., 1995), 15.

19  Ibid., 27–28. See also Fernández-Armesto's contribution to this volume.

20  "The First Charter of Virginia; April 10, 1606," The Avalon Project at Yale Law School, http://www.yale.edu/lawweb/avalon/avalon.htm.

21  David Armitage, *The Ideological Origins of the British Empire* (Cambridge, 2000), 99. See also J. H. Elliott, *Britain and Spain in America: Colonists and Colonized* (Reading, England, 1994); and J. H. Elliott, *Empires of the Atlantic World: Britain and Spain in America, 1492–1830* (in press).

22  Begin with J. H. Elliott, "A Europe of Composite Monarchies," *Past and Present* 137 (1992): 48–71; see also Mark Greengrass, "Introduction: Conquest and Coalescence," in *Conquest and Coalescence: The Shaping of the State in Early Modern Europe*, ed. Mark Greengrass (London, 1991), 1–24, and the superlative collection edited by Daniels and Kennedy, *Negotiated Empires* (cited in note 1).

23    A qualification is in order on this point. After the early mainland conquests of Hernán Cortés and Francisco Pizarro, as the scale of the demographic collapse of many indigenous groups became evident and as riches became less readily available, characterizations of protection and pacification took precedence.

24    See C. R. Boxer, "Faith in Empire: The Cross and the Crown in Portuguese Expansion, Fifteenth to Eighteenth Centuries," in *The Globe Encircled and the World Revealed*, ed. Ursula Lamb (Aldershot, 1995), 244, 241–56.

25    Charlotte de Castelnau-L'Estoile, *Les ouvriers d'une vigne stérile: Les jésuites et la conversion des Indiens au Brésil, 1580–1620* (Lisbon, 2000); Serafim Leite, *História da Companhia de Jesus no Brasil*, 10 vols. (Lisbon, 1938–1950), esp. vols. 1–3; and, investigating the Jesuits' roles within the broader Portuguese world, Dauril Alden, *The Making of an Enterprise: the Society of Jesus in Portugal, Its Empire, and Beyond, 1540–1750* (Stanford, Calif., 1996).

26    A recently published survey of the history of French North America underlines this pattern: see Gilles Havard and Cécile Vidal, *Histoire de l'Amérique française* (Paris, 2003), 188–99. Note that similar strategies of imperial expansion through alliance were also followed in many areas of Spanish America.

27    Armitage, *The Ideological Origins of the British Empire*, 45.

28    Pagden, *Lords of All the World*, 36–37.

29    Frank Moya Pons, *Historia colonial de Santo Domingo*, 3rd ed. (Santiago, 1977), 68–69; see also José García Oro, *Cisneros: El cardenal de España* (Barcelona, 2002), esp. 211–44.

30    Pagden, *Lords of All the World*, 30–31.

31    Antonio Ruiz de Montoya, *The Spiritual Conquest accomplished by the Religious of the Society of Jesus in the Provinces of . . .* (St. Louis, Mo., [1639] 1993).

32    Reuben Thwaites, ed., *The Jesuit Relations and Allied Documents*, 73 vols. (Cleveland, 1896–1900) [hereafter JR], 28:55. See Carole Blackburn, *Harvest of Souls: The Jesuit Missions and Colonialism in North America, 1632–1650* (Kingston, 2000), 105–28.

33    Our characterization of Protestant ideologies of empire is overly schematic. If this were a longer chapter and its subject the "Christian Atlantic," our remarks would certainly require extensive qualification in light of Jean de Léry's writings on Brazil, John Eliot's missions in Massachusetts, and other manifestation of Protestant cross-currents. As it is, we hope to prompt others' explorations.

34    See, notably, Richard White, *The Middle Ground: Indians, Empires, and Republics in the Great Lakes Region, 1650–1815* (Cambridge, 1991), and Ignacio J. Gallup-Díaz, *The Door of the Seas and Key to the Universe: Indian Politics and Imperial Rivalry in the Darién, 1640–1750* (New York, 2001, an electronic monograph in the Gutenberg-e online series of the American Historical Association: http://www.gutenberg-e.org/index.html).

35    Though, admittedly, there was a strong current of institutional "Church history" in Latin America and French Canada. Works in this tradition, often written by clerics, continue to be important down to the present day. See, for example, the thorough and internally rigorous works of Mariano Cuevas and Lucien Campeau: Lucien Campeau, *La Mission des Jésuites chez les Hurons 1634–1650* (Montreal, 1987); P. Mariano Cuevas, *Historia de la Iglesia en Mexico*, 4 vols. (Mexico City, 1942).

36    Robert Ricard, *The Spiritual Conquest of Mexico: An Essay on the Apostolate and the Evangelizing Methods of the Mendicant Orders in New Spain, 1523–1572*, trans. Lesley Byrd Simpson (Berkeley, 1966), 277. The phrase, it should be noted, is less egregious when properly placed in context. One of the more systematic critiques of the Ricard thesis that repays consideration is still that of J. Jorge Klor de Alva, "Spiritual Conflict and Accommodation in New Spain: Toward a Typology of Aztec Responses to Christianity," in *The Inca and Aztec States 1400–1800: Anthropology and History*, ed. G. A. Collier, R. I. Rosaldo, and J. D. Wirth (New York, 1982), 345–65, though see also the earlier insights of

Ursula Lamb, "Religious Conflicts in the Conquest of Mexico," *Journal of the History of Ideas* 17 (1956): 526–39.

37  James Axtell, *The Invasion Within: The Contest of Cultures in Colonial North America* (New York, 1985).

38  See, for example, James P. Ronda, "The Sillery Experiment: A Jesuit Indian Village in New France, 1637–1663," *American Indian Culture and Research Journal* 3 (1979): 1–18; Karen Anderson, *Chain Her by One Foot: The Subjugation of Women in Seventeenth Century New France* (London, 1991).

39  Clendinnen, *Ambivalent Conquests: Maya and Spaniard in Yucatan, 1517–1570* (Cambridge, 1987); Karen Spalding, *Huarochirí: An Andean Society under Inca and Spanish Rule* (Stanford, Calif., 1984), 239, 244, and 240, within chap. 8, 239–69. "Tempered steel" is only our paraphrase of Spalding's image of the strains of the Counter-Reformation giving "a cast to the temper and the actions of the Church in the Andes that was lacking for much of the first decades of the Spanish presence in Mesoamerica" (244).

40  Examples of the new approaches include William B. Taylor, *Magistrates of the Sacred: Priests and Parishioners in Eighteenth-Century Mexico* (Stanford, Calif., 1996), esp. chap. 3; Serge Gruzinski, *La colonisation de l'imaginaire: Sociétés indigènes et occidentalisation dans le Mexique espagnol, XVIe–XVIIIe siècle* (Paris, 1988); Inga Clendinnen, "Ways to the Sacred: Reconstructing 'Religion' in Sixteenth-Century Mexico," *History and Anthropology* 5 (1990): 105–41; Kenneth Mills, *Idolatry and Its Enemies: Colonial Andean Religion and Extirpation, 1640–1750* (Princeton, N.J., 1997); Allan Greer, "Conversion and Identity: Iroquois Christianity in Seventeenth-Century New France," in *Conversions: Old Worlds and New*, ed. Kenneth Mills and Anthony Grafton (Rochester, N.Y., 2003), 175–98.

41  Richard Gray, *Black Christians and White Missionaries* (New Haven, Conn., 1990), esp. chap. 3. See also John K. Thornton, "The Development of an African Catholic Church in the Kingdom of Kongo, 1491–1750," *Journal of African History* (1984): 147–67.

42  See Castelnau-L'Estoile, *Les ouvriers d'une vigne sterile*, and, among the works of Jean-Pierre Tardieu, esp. *L'Eglise et les noirs au Pérou: XVIe et XVIIe siècles*, 2 vols. (Paris, 1993); on midcolonial Mexico, Herman L. Bennett, *Africans in Colonial Mexico: Absolutism, Christianity, and Afro-Creole Consciousness, 1570–1640* (Bloomington, Ind., 2003).

43  The Jesuit Alonso de Sandoval is a good example of a voice who responded. His 1627 work *De instauranda Aethiopum salute* grew out of experience in early seventeenth-century Cartagena de Indias; see Sandoval, *Un tratado sobre la esclavitud (De instauranda Aethiopum salute)*, ed. Enriqueta Vila Vilar (Madrid, 1987). Recent scholarship includes Margaret M. Olson, *Slavery and Salvation in Colonial Cartagena de Indias* (Gainesville, Fla., 2004) and Jean-Pierre Tardieu, "Du bon usage de la monstuosité: La vision de l'Afrique chez Alonso de Sandoval (1627)," *Bulletin Hispanique* 86, no. 1–2 (1984): 164–78.

44  Elisabetta Corsi searches for "common modalities of fruition and response provoked by exposure to . . . sacred images" in her "Masons of Faith: Images and Sacred Architecture of the Jesuits in Late Imperial Beijing" (unpublished paper presented at the Workshop on Court, Ritual Community, and the City: Chinese and Christian Rituality in Late Imperial Beijing, Katholieke Universiteit Leuven, Leuven, Belgium, 18 June 2004).

45  *The Rise of Western Christendom*, 2nd ed. (Oxford, 2003), esp. introduction and chap. 16.

46  Kenneth Mills, "The Naturalisation of Andean Christianities," in *The Cambridge History of Christianity*, vol. 6, *Re-Formation and Expansion, c. 1500–c. 1660*, ed. R. Po-chia Hsia (Cambridge, in press).

47  Ines G. Županov, "The Prophetic and the Miraculous in Portuguese Asia: A Hagiographical View of Colonial Culture," *Santa Barbara Portuguese Studies* 2 (1995): 137, 135–61, and her *Disputed Mission: Jesuit Experiments and Brahmanical Knowledge in Seventeenth-Century India* (New Delhi, 1999).

*Scholars of Puritan New England and colonial Spanish America have rarely spoken to each other. When one thinks of the European colonization of the New World, images of the daring yet brutal conquistadores in Mexico bubble up along with those of the Pilgrims in New England: these are images of two allegedly radically different experiences of colonization. Greer and Mills also draw these distinctions. Their "Atlantic," although truly rooted on both sides of the ocean, is nevertheless distinctively Catholic. Jorge Cañizares-Esguerra works against the grain of this tradition and suggests that there were indeed the likes of Cortés and Pizarro in New England. He argues that there were to be sure important religious differences between English Calvinists and Spanish Catholics in the New World. But the literature on the Reformation has exaggerated these differences, overlooking striking resemblances. For the Puritan and Spanish clergies, the colonization of the New World was an act of Reconquista, of taking the continent from the Devil back to God. In the imagination of these two groups, the Devil and his armies of demons had ruled uncontested over the fauna and flora and the peoples of the New World. Both the Puritan and the Spanish clergies thought that the Devil was a tyrant and therefore that colonization was an act of liberation. Both groups, however, thought that Satan fought back and was determined to uproot the settlers from America by manipulating nature (tempests at sea and plagues) and by lining up allies (Indians, metropolitan officials, foreign enemies, and heretics and witches within). According to Cañizares-Esguerra, studying the Atlantic solely along national lines obscures a world of similarities and shared values. This, of course, begs the question: did the French, the Portuguese, and the Dutch also share similar demonological views?*

# The Devil in the New World:
# A Transnational Perspective

## Jorge Cañizares-Esguerra

The historiographies of the British and Spanish Atlantics have gone their own separate ways. Behind these separate trajectories lies the assumption that the United States and "Mexico" (that opaque and seemingly homogeneous space south of the Rio Grande comprising dozens of nation-states and peoples) are in fact two essentially (ontologically) different spaces. The literature on the British Atlantic is about the making of the United States, whereas that on the Spanish Atlantic is about elucidating the colonial roots of "Latin America." These two worlds are destined never to meet.

The purpose of this chapter is to undermine this assumption through a case study. I maintain that the discourses the Puritan and the Spanish clergies used to make sense of their presence in the New World were remarkably similar. I argue that both groups saw colonization as an epic struggle against the Devil. Although the languages of conquest, the chivalric, and the crusading have come to be seen as typical of Spanish colonialism in the New World, I maintain that they were also central to Puritan colonization. Puritans and Catholics felt threatened and harassed by Satan and his armies of demons. Christians, consequently, waged a war of attrition against Lucifer, who in turn used various strategies to defeat the heroes. Puritans and Spanish Catholics encountered Satan everywhere: in nature (in storms at sea and in the landscapes, plants, and animals of America), in foreign enemies (pirates, Indians, and frontier armies), and inside their own communities (heretics, metropolitan authorities, and rebellious and rapacious individuals). Puritans and Spanish Catholics conceptualized the Devil and his actions in the New World in remarkably similar terms and with similar consequences for colonization.

Historians have been only partially right to argue that the English were more "modern" than the Spaniards when justifying territorial possession. It is now common to maintain that the English deployed Lockean theories of property: land and objects belonged to those who had transformed them through labor. Since English colonists did not find traces of "labor" in the New World, they considered the lands of the natives empty and ready for the picking. Spaniards, on the other hand, were more "medieval." They justified territorial possession by claiming that the pope had "dominium" and "imperium" over pagan territories. As the pope transferred that sovereignty over the Spanish kings, the kings' vassals felt entitled to the newfound lands.[1] This distinction not only blurs important chronological differences (Puritan colonization was launched some 150 years after the Spaniards first arrived in the New World) but also leaves out the more important biblical foundations of European colonial expansion. For Puritans and Catholics, colonization was an act foreordained by God, prefigured in the trials of the Israelites in Canaan. Just as the Israelites had fought against the stiff resistance of Satan's minions (the Philistines), Puritans and Spanish clerics felt entitled to take over America as they battled their way into a continent infested by demons. Ultimately, the objective of both religious communities became to transform the "wilderness" into blossoming spiritual "plantations."

This common demonological discourse is the subject of this chapter. But before plunging into it, a question needs to be answered: Why compare only the Puritans of New England, instead of some other group in British North America, to the Spanish Catholics? Given that Jack P. Greene has demonstrated that New England's politics, culture, and economy were not representative of the British American experience, it would appear to make more sense to focus on the ideologies that surfaced in the middle and southern colonies.[2] In fact, as the work of Edward L. Bond suggests, the crusading discourse of colonization as an epic battle against the Devil seems to have run as deeply in seventeenth-century Virginia as it did in Puritan New England.[3] Furthermore, there is the issue of sources. Simply put, Puritans left behind a far larger cache of primary sources than other English colonists. But most importantly, the warnings of scholars like Greene have not yet dislodged the Puritans from the public imagination as the quintessentially "American" colonists. This reason alone justifies my choice: I want to reach and challenge a wide audience.

At first sight, positing resemblances between the Puritan and Spanish clergies makes little sense, for the literature on the Reformation has familiarized us only with differences. The Puritans were followers of John Calvin (1509–1564), whereas Spaniards were staunch defenders of the pope, leaders of the Counter-Reformation. Therefore, these two communities developed very different views of God, salvation, church organization, and conversion. As followers of Calvin, the Puritans, for example, believed that God was an almighty sovereign whose plans for humanity were inscrutable. In the Puritan view of things, Catholics who thought that it was up to them to be saved (by either behaving well or praying to God) were full of themselves. According to the Puritans, Catholics had a ridiculous view of God as a petty merchant whose will could be bought (such as by buying indulgences) or bent at will (through confession and prayers). Salvation was a preordained act of God, and nothing humans did could change the outcome. According to the Puritans, Catholics had deviated from the original message of God as revealed in the Old and New Testaments. Over the centuries Catholics had added institutions and ceremonies never mentioned in the original scriptures. The Puritans in fact owed their name to their efforts to "purify" the church from these inventions as they sought to live according to the religious, social, and political institutions found in the Bible. For the Puritans, Catholic "inventions" were not really the product of the human imagination but of demonic deception: Counter-Reformation Spain stood for the Antichrist.[4]

These theological differences manifested themselves concretely in the ways these two religious communities approached colonization. Spanish Catholics, for example, had laxer standards of who should belong to the church, along with a more hierarchical understanding of how to communicate with God. Spaniards therefore approached conversion by demanding that indigenous peoples conform to certain rituals and external behaviors, allowing in practice great variations. As Greer and Mills have shown in the previous chapter, this attitude toward conversion allowed for the multiplication of micro-Catholicisms all across the empire. The Puritans, however, saw things differently. For them, conversion implied God's election: the individual had to be touched by God's grace after protracted "preparation." God acted like a seal over the wax of the body and soul (justification), transforming them forever (sanctification). To belong to a Puritan church, individuals needed to prove, through protracted interviews and testimonials (which could last several months), that they had in fact been touched by the grace of God. When the Puritans arrived in the New World, they instituted such strict rules of conversion that not even the sons and daughters of the members of the church could be guaranteed membership. Although some Puritans did seek to convert Amerindians to hasten the arrival of the millennium, in practice Indian converts were few and far between.[5] In short, whereas by the seventeenth century there were thousands if not millions of Amerindians in Spanish America practicing their own versions of Catholicism, only a handful of Amerindians in New England could bear witness to the grace of God.

It is clear that there were important differences separating the Puritans from the Spanish Americans. But there were also significant resemblances, and the scholarship on the Atlantic has paid little attention to them because it has imagined the Atlantic in largely national terms. In the pages that follow, I explore the discourse of demonology and spiritual gardening and argue that Anglo-American Puritans and Spanish American Catholics saw the world of colonization in strikingly similar terms.

## THE DISCOURSE OF DEMONOLOGY

For us, the Devil is largely an abstract figure that stands for various manifestations of human evil, be they genocide or imperial hubris. But in the early modern period, the Devil was a real physical force who had his abode in the sphere of air (thus his power over the weather and the chiming of church bells to drive him away) but who could be incarnated in plants, animals, and human beings. The Devil had armies of millions of demons who were capable of setting off storms and earthquakes. He enjoyed absolute mastery of the preternatural (those laws of nature beyond the understanding of humans, including occult forces and natural sympathies) and could use his knowledge to deceive humans. The Devil was a master of deception by altering physical reality or by manipulating the mind, creating illusions. Thus, no one could be sure that what he or she saw or experienced was true or a demonic trick. The Devil was also a master of mockery and inversion; wherever he went, he created institutions that mimicked those established by God.[6] Finally, the Devil chose either the strongest or the weakest to attack, so he tempted Christ but also spinsters. He especially liked to sexually harass unmarried women.[7] This is the physical force that both Puritans and Spaniards confronted every day.

In the New World, the Devil was even more powerful. Puritan and Spanish American clerics concurred that the Devil had enjoyed uncontested sovereignty over the New World prior to the arrival of the Europeans. When the apostles took the gospel into Eurasia, the Devil felt threatened and took a handful of Scythians to America through the Bering Strait. Once in the New World, Lucifer elected one nation, namely, the Aztecs, to play the role of Israelites in a parody of the Pentateuch in the New World.

Like the Israelites, the Aztecs experienced an exodus, arrived in a promised land, endured subordination to American versions of the Canaanites, witnessed David- and Solomon-like monarchies, built a temple to their god Lucifer, and endured the destruction of their capital by foreign (Spanish) invaders. Over the course of 1,500 years, Satan entrenched himself in the landscape, plants, animals, and peoples of the continent. He made a point of blocking any attempt to reach America through Atlantic navigation. This view of Satan was widely shared by both Puritans and the Spanish clergy.[8]

The demonology of the Puritan and the Spanish clergies was remarkably similar. Both groups believed that demons enjoyed great geographical mobility as Satan and God engaged in a geopolitical struggle, that Satan had maintained uncontested sovereignty and feudal control over the New World until the European arrival (including developing tyrannical rule and building difficult-to-uproot "fortifications"), that cannibalism was a reflection of the hellish world Satan had instituted in America, that the Devil mimicked God both through Amerindian rituals that inverted Christian church structures and through Amerindian historical narratives that perversely imitated those in the Bible, that Amerindians were collectively infected by Lucifer because they were collectively effeminate, that colonization was an epic struggle of liberation, and that colonization was about expelling demons from the land, using either crosses (Catholics) or Bibles (Puritans) as charms.

It would take too much space to explore each one of these shared views. But take, for example, the idea that Satan was a tyrant who had ruled over the natives as a slave master or an unforgiving feudal lord. There is perhaps no more powerful statement of this vision than that offered in 1570 by the Mexican Franciscan Diego de Valadés (b. 1533) in an image he designed for his *Rhetorica Christiana*. A mestizo who wound up representing the Franciscans in Rome, Valadés has his natives parade in shackles and pillories before a monstrous Devil presiding over a court of obsequious demons and Amerindians (fig. 1).

Valadés was convinced that Europeans had brought "freedom" to Mexico. But to do this, Europeans needed to attack the mechanisms used by the Devil to ensnare and trap his victims. Standard theological doctrine held that the Devil operated at an individual level. Free will made individuals originally responsible for their sins, but once they caved in to alluring temptations, they became Satan's indentured servants. Andrés de Olmos (1491–1570), a Franciscan in Mexico one generation before Valadés, illustrated this process: "Demons do all they can to appropriate themselves of an individual, to be his owners, to humiliate him, to rule over him, to oppress him, to tie him up in chains in a dungeon."[9]

It was the Puritan Cotton Mather (1663–1728) who most keenly captured the stages toward individual moral serfdom first elucidated by Valadés. "The Devil first *enters* the heart of the sinner," Mather argued, "[and the] poor man delivers up the keys of the castle . . . [and] the devil gets [into] all the faculties of the soul [intellect, memory, and affections]." In the second phase, the Devil *commands* the heart. It is at this stage that "the Devil can drag [the sinner] hither and thither and even do what he will with [the sinner]. The devil becomes the absolute commander of [the sinner's] undone Soul." Satan acts like a spider, Mather explained, and the sinner as a fly in its web. It is here that the devil-spider "sucks out the heartblood of [the sinner-fly] when he pleases."[10] Thus, Mather concluded, "the devil is an Absolute Lord over the hearts of them that are

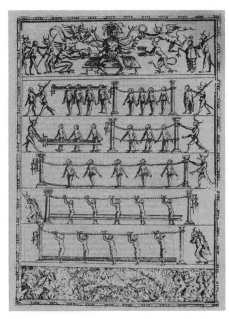

**Figure 1**   The Devil enslaves Amerindians. Diego de Valadés, *Rhetorica Christiana* (Perugia, 1579).

not born again; he Rules and reigns like a Bloody Tyrant. . . . Come then, shake off the yokes of that Hellish Tyrant, by entering into Covenant with God in Christ"[11]

Just as much as the Spanish Catholics, the Puritans insisted that the natives were enslaved collectively. John White (1575–1648), rector of the Church of the Holy Trinity in Dorchester, in the county of Dorset, England, argued in 1630 that the Indians of New England were the "bondslaves of Sathan," and John Eliot (1604–1690) found in 1653 the inhabitants of Massachusetts to be "poor captivated men (bondslaves to sin and Satan)."[12] It was the Puritan magistrate Samuel Sewall (1652–1730), however, who explored in greater detail the nature of this collective serfdom. Sewall saw the Devil in America as an Oriental despot, an absolute overlord: "For Satan was here as in his House strongly Fortified, and well Moted in. [He] was abundantly stored with Arms and Ammunition. Here [in the New World] he had his headquarters, his Palaces; his Throne, kept his Court; exercised an Universal, Unlimited, Unquestioned Jurisdiction." Like alienated serfs, the natives took the side of the Devil, their slave master, in the epic struggle against the Europeans. "Being in love with Bondage," Sewall explained, "[Amerindians] take up Arms against their Deliverer; and strive with all their might to continue the Tyrant in quiet Possession. . . . He will not fail therefore to use all his Policy and Power, all his Methods and Stratagems of War against these recruits, coming over to reinforce the Invasion of his Dominions." Such an alliance of the slave and the slave master made the struggle all the more dangerous for the Europeans, for "Old and experienced Souldiers may be wounded and worsted in particular Encounters; specially in great Expeditions that are New and Unusual."[13]

The association of Amerindian cannibalism with the Devil's control over the continent is another good example of how both the Puritan and the Spanish clergies saw eye to eye. According to both, Satan's collective control of the natives had forced indigenous peoples to model their behavior after what demons do best in hell, namely, the processing and dismembering of bodies. As Caroline Walker Bynum has elegantly shown, Christian patristic and medieval debates over hell and the Last Judgment were in fact arguments over the nature of the holy and the resurrected body. According to the theologians that Bynum studies, holiness consisted of the avoidance of bodily change, decay, and putre-faction. All processes that dismembered and mixed human bodies, such cannibalism, quartering martyrs, and feeding them to the lions, threatened holy bodily resurrection. At the Last Judgment, however, God would put back together the bodies of the blessed, piece by piece, hair by hair, nail by nail. It is no wonder therefore that in medieval representa-tions of hell, demons often appear busy mutilating and boiling bodies.[14]

A closer look at Diego de Valadés's image of tyrannical oppression shows that for the Franciscan, the ritual dismemberment of bodies in Mexico lay at the core of his con-ception of Amerindian collective servitude to the Devil. A clawed Hydra with multiple arms presides as emperor. This monstrous Satan wears a necklace strung with skulls; at the bottom of the picture, demons boil and dismember bodies in hell while two natives busily carry buckets of chopped heads (fig. 2).

For Valadés, the most radical expression of Satan's tyranny in the New World was that the Devil demanded that the natives immolate their own children, deform their own bodies, and shed their own blood.[15] The Spanish friars had finally arrived to liberate these souls and bodies from Satan's intolerable oppression.[16]

Puritans shared these same ideas with the Spaniards. If the Puritan literature on King Philip's War (1675–1676) is remarkable for its anti-Indian virulence, Benjamin

**Figure 2**    Cannibal detail. The Devil enslaves Amerindians. Diego de Valadés, *Rhetorica Christiana* (Perugia, 1579). Notice the Devil's necklace made up of skulls and an Amerindian in hell carrying a bucket full of heads.

Tompson's epic poems on the war are breathtaking in their glorification of settlers' violence.[17] In *Sad and Deplorable Newes from New England* (1676) and *New-Englands Tears for her Present Miseries* (1676), Tompson (1642–1714) sought to present King Philip's War as New England's Trojan War. In this American *Illiad*, the natives appear as cannibal demons who "with bloody hearts" dismember, fleece, kill, and "butcher at their feet" like beasts.[18] They are wild men whose clubs are wielded to smash brains and who wear Medusa-like hairdos, employ the forest as their "fortifications" and "castles," belch fire like dragons, and use the blood and fat of white bodies as anointing oil for their demonic ceremonies.[19] So as not to leave anything to the reader's imagination, Tompson made clear how the demonic and the cannibal were intimately connected in America. According to Tompson, the natives not only burned down houses in their raids on Puritan towns but also burned people and cattle because they wanted to feed the demonic spirits hovering over the land with the smoke of roasted bodies.[20] King Philip himself appears in Tompson's epic as the Devil presiding over hell.[21]

Puritans likewise used the discourse of the demonic and the cannibal to castigate dissenters and atheists. Cotton Mather, for example, argued in 1695 that "Atheists eat up the people of God as they eat bread. They destroy the People of God with open mouth; and they do it with as little remorse they do it with as much fury as much delight; as they can eat a meal when they are hungry. Such Cannibals doe the People of God often meet withal."[22] Puritans also linked cannibalism and the demonic to Spanish colonialism. Samuel Sewall, for example, castigated the Spaniards for having brought "hell" to the New World. The conquistadores had dispatched 20 million Indians; Spanish hounds then had torn many of the slaughtered to pieces. The bodies of the Amerindians had ended up dismembered and fragmented in the bellies of dogs, thus proving the link between Spanish colonialism and the Devil.[23]

Lest we assume that this demonization of the Spanish conquest was something that set the Puritans apart from their Iberians cousins, we need to remember that Sewall took the idea from Bartolomé de las Casas (1474–1566), a Dominican who cast the Spanish conquest as a tragedy in which America played the role of prelapsarian paradise, the conquistadores the part of demons, and the colonial regime a stage for hell. Las Casas repeatedly denounced the conquistadores as "the precursors of Anti-Christ and imitators of Mahomet, being thus Christian only in name" or as men "governed and guided by the Devil."[24] In his massive *Historia de las Indias* (completed 1552–1561), Las Casas created an image of the Caribbean as prelaspsarian paradise, located in a temperate climate and under the influence of numerous and mostly benign constellations. It is this prelapsarian paradise that the Devil attacked through his agents, the Spanish conquistadores. The demonic character of the conquistador is revealed in his readiness to dismember the bodies of Indians through the use of hounds: "As many other exquisitely evil and most hurtful inventions against the human race that were created and fostered here [in the Caribbean] and that led to total destruction of the natives, [setting hounds loose to kill and dismember Indian bodies] was an invention first conceived, thought of, and sanctioned by the Devil here."[25] But of all the institutions the satanic conquistadores introduced in the Caribbean, it was the *encomienda* (the assignment of entire communities to serve a given conquistador) that Las Casas most detested, for it had sanctioned a form of institutionalized cannibalism in which all settlers were allowed to "drink [the natives'] blood and eat their bodies."[26]

## THE SATANIC EPIC

Both Puritans and Spaniards saw themselves as fighting an epic battle to liberate the New World from the grip of the Devil and his armies of demons. The Devil, however, fought back as he sought to uproot the new European settlements. It was not only that Satan made Atlantic crossings very difficult by setting off tempests but also that he created conflict and hardships once the Europeans set foot in the Indies. The struggle to maintain colonial settlements in the New World was thus seen as a monumental effort in which colonists were pitted against poisons; treacherous, monstrous animals; satanic landscapes; Indian revolts; European enemies (either Protestant pirates or the Spanish Antichrist); tyrannous metropolitan officials; heretics; and internal rivalries.

The frontispiece to Juan de Castellanos's epic *Primera parte de las elegías de varones illustres de Indias* (Eulogy to the Illustrious Conquistadors of the Indies. Part One) (1589) typifies this view of colonization as an epic struggle against the Devil (fig. 3). Here, nature in the Old and New Worlds is united by the sheer crusading prowess of Hispania, a faithful maiden wielding the sword of the cross who slays Leviathan, a nasty dragon whose tail encircles the ocean and now lies dead, belly up at the feet of Hispania. The triumphant Hispania stands for Philip II, the monarch who rules over the ocean and the earth and the shepherd who is about to bring the Amerindians into the flock of Christianity. The naked natives, however, are represented as staunch allies of Satan, shooting arrows at Hispania. Hispania, the faithful maiden, has single-handedly united two radically different worlds that Leviathan sought to keep apart. She not only opens up the riches of the fauna and flora of America but also is about to step into the wilderness of America in which dismembered bodies lie scattered.

The illustration's meaning is further elucidated by an accompanying poem by the Dominican Alberto Pedrero, who lionizes Castellanos (1522–1607) for outdoing both Homer and Virgil. Whereas Virgil misleadingly cast the narrow and provincial adventures of the hero Aeneas as having earth-shattering significance and whereas Homer dealt with heroes and monsters who were fictional, Castellanos wrote about real heroes whose terrifying adventures were truly global. Thus, unlike the heroes of Homer, who faced three-headed monsters and visited fictional gardens, the heroes of Castellanos, according to Pedrero, battled the Great Dragon of the Ocean. The Devil had kept Europeans from crossing the Atlantic and had kept native peoples tyrannized and the resources and marvels of the New World hidden.[27] Castellanos himself made that point explicit in a poetic interpretation of the image: Hispania the warrior maiden had launched an assault on the dragon-Leviathan guarding the New World. The dragon was a huge serpent biting its own tail, a tail so long that it circled the ocean at both ends. It had fallen to Philip II to preside over the slaying of this monstrous serpent.[28]

Spaniards also found the Devil among their own. Spanish American Creoles presented peninsular newcomers (including conversos, merchants, and centralizing crown officers) as Satan's allies. As we have already seen, it was Las Casas who first presented conquistadores as demons and the colonial regime as hell. Iberians also readily demonized Protestants. *Vida de Santa Rosa de Lima. Poema Heroyco* (Life of St. Rose of Lima. Heroic Poem) (1711) typifies this approach. In this epic poem, the author Luis Antonio de Oviedo y Herrera (1636–1717) presents St. Rosa (1586–1617) as a godly heroine who, to save Lima from being destroyed, fights great preternatural battles

**Figure 3**   Hispania slays Leviathan, who has kept a lock over the Atlantic Ocean. Juan de Castellanos, *Primera parte de las elegías de varones illustres de Indias* (Madrid, 1589). Courtesy John Carter Brown Library, Brown University. The coat of arms of the king unites the two halves of the composition, one in which the fauna and flora of the Old and New Worlds stand at opposite sides of the image. The words around the coat of arms declare the power of Philip II Catholic monarch over both the oceans and the earth (*Philip 2 Rex Chatolicus atque ri (Rex Indorum?) super maria terrasque fadi(?)*) and praises God's mercifulness over the whole of the earth (*Misericordia Dei plena es terra*). The escutcheon is held up by an Old World lion and by what appears to be an American "tiger." For every Old World animal, there is one match from the New, and so the peacock stands equidistant to the turkey (palms, monkeys, parrots, and turkeys stand for America). On the ground right below the escutcheon and next to the European rabbit lies a dismembered Amerindian corpse, a symbol of the terrors that the hero should overcome. Yet written on the leaves and trunks of the American palm and the Old World olive tree seem to be passages of Psalm 97 (peoples and nature singing praises to the lord). Engraved around the escutcheon are passages of Mathew 11:28 ("come to me all" / *Venite ad me omnes*) and John 10:16 ("I have other sheep, too, which do not belong to his fold; I must bring them also, and they will listen to my voice" / *Alias oves habeo que non sunt ex hoc ovili et illas oportet me adducere et vocem meam audient*). The escutcheon represents Spain, faithful maiden (*Hispania Virgo fidelis*) carrying the cross and the Bible, standing in the middle of the sea on a seashell, and slaying the dragon (*dan [Dan 14:26] io diruptus est draco*) that guards the entrance to the New World. The dragon bites its own tail, which is long and encircles both the ocean and the two continents. Angels and the Holy Spirit descend over the New World, while Indians (allies of the dragon) shoot arrows at Hispania. (I am grateful to David Lupher for correcting some of my Latin transcriptions and identifying Dan 14:26 as one of Castellanos's sources in the Vulgate.)

against Lucifer's allies: earthquakes; Indian rebellions triggered by Yupanqui, Satan's Inca ally; and English and Dutch pirate attacks.[29] In the poem, demons fly all over the world lining up English, Dutch, and Amerindian allies to expel the Iberians.[30]

This siege mentality is also obvious in Puritan versions of the satanic epic. Take, for example, Cotton Mather's *Magnalia Christi Americana*. Like Castellanos, Mather cast his history of colonization in epic, cosmic terms. As Timothy Woodbridge, minister of Hartford, Connecticut, put it in a praising, introductory poem, Mather's *Magnalia* was about tracing "out paths not known to mortal eye" of how providence had guided "those [Puritan] brave men" through the terrors of Atlantic crossings and the ordeals of settlement: "Such were these *heroes*, and their *labours* such."[31] Woodbridge's poem captures accurately the pervasive epic tone of Mather's narrative, for Mather's history is about Herculean heroes pitted in battle against Lucifer in the New World.

The epic tone of the *Magnalia Christi Americana* (1702) comes through everywhere. Book One describes the Atlantic crossing as an act of heroism against Leviathan who had long enjoyed control over the ocean and kept Europeans in the dark (1:41). Colonization itself is presented as an ongoing battle against the Devil, who has his minions, the shamans, cause shipwrecks and poisonings as soon as the Puritans arrive (1:52 and 62). Book Two, suggestively titled "Ecclesiarum Clypei" ("Shields of the Churches"), recounts the deeds and lives of Puritan leaders as modern Argonauts. Typical of Mather's biographies is that of Sir William Phipps (1650–1695), captain-general and governor of Massachusetts. Mather presents Phipps as the English version of Francisco Pizarro, who, although from lowly social origins, through sheer chivalric prowess became both a marquis and the viceroy of Peru (1:152). Phipps appears as a hero who confronts the Devil in New England at every turn. For example, Phipps abolishes the Salem trials because he is the first to realize that the Devil was manipulating the trials by taking on the appearance of the innocent. Phipps also "saves the lives of many poor people from the rage of the diabolical Indians in the eastern parts of the country" by putting "those worse than Scythian wolves" to flight (1:193). His ordeals in America are in fact so trying that Hercules' labors appear as "pleasures" in comparison (1:208). The final Book Seven is titled "Ecclesiarium Praelia" ("The Battles of the Churches") and describes in exquisite detail all the enemies of the Puritans who for over a century sought to cause the plantations to fail. The battles against the Devil in the guise of dissenters such as Quakers and Familists take up most of this narrative. Chapters such as "Milles Nocendi Artes" ("The Thousand Arts of Harming"), on satanic temptations to weaken the church, give way to chapters recounting the elimination of religious dissent: "Hydra Decapitata" (2:440). The last chapter of the book, "Arma Virosque Cano" ("I Praise Arms and the Men"), a slightly modified version of the introductory words of Virgil's *Aeneid*, is devoted to painstaking descriptions of the frontier battles against the satanic Indians: the Pequot, King Philip's, and King William's wars.[32]

It is interesting that scholars are beginning to notice this siege mentality to explain important events in New England's history. Alfred Cave has shown that it was this mentality that rendered the Puritans so uncompromising in their negotiations with the Pequot leading to the war of 1637, for the war happened in the context of the so-called Antinomian controversy (in which Anne Hutchinson and her followers were seen as demonic agents) and in the wake of attempts at court (led by Sir Ferdinando Gorges) to take the colony's charter away. Indians, heretics, and absentee overlords were part of the same demonic plot to oust the Puritans from America.[33] Richard Godbeer has shown that Salem's witchcraft outbreak can be explained only if we are willing to enlarge our vision of whom the Puritans considered their satanic enemies to be (not only witches). Godbeer has argued that the Puritan laity brought witches to trial often but without much success. There were, to be sure, other prior isolated cases of witch prosecution, but it was only in 1692 that the laity succeeded in having magistrates and ministers punish and even execute witches on a large scale. This unusual behavior of the Puritan clergy, he argues, can be explained only in the context of the siege mentality that began to develop in Essex County in the wake of King Philip's War. For two decades, Puritans experienced all sorts of setbacks, including epidemics, loss of political autonomy vis-à-vis the English crown, Quaker encroachment, failed campaigns against the French, and constant Indian frontier warfare. Puritan magistrates saw Satan as an enemy not only working within the soul but also harassing the community from without. Thus, the clergy during the Salem crisis found itself willing to punish as demonic anyone deemed to be an outsider (spinsters with connections to Quakers and to the Indian frontier).[34] Mary Beth Norton has more recently made a similar argument. According to Norton, Salem witches were deemed by Puritans to be allies of the Indians or the French and thus Satan's minions in the larger struggle over control of the northeastern frontier.[35]

# PLANTATIONS

For every fortification Satan had in the New World, Christians built one of their own. The barricades Puritans and Spaniards erected in the Indies were churches and saints. Yet saints and churches were imagined as walled gardens, not ramparts: beautiful plantations with hedges to keep threats out. Historians have thought of the term "plantations" in strict economic terms: lands on which to grow cash crops to be sent to Europe. But the historical actors themselves thought that plantations meant something else, namely, well-tended gardens in the hostile environment that was the satanic wilderness.

The idea that pious souls and churches were "gardens" comes straight from the Song of Songs. This odd text in the Bible describes male and female lovers as flowers and trees, gardeners and gardens.[36] Theologians came to identify at least three lovers of God as they sought to make sense of the Canticles: the soul, the church, and, for Catholics, the Virgin Mary. Exegetes interpreted the soul to be a fertile ground for flowers of spiritual virtues to blossom, a garden for the individual to tend. Thus, it is not surprising that in sixteenth-century Spain, St. Teresa of Avila (1515–1582) not only wrote an interpretation of the Song of Songs but also conceived of her mystical union to God in gardening metaphors: "It was delightful for me to think of my soul as a garden where God strolled. I prayed for the odorous, little flowers of virtue, that seemed were beginning to sprout [in me] for the glory of God, to be tended by him."[37]

The most pious individuals in Spanish America were quickly associated with flowers. Lima, for example, produced a rose: St. Rose of Lima (1586–1617), whom Clement X canonized in 1671. In 1675, her piety and preternatural powers moved Manuel de Ribero Leal to argue in a sermon commemorating her canonization that "Her virtuous fragrances have converted into paradise of holy delights the previously barbarous jungle of our South America."[38] Quito produced St. Mariana of Jesus (1618–1645), the Lily of Quito.

The hagiography of Mariana published in Madrid in 1724 by the Quiteño Jesuit Jacinto Morán de Butrón (1668–1749) typifies the views of the Spanish American clergy that sought to build plantations in the New World. Mariana, he argued, was a flower of the Church as remarkable as Rosa of Lima. She was a second new blossoming in the bountiful garden of the Indies, for God had foreordained that a lily flourish in the Indies along a rose. Turning to the Fourth Book of Azrael (4 Esdrae), Morán de Butrón interpreted 2:16–19—"And those that be dead will I raise up again from their places, and bring them out of the graves. . . . I have sanctified and prepared for thee twelve trees laden with divers fruits, And as many fountains flowing with milk and honey, *and seven mighty mountains, whereupon there grow roses and lilies*, whereby I will fill thy children with joy"—as evidence that roses and lilies were meant to surface *together* in the Andes, which were no other than the seven mighty mountains of 4 Esdrae. Since this passage linked the blossoming of roses and lilies with the Last Judgment and the Resurrection, Morán de Butrón managed to put the lives of Rose and Mariana into a much larger eschatological framework. These two saints and the Andes of Quito and Peru appeared central to any narrative of universal salvation.[39]

Like their Iberian cousins, the Anglo-American Puritans tied the language of spiritual gardening to a discourse of providential election. Also like their Iberians cousins, Creole Puritans wove the history of their spiritual gardens into millenarian narratives. Millennialism was in fact a Puritan obsession, a longing for a time when the primitive structures of the Apostolic Church would finally be restored by the second coming of Christ. The connections between millennialism and the discourse of spiritual gardening can be seen in the writings of the great eighteenth-century theologian Jonathan Edwards, a contemporary of the Jesuit Morán de Butrón.

Edwards emerged out of Northampton, Connecticut, to become one of the most important and influential preacher-theologians of the evangelical movement of the mid-eighteenth-century British Atlantic. As the successor of his formidable grandfather Solomon Stoddard, Edwards witnessed how Stoddard had on several occasions produced "harvests" of souls through the sheer persuasion of his preaching, causing some individuals to "convert." Stoddard himself had cultivated the reputation of being like John the Baptist: a stout tree, not a bending reed. William Williams likened the passing of Stoddard to "the felling of a mighty spreading Tree in a Forest [that caused] all the trees about it to shake."[40] It is not surprising therefore that Edwards would describe his own experience of being suddenly touched by the grace of God in the spring of 1721 in horticultural terms. Like St. Teresa of Avila, Edwards felt holiness "of a sweet, pleasant, charming serene, calm, nature." Being touched by God's grace felt like "an inexpressible purity, brightness, peacefulness and ravishment of the soul." His soul was "like a field or garden of God, with all manner of pleasant flowers."[41] But Stoddard's harvests and Edwards's experiences were ultimately about individual conversions (fig. 4).

By the 1730s, however, New England witnessed a new phenomenon, namely, mass conversions. The Great Awakening first started in Northampton in 1734 when the

**Figure 4** Connecticut's seal (1636). Fifteen vines crawl up arbors while a hand holds a banner with the motto "He, who brought us here, sustains us" (*Sustinet qui transtulit*). Similar to Spanish Americans, the Puritans considered colonization an act of spiritual gardening. The seal speaks volumes on the motivations behind the foundation of the new colony, created when the Puritan theologian Thomas Hooker took a group of disenchanted Newtown colonists to found Hartford. The migration was prompted by land shortages but also by theological concerns. Hooker and his followers thought that Puritan ministers of Massachusetts like John Cotton had limited membership in the church only to those who could prove they had been touched by the inscrutable grace of God. Hooker sought to enlarge membership by emphasizing the act of "preparation" of the soul prior to the reception of grace. According to Hooker, the soul needed to be plowed prior to its "ingrafting" into "the tree of Christ." Hooker articulated his views on preparation repeatedly in horticultural terms in such treatises as the *The Soules Ingrafting into Christ* (1637) and *The Soules Implantation into the Naturall Olive* (1640).

rather dull Edwards managed to touch the soul of the loitering youth of his town.[42] The youth began to attend church in droves and to declare their passion for Christ. Things got even more dramatic in the 1740s when the new persona of the itinerant preacher began to crisscross the Atlantic, unleashing massive conversions in open-air revivalist meetings. The Great Awakening spread over Scotland, England, and the British colonies like wildfire. The scenes of collective conversion convinced Edwards that he was witnessing the beginning of the millennium, for it was "probable this work will begin in America."[43]

The sudden, massive transformation of hundreds of souls into gardens was a sign that the experiences of Creole British America were central to any narrative of universal salvation (and damnation). Soon, however, Edwards came to realize that many of these conversions were not really manifestations of God's grace (which should have led to permanent changes of behavior). Edwards was disappointed. But even when it became clear that the Great Awakening had been a passing, even misleading, event, Edwards hung on to both his millenarian and horticultural hopes. In his *Treatise Concerning the Religious Affections* (1746), Edwards likened the Awakening to the blossoms of spring: "It is with professions of religion, especially such as become so in a time of outpouring of the Spirit of God, as it is with the blossoms in the spring." All blossoms "look fair and promising; but yet very many of them never come to anything." All blossoms smell sweet and "look beautiful and gay as the others," so it was impossible through the use of the senses alone to "distinguish those blossoms which have in them the secret virtue, which will afterwards appear in the fruit." It was "mature fruit which comes afterwards, and not the beautiful colors and smells of the blossoms," Edwards argued, that should help assess whether the reformed churches had become plantations and whether the millennium was indeed near.[44]

## CONCLUSIONS

It is clear that Puritan and Spanish American clerics shared a common view of the meanings and significance of colonization. For both, colonization was an epic battle to uproot the Devil and to set up spiritual plantations. Historians have largely overlooked these two rather basic theological tenets because they have failed to see the hemisphere as a whole. Only by doing away with narratives that anachronistically follow the trajectories of single nation-states can we reconstruct the historical experiences of past historical actors. It is time for the historiographies of the various national Atlantics (British, Dutch, French, Portuguese, and Spanish) to merge.

## Notes

1    See, for example, Patricia Seed, *Ceremonies of Possession in Europe's Conquest of the New World, 1492–1640* (Cambridge, 1995); Patricia Seed, *American Pentimento: The Invention of Indians and the Pursuit of Riches* (Minneapolis, 2001); Anthony Pagden, *Lords of All the World: Ideologies of Empire in Spain, Britain and France c. 1500–c. 1800* (New Haven, Conn., 1995); and James Muldoon, *The Americas in the Spanish World Order: The Justification for Conquest in the Seventeenth Century* (Philadelphia, 1994). On Lockean conceptions of property as distinctive of British colonization, see Joyce E. Chaplin, *Subject Matter: Technology, the Body, and Science on the Anglo American Frontier, 1500–1676* (Cambridge, Mass., 2001).

2   Jack P. Greene, *Pursuits of Happiness: The Social Development of Early Modern British Colonies and the Formation of American Culture* (Chapel Hill, N.C., 1988).

3   Edward L. Bond, "Source of Knowledge, Source of Power: The Supernatural World of English Virginia, 1607–1624," *Virginia Magazine of History and Biography* 108 (2000): 105–38. I am grateful to James Sidbury for this reference.

4   My views on Puritan seventeenth-century theology in the New World rely on the superb scholarship of Theodore Dwight Bozeman, *To Live Ancient Lives: The Primitivist Dimensions in Puritanism* (Chapel Hill, N.C., 1988); Edmund S. Morgan, *Visible Saints: The History of a Puritan Idea* (New York, 1963); Perry Miller, *Errand into the Wilderness* (Cambridge, Mass., 1956); Michael Winship, *Making Heretics: Militant Protestantism and Free Grace in Massachusetts 1635–1641* (Princeton, N.J., 2002); and E. Brooks Holifield, *Theology in America: Christian Thought from the Age of the Puritans to the Civil War* (New Haven, Conn., 2003).

5   Morgan, *Visible Saints.*

6   There is perhaps no better introduction to early modern demonology than Stuart Clark's groundbreaking *Thinking with Demons: The Idea of Witchcraft in Early Modern Europe* (Oxford, 1997).

7   Clark, *Thinking with Demons*, 106–33; Moshe Sluhovsky, "The Devil in the Convent," *American Historical Review* 107 (2002): 1379–411. On sexual intercourse with demons, see Walter Stephens, *Demon Lovers: Witchcraft, Sex, and the Crisis of Belief* (Chicago, 2002). For the case of the Puritans, see Carol F. Karlsen, *The Devil in the Shape of a Woman: Witchcraft in Colonial New England* (New York, 1989), and Elizabeth Reis, *Damned Women: Sinners and Witches in Puritan New England* (Ithaca, N.Y., 1999).

8   On a distinctly New World demonological discourse as it relates to colonization and European–Amerindian interactions, I have profited greatly from the following works: M.C. Pioffet, "L'arc et l'épée: Les images de la guerre chez le jésuite Paul le Jeune," in *Rhétorique et conquête missionnaire: Le jésuite Paul Lejeune*, ed. R. Ouellet (Sillery, 1993), 41–52; Peter A. Goddard, "The Devil in New France: Jesuit Demonology, 1611–50," *Canadian Historical Review* 78 (1997): 40–62; Daniel T. Reff, "The 'Predicament of Culture' and Spanish Missionary Accounts of the Tepehuan and Pueblo Revolts," *Ethnohistory* 42 (1995): 63–90; David S. Lovejoy, "Satanizing the American Indian," *New England Quarterly* 67 (1994): 603–21; John McWilliams, "Indian John and the Northern Tawnies," *New England Quarterly* 69 (1996): 580–604; Mary Beth Norton, *In the Devil's Snare: The Salem Witchcraft Crisis of 1692* (New York, 2002); Laura de Mello e Souza, *Inferno Atlântico. Demonologia e colonização. Séculos XVI–XVIII* (São Paulo, 1993); Fernando Cervantes, *The Devil in the New World: The Impact of Diabolism in New Spain* (New Haven, Conn., 1994); and Sabine MacCormack, *Religion in the Andes: Vision and Imagination in Early Colonial Peru* (Princeton, N.J., 1991).

9   "*Hacen todo lo que pueden para apoderarse, para hacerse dueños de alguien, para mofarse de el, para gobernarlo, para someterlo para agarrarlo con lazos, en un agujero, en una cuerda.*" Andrés de Olmos, *Tratados de hechicerías y sortilegios*, ed. George Baudot (Mexico City, 1990), 7.

10  Cotton Mather, *Bateries upon the Kingdom of the Devil* (London, 1695), 9–10, emphasis in the original.

11  Mather, *Bateries upon the Kingdom of the Devil*, 36.

12  John White, *The Planters Plea or the Grounds of Plantations examined and usual Objections Answered* (London, 1630), 22; John Eliot, *Tears of repentance: or, A further narrative of the progress of the Gospel amongst the Indians in Nevv-England* (London, 1653), 202.

13  Samuel Sewall, *Phaenomena quaedam Apocalyptica Ad Aspectum Novi Orbis configurata. Or, some few lines towards a description of the New Heaven as it makes those who stand upon the New Earth* (Boston, 1697), 51–52.

14   Caroline Walker Bynum, *The Resurrection of the Body in Western Christianity, 200–1336* (New York, 1995).

15   Diego de Valadés, *Rhetorica Christiana ad concionandi, et orandi usum accommodata* (Perugia, 1579), 172.

16   Valadés, *Rhetorica Christiana*, 172.

17   On the Puritan literature on King Philip's War, see Jill Lepore, *In the Name of War: King Philip's War and the Origins of American Identity* (New York, 1998).

18   Benjamin Tompson, *Sad and Deplorable Newes from New England* (London, 1676), 8.

19   Tompson, *New-Englands Tears for her Present Miseries* (London, 1676), 2–3.

20   Tompson, *Sad and Deplorable Newes*, 15–16.

21   "And here, methinks, I see this greasy Lout
With all his pagan slaves coil'd round about,
Assuming all the Majesty his throne
Of rotten stump, or of the rugged stone
Could yield; casting some bacon-rine-like looks,
Enough to fright a Student form his books,
Thus treat his peers, and next to them his commons,
Kennel'd together all without summons."
(Tompson, *Sad and Deplorable Newes*, 7).

22   Mather, *Bateries upon the Kingdom of the Devil*, 46.

23   Sewall, *Phaenomena quaedam Apocalyptica*, 8–9.

24   Quoted in David Brading, *First America: The Spanish Monarchy, Creole Patriots, and the Liberal State, 1492–1867* (Cambridge, 1991) 65, 74.

25   Bartolomé de Las Casas, *Historia de las Indias* [1552–61], ed. Miguel Ángel Medina, Jesús Ángel Barreda, and Isacio Pérez Fernández, 3 vols., *Obras Completas*, vols. 3–5 (Madrid, 1994), 2:928 (bk. 1, chap. 104).

26   Las Casas, *Historia de las Indias* 2:1286 (bk. 2, chap. 1).

27   Alberto Pedrero, Epigramma, in Juan de Castellanos, *Primera parte de las elegías de varones illustres de Indias* (Madrid, 1589), 1–2.

28   *Hispanum regnum declarat bellica virgo*
*Est maris oceani littus & ipse draco.*
*Hic serpens ingens orbem circundat utriunque*
*Coniungenscaude, perfreta, longa, caput.*
*Ergo, quicquid erit, quod continet orbis uterque*
*Magne Philippe tuo serviet imperio*
(Castellanos, *Primera parte de las elegías de varones illustres de Indias*, n.p.).

29   By Francis Drake (1543?–1596), John Hawkins (Juan de Aquines) (1532–1595), and "Janis van Speilberg," who attacked Callao in 1615.

30   Luis Antonio de Oviedo y Herrera, *Vida de Santa Rosa de Lima. Poema Heroyco* (reprint of 1711 Madrid original; Mexico City, 1729).

31   Cotton Mather, *Magnalia Christi Americana* [1702], 2 vols. (Hartford, 1820), 1:18.

32   Sacvan Bercovitch has offered a reading of Mather's *Magnalia Christi Americana* as a satanic epic emphasizing its eschatological aspects in "New England Epic: Cotton Mather's 'Magnalia Christi Americana,'" *English Literary History* 33 (1966): 337–50.

33   Alfred A. Cave, *The Pequot War* (Amherst, Mass., 1996), 6, 139, and passim.

34   Richard Godbeer, *The Devil's Dominion: Magic and Religion in Early New England* (Cambridge, 1992).

35   Norton, *In the Devil's Snare*.

36   E. Ann Matter. *The Voice of My Beloved: The Song of Songs in Western Medieval Christianity* (Philadelphia, 1990); Ann W. Astell, *The Song of Songs in the Middle Ages* (Ithaca, N.Y., 1990).

37  *"Me era un gran deleite considerar ser mi alma un huerto y al Señor que se paseaba en él. Suplicábale aumentase el olor de las florecitas de virtudes que comenzaban, a lo que parecía, a querer salir, y que fuese para su gloria, y las sustentase."* Saint Teresa de Avila, "Vida de Santa Teresa de Jesús y algunas de las Mercedes que Dios le hizo, escritas por ella misma por mandato de su confessor, a quien lo envia y dirige, y sice asi." In *Obras Completas*, ed. Luis Santullano (Madrid, 1951), 62 (chap. 14). There are countless other passages in the autobiography in which Teresa de Avila conceives of her soul as a garden or flower and God as a gardener; see, for example, 70 (chap. 16), 73 (chap. 17). See also her exegesis of the Song of Songs, "Conceptos del amor de Dios. Escritos por la beata Madre Teresa de Jesús, sobre algunas palabras de los Cantares de Salomón." In *Obras Completas*, 503–35.

38  Manuel de Ribero Leal, quoted in Kathleen Ann Myers, "'Redeemer of America': Rosa de Lima (1586–1617), The Dynamics of Identity, and Canonization," in *Colonial Saints: Discovering the Holy in the Americas*, ed. Allan Greer and Jodi Bilinkoff (New York, 2003), 260.

39  Jacinto Morán de Butrino, *Vida de Santa Mariana de Jesús*, ed. Aurelio Espinosa Polit S.I. (Quito, 1955), 59–64, esp. 63 (see also 24–25, 42).

40  William Williams, *The Death of a Prophet Lamented and Improved,* quoted in Philip F. Gura, *Jonathan Edwards: America's Evangelical* (New York, 2004), 57.

41  Jonathan Edwards, "Personal Narrative," quoted in Gura, *Jonathan Edwards*, 41. On Stoddard's harvest, see Gura, *Jonathan Edwards*, 48–49.

42  On the Great Awakening, see Frank Lambert, *Inventing the "Great Awakening"* (Princeton, N.J., 1999).

43  Jonathan Edwards, *Some Thoughts*, quoted in Gura, *Jonathan Edwards*, 126.

44  Jonathan Edwards, *The Religious Affections*, quoted in Gura, *Jonathan Edwards*, 130–31.

Like Greer and Mills and Cañizares-Esguerra, Erik R. Seeman uses religion to undercut the primacy of the nation-state in our understanding of the early modern Atlantic. Contrasting with the previous essays' examination of Christians, Seeman turns our attention to Jews. Jewish deathways in the early modern Caribbean, he argues, demonstrate that historians' use of nation-based Atlantics (French Atlantic, Spanish Atlantic, and the like) can obscure local variations that did not adhere to imperial boundaries. Jewish deathways in the Dutch colony of Surinam, for example, were shaped by the unique context of large numbers of Jewish owners of slave plantations in the colony. Thus, in the fashion of Greer and Mills, Seeman makes a case for attention to local dynamics. Whereas Greer and Mills argue for the importance of "micro-Christianities," Seeman points toward what might be termed "micro-Judaisms," variations in practice shaped by local conditions. Thus, histories based on a false assumption about the unity of the nation-state should not be replaced by one that falsely posits the unity of the Jewish "nation."

Moreover, Seeman's chapter contributes to the comparative study of diasporas in the Atlantic World. Whether the subject is involuntary African migrants as in Pier Larson's and Jason Young's chapters or voluntary European migrants as in Jose Moya's and Patrick McDevitt's chapters, this collection includes numerous pieces that touch on the dispersal of peoples around the Atlantic and beyond. For all these dispersed peoples, the traditions they brought with them were inevitably altered by their new surroundings, though the depth and rapidity of change varied from group to group. Judaism was clearly not impervious to change, but did it change more slowly than other religions transplanted to the New World?

# Jews in the Early Modern Atlantic: Crossing Boundaries, Keeping Faith

## Erik R. Seeman

When writing about the early modern Atlantic, historians commonly approach their topic from the perspective of the modern nation-state. They write about the "Dutch Atlantic," the "French Atlantic," the "Spanish Atlantic," and so on through the great (and not-so-great) European imperial powers of the early modern period.[1] There is no doubt that this can be a useful perspective. These authors have taught us a great deal about imperial rivalries, about the commonalities between such disparate colonies as Quebec and Martinique, and about the importance of colonial exports in the economy of the metropole.

But a nation-based approach to the Atlantic can be limiting and even ahistorical. The "persistent localism" of early modern colonists meant that—especially by the eighteenth century—they often identified themselves as, for example, "Virginians" or "Barbadians" first and "Britons" second.[2] Moreover, historians who confine themselves to the relations between one European nation and its colonies can inadvertently diminish the dynamic interplay across national boundaries that characterized the early modern Atlantic. In the Caribbean, in particular, the close proximity of islands claimed by the Dutch, Spanish, English, and French meant that colonists and slaves continually interacted with counterparts from different national traditions. French sugar planters purchased wheat and salt cod from British North American merchants, Dutch smugglers sold French sugar to Spanish colonists in Mexico, and slaves whispered news of the latest uprising from Saint-Domingue to Jamaica and on to Cuba.[3]

This last example, of slaves and free people of color communicating across national boundaries, points to the importance of the Black Atlantic for providing a conceptual model that does not unduly privilege the European nation-state. Historians of slavery and the African American experience have long crossed national boundaries in their studies.[4] But not until Paul Gilroy's 1993 *The Black Atlantic* did a scholar so clearly and emphatically demonstrate the value—and political implications—of an analysis that examines connections across national lines. Gilroy took his cue from twentieth-century pan-Africanism, which "challenges our understanding of modern politics precisely because it overflows from the confining structures of the nation state and comprehensively queries the priority routinely attached to those structures in historical and sociological explanations of social and cultural change."[5] Since Gilroy wrote these words, several scholars have taken his insights and applied them to the early modern period, which did not form the chronological center of Gilroy's analysis.[6]

But focusing on people of African descent is not the only way to escape the confines of the European nation-state. Religious cultures also flowed across national boundaries. Elsewhere in this volume, Allan Greer and Kenneth Mills demonstrate how a focus on Catholicism allows us to see previously hidden connections between French and Spanish imperial ambitions in the New World. Likewise, Jorge Cañizares-Esguerra compares Protestant and Catholic demonology to highlight previously ignored similarities between English and Spanish attitudes toward the New World's native inhabitants. Other religious groups not examined in this volume, like Quakers and Huguenots (French Protestants), established far-flung trading networks based on ties of kinship and religion that spanned the French, English, and Dutch empires. But no group crossed as many national boundaries as Jews.

Jews allow us to see how a focus on nation-based Atlantics can sometimes obscure the actual experience of life in the early modern Atlantic. Jews established communities around the Atlantic, from West Africa to Recife (Dutch Brazil), from Barbados to Montreal, and from Newport to Amsterdam. For centuries, Jews had been denied the right to own land in most of Europe, so they turned to mercantile activities for their livelihood. When northern European states began to establish colonies in the seventeenth century, Jewish merchants followed the shipping lanes to new homes around the Atlantic. Significantly, Jews did not migrate and then lose touch with their coreligionists in other lands. Instead, they maintained their economic and kinship ties across thousands of miles of ocean. Indeed, economics and kinship were intertwined: a Curaçaoan merchant whose daughter married into a Jewish family in Newport, Rhode Island, made a shrewd economic decision even as he followed his religion's call for endogamous marriage (i.e., marriage within one's group).

Thus, a focus on Jews necessarily shifts our attention away from the European nation-state as a category of analysis. But the story of Jews and nationhood is even more complex than at first glance: Sephardic (Iberian) Jews referred to themselves as a "Nation." This usage began in the late sixteenth century after Spain annexed Portugal in 1580. At this time, numerous Portuguese conversos—Jews who converted to Christianity with varying degrees of sincerity—migrated to Spanish cities like Seville and Madrid. To distinguish them from Spanish conversos, who were much more likely to be sincere Christians, Spaniards dubbed the Portuguese conversos *portugueses de la nación hebrea*, or "Portuguese of the Hebrew Nation." Many of these individuals would migrate again after 1600, this time to Amsterdam and its relatively tolerant religious climate. In this context, they took up with pride the label that had suggested some ambivalence in Spain, calling themselves *homens da nação*, or "Men of the Nation."[7]

By the second half of the seventeenth century, Sephardic Jews used the term "the Nation" to refer to the Sephardic diaspora in Europe and the New World. Even when increasing numbers of Ashkenazic (German) Jews came to the New World in the eighteenth century, the older Portuguese concept of "the Nation" persisted and was translated into the local vernacular in Dutch and English colonies. As late as 1789, when Barbadian Jews authored a message to King George III expressing their happiness that he had recovered from his "late dangerous and alarming malady" (a tactful way of saying he had been mad as a hatter), they called themselves "the People of the Hebrew Nation resident in this island of Barbados." Their usage was quite deliberate. Even in a fawning message like this, penned by His Majesty's "ever dutiful and loyal subjects," these writers made clear that they did not identify themselves as Britons or even as Barbadians but as Jews "resident in" Barbados.[8]

Thus, a group that helps us see the limits of a nation-based approach to understanding the early modern Atlantic considered itself a nation within nations. Though this may seem ironic or paradoxical to the modern sensibility, it helps us recover a contemporary usage of the word "nation," which in the sixteenth and seventeenth centuries could mean a local community of foreigners.[9] Not until the late nineteenth century would the term "nation" (and its cognates in Spanish, French, and Portuguese) come to include the idea of government.[10] An analysis of Jews, therefore, forces us to separate analytically the concepts of "nation" and "state," conventionally yoked together in the modern phrase "nation-state." Early modern Jews were a nation without a state.[11] This allowed them to occupy geographic territory claimed by several European states. Across national boundaries, men and women of the Hebrew Nation maintained and formed connections that helped preserve their distinctive identity even as that identity evolved in a New World context.

## JEWISH DEATHWAYS IN THE DUTCH AND ENGLISH CARIBBEAN

In what follows, I focus on Jewish deathways as a way to understand Jewish religious practice and identity in the New World. There are several reasons why deathways are especially valuable for understanding these issues. Death rituals were (and are) one of the primary sites of Jewish self-definition. The very first thing a fledgling Jewish community in the New World sought to do—long before it tried to build a synagogue—was to secure a burial ground. Indeed, the very presence of a Jewish burial ground within a predominantly Christian colony would have been a visible symbol of Jewish nationhood. Even Jews without a firm commitment to their religion's dietary or marital strictures sought burial in a *beth haim* ("home of the living," a pious euphemism for a Jewish burial ground). Because death was such a central concern of Jewish religion, Jewish colonists generated numerous sources that survive today: wills, tombstones, and descriptions of deathbed scenes, to name a few.

To demonstrate how Jews complicate any attempt to understand the early modern Atlantic based on the European nation-state, I turn to the Dutch and English colonies in the Caribbean, where Jews formed a sizable presence in the seventeenth and eighteenth centuries. I employ two strategies in this analysis. First, I explore some of the similarities in Jewish ritual practice that crossed national boundaries. Jews in the Dutch colonies and their coreligionists in English colonies treated their dead in many similar ways. In these cases, whether the Jews lived in an English or a Dutch national context mattered precious little for many of their deathways. Second, I examine some of the differences that emerged in Jewish practices within a single national context. Although both Surinam and Curaçao were Dutch, some important differences emerged in Jewish deathways as practiced in the two colonies (Map 1).[12]

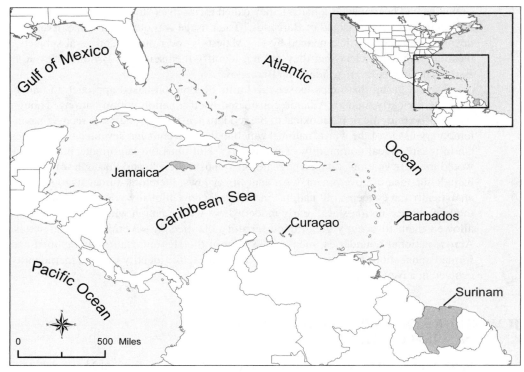

**Map 1**    The Caribbean.

Dutch interest in the New World began in the 1590s as the Dutch were fighting for their independence from Spain. A century of New World colonization efforts had made Spain the richest country in Europe, and the Dutch sought to make inroads of their own, partly to help finance their war effort and partly to put a crimp in Spain's economic fortunes. The Dutch established their first colonies in the New World in the 1590s on what the Dutch called the "Wild Coast" of South America, the northeastern shoulder of that continent where the modern nation of Guyana sits. But these colonies were tiny and did not capture the imagination of the Dutch public. When in 1630 the Dutch captured Recife in present-day Brazil from the Portuguese, however, this looked like an opportunity to cash in on the lucrative sugar economy already flourishing there.[13] Along with numerous Christians, approximately 1,500 Jews from Amsterdam migrated to Recife to try their hand at the mercantile activities at which they had become expert in Europe.[14] When the Portuguese captured Recife for good in 1654, many Jews looked to continue their residence in the New World. Some went to the Dutch island of Curaçao, and, later, others went to Surinam after the Dutch took this colony on the South American mainland from the English in 1667. Most Jews who went to Curaçao participated in mercantile or maritime trades, whereas many Surinam Jews owned sugar plantations.

Other Jewish migrants from Recife found their way to English Caribbean colonies. The English were relative latecomers to the European quest for New World colonies, but by the time they entered the fray seriously in the late sixteenth century, they were aided by a powerful navy. In 1627, the English laid claim to Barbados, which, despite its Spanish name, had not been occupied by the Spanish. Unlike most Caribbean colonies, which changed hands between European powers with dizzying frequency (witness St. Eustatius, which was possessed by three different European nations in succession between 1665 and 1667), Barbados remained English until independence in 1966.[15] Jamaica had been a Spanish colony until the English captured it in 1655. Both Barbados and Jamaica received some migrants from Recife after its fall, and both also were the destination of Sephardic Jews migrating directly from Amsterdam and London. As in Curaçao, most Jewish men in the English Caribbean worked as sailors, shopkeepers, or merchants.

Although Amsterdam tolerated Jews, Dutch colonies were not all so welcoming. New Netherland (later New York) bore the stamp of its anti-Semitic leader, Peter Stuyvesant. The man who led New Netherland from 1646 until its handover to the English in 1664 called Jews a "deceitful race" and worried that religious diversity would undermine social harmony.[16] But Curaçao and Surinam were different. In Curaçao, Jews worshiped openly and were not subject to any discriminatory taxes. In Surinam the situation was even better. The leading historian of Jews in Surinam writes that "legally, Surinamese Jews formed perhaps the most privileged Jewish community in the world."[17] Originally, these legal rights were an English inducement to encourage Jewish migration to Surinam when it was in English hands; the Dutch retained and expanded them. Crucially, the Dutch gave the Jews the right to adjudicate their own disputes up to the value of 10,000 pounds of sugar. Jews thus had their own legal institutions in Surinam.[18] Because of this tolerant climate, Jews flocked to these colonies, and Jews eventually formed one-third of the white population of both Surinam and Curaçao.[19]

The legal situation was not as rosy in the English colonies. Barbadian Jews complained in 1669 that their testimony was not accepted in the colony's courts. Moreover, between 1688 and 1706, there were restrictions placed on the number of male slaves whom Jewish merchants in Barbados could employ.[20] Jamaican Jews faced even harsher legal discrimination. They could not vote or hold office. A discriminatory "Jew tax" was instituted in 1692. The justification for this was that Jews were allegedly unproductive economic parasites. Anglo-Barbadians accused Jewish shopkeepers of "furnish[ing] our people with materials of luxury, tempt[ing] them to live and dress above their circumstances."[21] Attitudes like this led to occasional flare-ups of anti-Semitic violence: an angry mob of Anglo-Barbadians pulled down the Speightstown, Barbados, synagogue in 1739 in response to a report that a Jew had badly beaten a Christian.[22] Partly as a result of this climate of intolerance, Jews were not as numerous in the English colonies as in the Dutch: Jews constituted perhaps 10 percent of the white population in Jamaica and about 3 percent in Barbados.[23]

Thus, there were important differences regarding the legal standing of Jews in Dutch versus English Caribbean colonies. But when one's attention turns from legal rights to religious experience, the picture divides less clearly along European national

lines. In fact, there were numerous similarities in Jewish deathways in the Dutch and
English colonies. This was, as historian Jonathan Sarna explains, the result of the conservative tendencies of Sephardic Jews. Like Catholics, Jews believed that "ritual could
unite those whom life had dispersed." They wanted any member of the Hebrew Nation
"to feel at home in any Sephardic synagogue anywhere in the world: the same liturgy,
the same customs, even the same tunes."[24] Sephardim consequently frowned on religious innovations, particularly in the realm of deathways. New World Jews looked back
to centuries of written Jewish laws to guide them in their handling of dying and the
dead. One key source they relied on was the *Shulhan 'Aruk*, a sixteenth-century codifi-
cation of Jewish law. The "nearly universal acceptance" of this code helped ensure a
degree of uniformity in early modern Jewish practice.[25]

Whether Jews resided in English or Dutch colonies, then, there were many similarities in their deathways. For analytical purposes, it will be useful to divide deathways
into four broad categories that roughly correspond to the ways in which a typical death
played out: the deathbed scene, preparation of the corpse and burial, mourning, and
memorialization.

Among early modern Jews, the deathbed scene was not improvised but carefully
scripted. It was considered a mitzvah (good deed or religious duty) to attend a deathbed
scene, so the dying person was typically surrounded by friends and relatives offering
prayers and support. Indeed, the community did all in its power to make sure that an
individual did not die unattended. If at all possible, the dying person was to offer a
"confession" before ten Jews—not a recounting of specific sins but a prayer with a set
text that began, "I confess before Thee O Lord, my God and the God of my fathers, that
my healing and my death are in your hand."[26] Women and young children were supposed to be sent away before the confession so that their weeping would not disturb the
dying person. But then they regathered, for following the example of the biblical patri-
arch Jacob (Israel), the dying person was supposed to offer blessings to family members. When the individual died, those present rent their garments from the neck
downward about a handbreadth.

In both the Dutch and the English Caribbean, the deathbed scene was accorded
great importance. Indeed, the first New World society for presiding at deathbeds was
founded in Curaçao between 1686 and 1692.[27] Members of the *Gemiluth Hasadim*
(Society of Mercies) paid an initiation fee and a small monthly allowance for the privilege of helping their fellow Jews in times of distress. Members also joined so that they
could have the pleasure of performing the valuable mitzvah of deathbed attendance.
That the community paid attention to the dying person's deathbed demeanor is
attested by the occasional gravestone, such as these two from Barbados: Esther
Pinheiro's 1802 stone reported that she was "resigned in death," and twelve-year-old
Sarah Nunes Castello was likewise reported in 1782 to have demonstrated "fortitude in
her last illness."[28]

When the dying person expired, the corpse demanded immediate attention. Jews
were expected to bury their dead as soon as possible, ideally before the following morning and certainly within twenty-four hours. Members of the Society of Mercies washed
the corpse with warm water, stopped all the corpse's orifices with clean linen, and then
wrapped the whole body in a linen shroud. Finally, those present eased the shrouded
body on its back into a simple wooden coffin, usually with a bag of earth placed under

its head. If available, a bit of earth from Israel was sprinkled into the coffin to symbolize that it would have been preferable to be buried in the Holy Land, where Jews believed all exiles would be gathered on the day of resurrection.[29]

Soon after the Society of Mercies washed and coffined the body, the procession began. The journey from the home to the *beth haim* was likely to be circuitous, for this was an opportunity for as many Jews as possible to join the procession. It was considered a "very meritorious work" to attend someone to the grave, so numerous people tried to get their shoulders under the coffin for part of the procession.[30] The presence of so many Jews snaking their way through narrow city streets would have been a very public display of nationhood to the Christians of these New World colonies. In Curaçao, the procession took on a unique cast, as the *beth haim* was located upriver from the synagogue. As many as fifteen to twenty barges, each carrying eighteen to twenty-four passengers, carried the deceased and the mourners to the *beth haim*.[31]

At the graveside people were supposed to praise the deceased (while being careful to avoid exaggerating the dead person's virtues).[32] Even someone who in life had been unpleasant was supposed to receive some lamentations. It had become customary in parts of early modern Europe, even though nothing in Jewish law required it, for ten of the "most considerable relations and friends of the deceased" to walk around the coffin seven times while reciting a prayer, the number seven having a variety of mystical associations.[33] At last, the coffin was lowered into the ground, and all present helped shovel earth into the hole. The mourners then said Kaddish (often called an *escaba* by Sephardim), an ancient prayer glorifying God that had surprisingly little direct connection to death or mourning: "May His great Name be magnified and sanctified," it begins. This prayer seems to have emerged in the Middle Ages in response to the depredations of the Christian Crusades.[34] Finally, the mourners washed their hands, both to cleanse themselves of impurities and also to signal the end of the burial ritual.

Once the deceased had been ritually prepared and buried, the work of mourning began. There were very specific requirements for those who had lost a near relation: a spouse, parent, sibling, or child. These individuals returned to the house where their kin had died for a period of sequestration. First they lit an oil lamp next to the deathbed that was supposed to burn for the entire seven-day period of deep mourning called shivah. During this period, the mourners wore no shoes, did not bathe or shave, and did not even prepare food for themselves. Members of the community provided sustenance, a symbol of how the mourners were not left alone during their time of grief. During these seven days, mourners could leave the house only to go to synagogue on the Sabbath. After the seven days of shivah, mourners could leave the home, but for the first thirty days after the death, mourners were supposed to continue their avoidance of bathing, shaving, and changing their clothes. The importance of this period of mourning in the Caribbean is suggested by the fact that the Hebrew word *abel*, meaning mourning, is used even today in Papiamento, Curaçao's Afro-Dutch dialect.[35]

We turn now to memorialization, the final stage of attention to the dead. For those Jews in the Caribbean whose families were wealthy enough to afford them, gravestones were an opportunity for the living to remember the dead. In addition to standard information such as name and birth and death dates and perhaps parents' names, epitaphs could include a favorite scriptural text or more elaborate details about the deceased. Jewish gravestones in the English and Dutch Caribbean shared numerous similarities. Because of a dearth of local carvers with the facility to render Hebrew letters accurately, Caribbean Jews usually ordered their stones from Europe. In his 1722 will, Isaac Henriques Alvin of Jamaica declared that his executors should "as soon as conveniently can be after my decease purchase in Great Britain three new large marble tombstones of dark blue colour and of a good thickness to be sent to Jamaica to cover three graves": his own, his brother's, and his sister's.[36] Like their coreligionists in Jamaica, the Jews of Barbados and Nevis imported their stones from London, while Surinam's and Curaçao's Jews sent out to Amsterdam.[37]

The iconography on these stones often surprises Jews today, who are taught that human images on gravestones violate the Second Commandment's prohibition against "graven images." Such concerns did not trouble Caribbean Jews. As relatively recent returnees to rabbinic Judaism (after more than a century in the Iberian Peninsula when the open practice of Judaism was prohibited), Caribbean Jews embraced the iconographic traditions of the lands in which they lived. In Jamaica, many gravestones can be found with skulls and crossbones, numerous stones depict a hand descending from the clouds to fell a tree, and at least two represent the faces of angels.[38] A Barbadian gravestone goes so far as to seemingly represent God—with face and body visible—cutting down the Tree of Life.[39] Numerous Curaçaoan stones, like their counterparts in Amsterdam's *beth haim* at Ouderkerk, depict human figures. Abraham Henriques's monument, made in Amsterdam from expensive Carrara marble in 1726, shows him confidently piloting his ship through a light chop.[40]

Ishac Haim Senior, who also died in 1726, went one step further than Henriques in the depiction of a recognizable human character: he is represented by Isaac Aboab da Fonseca, an Amsterdam rabbi, as copied from a 1686 mezzotint by the artist Aernout Naghtegael (fig. 1).[41] If a Christian's engraving of a rabbi seems an unlikely source for a Jewish Curaçaoan stone, consider the source for the human figures on Esther Senior's 1714 marker. The representation of the biblical Esther pleading her case before King Ahasuerus is "almost a line-for-line copy" of a woodcut from a Christian Latin Bible published in Lyon in 1562 (figs. 2 and 3).[42] Jews in the Dutch and English Caribbean, remembering the dark decades when Catholics forced Sephardim to convert or keep their beliefs secret, seem to have rejoiced in their ability to proclaim to the world their faith and their varied cultural inheritances. Moreover, their distinctive stones—most with Hebrew lettering—stood as silent reminders of Jewish nationhood within a Christian context.

But gravestones were not the only way deceased Jews lived on in the Caribbean: a complex range of mourning prayers ensured that the memory of the dead lingered among the living. Traditionally, people counted on their family—and in particular their children—to ensure that Kaddish was said for them during the year after their death. But if one did not have any children or wanted a little extra insurance, one might include a bequest in one's will in exchange for someone offering prayers. In some cases, this could be a form of charity, as in 1737 when the Jamaican merchant Mordecai da Silva willed £5 to a young orphan boy "for to say a funeral prayer used in our Synagogue during the time of Eleven Month after my decease."[43] Although da Silva, like most testators, did not explicitly state his reasons for paying for memorial prayers, Abraham Mendes de Castro of Curaçao did. According to his 1752 will, de Castro left 100 pesos

**Figure 1**  Amsterdam rabbi Isaac Aboab da Fonseca, represented on the gravestone of Ishac Haim Senior (upper left). This 1726 Curaçaoan stone was copied from a mezzotint by Aernout Naghtegael. Courtesy of the Jacob Rader Marcus Center of the American Jewish Archives, Cincinnati, Ohio.

**Figure 2**    *Esther Before Ahasuerus*, woodcut by Pierre Eskrich, *Biblia Sacra* (Lyon, 1581). Courtesy of the Rare Books Division, New York Public Library, Astor, Lenox and Tilden Foundations.

for memorial prayers simply so that "God may receive me."[44] Because this goal was so important, some Jews worried that those they entrusted to say Kaddish for them would neglect their duties. As a result, some testators made their bequests provisional. Before Jacob Hisquiau de Leon of Curaçao died in 1760, he included this legacy in his will: "I leave Jeudah Alva the sum of one hundred pesos to say 'Cadis' for me only on condition that he say it for the eleven months [of mourning] when he shall be paid, and in default thereof this bequest shall remain null and void."[45] No leaving such an important matter to chance for de Leon.

Although formal mourning ended on the one-year anniversary of the person's death, children were supposed to fast and say Kaddish on every anniversary of a parent's death. In addition, some people's wills included bequests to the local synagogue to pay for memorial prayers, sometimes in perpetuity. But Caribbean congregations began to find that people's strong desire for perpetual memorialization led to some problems. In Kingston, Jamaica, the congregation was faced with at least two individuals who wanted their memorial prayers to be set off from those of the common hordes. David Bravo left the hefty sum of £100 to his synagogue in 1749 in exchange for an annual "prayer called Scava," but he attached the following proviso: "I do hereby further direct that no other person or persons name or names shall be named or read in the reading the

**Figure 3** Tombstone of Esther Senior, 1714, Curaçao. Copied from the Christian Bible shown in figure 2. Courtesy of the Jacob Rader Marcus Center of the American Jewish Archives, Cincinnati, Ohio.

said Scava but my own."[46] It seems that the congregation accepted this rather self-aggrandizing restriction, though they may have regretted the decision, for less than five years later Abraham Gonsales demanded similar treatment in return for his own bequest of £100. The synagogue could collect the cash "upon this condition, that there be had for me an Escava on our fast day called Kippur in the same manner as was done for the late David Bravo deceased."[47] The congregation may have decided to nip this trend in the bud and refuse Gonsales's money, as there are no further examples of Jamaican testators invoking the Bravo precedent.

As these examples of Jewish deathways indicate, numerous Jewish rituals and beliefs crossed national boundaries. Deathbed scenes, corpse preparation and burial, mourning, and memorialization all had similar elements, whether they took place in the Dutch or the English Caribbean. But Judaism was not a religion frozen in amber. Although conservative impulses were strong, Jewish practices did change—at least to a certain extent—in relation to local conditions. And sometimes variations in local conditions did not occur along national lines. The clearest example of this occurred in the Dutch Caribbean. The divergent economies of Surinam and Curaçao resulted in differing social and demographic contexts that in turn caused Jewish deathways to evolve differently in the two colonies.

The key variable was plantation slavery. Surinam was a sugar colony with a population that was overwhelmingly African in origin. Unlike anywhere else in the New World, large numbers of Jews were plantation owners. In 1730, Jews owned 115 of Surinam's 401 plantations and held perhaps 20,000 slaves.[48] The average Jewish-owned sugar plantation, therefore, exploited the labor of nearly 175 slaves. Slavery existed on the island of Curaçao, but not in the same form as in Surinam. Curaçao's arid climate did not support sugar agriculture or plantation agriculture of any kind. Instead, Curaçao's economy thrived because the island served as an entrepôt, or trading post, for the southern Caribbean and mainland South America. According to a slave census of 1764–1765, Curaçao's 159 slave-owning Jews owned only 867 slaves, or roughly 5.5 per owner.[49]

Jews in Surinam, therefore, lived surrounded by many more people of African descent than did Curaçaoan Jews. As a result, Surinam was the only place in the New World where a community of mulatto Jews developed. In Curaçao, Jamaica, and other places where Jews owned slaves, there are no recorded examples of Jews trying either to convert their slaves to Judaism or to raise their mulatto offspring as Jews. Partly this is because of Judaism's nonproselytizing character: this is a religion by birth and not, generally, by conversion. And partly this is because Judaism had for millennia evolved regulations for treating slaves as something less than human, as is clear from this statement in the *Shulhan 'Aruk* regarding mourning rites for slaves: "For male and female slaves no line [of comforters] is made, nor is consolation offered [to their master], but they say to him, 'May the Lord replace your loss,' even as they say to a man regarding his ox and ass."[50] Only in a plantation setting like Surinam would the extreme demographic imbalance between Africans and Jews overcome these hurdles to the creation of a Jewish mulatto community.

Surinam's Jewish mulattoes were almost all the result of sexual liaisons between Jewish men and African women. In some cases, mulattoes resulted from slave owners sexually exploiting their female slaves, but these offspring were not likely to be raised as Jews. More likely to be raised as Jews were the children who resulted from a "marriage Surinam-style," the contemporary term for a marriage or, more often, cohabitation between a free mulatto woman and a European (Christian or Jewish) man.[51]

But one should not imagine that these familial bonds meant that mulatto Jews were warmly welcomed into Surinam's Jewish community. By the 1760s, there were at least several dozen Jewish mulattoes who sought to practice their religion with their white coreligionists. Surinam's Jewish leaders made it clear that mulattoes could participate only as second-class citizens. As early as 1754, the Paramaribo congregation passed a series of rules codifying the lower status of the Jewish mulattoes. The mulattoes could never be *Yahidim* (full members), only *Congreganten* (congregants). They were relegated to the mourners' bench in the synagogue, and they could not receive a *Misheherah*, or blessing, in the synagogue.[52]

Although Surinam's Jewish mulattoes had no choice but to accept these demeaning regulations, the humiliations inspired by the new rules led them in 1759 to form a religious brotherhood called *Darhe Jesarim* (Way of the Righteous).[53] This fraternity existed inconspicuously for over thirty years before it became the center of controversy in the 1790s. It began with the April 1790 burial of a Jewish mulatto, Joseph de David Cohen Nassy. The brotherhood, as usual for one of its members, prepared the corpse and organized the procession to the cemetery. But when they arrived at the *beth haim*, they found that the grave opened by the congregation's white grave diggers was "in a swamp" (and thus full of water) and dug "only one foot deep." When they protested to the grave diggers, they were told, "You cannot give orders here, and if you folks do not shut up we will shut you up."[54]

The mulattoes complained to the synagogue's leaders, but they were surprised when the incident caused the leaders to investigate *Darhe Jesarim*. David Cohen Nassy, the secretary of the executive committee, led the inquiry. This wealthy Nassy seems to have been the former owner of the poor mulatto Nassy—could he have been the deceased man's father too? This latter possibility seems unlikely, for Nassy's ruling contained no shred of paternal feeling. Instead, Nassy complained that the fraternity was not burying its members according to proper Jewish law. It turned out that the religious brotherhood of mulattoes had buried Joseph de David Cohen Nassy—and perhaps others—with ceremonies reserved for a *parnass* (president of the congregation). They had used wax candles in the procession, and the mourners themselves, instead of the cantor, had recited the mourning prayers. By these small gestures, the members of *Darhe Jesarim* had tried to add a hint of pomp to an otherwise humble burial. David Cohen Nassy and the congregation's other white leaders would not allow such usurpations of the postmortem symbols of esteem, and in 1793 they proscribed and disbanded the Way of the Righteous.[55] In contrast, although the island of Curaçao witnessed numerous conflicts among Jews in the eighteenth century, none of those conflicts occurred across a color line the way they did in Surinam.

Perhaps one of the reasons that there was tension between mulatto and white Jews in the 1790s was that this period coincided with bloody warfare against black maroons: runaway slaves who had formed their own communities in the jungles of Surinam. From the 1760s through the 1790s, a state of on-again, off-again war existed between

**Figure 4** Marker with *sankofa* symbol in Surinam's Creole cemetery. Photograph by Rachel Frankel.

Surinam's whites and its maroon communities. In 1788, maroons attacked four plantations near the main Jewish settlement. An undated Jewish prayer from 1789 or 1790
shows the impact that this warfare was having on Jewish religious practice. This printed
prayer, written by the cantor David Hisquiau Louzada, hoped that God would "pity, save,
succor, and protect all those who, going to war against our enemies the cruel and rebellious Blacks, are fearful of the foe." The prayer invoked biblical language of conquering
another people when it asked God to "be a refuge and citadel to them [those going to war
against the maroons], so that they may put down, conquer, and destroy under their feet all
the enemies, the rebellious cruel Negroes who plot against our welfare."[56]

Although the attitudes of Surinam's white Jews toward mulatto Jews and maroons
seem to represent an unbridgeable divide, a longer view suggests that African practices
ultimately influenced Jewish deathways.[57] Some Jewish gravestones in nineteenth- and
twentieth-century Surinam adopted distinctively African iconography. To understand
this connection, we first must examine a "Creole" cemetery in Jodensavanne, the original locus of Jewish sugar plantations. In Surinamese usage, "Creole" denotes descendants of African slaves who trace their freedom to manumission rather than
marronage.[58] The graves in this cemetery, which date to the nineteenth and twentieth
centuries, belong to people of African descent who were not Jewish. Some surviving
stones include Christian crosses. Numerous stones also use the heart-shaped *sankofa*
symbol of the Akan people of West Africa, many of whom became slaves in Surinam
(figs. 4 and 5). "Sankofa" means "go back and fetch it," and the symbol stands for an

**Figure 5**  Another marker with *sankofa* symbol in Surinam's Creole cemetery. This
cemetery holds the descendants of manumitted slaves. Photograph by Rachel Frankel.

**Figure 6**    Nineteenth- and twentieth-century markers with *sankofa* finials in the Sephardic Cemetery, Paramaribo, Surinam. Photograph by Rachel Frankel.

**Figure 7**　Nineteenth- and twentieth-century markers with *sankofa* finials in the Sephardic Cemetery, Paramaribo, Surinam. Photograph by Rachel Frankel.

Akan proverb, "it is not a taboo to go back and retrieve if you forget." The *sankofa* symbol has been found in other African American cemeteries in the New World, including New York's eighteenth-century Negro Burial Ground.[59]

This is interesting but hardly surprising; it makes sense that descendents of Africans would use an African symbol in their gravestone iconography. But travel downriver from Jodensavanne to Paramaribo, just as many Jews did as they relocated to the city when their plantations began to fail in the second half of the eighteenth century, and one finds a remarkable collection of Jewish-African gravestone iconography. In Paramaribo's weedy Sephardic cemetery stand numerous nineteenth- and twentieth-century Jewish gravestones with *sankofa* finials, Stars of David, and Hebrew lettering (figs. 6 and 7). The *sankofa* symbols are numerous enough to indicate that their use "does not reflect the idiosyncratic taste of a few individuals, but rather a widely accepted consumer pattern."[60] It is unclear what the Jews memorialized by these stones thought about the *sankofa* symbols. Did they even realize they were African in origin, or did they see them simply as hearts? But even if Paramaribo's Jews did not fully perceive the connection with African iconography, the significance is clear. Nowhere else in the New World, certainly not in Curaçao, did Jews adorn their gravestones with heart-shaped finials. Clearly this was the result of Surinam's unique history as the only Jewish plantation society the world has ever known.

Ultimately, then, the men and women of the Hebrew Nation in the New World defy our expectations about the relationship between nationhood and society in the early modern Atlantic. Although they lived in territories claimed by European nation-states, they saw themselves as Jews first and members of European empires second. When they crossed the boundaries of European empires, therefore, they worked to keep their rituals in line with those of earlier generations of Jews. But like all religious groups in the New World, Jews found their faith shaped and tested by the new contexts in which they found themselves. As Surinam's Jewish mulattoes attest, the boundaries of the Hebrew Nation—like the boundaries of European nation-states—were permeable and contested. People of color who wished to join the Hebrew Nation were held at arm's length, just as white members of the Hebrew Nation themselves were held at arm's length by some Caribbean Christians. Thus, it is all the more important that we examine the early modern Atlantic not only from the perspective of the modern nation-state but also from the perspective of religious cultures—even as they crossed national boundaries.

## Notes

1   See, for example, Pieter C. Emmer and Wim Klooster, "The Dutch Atlantic, 1600–1800: Expansion without Empire," *Itinerario* 23 (1999): 48–69; Silvia Marzagalli, "The French Atlantic," *Itinerario* 23 (1999): 70–83; David Hancock, "The British Atlantic World: Coordination, Complexity, and the Emergence of an Atlantic Market Economy, 1651–1815," *Itinerario* 23 (1999): 107–26; David Armitage and Michael J. Braddick, eds., *The British Atlantic World, 1500–1800* (New York, 2002); Ian K. Steele, *The English Atlantic, 1675–1740: An Exploration of Communication and Community* (New York, 1986); and W. J. Eccles, *France in America*, rev. ed. (East Lansing, Mich., 1990).

2   The phrase is used in a different context by T. H. Breen, "Persistent Localism: English Social Change and the Shaping of New England Institutions," *William and Mary Quarterly* 32 (1975): 3–28.

3   Laurent Dubois, *Avengers of the New World: The Story of the Haitian Revolution* (Cambridge, Mass., 2004), 304–5, and several of the essays in David P. Geggus, ed., *The Impact of the Haitian Revolution in the Atlantic World* (Columbia, S.C., 2001).

4   Two classics are Melville J. Herskovits, *The Myth of the Negro Past* (Boston, 1958 [1941]), and Frank Tannenbaum, *Slave and Citizen: The Negro in the Americas* (New York, 1963 [1946]).

5   Paul Gilroy, *The Black Atlantic: Modernity and Double Consciousness* (Cambridge, Mass., 1993), 151.

6   For example, John Thornton, *Africa and Africans in the Making of the Atlantic World, 1400–1680*, 2nd ed. (New York, 1998); Deborah Gray White, "'Yes,' There Is a Black Atlantic," *Itinerario* 23 (1999): 127–40; and Peter Linebaugh and Marcus Rediker, *The Many-Headed Hydra: Sailors, Slaves, Commoners, and the Hidden History of the Revolutionary Atlantic* (Boston, 2000).

7   Miriam Bodian, *Hebrews of the Portuguese Nation: Conversos and Community in Early Modern Amsterdam* (Bloomington, Ind., 1997), 11–18.

8   Zvi Loker, *Jews in the Caribbean: Evidence on the History of the Jews in the Caribbean Zone in Colonial Times* (Jerusalem, 1991), 197.

9   Bodian, *Hebrews of the Portuguese Nation*, 6, and the *Oxford English Dictionary Online*, definitions 1.a and 1.c.

10  E. J. Hobsbawm, *Nations and Nationalism since 1780: Programme, Myth, Reality* (New York, 1990), 14–17.

11  Paolo Bernardini, "A Milder Colonization: Jewish Expansion to the New World, and the New World in the Jewish Consciousness of the Early Modern Era," in *The Jews and the Expansion of Europe to the West, 1450–1800*, ed. Bernardini and Norman Fiering (New York, 2001), 21.

12  For another example of this latter approach, see James Homer Williams, "An Atlantic Perspective on the Jewish Struggle for Rights and Opportunities in Brazil, New Netherland, and New York," in Bernardini and Fiering, *Jews and the Expansion of Europe*, 369–93.

13  Wim Klooster, *The Dutch in the Americas, 1600–1800* (Providence, R.I., 1997), 6–67. See also Benjamin Schmidt, *Innocence Abroad: The Dutch Imagination and the New World, 1570–1670* (New York, 2001).

14  Jonathan I. Israel, "The Jews of Dutch America," in Bernardini and Fiering, *Jews and the Expansion of Europe*, 342.

15  Hilary McD. Beckles, *A History of Barbados: From Amerindian Settlement to Nation-State* (New York, 1990).

16  Williams, "An Atlantic Perspective on the Jewish Struggle," 378–79.

17  Robert Cohen, *Jews in Another Environment: Surinam in the Second Half of the Eighteenth Century* (Leiden, 1991), 1.

18  Cohen, *Jews in Another Environment*, 124–26; J. A. Schiltkamp, "Jewish Jurators in Surinam," in *The Jewish Nation in Surinam: Historical Essays*, ed. Robert Cohen (Amsterdam, 1982), 60.

19  Wim Klooster, "The Jews in Suriname and Curaçao," in Bernardini and Fiering, *Jews and the Expansion of Europe*, 361.

20  Holly Snyder, "A Sense of Place: Jews, Identity, and Social Status in Colonial British America, 1654–1831" (Ph.D. diss., Brandeis University, 2000), 85 n.100.

21  *Journal of the Assembly of Jamaica*, 7 May 1741, quoted in Snyder, "A Sense of Place," 106.

22  Samuel Oppenheim, ed., "The Jews in Barbados in 1739," *Publications of the American Jewish Historical Society* 22 (1914): 197–98.

23  Snyder, "A Sense of Place," 135 n.70; Joanna Westphal, "Jews in a Colonial Society: The Jewish Community of Barbados, 1654–1833" (M.A. thesis, University College London, 1993), 7.

24  Jonathan D. Sarna, "The Jews in British America," in Bernardini and Fiering, *Jews and the Expansion of Europe*, 522.

25  Bodian, *Hebrews of the Portuguese Nation*, 30. The edition of the *Shulhan 'Aruk* that I use is Chaim N. Denburg, ed., *Code of Hebrew Law: Shulhan 'Aruk* (Montreal, 1954), which I will cite by chapter and paragraph.

26  *Shulhan 'Aruk*, 338 § 2.

27  Isaac S. Emmanuel, *Precious Stones of the Jews of Curaçao: Curaçaon Jewry, 1656–1957* (New York, 1957), 60.

28  E. M. Shilstone, *Jewish Monumental Inscriptions in the Burial Ground of the Jewish Synagogue at Bridgetown, Barbados* (New York, 1956), 163, 164. See also Emmanuel, *Precious Stones*, 381.

29  Emmanuel, *Precious Stones*, 75–77.

30  Leo Modena, *The History of the Rites, Customes, and Manner of Life, of the Present Jews, throughout the World* (London, 1650), 235.

31  Emmanuel, *Precious Stones*, 80–81.

32  *Shulhan 'Aruk*, 344 § 1.

33  Bernard Picart, *The Ceremonies and Religious Customs of the Various Nations of the Known World*, 7 vols. (London, 1733–1737), 1:243. See also Modena, *History of the Rites*, 237,

and Sylvie Anne Goldberg, *Crossing the Jabbok: Illness and Death in Ashkenazi Judaism in Sixteenth- through Nineteenth-Century Prague*, trans. Carol Cosman (Berkeley, 1996), 116. This custom seems not to have existed in the thirteenth century, but by the sixteenth century it was integral to Jewish burial practices throughout Europe. Goldberg, *Crossing the Jabbok*, 133–35.

34 Goldberg, *Crossing the Jabbok*, 38–39.

35 Emmanuel, *Precious Stones*, 88.

36 Richard D. Barnett and Philip Wright, *The Jews of Jamaica: Tombstone Inscriptions, 1663–1880* (Jerusalem, 1997), 3. See also the 1721 will of Daniel Lopez Laguna of Kingston. Jacob A. P. M. Andrade, *A Record of the Jews in Jamaica from the English Conquest to the Present Time* (Kingston, 1941), 180.

37 Shilstone, *Jewish Monumental Inscriptions*, xxviii; Emmanuel, *Precious Stones*, 129.

38 The first two motifs are too numerous to cite. For angels, see Barnett and Wright, *Jews of Jamaica*, 49, 89.

39 Karl Watson, "The Iconography of Tombstones in the Jewish Graveyard, Bridgetown, Barbados," *Journal of the Barbados Museum and Historical Society* 50 (2004): 195–212, esp. 203–4.

40 *They That Are Born Are Destined to Die and the Dead Brought to Life Again: The Jewish Cemetery Beth Haim Curaçao* (Curaçao, 2001), 20.

41 Rochelle Weinstein, "Stones of Memory: Revelations from a Cemetery in Curaçao," in *Sephardim in the Americas: Studies in Culture and History*, ed. Martin A. Cohen and Abraham J. Peck (Tuscaloosa, Ala., 1993), 118. See illustrations on 88 and 107.

42 Weinstein, "Stones of Memory," 124. See illustrations on 86 and 125.

43 Snyder, "A Sense of Place," 234–35.

44 Isaac S. Emmanuel and Suzanne A. Emmanuel, *History of the Jews of the Netherlands Antilles*, 2 vols. (Cincinnati, 1970), 1097.

45 Emmanuel, *Precious Stones*, 92.

46 Will of David Bravo, 1 June 1749, "Jamaica Wills, 1692–1798," American Jewish Archives, Cincinnati.

47 Will of Abraham Gonsales, 1 November 1753, "Jamaica Wills, 1692–1798."

48 Jacob R. Marcus, *The Colonial American Jew, 1492–1776*, 3 vols. (Detroit, 1970), 159.

49 Statistics calculated from Emmanuel and Emmanuel, *History of the Jews of the Netherlands Antilles*, 1036–1045. A 1680 census of Bridgetown, Barbados, demonstrated a similarly small number (3.0) of slaves per Jewish household. Richard S. Dunn, *Sugar and Slaves: The Rise of the Planter Class in the English West Indies, 1624–1713* (Chapel Hill, 1972), 107.

50 *Shulhan 'Aruk*, 377 § 1.

51 Cohen, *Jews in Another Environment*, 158.

52 Ibid., 161.

53 Jonathan Schorsch, *Jews and Blacks in the Early Modern World* (New York, 2004), 252.

54 Cohen, *Jews in Another Environment*, 163. These quotations are from the mulattoes' 1793 letter to the governor.

55 Ibid., 165–67.

56 Z. Loker and R. Cohen, "An Eighteenth-Century Prayer of the Jews in Surinam," in Cohen, *The Jewish Nation in Surinam*, 75–87, quotations on 78 and 81–82.

57 My analysis is heavily indebted to Rachel Frankel, "Antecedents and Remnants of Jodensavanne: The Synagogues and Cemeteries of the First Permanent Plantation Settlement of New World Jews," in Bernardini and Fiering, *Jews and the Expansion of Europe*, 394–436, esp. 425–26. I am grateful to Frankel for allowing me to use her cemetery

photographs. See also Aviva Ben-Ur, "Still Life: Sephardi, Ashkenazi, and West African Art and Form in Suriname's Jewish Cemeteries," *American Jewish History* 92 (March 2004): 31–79. Ben-Ur kindly gave me access to her article before its publication.

58 Ben-Ur, "Still Life," 76.

59 Kwaku Ofori-Ansa, "Identification and Validation of the Sankofa Symbol," *Update: Newsletter of the African Burial Ground* 1, no. 8 (summer 1995): 3.

60 Ben-Ur, "Still Life," 77.

*Claudio Saunt takes a different approach to comparing various nation-based Atlantics. He examines the ways in which the imperial rivalry between France and Great Britain played out with devastating consequences for American Indians in what would become the southeastern United States. Saunt sets aside the tired historiographical cliché that posits essentialist nation-based differences between the ways different European powers interacted with Indians. As Francis Parkman, the originator of this tradition, wrote in the mid-nineteenth century, "Spanish civilization crushed the Indian; English civilization scorned and neglected him; French civilization embraced and cherished him." In the eighteenth-century world that Saunt describes, the French showed little propensity to "embrace and cherish" their Choctaw allies. In fact, the French used the Choctaws as proxies in their worldwide rivalry with Great Britain, in a way not dissimilar to how the United States and the Soviet Union used armed insurgents in twentieth-century Angola and Afghanistan to play out their geopolitical competition. Like its later counterpart, the eighteenth-century proxy war in the homeland of the Choctaws left a legacy of death and dislocation. For these Indians, living between imperial rivals left them less with the opportunity to play European powers off one another, as most historians today assert, than with the unfortunate role of foot soldiers in a bloody war for empire. Nonetheless, Choctaws were not completely without agency. At what points in this story were the Choctaws able to shape their destiny?*

# "Our Indians": European Empires and the History of the Native American South

## Claudio Saunt

Atlantic World histories, like more familiar narratives of the rise of the nation-state, frequently seem to convey a sense of European omnipotence. Capitalism reaches across the Atlantic to engulf the Americas, Old World biota invade the New World and push out indigenous species, and historical narrative replaces oral traditions about the past. Searching the frayed edges of transatlantic empires, however, historians have located peripheral regions, variously described as frontiers, borderlands, or middle grounds, that lay just beyond the reach of imperial control.[1] Once characterized as the proving grounds of empire, scholars now recognize that these regions were sites of negotiation and compromise, where Indians and colonists together forged new worlds.[2]

In a 1999 article, Jeremy Adelman and Stephen Aron summed up recent literature on borderlands, the contested regions lying between empires. These regions, they observed, were characterized by "fluid and 'inclusive' intercultural frontiers." They were places of "mutual acculturation," "replete with ethnic mixing, syncretism, and cohabitation." Where borderlands existed, Adelman and Aron concluded, "Indian peoples deflected imperial powers from their original purposes and fashioned economic, diplomatic, and personal relations that rested, if not entirely on Indian ground, at least on more common ground."[3] Since Adelman and Aron's essay, the emphasis on "fluid" borderlands has shown no signs of waning.[4] One historian describes the "relatively harmonious past" of the Deep South, where Indians and colonists participated in a system of "mutually beneficial economic interactions."[5] Another writes about a "world of equals" in the Texas borderlands, where Indians and Europeans "brought together respective traditions of ceremony, gift giving, and protocol to forge new systems of diplomatic exchange with one another."[6]

Paradoxically, this historiographical turn toward borderlands may in fact perpetuate rather than destabilize a Eurocentric perspective of the Atlantic World. Metaphorically, "middle ground" and "borderland" suggest a sense of in-betweenness, of negotiation and compromise, but literally they reflect the viewpoint of colonial ministers in Paris, Madrid, and London who eyed the possessions of their European rivals and dreamed of extending their territorial claims across Indian lands. To Native Americans, by contrast, middle grounds and borderlands were simply homelands. Narratives that foreground negotiation, compromise, and boundary crossing between races and cultures perhaps reflect more the emancipatory fantasies of twenty-first-century scholars than the lives of eighteenth-century Indians, whose nations were invaded and reduced, if not destroyed.[7] Any account of Indians in this period must consider the imperial dimensions of the Atlantic World without resorting to older narratives that assumed that conquest was inevitable and total.

To understand the dynamics of regions that were, from different perspectives, both imperial borderlands and Indian homelands, a twentieth-century neologism may be helpful. Where European empires fought each other and Indian nations for Indian lands, they frequently did so by means of proxy warfare.[8] Loosely defined, proxy wars are local or regional conflicts in which competing imperial states covertly invest. They are "large small wars," as two scholars said of the thirty-five-year civil war in Angola that began in the 1960s.[9]

There are a number of obvious differences between the well-known proxy wars of the twentieth century in places such as Angola and Afghanistan and those in the eighteenth century in the Choctaw Nation, Iroquoia, and elsewhere, but there are a number of revealing similarities too.[10] First, in the eighteenth-century Atlantic World, European empires exported their conflicts to other nations, and those conflicts were deeply imbricated in international imperial rivalry as well as in regional colonial ambitions. Second, imperial administrators displayed a deep contempt for the people who lived in battlegrounds, arrogantly and erroneously imagining that they could control the actions of local residents. Third, although administrators' fantasies of control were not in the least warranted, the guns, textiles, and other trading goods that they poured into battlegrounds in the interest of manipulating native peoples frequently had devastating consequences for indigenous communities, not unlike the effects that machine guns and mortars had more recently on Angolans and Afghanis.[11] There is a significant disparity in the scale between eighteenth- and twentieth-century proxy wars, reflected in the deadliness of modern weapons and the tremendous reach of today's superpowers, yet the parallels remain compelling.

This chapter explores one European borderland and Indian homeland, the Choctaw Nation, where French and British empires fought a proxy war in the first half of the eighteenth century.[12] It outlines how France and Britain exported their imperial rivalry to the Choctaw Nation. It explores the French administrators' fantasies of control over native peoples. And it concludes by arguing that the proxy war in the Choctaw Nation, though hardly controlled by French and British officers, nevertheless had devastating consequences for native peoples.

\*\*\*

In the early eighteenth century, the lower South was shared by three large Indian nations (Map 1). The Choctaw Nation in east-central Mississippi numbered about 17,000 people. On its northern border (present-day northern Mississippi), the Chickasaw Nation had 14,000 residents. And farther east, in present-day Alabama and western Georgia, the Creek Nation comprised 10,000 people.[13] The European presence in the lower South remained negligible until 1670, when Britain established a settlement in Charleston. Some thirty years later, France established a competing colony along the Mississippi River. Separated by more than 600 miles and by the Choctaw, Chickasaw, and Creek nations, these two imperial outposts would spend the next sixty years struggling for control of the land lying between them. (Although Spain had settlements in present-day Florida, by the eighteenth century it was no longer able to mount a significant challenge to its imperial competitors.) For much of the time, France and Britain chose to fight by proxy rather than overtly.[14]

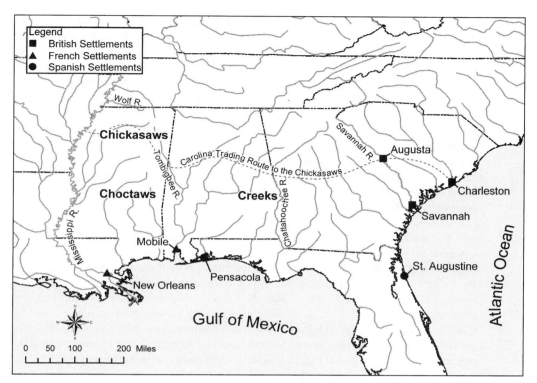

**Map 1** The Colonial Southeast.

The Choctaw and Chickasaw nations, with their relatively large populations and their strategic location, held the key to controlling access to the Mississippi River. In 1715, French colonists and their slaves numbered only 400, and even fifty years later, when the French abandoned their claim to the colony, their numbers would barely exceed 9,000.[15] By making "striking comparisons" between the great numbers of people in France and the small numbers of Choctaws and Chickasaws in the South, Jean Baptist le Moyne de Bienville, the colony's governor from 1701 to 1713, tried to elide the power imbalance in Louisiana, but the fact remained, as the Indians pointed out to him in 1707, that "instead of increasing you are diminishing."[16]

It should be noted that eighteenth-century states were far less cohesive than their twentieth-century counterparts. Dependent on slow-moving and unreliable ships, colonial officials sometimes received their orders months after they had been issued. Moreover, when it came to implementing Indian policy, traders played a critical role, and both French and British officials complained that these men had little allegiance to the crown.[17] Britain faced the added disadvantage of managing affairs through several competing colonies.[18] But the fact remains that French and British officials, schooled in the theory of mercantilism, believed they were engaged in a zero-sum game for control of the world's wealth.[19] Even local traders, looking out for their own interests rather than those of the crown, spent a great deal of time trying to monopolize commerce for their own nation.

Despite the powerful presence of the Choctaws and Chickasaws, both France and Britain imagined that their true adversary for control of the lower South lay on the other side of the English Channel, not across the Atlantic Ocean. As one British agent put it, with the establishment of Louisiana, the "English American Empire" might become "unreasonably Crampt up."[20] The key to thwarting the French colony, British officials believed, was the establishment of a western Indian trade. Carolina consequently organized an expedition in 1699 to forge commercial ties with Louisiana Indians and to claim the Mississippi region for the British crown, and that same year it began arming Indians against the rival colony.[21] Friendly Indians, declared a Carolina governing committee, should be encouraged to make war "upon those Indians that are our and their Enemies."[22] By offering high prices for enslaved Indians, Carolina and Virginia created a market that sent their native allies as far as east Texas in search of potential victims. Between 30,000 and 50,000 Indians were captured and sold into the British slave market between 1670 and 1750.[23]

These actions did not go unnoticed in French Louisiana. "The English of Carolina are sparing nothing to have our Indians destroyed by theirs," Bienville wrote in 1709, using an expression of possession that became common among both French and British officials.[24] By the end of Louisiana's first decade, it was clear to the governor that the Chickasaws would be "theirs." These people, whom the French could reach only with difficulty by ascending the winding path of the Tombigbee River, lay on a route frequently traveled by Carolina traders.[25] As the Chickasaws expanded their relations with Carolina, Bienville announced that the more populous and more centrally located Choctaws were "the key to this country," an opinion that French officials would share for the next fifty years.[26]

Like proxy wars in the twentieth century, the Choctaw–Chickasaw war was a regional conflict with connections to remote locales. The great distance between Paris and the lower South as well as the interest of French administrators in their far-flung colony is captured by the brief yet strongly worded comments left by Parisian officers in the margins of reports on Louisiana. "Last autumn, these savages killed two English," read one such report, to which a colonial minister noted in the margin, "*bon.*"[27] When French-allied Indians failed to attack the Chickasaws, another administrator wrote in the margin, "*tant pis*" ("too bad").[28] The King encouraged measures to have the Choctaws destroy the Chickasaws "as soon as possible," a more effusive marginal note explained in 1735, because if conflict with England became overt, the war with the Chickasaws would become especially costly.[29] "I will spare no expense [*Je n'épargnerai aucun soin*] to achieve the total defeat of the Chickasaws," Bienville wrote to the minister of the Marine soon afterward.[30]

The imperial dimensions of the conflict were made real when Louisiana governors coordinated forces against the Chickasaw Nation with their ministerial counterparts in distant New France. In 1730, Governor Étienne Boucher de Périer (1726–1733) wrote to Governor Beauharnois in Quebec, requesting that Hurons, Iroquois, Miamis, and other northern Indians be sent against the Chickasaws. In that year, Hurons killed or captured some thirty Chickasaws.[31] In later years, orders were relayed from New Orleans to Quebec to Fort Detroit to organize war parties against the Chickasaws.[32] "The savages from the north are relentlessly harassing the Chickasaws," an officer reported from Mobile in 1738.[33] Given the concerted French efforts spanning nearly half a century to set their Indian allies against the Chickasaws, it is not surprising that more than one Choctaw concluded that the French themselves should be doing the fighting. "For a number of years," one Choctaw reportedly said in 1745, they have fought the Chickasaws, who "never did anything to them except fail to be allied with the French."[34]

\*\*\*

French officers believed that with well-directed gifts, cleverly timed encouragements, and occasional threats they could manipulate Choctaws to conform to their strategic plans. They manifested a deep conviction in their own superiority.[35] The Choctaws might "take a few scalps here and there," Périer wrote in 1731, but they would never be able to destroy a well-fortified nation such as the Chickasaws. By contrast, he wrote, "nothing is impossible for the well-led Frenchman," especially when "the glory of the King" was at stake.[36] But French arrogance was undercut by two disastrous military campaigns in 1736 and 1740. In the first, Bienville, frustrated with the lack of progress against the Chickasaws, decided to organize two French forces to invade their homeland simultaneously. One, led by Martin d'Artaguette, would descend from Fort Illinois on the Mississippi River, while the other, commanded by Bienville himself, would ascend from Mobile.

Although Bienville was delayed by a lack of supplies for two months, d'Artaguette did not receive word until his party of 130 French soldiers, 38 Iroquois, and 190 Illinois and Miami Indians was already on the march. He decided not to turn back. When his troops arrived in the Chickasaw Nation in late March 1736, 400 to 500 warriors rushed over a nearby hill and pursued the panicked soldiers back to their camp. The Chickasaws killed d'Artaguette and forty other men and seized their supplies.[37] When news filtered back that ten prisoners were burned alive, the French took consolation by reporting that their compatriots had sung bravely during their immolation. One officer explained, "That is the custom of the savages, who judge the valor of a warrior only by the strength or weakness of his voice at the moment when they have him killed."[38] The stunning defeat, coupled with their painful adoption of Indian standards of valor, must have made colonists uncomfortable. Unwilling to attribute the rout to the skill of the Chickasaws, Bienville concluded that the English were to blame.[39]

Bienville's belated foray into the Chickasaw Nation, two months after D'Artaguette's, fared no better. Numbering over 1,000 men, the expedition quickly got itself into trouble when French soldiers thoughtlessly set fire to several Chickasaw cabins providing cover from hostile gunfire. Forced into the open by the roaring flames, the soldiers were shot down by their own rear guard as well as by the Chickasaws. As their officers fell around them, the troops hurriedly took flight.[40] Roughly eighty French soldiers were killed or wounded in the fighting, compared to perhaps twenty Chickasaws. Adding insult to injury, Bienville had to plead with his Choctaw allies to help carry the French wounded back to Mobile.[41] A month later, Bienville humbly reported to the minister of the Marine that the campaign "occasioned the vacancy of several officers' positions."[42] Once again, he attributed the defeat to the English: "What happened against my expectation was the assistance of the English, whom I did not think would take sides."[43] Bienville also blamed the stature of his troops. Of fifty-two recent recruits, he wrote with dismay, only two were taller than five feet.[44] Nevertheless, he recognized that this time he might not be able to avoid shouldering some of the responsibility. "Your silence, Monseigneur, regarding what I suggested about the cowardice of our soldiers," he wrote to the minister of the Marine, "leads me to believe that you are not well persuaded that it was the only cause of the poor success." This cowardice, he insisted, "was only too real and too public."[45]

The 1736 expeditions did nothing to improve the image of the French in the minds of local Indians. Red Shoes, a noted Choctaw warrior, visited Mobile in May 1737 and told the commander that the French "know nothing about making war." They were unable to take even a small village of thirty or forty men, he observed, and in their failed attempt lost scores of soldiers without killing a single Chickasaw. French troops, encumbered by their heavy clothing, marched too slowly and too closely together, Red Shoes said, making it possible for the Chickasaws to fire blindly and still kill or wound several of them. Bernard Diron d'Artaguette, whose nephew had led the first expedition, listened to Red Shoes's humiliating reproach and responded as best he could: French soldiers had sacrificed themselves on the King's orders, he explained, to see if the Chickasaws were "true men" and if they, as "great warriors," merited a worthy attack. The Choctaws, he reported to the minister of the Marine, returned home impressed with the "great courage" and "obedience" of French soldiers, but his response could scarcely have soothed French doubts about their military prowess or bolstered the Indians' waning opinion of their neighbors.[46] Bienville immediately began planning a 1740 campaign to redeem French honor.[47]

This time Bienville intended to sail up the Mississippi and Wolf rivers, cross overland, and descend on the unwitting Chickasaws. The expedition, put into motion in the middle of 1739, ended in disaster because of a fatal oversight: there was no route from the Wolf River to the Chickasaw Nation that permitted a thousand French soldiers to pass with their artillery.[48] Although by September the French troops were positioned on the Wolf River at Fort Assumption, not far from present-day Memphis, they could only bide their time while several parties desperately tried to discover a route that did not demand the construction of dozens of bridges or the fording of deep waters. Three months later, the number of Frenchmen, Indians, and slaves at Fort Assumption had risen to close to 3,000, but Bienville still had not discovered a road to the Chickasaw Nation. Winter set in, and the waters rose, flooding the lands and making overland routes even more impassable. In the cold weather, the army's horses and cattle, many of which had already drowned in the high waters, began to starve to death. Although it was clear by the end of the year that the entire campaign would have to be abandoned, Bienville maintained the charade until mid-February, when he finally called off the disastrous expedition.[49] How disastrous is illustrated by the extraordinary cost to the French crown: over a million livres, more than three times the annual budget of the entire colony, expended on a war that Bienville abdicated before it began.[50] Along with this immense sum, Louisiana lost 500 soldiers, who died of disease during the long, fruitless wait at Fort Assumption.[51]

"Even if we did not get out of this fix as successfully as we had the right to expect we would," Bienville wrote, "the glory of the king's arms did not suffer."[52] But no one shared his opinion, least of all the Choctaws. They wondered aloud why their allies had tried to carve out such a difficult route to the Chickasaws.[53] They "have an infinite scorn for the French," reported one officer.[54] Even as late as 1750, the expeditions of 1736 and 1740 were inspiring "such a great scorn for our inability to subdue the savages that they all boast of it." "I see it every day," wrote Governor Vaudreuil, "which pains and embarrasses me."[55]

***

Considering these French military fiascos, it is hard to imagine how southern Indians could have been put at risk by a proxy war mounted by France and Britain. Indeed, the self-aggrandizing pronouncements of colonial officials must be read with skepticism. "At present, I am . . . the master of reestablishing the tranquility and peace of the colony," Bienville claimed in 1733, insisting that the Chickasaws were desperate to settle at all costs.[56] Seven years later, after his embarrassing 1740 defeat, Bienville announced another truce with the Chickasaws. This time, however, even his inferiors reported (with some exaggeration) that the peace was a sham, agreed to by a single elderly Chickasaw and obeyed by no one. To sustain the pretense, Bienville ordered his officers to refrain from reporting on Indian affairs.[57] It would be wrong to believe that Indians were merely victims in the French–English proxy war. But if they did not passively participate in their own destruction, as historians used to maintain, neither did they preserve "indomitable tribal independence in the face of relentless European intervention," as scholars more commonly assert today.[58] Like the chaotic and dangerous worlds created by twentieth-century imperial rivalries in Angola, Afghanistan, and elsewhere, the French and British competition for the lower South destabilized the region and created a situation dominated by no one.[59]

The impact of French interference in Choctaw affairs can be seen in three related arenas: the enrichment of Choctaw leaders through French presents, the introduction of firearms, and the creation of a scalp market. Although French trade with the Choctaws remained minimal, the governor of Louisiana annually awarded Choctaw leaders thousands of livres worth of cloth, guns, knives, and other items. The French were "masterly" at managing Indian affairs by the "great quantities of valuable goods they gave them with," observed one English competitor.[60] In the early 1740s, these items averaged about 20,000 livres, rising to twice that amount by mid-decade.[61] The goods were distributed to a little over 100 Choctaw leaders in the 1730s.[62] Even if, in response to Choctaw demands, that number rose to 200 by the 1740s, it meant that each leader received 200 livres worth of commodities, the equivalent market value of fifty-four deerskins.[63] By the measure of the Louisiana governor, who made 12,000 livres per year, this sum was not extraordinary, but for a common soldier, who made fifty-four livres, it was significant.[64] More important, for Indians, the market value of fifty-four deerskins represented the profits of two years of hunting.

"The savages . . . learned from us to have true needs [*de vrais besoins*]," remarked Périer in 1731. Indians, he therefore concluded, could be manipulated with a plentiful supply of textiles and firearms.[65] The truth was more complicated. "They are insolent," wrote one of Périer's fellow officers, "and one can say that they demand as tribute what we call presents."[66] Whether textiles and guns were gift or tribute, the French distributed them to Choctaws inclined to kill Chickasaws and withheld them from those who were not.[67] As a consequence, Choctaws always had to keep in mind the costs of opposing the French. When Alibamon Mingo agreed to the establishment of an English trading post in his town, he quickly realized that the disadvantages outweighed the benefits. "It turned me against the French leaders, who, to punish me," he explained, "deprived me for two years of the presents I was accustomed to receiving." This "disgrace," he continued, "made me lose all credit in the nation."[68] Presents, concluded Governor Vaudreuil, "are indisputably the strongest ties that keep the Choctaws in our interest and the principal motive behind their actions."[69]

Vaudreuil's dismissive assertion that the Choctaws were driven mainly by the desire for European goods flatly ignores the many other factors that influenced them: friendship; strategic considerations toward France, Britain, and Spain and toward other Indian nations; political competition within the Choctaw nation; and religious convictions. The French could not control the Choctaws merely by distributing textiles and firearms, but neither could the Choctaws control the effect of this new source of wealth flowing into their nation. The French first tried to channel goods through the great chief, an office created by them to facilitate the political manipulation of the Choctaw Nation. The great chief in turn redistributed the merchandise to the principal chiefs, who, according to French plans, were supposed to become beholden to their leader. Unfamiliar with such hierarchy, however, the principal chiefs successfully pressured the French to distribute goods more broadly.[70]

The goods did not sow disorder because Choctaws abandoned their beliefs for the pursuit of wealth, as the French imagined. Rather, the stream of wealth traveled down traditional lines of distribution in such great quantities that the number of influential leaders multiplied without precedent. Customarily, Choctaw leaders redistributed goods to their extended families, sustaining a network of people who were beholden to them.[71] With the practice of French gift giving, Bienville explained, "each of these chiefs, by means of the presents that he receives and that he knows how to distribute appropriately, forms a party that he employs independently of the great chief, who is now so only in name."[72] The new sources of wealth in Louisiana and Carolina strengthened and enlarged these parties and introduced a heated competition between leaders for recognition from colonial authorities, as Red Shoes revealed. "I will be as faithful to the English as you want to be to the French," he challenged Alibamon Mingo, "and we will see whether my warriors or yours will return more satisfied with the presents they receive."[73]

The presents also introduced another element of disorder into the nation. Common warriors watched the growing wealth and power of the principal chiefs with envy. Hoping to become chiefs themselves one day, they explained, they did not object to the gift-giving practices of the French. Nevertheless, "their needs were not any less great" than those of the chiefs, nor did they lack "a sound ambition [*une honnête ambition*]," both unfulfilled by French presents. "It was not surprising," the Choctaws therefore explained, "that they sought their advantage elsewhere," that is, in South Carolina.[74] This dynamic was evidently at work in 1738 when Red Shoes convinced a large number of warriors to welcome the English into the nation. They did so, Alibamon Mingo explained, because "all of the warriors were very discontent after returning last winter from Mobile, where the presents were delivered to the chiefs, who shared them among themselves and their relatives."[75] The result of French gift giving was a more turbulent Choctaw Nation that experienced social upheavals controlled by neither the French nor the Choctaws themselves.[76]

Among the gifts distributed by the French were muskets, which led to an increase in violence in the lower South. Historians have questioned the prevalence of guns in the Choctaw Nation before the American Revolution.[77] There have been virtually no archaeological excavations in the old Choctaw Nation to settle this question, but there is enough documentary evidence to suggest that firearms were more widespread in Choctaw communities than previously thought.[78] The French clearly believed that their Indian allies were dependent on them for munitions, especially powder and lead, which were prohibitively difficult for the English to transport on horseback from South Carolina. Governor Vaudreuil even suspected that the Choctaws would abandon Louisiana entirely if it were not for their dependence on French ammunition and French alcohol.[79] In fact, English-allied Indians occasionally found themselves without any ammunition, as one Choctaw warned they would in 1746. "They will completely lack munitions," he reportedly said, "unless they want to load their muskets with Limbourg [a textile] and other merchandise."[80] He was proven right two years later when Red Shoes's English-allied followers desperately substituted pieces of hardwood knot and fire-dried oak for lead balls.[81]

The importance and prevalence of firearms are best attested to not by the French but by the Choctaws themselves. In 1732, during a speech encouraging his men to go to war, the Choctaw great chief urged that "they had only to prepare their muskets and their war clubs to go take scalps."[82] His reference suggests that guns already occupied a central place in Choctaw military campaigns. Indeed, Choctaws painted a bleak picture when they imagined what life would be like without firearms. In 1734, one Choctaw recalled when the British first began arming the Chickasaws, asserting, "Without M. de Bienville, our father who gave us muskets and munitions, we would no longer exist."[83] At least one Choctaw considered the possibility of abandoning the French and "taking up the bow and arrow again," but others thought the prospect ruinous. The bow and arrow are a "pitiful resource for those who have a family to feed and support," said one Choctaw in 1748, "all the more because we have completely lost the ability to use them." Another, making the same point more forcefully, showed up with a bow and arrow at a debate about French alliance. He had just tried "his old weapons," he told this audience, but "he could no longer use them, having lost the ability." The Choctaws would be "miserable," he concluded, if the French abandoned them.[84]

The Choctaw reliance on firearms, hastened by the violence unleashed by the French–English proxy war and encouraged by the French policy of supplying their Indian with muskets, had two consequences. First, the Choctaws became dependent on a steady supply of weapons, severely limiting their ability to respond to the French and British invasion of their nation. Second, the violence in the Southeast became bloodier and deadlier. Musket balls pierced leather clothing, tore flesh, broke bones, and, if the victim survived, left irregular gashes that were more likely than arrow wounds to host fatal infections. The result was a Chickasaw population that, under sustained attack by French-armed Choctaws, plummeted by 50 percent between 1730 and 1760.[85]

It is undeniable that the French–English proxy war made the Choctaw and Chickasaw nations more dangerous places to live. Periodically, to drive a wedge between their Indian allies and enemies, the French sponsored and hosted the burning alive of Chickasaw prisoners.[86] One such fire occurred in October 1731 in New Orleans when Governor Périer sent three Chickasaw men to the flames despite pleas of clemency from Périer's Indian allies.[87] "It will serve to enflame even more the war between the Choctaws and Chickasaws," he calculated.[88] On another occasion, Périer reported that the Choctaws had burned to death twelve Chickasaws on the field of battle. He noted with satisfaction that "the war is more bitter than ever between these two nations" and suggested that the French should encourage "the Choctaws' fervor."[89]

The role of the French in this upsurge in violence is visible in the transformation of scalping in the eighteenth century. Although likely an ancient practice among the Choctaws, scalping became both more frequent and commercially motivated as a result of the French–English proxy war.[90] As early as 1708, the governor of Louisiana was encouraging Choctaws to bring him the scalps of English-allied Indians, and some time before 1721, the colony adopted an official policy of paying the Choctaws a gun, a pound of powder, and two pounds of bullets for each Chickasaw scalp in order to "encourage better the nation of the Choctaws to carry on vigorously the war against the Chickasaws."[91] This bounty produced 400 scalps in a single winter, Bienville reported in 1723.[92] When Choctaw ardor faded, French messengers appeared in the Choctaw Nation to reconfirm that Chickasaw scalps had a price, and when French governors wished to show special gratitude for a lock of enemy hair, they paid more "handsomely" than usual.[93] No wonder Choctaws concluded that scalps were the "best gift" they could give the French governor. They would search out the Chickasaws "so as not to appear before him empty-handed," they announced to Bienville in 1736.[94] The results of the French bounty on scalps are impressive: French governors collected at least 1,000 scalps in the twenty-year period beginning in 1732, averaging about fifty per year, and they likely received many more not accounted for in the official records.[95] It is not clear what the French did with their gruesome purchases (fig. 1).

Before the arrival of the French, it is unlikely that there was an Indian market for scalps, for the practice of scalping seems to have been linked to rites of passage rather than to commerce. One eighteenth-century visitor recalled that among the neighboring Creeks, boys took their first scalps to establish their manhood. "When a young warrior brings back a scalp, for the first time," Louis Milfort explained, "the chiefs of the place where he lives assemble in the grand cabin to give him a name, and to take from him that of his mother." Later in life, men took scalps to establish their bravery and to rise in the estimation of their families and communities.[96] James Adair noted an additional purpose for these "joyful trophies of a decisive victory." Mounted atop the houses of deceased family members, scalps marked the avenging of dead relatives and enabled their spirits to go to a place of rest.[97] Although these uses persisted to the end of the eighteenth century, by the 1730s scalps had also become commodities. Responding to market incentive (albeit deceitfully), Choctaws adopted the practice of cutting enemy scalps into several pieces so as to receive more than one payment for a single scalp. "We paid them the price of ten scalps for a single enemy," Bienville complained.[98] For a brief

**Figure 1** "Savages Tchaktas matachez en Guerriers qui portent des chevelures" [Choctaw savages in war paint carrying scalps]. This water-color, painted by French architect Alexandre de Batz in the 1730s, reflects the prevalence of scalping in eighteenth-century Louisiana, a practice encouraged by French policy in the region. Courtesy Peabody Museum of Archaeology and Ethnology, Harvard University.

period, French officers closely inspected their grisly purchases, paying for pieces in proportion to the whole, but this cost-saving measure soon had to be abandoned when Choctaws objected to such market regulation.[99]

The Chickasaws highlighted the disturbing logic of assigning a market value to a human scalp. One warrior asked, "What do the French claim to be doing? What use are our scalps to them to pay for them? . . . Do they find treasure in our scalps?"[100] He knew the answer but wished to draw out the link between money and violence in the South. Another warrior looked forward to the time when the Choctaws would "tire of selling our scalps." But the Choctaws, the beneficiaries of this new market, said they would continue selling scalps until the French ceased paying for them.[101] By mid-century, Indians far and wide associated the French with scalping. One Cherokee said he had "little Knowledge" of the French but heard that they raised a "constant Cry": "go kill and destroy, bring us plenty of Hair, plenty of Scalps."[102]

\*\*\*

Divided between the French and the English, the Choctaws fought a deadly civil war between 1748 and 1750. Governor Vaudreuil boasted that, because he was short of troops, he "made use of the eastern Choctaws" to destroy the English-allied Choctaws. The violence was extraordinary. French allies shot and eviscerated the captain of Boukfouka, stomping his intestines into the ground before pursuing and killing eighty of his followers. They exterminated Red Shoes's family, including his children, and they destroyed several towns entirely.[103] Vaudreuil estimated that more than 800 English-allied warriors died in the conflict, or almost one out of every four Choctaw men.[104] "I engaged them as much as I could to make war against their rebellious brothers . . . ," Vaudreuil boasted, "persuaded that while [the English] see a civil war among the Choctaws, they would not risk going there in significant numbers or with lots of merchandise."[105] Purchasing hundreds of scalps and supplying firearms was costly, he admitted, but well worth the price.[106]

By virtue of their numbers, political skill, and military acumen, Indians remained a significant presence in the lower South through the American Revolution. Nevertheless, describing the region as a borderland elides the destructive interference of France and Britain in the affairs of native nations. The analogy to twentieth-century proxy warfare captures the deadly influence of imperial powers as well as the chaotic and uncontrollable world that resulted. Regional conflicts and local communities in the lower South became part of a much larger hemispheric war between France and Britain. Although the number of French colonists in the region remained minimal, French officers, calling down Indian allies from the Great Lakes and ordering guns and munitions from across the Atlantic, drew on imperial networks that extended for thousands of miles. Choctaw warriors who carried muskets forged in France in place of their own hand-carved bows and arrows did not become the obedient foot soldiers of the French king. But neither did they remain immune from the rapid, unpredictable, and uncontrollable social transformations that were set off by the arrival of the French and English. As in Angola and Afghanistan in the twentieth century, the scale of geography in the lower South changed suddenly. Community rivalries, local economies, and regional conflicts all became international, immersed in networks of trade and warfare that encompassed millions of people and drew on vast amounts of capital.[107] As the scale grew, so too did the order of violence. In the Atlantic World, it was sometimes a misfortune to have your homeland deemed a borderland.

## Notes

1   On the middle ground, see Richard White, *The Middle Ground: Indians, Empires, and Republics in the Great Lakes Region, 1650–1815* (New York, 1991). In the hands of other historians, the metaphorical middle ground has come to be associated almost entirely with negotiation and compromise, even though White makes violence a central component of the middle ground of the Great Lakes region.

2   Daniel J. Herman, "Romance on the Middle Ground," *Journal of the Early Republic* 19 (1999): 280.

3   Jeremy Adelman and Stephen Aron, "From Borderlands to Borders: Empires, Nation-States, and the Peoples in between in North American History," *American Historical Review* 104 (1999): 816, 820, 827, 838. See also Mary E. Young, "The Dark and Bloody but Endlessly Inventive Middle Ground of Indian Frontier Historiography," *Journal of the Early Republic* 13 (1993): 193–205.

4   Alan Taylor, "The Divided Ground: Upper Canada, New York, and the Iroquois Six Nations, 1783–1815," *Journal of the Early Republic* 22 (2002): 55–75. Quotation on 55.

5   Joshua Piker, "Colonists and Creeks: Rethinking the Pre-Revolutionary Southern Backcountry," *Journal of Southern History* 70 (2004): 505–6, 509.

6   Juliana Barr, "A Diplomacy of Gender: Rituals of First Contact in the 'Land of Tejas,'" *William and Mary Quarterly* 61 (2004): 401.

7   Indians were not "people in between," observes Colin Calloway; rather, Europeans were "people on the edge." Calloway, *One Vast Winter Count: The Native American West before Lewis and Clark* (Lincoln, Nebr., 2003), 313. On ethnohistorians and boundary crossing, see Jennifer Brown, "Ethnohistorians," *Ethnohistory* 38 (1991): 113–23.

8   For an overview of imperial and Indian warfare in colonial North America, see Ian K. Steele, *Warpaths: Invasions of North America* (New York, 1994).

9   Christine M. Knudsen and I. William Zartman, "The Large Small War in Angola," *Annals of the American Academy of Political and Social Science* 541 (1995): 130–43.

10  For a highly readable history of proxy wars in the twentieth century, see Mahmood Mamdani, *Good Muslim, Bad Muslim: America, The Cold War, and the Roots of Terror* (New York, 2004). On Iroquoia as a borderland, see Taylor, "The Divided Ground."

11  Evan Haefeli perceptively notes that imperial rivalries, rather than granting Indians more options, may have actually been unusually destructive to native peoples. Evan Haefeli, "A Note on the Use of North American Borderlands," *American Historical Review* 104 (1999): 1223.

12  For other interpretations of the Choctaw Nation and its relations with France and England, see Richard White, *The Roots of Dependency: Subsistence, Environment, and Social Change among the Choctaws, Pawnees, and Navajos* (Lincoln, Nebr., 1983); James Taylor Carson, *Searching for the Bright Path: The Mississippi Choctaws from Prehistory to Removal* (Lincoln, Nebr., 1999); and Greg O'Brien, *Choctaws in a Revolutionary Age, 1750–1830* (Lincoln, Nebr., 2002).

13  Peter H. Wood, "The Changing Population of the Colonial South: An Overview by Race and Region, 1685–1790," in *Powhatan's Mantle: Indians in the Colonial Southeast*, ed. Peter H. Wood et al. (Lincoln, Nebr., 1989), 38–39, 68–71.

14  France and Britain waged a similar proxy war in New England in the early eighteenth century. Emerson W. Baker and John G. Reid, "Amerindian Power in the Early Modern Northeast: A Reappraisal," *William and Mary Quarterly* 61 (2004): 93–96.

15  Wood, "The Changing Population of the Colonial South," 38–39.

16  Bienville to Pontchartrain, February 20, 1707, in *Mississippi Provincial Archives, 1704–1743: French Dominion*, ed. Dunbar Rowland and Albert Godfrey Sanders, 3 vols. (Jackson, Miss., 1927–1932), 3:38 (hereafter *MPA*).

17 "Memoir sur la Louisianne," ca. 1731, p. 231, COL-20, C13A-13, Centre historique des Archives nationales, Paris (hereafter ANP); Alan Gallay, *The Indian Slave Trade: The Rise of the English Empire in the American South, 1670–1717* (New Haven, Conn., 2002), 292–94.

18 This perceived disadvantage eventually induced Britain to centralize Indian affairs. Wilbur R. Jacobs, ed., *The Appalachian Indian Frontier: The Edmond Atkin Report and Plan of 1755* (Columbia, S.C., 1954).

19 "Memoire sur l'importance du commerce du tabac," 1739, p. 259, COL-31, C13A-24, ANP; C. M. Andrews, "Anglo-French Commercial Rivalry, 1700–1750: The Western Phase, I," *American Historical Review* 20 (1915): 142–43.

20 Thomas Nairne to Charles Spencer, July 10, 1708, in *Nairne's Muskhogean Journals: The 1708 Expedition to the Mississippi River*, ed. Alexander Moore (Jackson, Miss., 1988), 73.

21 Verner W. Crane, *The Southern Frontier, 1670–1732* (Ann Arbor, Mich., 1929), 64–65; Marcel Giraud, *Histoire de la Louisiane Française: Le Regne de Louis XIV* (Paris, 1953), 1:72–78 (hereafter *HL*).

22 Quotation in Crane, *The Southern Frontier*, 75.

23 Gallay, *The Indian Slave Trade*, 299.

24 Bienville to Pontchartrain, August 20, 1709, in *MPA*, 3:136.

25 Giraud, *HL*, 1:192–93; Bienville to Pontchartrain, October 27, 1711, in *MPA*, 3:159–60.

26 Bienville to Pontchartrain, October 27, 1711, in *MPA*, 3:160.

27 Bienville, "La Louisianne, sur les Sauvages," April 25, 1733, p. 206, COL-23, C13A-16, ANP.

28 "La Louisianne," April 26, 1738, p. 52, COL-30, C13A-23, ANP.

29 Bienville sur les Sauvages, July 27, 1734, p. 217, COL-25, C13A-18, ANP.

30 Bienville to Maurepas, September 30, 1734, p. 192, COL-25, C13A-18, ANP. Shortly afterward, Bienville decided to pursue a peace with the Chickasaws, but his determination was short lived. Bienville to Maurepas, April 30, 1735, p. 150, COL-27, C13A-20, ANP.

31 Périer to Maurepas, March 25, 1731, p. 46, COL-20, C13A-13, ANP; "La Louisianne," May 14, 1732, p. 144, COL-21, C13A-14, ANP. See also Eric Hinderaker, *Elusive Empires: Constructing Colonialism in the Ohio Valley, 1673–1800* (New York, 1997), 116–17.

32 Bienville and Salmon to Maurepas, May 20, 1732, p. 110, COL-23, C13A-16, ANP.

33 Beauchamp to Maurepas, February 26, 1738, p. 176, COL-30, C13A-23, ANP.

34 Vaudreuil to Maurepas, October 28, 1745, p. 45, COL-36, C13A-29, ANP. One Choctaw expressed a similar surprise at the lack of direct French participation in a copy of a letter from Baudouin to Salmon, November 23, 1732, p. 182, COL-21, C13A-14, ANP.

35 As Guillaume Aubert suggests, the common assertion by historians that the eighteenth-century French were somehow more tolerant than the English of other peoples and cultures is without any substance. Aubert, " 'The Blood of France': Race and Purity of Blood in the French Atlantic World," *William and Mary Quarterly* 61 (2004): 439–78.

36 Périer to Maurepas, March 25, 1731, p. 46, COL-20, C13A-13, ANP.

37 Bienville and Salmon to Maurepas, June 1736, p. 20, COL-28, C13A-21, ANP; Bienville to Maurepas, June 28, 1736, p. 207, COL-28, C13A-21, ANP.

38 LaVelle to Maurepas, February 21, 1737, p. 251, COL-29, C13A-22, ANP.

39 Bienville and Salmon to Maurepas, September 1, 1736, p. 79, COL-28, C13A-21, ANP.

40 "Relation de la guerre des Tchicachas," June 1736, p. 164, COL-28, C13A-21, ANP; "La Relation Véritable de l'attaque des francois contre les chycachats," June 1736, p. 228, COL-28, C13A-21, ANP.

41 Salmon to Maurepas, June 15, 1736, p. 269, COL-28, C13A-21, ANP; Bienville to Maurepas, June 28, 1736, p. 188, COL-28, C13A-21, ANP.

42 Bienville to Maurepas, June 29, 1736, p. 181, COL-28, C13A-21, ANP.

43 Bienville to Maurepas, February 15, 1737, p. 70, COL-29, C13A-22, ANP.

44 Bienville to Maurepas, June 28, 1736, p. 188, COL-28, C13A-21, ANP.

45    Bienville to Maurepas, February 15, 1737, p. 70, COL-29, C13A-22, ANP.

46    Diron to Maurepas, May 8, 1737, p. 223, COL-29, C13A-22, ANP.

47    Bienville and Salmon to Maurepas, September 16, 1737, p. 57, COL-29, C13A-22, ANP.

48    Bienville's poor planning, discussed by a number of French officers in Louisiana, seems the central reason for the failure of the 1740 expedition. But see Daniel H. Usner Jr., *Indians, Settlers, and Slaves in a Frontier Exchange Economy: The Lower Mississippi Valley before 1783* (Chapel Hill, N.C., 1992), 84 n. 13. See also Michael J. Foret, "The Failure of Administration: The Chickasaw Campaign of 1739–1749," *Revue de Louisiane/Louisiana Review* 11 (1982): 49–60.

49    Journal of Nouailles d'Aymé, June 1739 to August 1740, p. 361, Marine, B4-45/2, ANP; Bienville to Maurepas, May 6, 1740, p. 42, COL-32, C13A-25, ANP; Journal of M. de Verges, June 28, 1740, p. 283, COL-32, C13A-25, ANP.

50    Charles Gayarré, *Histoire de la Louisiane* (New Orleans, 1846), 1:354.

51    Ibid., 1:352.

52    "Si nous ne sommes pas sortis de cette affaire avec tout le success qu'on avait droit de se promettre, la gloire des armes du roi n'en a pas souffert." Quoted in ibid., 1:352.

53    Beauchamp to Maurepas, March 19, 1740, p. 249, COL-32, C13A-25, ANP.

54    Louboey to Maurepas, October 6, 1745, p. 189, COL-36, C13A-29, ANP.

55    Vaudreuil to Rouillé, February 1, 1750, p. 231, COL-41, C13A-34, ANP.

56    Bienville to Maurepas, July 26, 1733, p. 277, COL-23, C13A-16, ANP.

57    Salmon to Maurepas, March 6, 1741, p. 115, COL-33, C13A-26, ANP; Salmon to Maurepas, October 4, 1741, p. 170, COL-33, C13A-26, ANP; Norman W. Caldwell, "The Chickasaw Threat to French Control of the Mississippi in the 1740s," *Chronicles of Oklahoma* 16 (1938): 475–76.

58    For "indomitable tribal independence," see Usner, *Indians, Settlers, and Slaves*, 95. For an essay that makes a similar case for indomitable Indian military power, see Baker and Reid, "Amerindian Power in the Early Modern Northeast," 77–106.

59    Despite the tremendous disruptions caused by the French–English proxy war, Richard White suggests that the Choctaws "achieved a tenuous balance—economically, ecologically, and socially—which preserved their independence for more than half a century." White, *The Roots of Dependency*, 64.

60    James Adair, *The History of the American Indians* (1775; reprint, New York, 1968), 286.

61    Les dépenses de la Louisianne, 1740, p. 342, COL-32, C13A-25, ANP; Les dépenses de la Louisianne, 1746, p. 199, COL-37, C13A-30, ANP.

62    Bienville, "La Louisianne, sur les Sauvages," April 25, 1733, p. 206, COL-23, C13A-16, ANP.

63    I am using Richard White's figure for the cost (30 sous/pound) and weight (2.5 pounds) of an average deerskin between 1743 and 1746. White, *The Roots of Dependency*, 67.

64    "Les dépenses de la Louisianne," 1742, p. 196, COL-34, C13A-27, ANP.

65    "Mouvements des sauvages de la Louisianne depuis la prise du fort des Natchez, par M. de Périer sur la fin de Janvier 1731," p. 85, COL-20, C13A-13, ANP.

66    Salmon to Maurepas, December 14, 1731, p. 185, COL-22, C13A-15, ANP.

67    Bienville to Maurepas, April 23, 1734, p. 153, COL-25, C13A-18, ANP; Bienville to Maurepas, March 25, 1739, p. 35, COL-31, C13A-24, ANP; Bienville to Maurepas, March 7, 1741, p. 53, COL-33, C13A-26, ANP.

68    Moyan to Maurepas, January 4, 1739, p. 224, COL-31, C13A-24, ANP.

69    Vaudreuil to Maurepas, November 5, 1748, p. 122, COL-39, C13A-32, ANP.

70    Copy of a letter from Baudouin to Salmon, 1732, p. 182, COL-21, C13A-14, ANP; Bienville, "La Louisianne, sur les Sauvages," April 25, 1733, p. 206, COL-23, C13A-16, ANP.

71    White, *The Roots of Dependency*, 41–46.

72    Copy of a letter from Baudouin to Salmon, 1732, p. 182, COL-21, C13A-14, ANP.

73    Moyan to Maurepas, January 4, 1739, p. 224, COL-31, C13A-24, ANP.

74    Vaudreuil to Rouillé, January 28, 1752, p. 36, COL-43, C13A-36, ANP.

75  Moyan to Maurepas, January 4, 1739, p. 224, COL-31, C13A-24, ANP.

76  See, by contrast, White, *The Roots of Dependency*, 64.

77  O'Brien, *Choctaws in a Revolutionary Age*, 47–48; White, *The Roots of Dependency*, 44–45.

78  James Adair, a trader in the Chickasaw Nation, claimed that the Chickasaws usually only had no more than five to seven guns in each town, but if a 1750 list of presents and goods is to be believed, Adair must have been mistaken. Adair, *The History of the American Indians*, 285; Etat des vivres . . . à envoyer de France à la Louisianne, pour les besoins de la Colonie en l'année 1750, p. 228, COL-40, C13A-33, ANP.

79  "Mouvements des sauvages de la Louisianne depuis la prise du fort des Natchez, par M. de Périer sur la fin de Janvier 1731," p. 85, COL-20, C13A-13, ANP.

80  Journal of Beauchamp, August–October, p. 222, COL-37, C13A-30, ANP. Quotation from October 12.

81  Beauchamp to Maurepas, October 24, 1748, p. 215, COL-39, C13A-32, ANP.

82  Extrait d'une lettre de M. de Cremont, August 18, 1732, p. 191, COL-22, C13A-15, ANP.

83  Bienville to Maurepas, September 30, 1734, p. 192, COL-25, C13A-18, ANP.

84  Journal of Beauchamp, August–October, 1746, p. 222, COL-37, C13A-30, ANP. Quotations are from the end of September and October 12.

85  Wood, "The Changing Population of the Colonial South," 68–69.

86  On empire and violence, see Eliga H. Gould, "Zones of Law, Zones of Violence: The Legal Geography of the British Atlantic, circa 1772," *William and Mary Quarterly* 22 (2003): 12–13, 19–25.

87  Salmon to Maurepas, June 20, 1732, p. 149, COL-22, C13A-15, ANP.

88  "Mouvements des sauvages de la Louisianne depuis la prise du fort des Natchez, par M. de Périer sur la fin de Janvier 1731," p. 85, COL-20, C13A-13, ANP; Vaudreuil and Salmon to Maurepas, July 21, 1743, p. 24, COL-35, C13A-28, ANP.

89  Périer to Maurepas, April 6, 1732, p. 44, COL-21, C13A-14, ANP.

90  On the origins of scalping in North America, see James Axtell and William C. Sturtevant, "The Unkindest Cut, or Who Invented Scalping," *William and Mary Quarterly* 37 (1980): 451–72.

91  Bienville to Pontchartrain, February 25, 1708, in *MPA*, 3:114; Minutes of the Superior Council of Louisiana, in *MPA*, 3:375–76.

92  Bienville to the Council, February 1, 1723, in *MPA*, 3:343.

93  "Extrait du Journal des Voyages faits par le Sieur Regis du Roullet, 1729–1733," August 18, 1732, p. 197, COL-22, C13A-15, ANP; Vaudreuil to Maurepas, March 15, 1747, p. 17, COL-38, C13A-31, ANP.

94  Bienville and Salmon to Maurepas, September 13, 1736, p. 117, COL-28, C13A-21, ANP.

95  This figure represents the scalps mentioned in correspondence in series C13A-15, ANP.

96  Luis Milfort, *Memoir; or, A Cursory Glance at my Different Travels and my Sojourn in the Creek Nation* (1802; reprint, Chicago, 1956), 109–10.

97  Adair, *The History of the American Indians*, 415, 425.

98  Bienville to Maurepas, August 26, 1734, p. 177, COL-25, C13A-18, ANP.

99  Diron to Maurepas, September 1, 1734, p. 127, COL-26, C13A-19, ANP.

100 Diron to Maurepas, October 24, 1737, p. 233, COL-29, C13A-22, ANP.

101 Bienville to Maurepas, September 30, 1741, p. 97, COL-33, C13A-26, ANP.

102 Information of George Johnston, October 2, 1754, William L. McDowell Jr., ed., *Documents Relating to Indian Affairs, Colonial Records of South Carolina* (Columbia, S.C., 1958), 2:10.

103 Vaudreuil to Maurepas, November 5, 1748, p. 122, COL-39, C13A-32, ANP.

104 Vaudreuil to Rouillé, January 12, 1751, p. 61, COL-42, C13A-35, ANP.

105 Vaudreuil to Maurepas, March 3, 1749, p. 12, COL-40, C13A-33, ANP.

106 Vaudreuil to Maurepas, November 5, 1748, p. 122, COL-39, C13A-32, ANP.

107 For a sense of the scale of European states in the eighteenth century, see John Brewer, *The Sinews of Power: War, Money and the English State, 1688–1783* (London, 1989).

*Historians often overlook the agency of nature in shaping both the past and how we remember it. Take, for example, the case of the Atlantic. Why were sailors able to cross the Atlantic for the first time only in the fifteenth and sixteenth centuries? Ironically, there is a lack of documentation to answer this question, for a 1755 Atlantic tsunami destroyed the archives of the first community ever to accomplish this deed, namely, the Portuguese. According to Patricia Seed, an answer to the puzzle lies in reconstructing the seamanship of Gil Eanes. In 1434, Eanes rounded Africa's Cape Bojador, opening up the navigation of the South Atlantic and making the new early modern global empires possible. Historians have traditionally found the key to the Portuguese success in their use of nautical charts, the compass, new ships, and star navigation. According to Seed, the answer lies elsewhere, namely, in understanding the winds and currents of the South Atlantic. Eanes managed to defeat the might of the ocean's currents and westerly winds by developing sailing techniques to correct course through the use of mathematics. Trigonometry lies at the core of Eanes's major breakthrough. Would the Polynesians, Arabs, or Chinese, all with greatly sophisticated seamanship, have been able to navigate the Atlantic had they found themselves in this ocean?*

# Navigating the Mid-Atlantic; or, What Gil Eanes Achieved

## Patricia Seed

As young children, we learn that Bartholomew Diaz rounded the Cape of Good Hope in 1487 and that Vasco da Gama set out in 1497 on the first successful voyage from Europe to India. Rarely do we learn much beyond those bare facts. Even delving deeper into Portugal's history, we encounter only similar details about earlier moments. Prince Henry "the Navigator" sponsored Portuguese navigational efforts, Gil Eanes rounded Cape Bojador in 1434, and Diogo Cao navigated the Congo River in 1471.

In short, the facts are well known; the story is scarcely known at all. How did the Portuguese manage to navigate from the mid–North Atlantic through the South Atlantic to the tip of the Southern Ocean and then northward through the treacherous Mozambique Channel? How important were these accomplishments? What sorts of knowledge and skills were required?

Despite the importance of these events in European history, today we have no answers; none of us has any inkling of how that expertise developed. This ignorance is surprising since European history ranks among the world's best studied. Thousands of years of literacy have yielded myriad accounts of Europe's past.

But histories abound in this region partly because the information needed to tell stories has survived. Neither man nor nature has managed to destroy it all. Periodically, wars, fires, and floods have ravaged pockets of knowledge about Europe's past, leaving the rest intact. But Portugal's history—and in particular the history of its seagoing adventures—has not been so fortunate. On November 1, 1755, the area of Portugal where information on Portuguese sailing exploits was stored suffered destruction so brutal that it devastated nearly every structure and every human life in its path. On that date, the largest earthquake to strike Europe in over 2,000 years shattered the Portuguese capital of Lisbon. Thirty minutes later, a giant wall of water engulfed the capital's port and surrounding buildings, leaving only a flattened landscape in its wake. Only those on higher ground—the seven hills that fringed the city—managed to survive. Portugal thus became the only European capital to have suffered both a magnitude 9.0 earthquake and a subsequent tsunami.[1]

The devastation inflicted on Lisbon on All Saints' Day 1755 paralleled that inflicted in the Indian Ocean on December 26, 2004; the magnitude of the catastrophe, the lack of advance warning, and the type of destruction were virtually indistinguishable. On both occasions, violent earthquakes of approximately equal force erupted on the ocean floor; quakes powerful enough to damage everything on land, the equivalent of 23,000 atom bombs, or 32 billion tons of TNT. Following closely on these deadly undersea quakes, the oceans rose up, traveling at 800 kilometers per hour, or the speed of a jet airliner, first sucking the waters far away from shore, and then slamming at full speed over the banks of the river, shoving people and tossing boats and buildings into a giant pile of debris. As it receded, the deadly waters swept people, buildings, and possessions out to sea. Pictures drawn of the shattered landscape of Lisbon in the aftermath of the quake and tsunami resemble photographs of towns along the Indian Ocean destroyed the day after Christmas 2004. Debris-strewn landscapes come into view where once buildings, houses, shops, and markets stood, scenes from which all human life has been violently and suddenly expunged, leaving behind only the shells of a few large buildings.[2]

The location of surrounding landmass differed between the events of the Indian and those of the Atlantic Ocean; fewer nations and coasts were affected by the 1755 tsunami; the Atlantic has fewer islands and hence fewer low-lying island nations than the Indian Ocean. North Africa and Portugal bore the brunt of the 1755 quake and tsunami, but the shaking was felt as far north as Finland and as far west as the Caribbean, where unusual ocean heights were recorded. In all of Europe, the only capital affected was Lisbon, twelve miles up the Tagus River from the ocean.

Stored in the giant libraries and archives near the quay along the Tagus were the records detailing how Portuguese sailors had conquered the Atlantic. While the 1755 quake leveled the buildings in which that knowledge was stored, the tsunami took all that understanding out to sea. The forces of nature thus destroyed an entire storehouse of knowledge in the blink of an eye, leaving nothing behind and no chance to save anything. Those brief catastrophic moments annihilated the rich documentary basis of Portugal's ventures into the Atlantic; the ocean does not respect stores of human knowledge more than any human endeavor. Portuguese sailors had mastered the ocean, but the ocean returned to claim its secrets.

While Lisbon housed the greatest collection of maps, charts, sailing guides, and instruments, another location, outside the capital, several hundred kilometers to the south, housed information on the earliest discoveries. Exploration of the Atlantic was first planned in Prince Henry's palace on Cape Saint Vincent in Europe's southwestern corner.[3] With the great irony that tragic events seem to generate, this second invaluable storehouse of knowledge resided even closer to the epicenter of the November 1, 1755, earthquake, and even more squarely in the tsunami's immediate path. Like the towns in Indonesia closest to the epicenter of the 2004 quake, nothing was left standing of Prince Henry's castle, only piles of debris. Even today, more than 250 years later, an utterly flat and desolate landscape remains where scientists and sailors who first planned the voyage past Bojador once ate and slept and drank and where once stood the palace where knowledge of sailing down the Atlantic was first assembled. A giant compass has been carved into the bedrock to remember what once stood on the cape. As in Lisbon, the ocean that Portuguese sailors first navigated destroyed all the evidence of how they succeeded in doing so.

No effort of will, no prayer, can bring back what the ocean destroyed in Lisbon and Cape Saint Vincent on November 1, 1755. All that remains to us are random scattered documents stored in a few hilltop convents out of the tsunami's reach and information illegally spirited out of Portugal during the fifteenth and sixteenth centuries on instructions of rulers from other European states. Most of this remaining knowledge reflects only what spies could learn, not the original information itself.

Also dragged out to sea was information on the men who manned those ships, who raised their sails, and who steered those vessels into the waters of the Atlantic. Even those who captained these ships remain only a name; all else rests in darkness carried off into the waters of the Atlantic.

To understand how that process of sailing the Atlantic began, however, we still have the ocean itself. Currents, winds, and tides still stream past the coast of Portugal. Squalls and dust storms still engulf vessels offshore. If the ocean deprived us of the means to tell the story, perhaps by examining its secrets—the mysteries that earth-observing satellites and the data provided by thousands of buoys have provided—we can begin to understand how the Portuguese confronted the challenge of the Atlantic.

Observing the patterns of the Atlantic winds, several historians have noted their importance. But the winds that filled the sails constituted only the most visually dramatic of the ocean's many powers to influence the path of Portuguese ships. Gravity, the earth's rotation, and solar heating—key elements of physical oceanography—directed the flow of currents beneath as well as the path of the winds. And the earth's geological past created sea floors and coastlines that shaped the routes that vessels could take. Employing both the physics and the geology of the ocean enables us to understand the forces that Portuguese ships had to contend with on ocean voyages.[4]

The youngest of the world's oceans, the Atlantic, did not exist until 100 million years ago when our ancestral supercontinent, Pangaea, began to separate. As North America pulled away from Europe and South America slid from Africa, the Atlantic Ocean appeared, an elongated letter S stretched out in a north-to-south direction.

If sheer numbers of people residing on its shore would suffice for navigation to begin, the Atlantic would have been one of the first oceans to be navigated instead of the last. Yet the mid- and South Atlantics were indeed the last oceans to be sailed. Indomitable Polynesians had crossed thousands of miles of the open Pacific, Arabs and Persians had mastered the northwestern quadrant of the Indian Ocean, Chinese sailors had navigated the South China Sea, and Vikings had shrewdly exploited the midnight sun traveling between Iceland, Greenland, and the eastern edge of North America. Other less adventurous sailors had safely kept land in sight as they moved like crabs along ocean coasts. In this fashion, boats managed coasts of northwestern Europe, eastern Africa, and Southeast Asia never more than a day out of sight of land. No group of sailors had traversed the mid-Atlantic and returned despite more than 3,000 years of sailing around the Mediterranean and despite the remarkable success of the Vikings along the Atlantic's northernmost edge. In 1430, virtually the entire Atlantic remained unnavigated—the last of the world's oceans to be traversed. Gil Eanes's rounding Cape Bojador on the northwestern coast of Africa in 1434 constituted a major step forward. It would have been significant even if Portuguese sailors had failed to follow up this voyage with even more spectacular breakthroughs.

For thousands of years, the oceans around Cape Bojador had been the barrier to sailing most of the North and the entire South Atlantics—the only oceans that traditional navigational techniques had never been able to master.[5] The Phoenicians tried to cross the barrier—the Greeks and Romans certainly failed,[6] as did all the other Arabs and Europeans who came after. And Africans who attempted the crossing—accidentally or intentionally—would have been carried by winds and currents to the eastern coast of South America, never to return to their ancestral homelands.[7]

Knowledge of the magnitude of the difficulty spread throughout Europe. Christians and Muslims and Venetians and Danes all understood that returning from sailing south of Bojador was impossible. Unlike many events in the past—when the significance of a particular moment is clear only in light of the events that have unexpectedly followed from it—participants in this event and those hearing the news knew that it was a significant breakthrough.

Despite its recognizable significance, Eanes's rounding Cape Bojador on the northwestern coast of Africa in 1434 remains one of the least well understood significant ocean crossings. While many textbooks correctly state the fact of the achievement—the first successful round-trip south of this point on the African coast—few can explain why the task was so difficult—they can only affirm that it was. Even viewing the maps that situate Bojador along the African coast fails to clarify the nature of the challenge or the degree of difficulty encountered.

To even the most thorough student of maps, Bojador (or Bulging Cape in English) does not appear to constitute any exceptional challenge for sailing. It does not particularly protrude into the Atlantic Ocean. Look at any globe, and you will see that both the White Cape (Cabo Blanco) and the Green Cape (Cabo Verde) farther to the south jut far more noticeably into the Atlantic. Even seen from outer space, the bulge does not particularly protrude; it resembles a squashed hat more than a cape.

But as much valuable information as maps disclose, they also conceal. Maps describe and locate natural features that either do not move or do so at a glacial pace—mountains, coastlines, or islands. Even when depicting these changes, maps do so by a series of snapshots—a "before-and-after" image—that allows us to see the results of change in the location or characteristics of physical objects but does not permit us to see the motions themselves.

Even when adjusting political boundaries, maps follow a similar pattern. In the second half of the twentieth century, decolonization redefined territories in Africa and Asia and the collapse of a major world empire, the Soviet Union, redrawing more political boundaries than at any previous time in history. But as with natural features, maps did not depict the process, only the "before" and "after" moments.

To understand why the Bulging Cape presented such a problem requires not locating fixed, defining space but rather trying to understand constantly moving objects—the world's oceans and winds. Maps portray only the sidelines—the comparatively stable edges of oceans—not the ceaseless sloshing of waves and the whispering and roaring of winds but only what remains stable in space.

Maps conceal other things besides movement. The depths of the ocean floor and the peaks of the mountains appear flattened on a sheet of paper. The most popular maps (and the ones we are most familiar with) level terrain with colors, replacing the peaks and valleys with a single shade. Only the less familiar, more specialized maps for sailors and mountain climbers employ techniques of drawing to provide hints of what lies beneath us at sea and above us on land.

Recent photographs from space provide clues to one of the unseen difficulties that sailors faced. The dramatic images that earth-observing satellites have captured of Saharan sands gusting out into the Atlantic show the direction of the otherwise invisible prevailing winds (fig. 1). South of the Canary Islands, the wind-borne sands of the Sahara streak right over Bojador and south of the smaller western Canary Islands. Over the course of a week, the Saharan dust captured in these images will cross the Atlantic and wind up fertilizing the rich soil of Brazil's Amazon. Thus, the first clue to the difficulties sailors confronted was the direction of the prevailing winds. The airstream would force westward any vessel attempting to sail south.

In response to such persistent winds, European mariners, including the Portuguese, tried their most conventional sailing strategy, staying close to the shore and keeping sight of land. Such coastal scuttling had allowed sailors on Europe's western coast to establish a flourishing trade within the Mediterranean.

However, the seemingly unexceptional Bulging Cape posed a substantial challenge for any would-be coast-hugging navigator. Portuguese chronicles report that many craft turned back, defeated by a giant sandy barrier that protruded out from the coast for twenty-one nautical miles.[8] At that distance, it became impossible to keep sight of the African coast while sailing southward. With water scarcely a meter high in many places, no European vessel could sail close enough to land in order to follow it.

**Figure 1**   Saharan dust blowing off the coast of Africa. Satellite view of Cape Bojador. Courtesy Patricia Seed.

Nor could sailors easily navigate around these sandy shoals because of another of this cape's unique characteristics: its breadth. Unlike most West African capes that sailors encountered, this cape's shallow waters extended for more than thirty nautical miles south. Thus, this cape's unique method of defeating sailors lay not in its sudden sharp protrusion into the sea but in its long, wide shape and endless off-shore shallows. Thus, what might have seemed a simple matter of rounding a cape became the endless miles of low waters during which land remained tantalizingly out of sight (fig. 2).

Most of today's maps emphasize boundaries such as the line between land and sea. Only sailors looking at today's specialized navigational charts would note the long sandy barrier off Bojador because it lies beneath the surface of the water. Fortunately for us, the earliest surviving maps of the African coast (drawn after Eanes's exploit) were nautical charts, designed with similar concerns as those drawn today. Every one of these fifteenth-century charts notes the shallow sands off Bojador employing the mapmaking convention established several hundred years before, a series of dots. Off Bojador, at least two carefully positioned dots appear in a straight line stretching out from the coast, thus warning navigators of a sandy hazard continuing for some

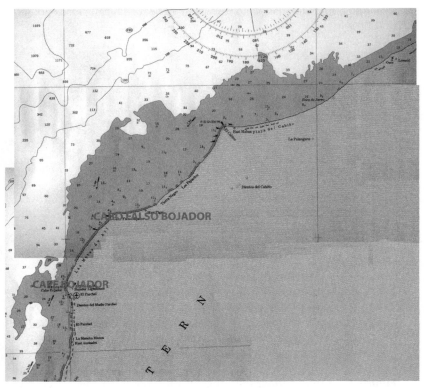

**Figure 2**   Sand banks off Cape Bojador. Courtesy Patricia Seed.

distance into the ocean.[9] Thus, the unprepossessing squashed appearance of the cape in fact contributed to the difficulties reaching its other side. This flattened shape portrayed by both photographs and maps taunted sailors, but even more features lay in motions these pictures cannot capture.

When Bojador's sandy shoals threw ships many nautical miles into the ocean, they tossed boats immediately into the path of the greatest difficulty they would encounter in the North Atlantic: currents. Thirty times more powerful than winds, currents carry tiny sailing craft in the direction that physics, not humans, demand. Solar heating causes water to expand. Through heating, the sea level near the equator becomes an average of eight centimeters higher than sea level in temperate ocean areas. This difference creates a slight slope, and warm equatorial water flows "downhill" toward the North and South Poles.

A second force of physics—the movement of the earth on its axis—introduces another characteristic to the flow of the ocean's currents. When large bodies of water such as the Atlantic encounter the rotation of the earth, they are deflected, moving to the right of their original path in the Northern Hemisphere. Because of this Coriolis effect, surface currents in the Northern Hemisphere flow to the right of the wind direction. Together with the poleward impact of solar heating, this wind-driven impact leads to water flowing in circular clockwise pattern around the periphery of an ocean basin.

Thus, the physics of the North Atlantic created a giant movement of waters toward the North Pole and veering clockwise around the Atlantic. Africa lies on the eastern boundary of the Atlantic; hence, north of the equator, waters move southward until they reach the zone where the equatorial sun heats the water and they begin flowing westward across the Atlantic. Just off the coast of Bojador (located on the edge of the North Atlantic), current flows south as physics requires. Today, this southward-flowing current off Bojador is known as the Canary Current. Eanes and his contemporaries, however, referred to it as the Guinea Current.

This ocean current had defeated Phoenician, Arab, and European Mediterranean sailors for thousands of years for one very simple reason. Shortly after it sails past Bojador, the Canary Current joins the North Equatorial Countercurrent, which flows unrelentingly westward. If you were to shove a barrel into the water at Bojador, sooner or later it would reach the New World—the Caribbean to be exact.[10] This westward-flowing current seemed intent on making America the final destination of ships heading toward Africa's southern Atlantic coast. The direction of ocean currents off the oddly shaped Bulging Cape worked against any southward-traveling vessel.

In addition to being dragged in the wrong direction, ships were compelled to contend with another difficulty in coping with the current, namely, its speed. The current traveling past Bojador was slow (0.03 to 0.07 meters per second), as are most currents along eastern edges of oceans. But the current moves fastest close to the shores of Cape Bojador, steadily weakening the farther it gets from shore. Thus, the closer you sailed to the shore, the faster you would be drawn into the westward-flowing North Equatorial Current. But if you sailed farther out into the ocean, the current would slow, and calm winds could bring the vessel to a virtual standstill.

One seemingly obvious solution, that is, sailing farther out and around the current, was also not a possibility. The final challenge the currents posed to sailors was their breadth (1,000 kilometers wide) from the African shores into the Atlantic.[11] A thousand kilometers out into the Atlantic, the current comes as close to stopping as a fluid possibly can. Being stalled over a thousand kilometers from land is just as dangerous as being carried too swiftly. Food and water can be exhausted and a crew driven to desperation.

None of the few surviving sources ever explained how Eanes managed to sail southward down Africa's coast. Since the few documents that survived the quake and tsunami were intended for broad distribution, these remain unlikely sources. To publicly give details of a voyage that no human had ever made before would have permitted competitors—including the Spaniards—to copy the feat. So the remaining official histories also tell us nothing, leaving us only to speculate on the methods of traveling. But armed with a smattering of knowledge of oceanography, we can begin to speculate on the timing and the nature of Eanes's successful strategy.

First, it seems likely that Eanes succeeded during the first half of the year. Between January and June, the Canary Current sliding past Bojador travels more directly and consistently south. The North Equatorial Countercurrent, which would put a barrel in the Bahamas, is pushed farther southward in those months, so sailing in the first half of the year would more likely have allowed a boat to travel farther to the south.

The knowledge that the Equatorial Countercurrent shifted southward during the first half of the year could have been gathered only by having ventured out into the current many times. The chronicles tell us that Portuguese sailors made more than twelve tries,[12] attempts that most likely resulted in knowing which months were the safest to attempt the southward journey. The first half of the year is additionally more likely because during those months, the North Equatorial Countercurrent flows more weakly than it does during the autumn and spring.

But by itself, knowing when to travel would not have solved his problems. Eanes also needed a new sailing strategy. Had sailing past Bojador been possible using any existing nautical technique, then other sailing nations would have rounded the cape earlier, and the vast continents of the Americas would have been discovered many centuries before they were.

By the start of the fifteenth century, many advances in nautical knowledge had surfaced. Among those achievements were the nautical chart, originally developed for the Mediterranean, and the navigational compass, originally developed by the Chinese for travel along lines where magnetic north and true north were identical. Polynesians had figured out the direction and movement of swells and discovered how to correct for wind direction. Persian, Arab, and Javanese navigators learned to use reversing monsoon winds in the tiny northwestern quadrant of the Indian Ocean and along the islands of what is now the Indonesian archipelago from Java to eastern Nusa Tengara. In short, on all other ocean voyages, sailors were able to hug the coast or to follow existing ocean currents, monsoons, magnetic fields, or ocean swells. To sail past Bojador, however, none of these techniques worked. Eanes needed to bring something new into existence. Where he began this process, however, likely resided with an existing well-known practice.

For centuries, sailors from the Viking North Atlantic to the Javanese Nusa Tengara (as well as those in many of the world's inland seas) had used a technique known as dead reckoning to determine their approximate position. Dead reckoning, however, counts distance only in a given direction—a simple straight line—and makes no allowance for either currents or winds that would push a vessel off course one way or another.

But in order to reach the Atlantic coastline south of Bojador, Eanes had to learn to compensate for the flow of the current, a sailing skill more advanced than mere dead reckoning. To plot a course toward and from an area south of the Bulge that would take even the slow-moving Canary Current into effect, Eanes (or those working with him) would have needed to invent a method of compensating for the direction in which a ship is pulled by a current. Sailing against a current demands significantly more sophistication than sailing against the wind primarily because current pushes a vessel far more powerfully than wind. A single knot of current pushes the same as thirty knots of wind. And unlike the wind, the direction and strength of which can be seen, the pull of the current remains unseen beneath the surface of the ocean.

Using the average speeds of the offshore waters of the modern Canary Current, a vessel would have been pulled between 1.3 and 11.55 kilometers southward in a single day's (twelve-hour) sail. Over a week of twelve-hour sails that distance would have magnified quickly to between 8.9 and 80.85 kilometers. Because of this pull, the direction the boat was heading and the actual course it traveled (course made good) would be different. When heading westward toward the coast, Eanes would have needed to steer his boat to the north of the direction in which he would have sailed without the current. And on the return voyage, he would have also had to point the vessel north of where he wanted to arrive. Today this technique is known as current sailing and is one of the basic techniques taught to every sailor.

To figure out which way to point his prow, Eanes would have needed to measure the current. At some point (and perhaps at several points) in the course of his journey, Eanes may have stopped, pulling down the sails or anchoring while measuring the speed and direction of the current. Only with that information could he redirect his vessel to compensate for that southward drift.

Eanes may well have initially guessed what direction he needed to sail in order to compensate for the current—but he may also have solved the problem of the direction in which to travel by what is now known as the current triangle. In the triangle, the first leg represents the ordered course (C) and speed (S). The other two legs were the estimated set (S) [direction] and drift (D) [velocity] of the current and the resultant track (TR) and speed of advance (SOA). Having the information on two legs of a triangle makes it possible to solve for the third leg of the triangle.

One additional fact seems to suggest that triangles were used. Two years after Eanes successfully traversed the Canary Current, a new diagram showed up in a drawing by an Italian chart maker known to keep close tabs on events in Portugal. In 1436, André Bianco drew a chart, including a table that allowed the exact measurement of distance traversed by a ship tacking back and forth.[13] While ships had been tacking back and forth across oceans for centuries without the need for any such tables, the sudden appearance of this diagram seems to suggest a new need for an exact measurement because the style of sailing had changed. Instead of tacking steadily in a single direction and then changing tack and sailing an equal period of time on another leg, the pilot on the journey across the Canary Current was constantly correcting the angle at which he was tacking because of the current.

Whether he guessed correctly or more likely used a triangle to figure out the correct angle he needed to sail with respect to the current, Eanes became the first successful current sailor who knew exactly how far to turn when facing opposing currents. Angling his boat too far to the north would have thrown him off course, just as the current would throw him off course. But Eanes clearly knew exactly what angle to take when crossing the offshore current at Bojador because he was able to repeat his journey almost exactly as he had journeyed the first time.

So remarkable was Eanes's success that even Prince Henry, the man directing these expeditions, was suspicious. Immediately after Eanes returned to Portugal with the news of his achievement, the prince demanded confirmation. He immediately ordered a second ship to accompany Eanes's ship and ordered him to make a return voyage.[14] Eanes succeeded, landing only slightly to the south of where he had gone ashore on his first momentous voyage, proving that he knew exactly what direction he needed to steer the boat to traverse the Canary Current and then return.

Regardless of whether he used triangles or, less likely, guesses, Eanes's success in piloting depended on careful observation of the direction and speed of the ocean currents. He had to measure the speed and direction of the unseen currents and employ those measurements to navigate. And as Portuguese sailors headed southward, gradually conquering the previously undefeated Atlantic, they would have to pay great attention to currents as well as winds, succeeding where none had succeeded before in navigating the mid-Atlantic and later the South Atlantic.

Eanes's use of triangles to solve the mystery of sailing past Bojador would have been the first application of mathematical principles to sailing. Everywhere else in the world, pilots had devised methods of sailing and implements to help them measure, using the materials available to them. Many measured the apparent movement of stars across the nighttime sky. Arabs and Persians had done so in the Indian Ocean, and Micronesians and Polynesians had memorized the names and paths of hundreds of stars across the sky. But none of these societies had utilized mathematics to reach their goals. Rough estimates, intuition, and measures based on the varying size of a navigator's hand all sufficed to make accurate-enough sailing possible.

Even the Arabs, whose mathematical knowledge was legendary, never applied their knowledge to the craft of navigation. The most likely reason, of course, is that they did not need to. The rough techniques of approximation sufficed for vessels to travel between African and Indian ports. No compelling need for mathematics had appeared. Yet mathematics and the use of triangles and trigonometry would prove crucial to all the further Portuguese voyages across the North and then South Atlantic, leading to their legendary voyages around the Cape of Good Hope and against the world's second-fastest current, the Agulhas, up into the previously navigated northeastern quadrant of the Indian Ocean.

Nor could simple perseverance have created a solution. Portuguese sailors were not the only ones to have tried repeatedly. "The sailors of Spain," a fifteenth-century chronicle reported, had attempted the journey for "almost a succession of generations."[15] At the time that Portuguese vessels were making their attempt, other Atlantic Ocean sailors from farther north were attempting the voyage as well.[16] But only the Portuguese vessels succeeded, because they acted differently.

All the existing high-seas navigational techniques relied on intuition—an instinctive response frequently the result of long experience—seeing which way the winds, currents, or magnetic fields blew or shifted. In other words, all relied on following existing natural phenomena to reach their destination. Portuguese sailors such as Eanes succeeded because rather than conforming to the path of nature, they acted against it. Put another way, rather than following currents instinctively, they acted counterintuitively. The source of their counterintuitive decisions involved measuring the unseen currents and applying mathematics to nature.

This counterintuitive use of measurement (of currents) and mathematics would eventually transform sailing into a science, for the principles of sailing did not depend on long years at sea for an individual to learn. Rather, the new principles of navigation could be taught in a classroom. Relatively inexperienced sailors could learn the techniques of navigation as they began to do in Portugal in the decade following Eanes's voyage.

A revolution in sailing had begun in 1434. Learning to measure the unseen in order to manage the seen and applying counterintuitive strategies based on abstract mathematical shapes changed the way sailing was done. The extent of this change, however, would become apparent only in the next sixty years as Portuguese navigators began the long, exhausting task of deciphering the difficulties of the South Atlantic.[17] During that time, they would have to turn repeatedly to unseen knowledge to be able to master the visible.

The devastation wrought by the tsunami and the quake at Lisbon reminds us how dependent we remain not simply on human volition but also on accidents of nature to preserve the past. Even the history of our most distinctive achievements can be wiped out in an instant—not by human hands but by those of nature.

## Notes

I would especially like to thank Felipe Fernández-Armesto and members of his Global History seminar at University College London for their helpful input into this chapter and Julie Sweet-kind-Singer of the Earth Sciences Library at Stanford for her help locating maps. I would also like to thank Jorge Cañizares-Esguerra and Erik Seeman, as well as members of the audience at the State University of New York at Buffalo for their suggestions.

1   Arch C. Johnston, "Seismic Moment Assessment of Earthquakes in Stable Continental Regions—III. New Madrid 1811–1812, Charleston 1886 and Lisbon 1755," *Geophysical Journal International* 126 (1996): 314–44, esp. 332–36, 341–42.

2   The National Information Service for Earthquake Engineering at the University of California Berkeley maintains an online collection of the images of Lisbon after the earthquake at http://nisee.berkeley.edu/lisbon/.

3   "Este principe mandar fazer ao cabo de S. Vicente, ali onde se comabane ambos mares, scilet: o grrande mar Ociano com o mar Medioterreno." Gomes Eanes da Zurara, *Crónica da Guiné*, ed. José de Bragança ([Porto] Livraria Civilizacao [1973]), cap. v, vol. I, 45–46.

4   The basic works on the oceanography of this region include A. Tejera, L. García, and M. Cantón, "Mesoscale Variability in the Canary Region from Altimetry," Earthnet Online, European Space Agency [online]; M. L. Batten, J. R. Martinez, D. W. Bryan, and E. J. Buch, "A Modeling Study of the Coastal Eastern Boundary Current System Off Iberia and Morocco," *Journal of Geophysical Research* 105 (2000): 14173–95; W. S. Wooster, A. Bakum, and D. R. McLain, "The Seasonal Upwelling Cycle along the Eastern Boundary of the North Atlantic," *Journal of Marine Research* 34 (1976): 131–40; A. Fedoseev, "Geostrophic Circulation of Surface Waters on the Shelf of North-West Africa," *Rapports et*

*procès-Verbaux des réunions/International Council for the Exploration of the Sea* 159 (1970): 32–37; E. Mittelstaedt, "The Ocean Boundary along the Northwest African Coast: Circulation and Oceanographic Properties at the Sea Surface," *Progress in Oceanography* 26 (1991): 307–55; L. Stramma and G. Siedler, "Seasonal Changes in the North Atlantic Sub-Tropical Gyre," *Journal of Geophysical Research* 93 (1988): 8111–18; and R. G. Peterson, L. Stramma, and G. Kortum, "Early Concepts and Charts of Ocean Circulation," *Progress in Oceanography* 37 (1996): 1–115.

5   "Ate aquele tempo, nem por escritura nem por memoria de nenhuns homens, nunca foi sabido determinadamente," *Crónica da Guiné*, cap. vii, vol. I, 59–60.

6   Most of the efforts to sail the Atlantic southward resulted in reaching the Canary Islands. *Crónica da Guiné*, cap. vii, vol. I, 59–60. Evidence of the Phoenecian attempts appears in recent archeological excavations. Fantastical stories of having rounded Africa, however, did appear, the best known being *The Periplus of Hanno*, which both the cautious Herodotus, *The Histories* 4.42 and Pliny the Elder (first century C.E.) dismiss as fabrications (*Natural History* 5.8). Hanno's description of the end of his journey describes circling several erupting volcanoes with lava flowing into the ocean—a very good description of the Canaries. Furthermore, since the craft they would have sailed was a Mediterranean vessel, it would have been unfit for stormy South Atlantic weather and disintegrated halfway into the South Atlantic. It took decades of ever-improving ship design, combining the strengthening techniques of medieval northern European shipbuilding with Mediterranean craft, to construct a sturdy-enough craft meet the challenge of the Atlantic. Seán McGrail, *Boats of the World from the Stone Age to Medieval Times* (New York, 2001).

7   Fifty African skulls from between 11,000 and 5,000 B.C. have been unearthed in Brazil. Even in the twentieth century, lost West African fishermen occasionally turned up off the northeastern coast of Brazil. On the most recent expedition, only half survived the thirty-day accidental crossing.

8   "O mar e tão baixo, que a uma legua de terra não ha de fundo mais que uma braça," *Cronica da Guiné*, cap. 7, vol. I, 66. The term "league" in this sentence signifies simply "far," not a precise measurement. The author calculated the distance using contemporary nautical charts.

9   The cape they rounded could not have been Cape Non because it lacks the sandbank described in all accounts. (At Non, shallow water extends only two nautical miles offshore.) Indeed, the only sandbank between the straits of Gibraltar and Cape Blanco resides off Bojador. João de Barros (*Décadas*, Dec. I liv 1, p. 4) mistakenly refers to "Non," as does one of the two versions in the Manuscrito Valentim Fernandes (De Prima iuentione guinea), 187. Both refer to "Non" as meaning no one passed beyond this point. In both cases, they seem to have confused the mnemonic for the significance of the place with the actual name of the cape. Examples of such charts include British Library, Additional ms. 31316 and British Library, Egerton ms. 73.

10  This phrase comes from Victoria Murden McClure, describing her effort to become the first person to row across the Atlantic. After failing to make the crossing from east to west, she turned to the Canaries, where the currents flowed most favorably, and she successfully traversed the Atlantic in a rowboat.

11  Contemporary oceanographers measure currents in kilometers.

12  "Com gran paciencia . . . sempre . . . o infante enviava . . . capitães de seus navios em busca daquela terra. . . . E finalmente, depois de doze anos," *Cronica da Guiné*, cap. ix, vol. I, 69.

13  Adolf Erik Nordenskiöld, *Periplus: An Essay on the Early History of Charts and Sailing-Directions*, trans. Francis A. Bather (reprint, New York, [1967?]), 53; Franco Masiero "La raxon de marteloio," *Studi Veneziani*, n.s., 8 (1984): 393–412.

14 "E acabado assim o recontamento de sua viagem, fez o Infante armar um barinel no qual mandou Afonso Gonçalves Baldaia, que era seu copeiro, e assim Gil Eanes com sua barca, mandando que tornassem lá outra vez," *Cronica da Guiné*, cap. ix, vol. I, 72.

15 *Cronica da Guiné*, cap. viii, vol. I, 65.

16 Prince Henry implies this: "Por opinão de quarto mareantes, os quaes, como são tirados da carreira de Flandres ou de algum outros portos para que communmente navegam, não saben mais." *Cronica da Guiné*, cap. vii, vol. I, 71.

17 Felipe Fernández-Armesto, "The Origins of the European Atlantic," *Itinerario* 24 (2000): 111–28, addresses some of the challenges at the end of the fifteenth century.

# Part II

# *Beyond the Atlantic*

Japanese drawing of the *Susquehanna*, Commodore Matthew C. Perry's ship, 1854. Perry was part of the process of connecting the Atlantic with the Pacific when in 1853 he led the first Western expedition to Japan since the 1630s.

*The five authors of part 2, "Beyond the Atlantic," question the very value of the Atlantic category itself. Can historians understand events that were actually global by limiting their analyses to a discrete area of the world? Is the Atlantic a useful category at all? Ironically, by calling into question the category itself, many of the authors in part 2 actually confirm its value and analytical power.*

*Felipe Fernández-Armesto, for example, demonstrates that the early modern European empires were not only Atlantic. By setting sail into the deep blue sea, European colonists were carried by the ocean's currents to the New World, Africa, India, and East Asia. The European maritime empires were global in reach and scope. Yet they were not the only world empires around. Russia and Qing China, to cite only two examples, were created at about the same time. They were not only larger but also far outlived any empire Europeans managed to put together. Historians have failed to place the early modern European empires into the larger context of expanding African, New World, and Asian contemporary empires, partly because the latter were landward and the former allegedly maritime. Fernández-Armesto argues that the early European empires were unremarkable: although they began solely as maritime, commercial enterprises, they as a matter of principle became landward. Compared to the Russian and Chinese empires, they followed similar principles of expansion: brokering deals with local elites and creating rickety multicultural bureaucracies. According to Fernández-Armesto, historians should not see the European empires as pioneering; rather they ought to be puzzled about why the European maritime empires came into being so late in time. But if these empires were unremarkable, the question remains, Why have scholars portrayed the colonization of the New World as an event that changed the course of world history?*

# Empires in Their Global Context, ca. 1500 to ca. 1800

### Felipe Fernández-Armesto

*Translated from the Spanish by Marielle R. Mecca
and Felipe Fernández-Armesto*

Every empire has its oddities. To understand the differences, we have to study them comparatively. So far, comparative study of empires in the so-called early modern period, from the fifteenth century to the end of the eighteenth, has been confined largely to empires originating in Europe and therefore to maritime imperialism. The effect is twofold. First, an impression is projected of a world increasingly susceptible to European hegemony, and this may be a false or an exaggerated impression. Second, the usual comparative trajectory privileges long-range maritime imperialism, which was an important new phenomenon of the era but which seems to me to have received disproportionate attention compared with landward imperialism. Therefore, I propose to broaden the framework of comparison and to attempt a genuinely global perspective, setting European empires in the context of indigenous imperialisms of other parts of the world and seaborne empires of the period in the context of those built up on land.

This approach has obvious virtues. European overseas empires, although fairly described as "maritime" in their origins and in much of their early history, can be seen gradually to have embodied imperialism of a type traditional in every part of the world: territorial imperialism, dedicated to landward expansion by adding contiguous domains. From a global perspective, imperialism of this type remained the most common throughout the period. The great empires of Africa and Asia and even, until Europeans conquered them in their turn, the indigenous empires of the New World had continued to expand, as always, through conquests of neighboring peoples. In existing comparative studies, there are too few references to such important empires as the Qing—the world's biggest and fastest-growing domains in the eighteenth century; nor Mwene Mutapa, which in the fifteenth and sixteenth centuries occupied the area between the Zambesi and Limpopo rivers and held off attempts at Portuguese conquest; nor Morocco, which succeeded in conquering Songhay across the vast sea of sand that was the Sahara in the 1580s; nor the Uzbeks, perhaps one of the largest empires of Central Asia; nor to any other of the non-European empires.[1]

Originally published in Spanish and reproduced in translation by kind permission of the editors of *Debate y Perspectivas* and the Fundación Tavera and with thanks for the kind assistance and advice of Professor Manuel Lucena Giraldo of the Consejo Superior de Investigaciones Científicas, Madrid.

Moreover, it is now generally acknowledged that the early modern period was a time of global expansion and that European impact—however important it may be—was only one thread in the complex fabric of cultural exchange, or "interculturation," to employ a useful neologism, much of which originated in other sources of influence. Non-European empires had and continued to have a profound influence on the Europeans with whom they came in contact or with Europe itself. Empires generally were of enormous importance as arenas of cultural exchange, as they encouraged the flow of tribute, trade, personnel, and migrant communities. Indeed, that is perhaps the main source of their impact on global history and, therefore, our main justification for studying them.

Exchanges of culture and, indeed, of power occurred between peoples as well as between empires. An enormous amount of late-twentieth-century scholarship has shown how peoples who took part in empires, as victims of conquest or hosts of colonizations, commonly maintained varying degrees of autonomy that permitted them to retain important forms of initiative apart from and often in defiance of imperial policy and to uphold their own identities and cultures, modifying them at times without abandoning them.[2] Retained elements of traditional culture often included indigenous forms of political rule, social structure, and religion. Traditional laws remained intact with few exceptions, and the elite continued to be as before, or continued to change as they had always changed. Communities sometimes incorporated European people and institutions into their own administrative, military, and judicial systems but often without radical substitutions. On the economic front, it was normal for means of production to change as the influence and power of new European empires grew, generating demand for new products or for traditional products on a new scale, but the process was very slow. Commercial networks multiplied and attained unprecedented scale and scope, but until the nineteenth century, the pace of change in this respect was modest.

The importance of indigenous contributions to European-led empires is now well attested in African and Asian cases. Similar findings seem increasingly applicable to the history of the New World, where the European impact broadened and deepened throughout the period without rupturing all the immense continuities of the indigenous past. In light of much current work, European empires seem weaker and less imposing than formerly supposed. The new historiography of imperialism focuses on peripheries rather than the metropolitan centers and on subject communities rather than colonial elites; we can now begin to see how often and how successfully indigenous peoples domesticated, transformed, and even exploited incoming Europeans. In some cases, the balance of cultural exchange tilted surprisingly: Europeans absorbed as much as or more than they transmitted. Even in the eighteenth century, the "equality of civilizations" was barely disturbed.[3]

Thanks to this new perspective, we can see some old problems in a new light. According to conventional wisdom, for example, relations between the Portuguese and Dutch were crucial in the decline of the Portuguese Empire in Asia in the seventeenth century. But in reality, the Portuguese yielded not only to their European rivals but also to the growing force of indigenous dynasties that challenged them: the Tokugawa, the Moguls, the Safavids, the Sayyids of Oman, and the empire personally created by Coxinga.[4] The fact that so many communities around the edges of maritime Asia—and with an even greater enthusiasm in the Andean and Mesoamerican worlds—welcomed European newcomers seems easier to understand when we take into account how threatening the expansion of indigenous empires must have seemed to the peoples concerned. Of course, none of this means that we should discount the importance of the kinds of imperialism that were new to the era. Long-range maritime imperialism was almost unprecedented. On a small scale, something of the kind existed in the Mediterranean among Greeks, Phoenicians, and Romans in antiquity and later in the Genoese, Catalan, Venetian, and Turkish cases. The Knytlinga Empire of the North Sea in the eleventh century and the "Norman Empire" of the English Channel are possible examples.[5] The so-called empire of the Cholas in the same period in southern India and neighboring seas remains little known, but it may be appropriate to put in the same category.[6] Commercial and, at times, political networks spread through the monsoon region of the Indian Ocean in what we think of as the Middle Ages, with centers in southern Arabia, Persia, India, and China.[7] In the early fifteenth century, Chinese expeditions, following routes that Indian Ocean merchants had used for centuries, intervened in the political lives of such diverse and distant places as Sri Lanka, Java, and Malacca. Until the fourth decade of that century, the possibility that the Chinese Empire would acquire a seaborne dimension seemed within the bounds of possibility.[8] At about the same time, Atlantic Africa became an arena of attempts of conquest and colonization by European adventurers.[9] But there had never before been maritime empires of the type and size created by Europeans from the sixteenth century on.

Some of them, in the long run, were genuinely world transforming. All of them displayed original features. That of the Spanish monarchy came to be, on a global scale, the greatest empire by land and sea constructed without the help of modern industrial technology. The French and British empires of the nineteenth century were larger but had at their disposal technological advances unavailable when the Spanish Empire was formed: new direction-finding and longitude-determining technologies, steam engines, rifles, steel cannon, machine guns, quinine pills and other measures against tropical diseases. The Dutch Empire was conspicuous simply for the remarkably widespread and diverse locations of Dutch colonies in the seventeenth century. With outposts as far apart as New Amsterdam in the northwest, the Cape of Good Hope in the south, and the Japanese island of Deshima in the east, the Dutch managed to exceed the range even of the Iberian empires. The Portuguese Empire resembled the maritime empires of Genoa and Venice more than its Spanish counterpart with its network of coastal settlements. The Portuguese effort was concerned more with the control of commerce than with direct forms of exploitation and tributary relations in conquered lands. The Portuguese command attention not only because they were relatively early pioneers in distant seas but also because of the contributions they made to new departures in imperialism, such as the transplantation of sugar to Brazil, which transformed the environment in the region affected, and the large-scale transportation of African slaves, in which Portuguese agents played a major role. In 1617, students from the Jesuit College in Goa performed a play in which a Brazilian parrot conversed with the Portuguese king in Tupi, the principal language of the Portuguese-ruled area of Brazil.[10] There could have been no clearer demonstration of the innovative character of long-range maritime imperialism, its extraordinary reach, the exchanges of all kinds that it produced across enormous distances, and the unforeseen mixture of cultures that resulted.

Moreover, although European influence in the early modern world has been exaggerated, that influence was tremendous in two contexts: ecological and demographic. In both, contact, conflict, and contagion had transforming effects. The New World endured a demographic disaster that killed millions of people and severely reduced or, in some areas, wiped out the indigenous population. In some areas, biological invaders—new populations of humans, animals, plants, and microbes—refashioned the physical environment.[11] Meanwhile, in certain areas in Africa, problems arising from the new scale of the slave trade had profound changes: provoking violence between buyers and suppliers of slaves, increasing the number of raptor states, and in some places probably provoking serious losses of manpower.[12] The scope of such effects, in Africa as well as in America, is hard to calculate and is open to dispute, but in the American case, even the most modest calculations are quite troubling.[13]

In short, despite all the revisions proposed by recent scholarship, European maritime expansion of the period remains undeniably important for the development of long-range navigation and related sciences, the establishment of extensive networks of communication between previously sundered zones, the contribution that Europeans made to maritime exploration, the exchanges of populations and cultures, and the ecological exchanges that transformed environments almost wherever Europeans went.

The basic problem in the history of modern imperialism therefore remains this: how did Europeans attain this new importance in the world? The region from which the European empire builders of the age came had previously displayed modest prospects compared with those of the great civilizations of the southern and eastern extremities of Eurasia. It was poorly equipped in resources and techniques, with a relatively underdeveloped economy, short of people, funds, and opportunities for wealth creation, compared with India and China, where all these advantages were abundant. The balance of trade in commerce, inventions, and perhaps ideas across Eurasia had long favored China and India. So how did people from such a backwater become the driving force of empires of such extensive and profound importance and impact? The problem of the "European miracle" reminds us of the story of the yokel who, when a passing motorist asked the way to a certain destination, replied, "I don't know. But I wouldn't start from here." As a starting point for creating an immense empire, Europe did not seem to be the ideal location.[14]

This raises a key problem in world history: until the middle of the nineteenth century, the superior technology and economies of civilizations in East and South Asia were a seemingly fixed feature of world history. Sometimes, empires are the product of excess resources, invincible might, or surplus population that demands lebensraum. The European empires of the sixteenth to eighteenth centuries were not of that kind. Their countries of origin more resembled present-day "third world" communities, searching desperately for new recourses, with foreign capital and expertise. In the most conspicuous examples—those of Castile, Portugal, and Holland—the technological and financial contribution from Italy and Flanders was of critical importance in launching the initial imperial effort.[15] These were, moreover, all places where what we might call "small-country psychosis" was manifest: menaced by bigger rivals, they had to increase their resources by means of conquest. Yet being small, poor, and peripheral does not necessarily disqualify people for empire. Some of the greatest commercial and colonizing forces in human history were launched from narrow shores and poor terrain. Where infertile or inaccessible hinterlands limit opportunities for expansion landward, empire-building ambitions naturally turn seaward. The classic case, in every sense of the word, is that of ancient Greece—"poverty's sister," as Hesiod called his homeland, a skeleton land, according to Plato, where the rocks poked like bones through the surface of the earth.[16] The Phoenicians, the Greeks' commercial and colonial rivals, inhabited a narrow coastal plain. From southern Arabia, Gujarat in India, and the maritime province of Fujian in China, great commercial and colonizing enterprises were launched by sea in antiquity and the Middle Ages. We do not usually count medieval and early modern Japan as a maritime empire, but it was: conditions of navigation in Japan's home seas are so difficult that the achievement of uniting so much of the Japanese archipelago in a single state was in itself a major achievement in the history of empires.[17]

In medieval Europe, the first great maritime initiatives we know of—the pilgrimages of Irish hermits and adventures of the Vikings—also began from relatively poor and peripheral places. The maritime empires of the medieval Mediterranean were launched from narrow shores in the Genoese and Catalan cases or from the salty, marshy soils of Venice. It is therefore not so surprising that Castile, Portugal, and the Netherlands should have produced more successful empire builders in the early modern period than such better-endowed places as France and England.

Usually, we describe these empires as "European." It would be more exact to say that they were empires founded from Europe's western edge, in the area I propose calling "Rimland"—the land at the water margin.[18] This seaboard stretches across diverse cultures and climates from Andalusia to Norway. To the coastal traveler, all seems to change except the inevitable presence of the sea. That sea has given the peoples that line its shores a tremendous role: almost all the great maritime empires of modern history started on its shores. There are only three candidates for consideration as exceptions. Italy had a relatively small and short-lived empire in Libya, the Dodecanese Islands, and the horn of Africa, laboriously erected between the 1880s and 1930, accessed through the Mediterranean and the Suez Canal. A small Russian maritime empire existed in the Pacific in the nineteenth century in the Aleutian Islands and (until the Alaskan Purchase in 1867) the Pacific coast of North America. And in the seventeenth century, merchants from Brandenburg and Courland in the Baltic Sea established modest networks of sugar-producing islands and slave posts in West Africa and the Caribbean.[19]

Almost all European overseas empires, therefore, were the work of communities on the Atlantic shore. In addition, no country on Europe's Atlantic failed to acquire such an empire. The only possible exceptions were Iceland, Ireland, and Norway. But these states achieved their own independence only in the twentieth century: they had no opportunity to participate, as states, in the business of overseas empire building. It is worth recalling, however, that while the Irish may not have had their own empire, they played a key role as participants in British imperialism as well as suffering from the encroachments of the English and Scots. Norwegians, too, thanks to their maritime tradition, served the Danish and Swedish interests in the slave trade. All the other states of Rimland embarked on overseas imperialism. Some (Portugal, England, the Netherlands, and even Scotland, for as long as it remained an independent state, and, later, Germany) had no seaward outlet except toward the Atlantic; others wore a Janus mask, with coasts open to the "internal" seas of Europe, the Mediterranean, or the Baltic: Spain, France, Sweden, and Denmark. When awarded the title of *honoris causa,* Salvador de Madariaga, well into in his eighties, congratulated himself on his "extraordinary precocity." European imperialism was precocious in the same sense. The biggest

"European miracle" is that for so long, until the early modern era, there was no miracle. We western Europeans like to think of ourselves as great makers of Europe because of our medieval expansion eastward and southward, our Renaissance, our scientific and industrial "revolutions," our Enlightenment, and our constitutional and democratic revolutions. All these movements, from points of departure in westerly parts of the continent, spread and helped form the culture that we now call European. Over a longer period, however, the story looks different. For most of recorded history, the West played a passive role, absorbing the imprint of cultural transmissions from the East: agriculture; metallurgy; Indo-European languages; Phoenician, Greek, and Jewish settlements; the coming of Christianity; Germanic, Slavic, and steppelander migrations; and the trajectories of technologies, aesthetics, and scientific ideas of Chinese, Indian, and Arab origin. Meanwhile, most Rimland communities remained stuck in their lands for centuries without turning seaward, trying to forge vast empires, or even penetrating very far into the ocean. Until the fourteenth century, the only oceangoing colonizing expeditions were those from Scandinavia. Other Rimland peoples discovered their maritime vocation little by little. The Atlantic gave them opportunities for fishing and coastal shipping. Their attempts at expansion—"reconquests" and crusades—made sporadic progress but were always interrupted or arrested or held back by enemy resistance or by the effects of plague or adverse changes of climate. Even when the history of Atlantic exploration began in earnest toward the end of the thirteenth century and in the first half of the fourteenth, it was Mediterranean navigators, from Mallorca and Italy, who took the initiative and not those from the Atlantic coast.

This part of the European past is hard to understand because it is so different from the present. In the nineteenth and twentieth centuries, the great civilizations of the East went through a period of exceptional inertia and economic stagnation. In consequence, people in the world's centers of power and wealth yielded predominance to formerly insignificant communities. The former center became the new periphery. Old peripheries in Europe and, ultimately, the New World became centers. Capitalism, imperialism, modern science, industrialization, individualism, and democracy—some of the most influential movements in the formation of the modern world—are supposedly European in origin. Up to a point, Western prejudices have suppressed the fact that other cultures have played a part in generating all these movements. Capitalism, for example, is an idea of great antiquity in Jain tradition, and, despite what is commonly supposed in the West, commercial values were much esteemed in ancient Buddhist and even Hindu tradition. Religions that have proved compatible with intense commercial activity include Jainism, Buddhism, Judaism, and Islam.[20] Paper money, without which capitalism would be unthinkable, was, like so much of the tool kit of modernity, of Chinese invention. Imperialism, now considered a white vice, is really a human vice. Nor is it only in the Christian tradition that it comes sanctified by missionary inspiration. In the eleventh to eighteenth centuries, Islam and Buddhism also took long-range "spiritual conquests." The empiricist basis of our modern science was known in China—in Taoist circles and in the tradition known as *khao-zheng*—many centuries before it was first expressed in surviving Western texts. Nineteenth-century industrialization began in Europe, but it has spread fairly quickly to other regions; in any case, we can now recognize it for what it was: one style of industrialization among many others. Individualism is an ideology that seems stronger in societies of European origins than in oriental civilizations, but it is found everywhere.

Buddhism, for instance, values human individuality as highly as Western traditions. The state system is often cited as one of the reasons for European dynamism, but a very similar system existed in Southeast Asia and, to some extent, in India until the completion of the Mogul conquests, as well as, in effect, daimyo Japan. Apparently, therefore, sociocultural explanations in the Weberian tradition do not help us understand the ascent of Europe. Culture is a concept so vast that it includes everything and explains nothing. Western culture, in the respects generally considered relevant, was not distinctive enough to explain a peculiar historical trajectory for Western civilization. That culture, in any case, was already in place during Europe's long stagnancy. If there is some ingredient in Western culture that might help explain why that stagnancy ended, it has to be something new to the period concerned: a trait, therefore, of late medieval origin.

A culture of adventure is detectable in western Europe at that time. Elites and those who aspired to join them idealized adventure and strove to embody in their lives the great aristocratic ethos of the age: the "code" of chivalry. Their models included heroes of romances of seaborne chivalry: such characters as Brut, who, in the medieval romance that bears his name, founded a realm in Albion after the fall of Troy; or Amadis of Gaul, who fought giants and won a kingdom on an enchanted island; or Prince Troian, who found his fortune aboard a ship and his love across an ocean. Their ships were caparisoned, and they mounted the waves like jennets. The "squires" of the Infante Dom Henrique of Portugal were desperadoes, pirates, and criminals, but they gave themselves chivalric airs and affected storybook names: on the isle of Madeira, "Tristão da Ilha" received, with all traditional rites, the homage of a vassal whom, because of an amorous imbroglio involving the vassal and Tristão's daughter, he subsequently emasculated: a perfect example of a culture of chivalric affectations and brutal realities. Columbus, whose life followed the plot of a romance of the sea and whose father-in-law was a follower of Dom Henrique, seems to have adopted the same literary tradition as a guide to how to behave. Although Vasco da Gama is hard to approach from surviving sources, one thing we do know is that he took seriously his knightly obligations as a member of the orders of Santiago and Christ. John Cabot departed from a land where English versions of the Arthur romances attributed to the king a series of ocean-borne conquests. Books of the same type nourished the self-perceptions of Spanish explorers and conquistadores until well into the seventeenth century. There was a kind of quixotic impulse at work in the imaginations of men who launched overseas enterprises and those who wrote them up with an admixture of chivalric language.[21]

The cult of chivalry ennobled deeds that might have been disparaged in other cultures. Among elites who did not read the chivalric literature of western Europe, interest in maritime adventures was slight or absent. The Chinese naval effort of the early fifteenth century came to an end because of opposition from the Mandarin class, animated by disdain for merchants, Buddhists, eunuchs, Muslims, mariners, and foreigners who supported the policy of maritime expansion.[22] In fifteenth-century Malacca, there were Muslim merchants who held titles of nobility and even Hindus who were accredited as "ninas"—a term signifying slightly lower rank; the higher reaches of the aristocracy, however, were not open to either group. Among the region's kings, there were many who dedicated themselves to commerce with a certain business élan but none who was called, like the king of Portugal, "Lord of commerce and navigation."

Although, as we have seen, the spirits of commerce and imperialism could be accommodated in various Asian traditions, only in the West did they get the extra impulse that chivalric literature imparted.[23]

More important than this peculiar feature of western European culture was Rimland's geographical location, bordering the ocean and with access to the northeast trade winds. However, because of their deficiencies in technology and resources, Western navigators could not profit from their advantageous location until the end of the fifteenth century. Naturally, the great maritime empires of the early modern period would have been impossible had navigators not succeeded in mastering the winds and currents that bound them. The Atlantic was the key to the global system because the winds of the southern half of that ocean lead directly to the great belt of westerlies that circles the world around the fortieth parallel south and leads to all the major oceans. Asian maritime civilizations, on the other hand, where merchants and mariners had a much longer tradition of daring navigation and long-range trade than their European counterparts, lived in a very different environment. The Indian Ocean constitutes a more or less closed system. During the southern summer, violent storms from the north block the way south. The vast Pacific extension discourages any attempt to find new opportunities in the east. The seamen of maritime Asia, whose markets were already the richest in the world, had no incentive to explore beyond their own seas or to breach the zone of storms. Meanwhile, internal conditions in the Indian Ocean were exceptionally favorable to sail-borne ships. The key lies in the regularity of the monsoon winds. North of the Equator, northeasterly winds prevail in winter. During the rest of the year, the winds blow from the south and west. Traditional navigators timed their voyages according to the monsoons so as to ensure favorable winds on both the outward and the return voyages.[24] Here, perhaps, is the most significant source of difference between European and Asian maritime imperialism: the latter made use of the monsoon system, whereas the former relied on fixed winds. The Spaniards did not use the monsoon since the routes that bound their empire crossed the fixed systems of the Atlantic and Pacific; the Dutch avoided it as much as possible, using, for their outbound voyages, winds and currents that flanked the system. The Portuguese route to and from the Indies, on the other hand, always involved both types of system, crossing the Atlantic with the trade winds and using the monsoon within the Indian Ocean.

All the maritime empires of the early modern period fit these categories. But we have now to turn to the landward empires, which, as claimed previously, were more important. Empires built up by traditional landward expansion continued to grow during the formative period of the new long-range maritime imperialism, and little by little, the maritime empires came increasingly to acquire a territorial character. The best approach to the study of land empires is to take a couple of examples: those of the Ottomans, Safavids, Moguls, and perhaps Thais might serve, but the two that grew fastest and became biggest in the early modern period, those of Russia and China, might make the most representative cases (Map 1). From today's perspective, these two empires were incomparably significant. All the maritime empires have disappeared, and of the territorial empires established at the time, only those of the Russians in Siberia and the Chinese in central Asia have survived.

We start with the Russians. The nature of Muscovite expansion is made visible in the Icon of the Hosts of the Heavenly King, a work of the mid-sixteenth century that adorns one of Moscow's principal churches. Led by the biblical kings Solomon and

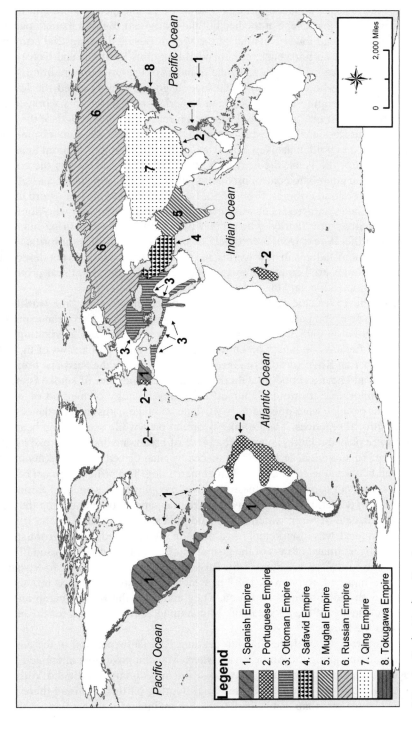

**Map 1** Early Modern Empires.

David, the Russians advance through a fantastic landscape of rivers and mountains, with Saints Boris and Glebe at the head of the rear guard. Behind them, a pagan city is in flames. They head toward an altar of the Virgin. Beside the terrestrial army marches another, celestial, on horseback, commanded by Saints Vladimir and Constantine, the emperors considered at the time to be the founders of the Orthodox tradition. "Although the martyrs were born on Earth," the legend goes, "they reached the level of the angels."[25] Two genuine leaps of Russian imperialism inspired this work. In the first place, the conquest of Kazan gave the tsars control of the entire length of the Volga and eliminated the Russians' greatest rival for the Siberian fur trade. Furs inspired Russian conquests, just as gold in the New World and spices in the Orient inspired Spaniards and Portuguese. For the tsars, the next task after the fall of Kazan was the conquest of Siberia and the attempt to control production as well as trade in "black and silver gold": sables, squirrels, and ermines. From 1555, Ivan IV exhibited the title "Lord of Siberia." Three years later, an agreement was struck with the entrepreneurs who dominated the trade—the Stroganov family, who were willing to help the tsar bring his dreams of conquest to life. A text from a chronicle of the conquest displays priorities typical of European conquistadores in new worlds and far frontiers: pagans do not deserve to have rights, their lands are "empty," they are like beasts or monsters, fiscal privileges will stimulate colonization, and the task is holy.[26]

From the 1570s, the Russians promised protection against "the warlike folk of Siberia" to tribes that paid tributes in furs. As in other areas of European expansion, the Russians relied on their technological superiority. The invaders, navigating the great rivers, used firearms, mounted on barges, against the bows and arrows of their defenders. The Siberian Khan was discouraged to hear that "when the Russians fire, you see a ring of fire and hear a sound, like thunder in the sky, and a lot of smoke is emitted . . . and it's impossible to protect yourself from any strategy or method of warfare."[27] Indigenous peoples were obliged to pay tribute and take oaths in accordance with their own traditional practices. The Ostiaks swore an oath while seated on a bear's pelt on which were placed a knife, an ax, and a piece of bread: anyone who broke his promise would die, be strangled, or be torn to pieces by men or bears. The Yakuts had to take their oath between the quarters of a dismembered dog. The principal object of conquest, however, was not to subjugate these "savage" peoples who wandered through frozen deserts but to defeat the only nation in that region capable of challenging the Russians: the Tatar khanate of Sibir, which dominated the eastern tributaries of the Irtysh River. So the conquest was "marketed" as a crusade, symbolized, in the frontispiece of a chronicle, by an image of rays of the gospel shining from Christ's eyes and illuminating a landscape full of cities founded by Russian colonists. According to Russian texts, Kuchum Khan had a vision in 1581 in which "the heavens opened up, and terrible warriors with radiant wings appeared. They encircled the Khan's camp and cried to him, 'Unclean son of the dark demon, Muhammad, leave this land, for the land and its fullness is the Lord's.' "[28]

Toward the end of the eighteenth century, Russian expansion in the east ran into that of the Qing along the Amur River, where Manchu governors attempted to impede the Russian advance. According to the Jesuit missionary Ferdinand Verbiest, who traveled the Chinese Empire with imperial hunting parties, the road there was more level and better kept than that "which Catholics maintain for processions of the Blessed

Sacrament."[29] The Treaty of Nierchinsk in 1689 formalized Chinese claims to vast and unexplored lands of doubtful extent in northeastern Asia, where some cartographers imagined a long tongue of land protruding toward and perhaps touching America. In large part, this territory remained outside the practical limits of Chinese dominion or the reach of settlers. In other imperial zones, however, the Qing promoted methods of exploitation far more intensive than those of the Russians. Their policies envisaged the settlement of colonists and the assimilation of conquered peoples as well as trade and the exploitation of natural resources. Before the end of the century, they had annexed Outer Mongolia, and more than 1.5 million people had colonized Szechwan with the promise of fiscal immunity. The next frontier, that of Xinjiang, was much less densely settled, with a mixture of fiscal privileges and forced deportations of exiles. Two hundred thousand settlers had been installed by the end of the century. Manchuria, the original homeland of the Qing, remained officially closed to colonization. But its rich lands continued to attract hundreds of millions of people, until the government had to face the facts and abolish the restrictions. Meanwhile, despite an attempt to preserve their identity, the Manchu began to redefine themselves as Chinese like all the others. On all fronts, the pressure of increasing colonization provoked a new cycle of problems and solutions, reminiscent of other cases of European colonization: tribes forcibly relocated or enclosed in reservations; military colonies where wheat, barley, vegetables, and corn were cultivated while the indigenous population was kept in stark subjection; and schools founded to increase the reach of Chinese cultures and language.

The maritime empires, too, were bound, sooner or later, to become territorial empires, following where traditional imperialism led. The difference between a maritime empire and a territorial empire is more than a matter of location. Maritime empires are empires of trade that they attempt to channel or, if possible, control. Land empires have different aims: to influence, manage, and even monopolize production of key commodities. Columbus's vision for Hispaniola when he discovered it was as a commercial center, a mercantile colony under the control of Castile, selling cotton, mastic, and slaves.[30] In reality, none of these products was available in adequate quantities. Instead, the economy was driven by the discovery and direct exploitation of gold mines. The wars of conquest Columbus fought in 1495–1496 can be understood as the first step toward the creation of a Castilian territorial empire in the New World. Mainland conquests consolidated the process whereby the Spaniards found themselves—somewhat to their surprise—obeyed across vast swaths of the most densely populated regions of the hemisphere. Furthermore, in the 1520s and 1530s in Mexico and Peru, the Spanish seized two of the fastest-growing and most ecologically diverse empires in the world.

The other European maritime empires, which lacked the advantage of abundant labor in their conquests, tended at first to eschew territorial acquisitions inland. In introducing new products for export and new production methods, they concentrated at first on crops that could grow in narrow zones close to the coasts, such as sugar on the islands and edges of the Caribbean, Brazil, and the Peruvian coast; tobacco in Virginia; and rice in the Carolinas. At times, impressive results were achieved in extremely restricted spaces. The French colony of Saint Domingue occupied scarce land but in the eighteenth century seemed to be an economic miracle where for a period of time much of the world's sugar and coffee was produced. In Brazil, the first local product of great importance was brazilwood, which was used to make dye, but sugar replaced it in the second half of the sixteenth century. Sugar demanded great investment and substantial labor. It could be successfully cultivated only in areas accessible to exterior commerce and to the slave trade. With an economy solely dependent on sugar, the idea of acquiring an inland empire might never have arisen.[31]

In Asia, similarly, there was at first no reason to conquer lands beyond the confines of the ports and garrisons occupied by European powers. Until the mid-seventeenth century, the only exceptions were the "Northern province" of Portuguese India between Chaul and Damian, where palms and rice were produced by the Portuguese in order to supply the coastal settlements, and Sri Lanka, where Portuguese garrisons could impose a monopoly of the cinnamon trade so complete that they were effectively in control of production. During the first half of the century, the total number of indigenous people under Portuguese rule did not exceed 500,000.[32] The Dutch took a decisive step toward territorial imperialism in the 1660s when they began to conquer areas of spice production in the Moluccas: this was significant not because of the extent of land involved, which was still very small, but because it represented a change of policy, from controlling trade to controlling production.[33] Even then, European territorial imperialism in Asia remained a very modest phenomenon. Only in the eighteenth century did the Dutch Empire begin to establish a solid presence in parts of inland Java. In a way paralleled in Brazil, Portuguese India began to expand inland from Goa into the "Novas Conquistas" of inland Goa. There was no other European territorial empire in mainland Asia until the British conquest of Bengal in 1757.

By that date, the British and French had succumbed to the temptation of creating territorial empires in the New World, imitating the Spanish example. The British Empire in North America had quite a substantial presence because of the large number of immigrants who made possible the colonization of the Ohio River Valley from the 1760s.[34] The French Empire in Louisiana, on the other hand, was little more than lines drawn on a map. Despite being a relatively populous country, France was unable to attract its people to its colonies.[35] Both France and Britain claimed vast spaces of the continental interior, although in a purely formulaic manner, until France abandoned its claim in 1763. To a certain extent, these "empires" were still speculations imperfectly achieved.

In its early stages, Portuguese interest in inland Brazil was of the same kind—a project for excluding Spain from territories about which little was known but which could prove beneficial in the future. Attempts by the Spanish to develop the Amazon and Orinoco as routes of navigation provoked a response by the Portuguese in 1630.[36] During the second half of the century, interest in the Brazilian colony increased enormously in Portugal after the withdrawal of so many Portuguese garrisons from Asia and East Africa. For lack of a better alternative, Brazil came to be the jewel of a more compact empire. Even so, the risks and costs of conquering the interior seemed uninviting. The exploitation of the interior was an affair of slavers and ranchers until the 1680s when news of gold and diamonds aroused renewed effort. The creation of the present linguistic frontier was the work of the next century.

To a certain extent, all empires functioned in the same way. For want of the industrial technology that eased communications, conquests, and policing in the nineteenth century, other means of exacting obedience and eliciting collaboration were needed:

braggadocio, for instance, such as Mandelslo observed among the Portuguese in India;[37] sleight of hand, such as Robert Clive used in seizing Bengal;[38] terrorism and intimidation, such as Cortés employed in Cholula and Pizarro at Cochabamba; and the use of alcohol and opiates in garrisons and remote settlements, such as the opium that sustained people in Portuguese fortresses on the Persian coast at the end of the sixteenth century.[39] More routine strategies were to ally with local elites or, if there were none, to attempt to appoint new ones. Another was to take advantage of the "stranger effect," that is, the deeply rooted custom in some cultures of respecting and obeying those who have newly arrived or using them for their objectivity, as arbitrators of social conflicts.[40] In any event, the imperialism in those centuries would have been impossible without local collaborators. The "Maya Conquistadores," recently identified by the research of Matthew Restall, are an example that turns out to be quite typical. Unknown until now, in the archives of the Yucatan, hidden in documents in the Yucatan language, is an entire series of affirmations by individuals and families who were proud of their role in serving the Spanish crown, subjugating their neighbors, and spreading the gospel.[41]

In short, the new European maritime empires seem, in a global context, less impressive than is usually supposed. In the early modern period, land empires continued to be the dominant type of trend. But the economic effects of new kinds of empire building must be taken into account. It is by no means certain that Europe's adverse balance of trade with China was paid for by American silver or that American gold ended up in India.[42] But it was paid for: indeed, Europeans and their American colonies proved capable of importing more than ever from China (especially in products new to the market in the period, such as tea, porcelain, and rhubarb) while also increasing their own capacity for production. The benefits of imperialism must surely have helped to make that improvement possible. From the Dutch example in the seventeenth century, it appears possible that increased trade with China and India was financed largely by freight charges, which were also important sources of income for other European trading communities in Asia, most of which dedicated much of their effort to securing a role as shippers in existing trades between Asian ports. The total increase of disposable cash in the economies of Europe and the European New World seem to have exceeded the value of the increase in trade between Europe and Asia.[43]

Nevertheless, whatever the particular role of American silver, it is probably fair to say that without a New World to deliver economic balance in the Old, Europe would have remained inferior, as ever, in wealth and power, to the great civilizations of Asia. After taking control of vast, underexploited resources in America, some western European states began to establish empires farther afield than the world had ever seen and collectively to erect the most complete hegemony that any civilization had ever imposed. Since the end of the eighteenth century, successive observers of the rise of the West have questioned whether there is any connection between the appropriation of America and the revolution in resources that wiped out ancient supremacies. Adam Smith, a privileged observer at a critical moment of the transition, published *On The Wealth of Nations* in the year of America's Declaration of Independence, and since then his name has been synonymous with the cause of global free trade. As an adversary of mercantilism, he could hardly have been expected to favor imperialism. It was apparent to him that Great Britain would be better off with an independent America than with a costly resentful colony. Regretfully, he said, it was not "the wisdom and policy, but the disorder and injustice of the European governments, which populated and cultivated America."[44] But he could not join those moralists of the Enlightenment who condemned unreservedly Europe's imperial projects. He thought that the opening of routes from Europe across the Atlantic and into the Indian Ocean was the greatest achievement of history. In particular, he saw in the gold and silver of the Americas the starting point of a change of fortune, for they helped to balance the long-standing disparities of wealth between Europe and the East; meanwhile, copious natural resources and new markets in the Americas remained at the exclusive disposal of the industries of western and central Europe.

The new empires' economic effects were clearly enormous, but the preoccupation of historians with economic and monetary affairs seems excessive. It is a side-effect of capitalist, industrialized modernity—part of a set of values appropriate to a world hectically bent on economic growth. The essential subject matter of world history ought not to be merely economic but also broadly cultural. Of course, economics is part of culture, but in terms of cultural exchanges, economics played a relatively minor role until the twentieth century (or at least the nineteenth) because, before then, trade was usually a small-scale activity, whereas other disseminators of culture, such as migrations, wars, pilgrimages, explorations, and missions of a religious, scientific, or diplomatic nature, exerted more influence. Finally, in its broadest global context, European expansion sowed seeds of another transcendentally important change: the great ecological revolution of early modern times, which transformed so many physical environments and reversed the direction of eons of evolution. From the moment, perhaps about 130 million years ago, when Pangea split into fragments, until the fifteenth century, biota—plants, animals, microbes, and even human types—were on a divergent course as the continents drew apart and their life forms grew ever more distinctive. Since then, because of the contacts that long-distance navigation inaugurated between the continents, convergence has replaced divergence. Increasingly, the same species occur worldwide. If for no other reason—and after discounting imperialist arrogance, racial supremacism, the collective guilt of the postcolonial era, and all the other discredited pretexts for studying the history of empires—the interest of the subject remains topical, lively, and urgent.

## Notes

1   Regarding the Qing, see also J. Waley-Cohen, *Exile in Mid-Qing China* (New Haven, Conn., 1991), and R. H. G. Lee, *The Manchurian Frontier in Ch'ing History* (Cambridge, Mass., 1970); on the Mwena Mutapa, see W. G. Randles, *The Empire of Monomotapa* (Harare, 1981); on Morocco, see H. de Castries, "La conquéte du Soudan par el Mansour," *Hespéris* 3 (1923): 433–88; on the Uzbeks, see J. Black, *War and the World: Military Power and the Fate of Continents, 1450–2000* (New Haven, Conn., 1998), 94–95.

2   "Anything which seems genuinely new . . . within cultural impact, in the final analysis appears to be imbedded in traditional structures." E. Zürcher, "Western Expansion and Chinese Reaction: A Theme Reconsidered," in *Expansion and Reaction: Essays on European Expansion and Reactions in Asia and Africa*, ed. H. Wesseling (Leiden, 1978), 77; R. Robinson, "Non-European Foundations of European Imperialism," in *Studies in the Theory of Imperialism*, ed. R. Owen and B. Sutcliffe (London, 1972), 120.

3   A. Disney, ed., *Historiography of Europeans in Africa and Asia, 1450–1800* (Aldershot, 1995), xii–xvi; J. R. Wills, "Was There a Vasco da Gama Epoch?," in *Vasco da Gama and the Linking of Europe and Asia*, ed. A. Disney and E. Booth (New Delhi, 2000), 350–60. The tradition was inaugurated with J. C. van Leur, "On the Eighteenth Century as a Category in Indonesian History," *Indonesian Trade and Society: Essays in Asian Social and Economic History* (La Haya, 1955), 268–89, an essay that was published for the first time during World War II.

4   E. van Veen, *Decay or Defeat? An Inquiry into the Portuguese Decline in Asia, 1580–1645* (Leiden, 2000).

5   J. Le Patourel, *The Norman Empire* (Oxford, 1978).

6   K. R. Hall, *Trade and Statecraft in the Age of the Colas* (New Delhi, 1980).

7   K. R. Hall, *Mandarin Trade and State Development in Early South-East Asia* (Honolulu, 1985); S. Subrahmanyam, *The Portuguese Empire in Asia, 1500–1700: A Political and Economic History* (London, 1993), 9–29; A. Reid, *Southeast Asia in the Age of Commerce*, 2 vols. (New Haven, Conn., 1988–1993), 2:277–303; K. Chaudhuri, *Trade and Civilization in the Indian Ocean* (Cambridge, 1985); *Asia Before Europe* (Cambridge, 1993).

8   Ma Huan, *Ying-yai Sheng-lan: The Overall Survey of the Ocean's Shores [1433]*, ed. J. V. G. Mills (Cambridge, 1970).

9   J. B. Hattendorf, ed., *Maritime History: The Age of Discovery* (Malabar, Fla., 1996).

10  J. Sardina Mimoso, *Relación de la Real Tragicomedia con que los Padres de la Compañía de Jesús en su Colegio de San Antón de Lisboa recibieron a la Magestad Catolica de Felipe II de Portugal y de su entrada en este Reino* (Lisbon, 1620).

11  W. McNeill, *Plagues and Peoples* (New York, 1976); A. W. Crosby, *Ecological Imperialism: The Biological Expansion of Europe, 900–1900* (Cambridge, 1986); H. Hobhouse, *Seeds of Change: Six Plants That Transformed Mankind* (Londres, 1999); A. Viola and C. Margolis, eds., *Seeds of Change* (Washington, D.C., 1991); F. Fernández-Armesto, *Civilizations: Culture, Ambition and the Transformation of Nature* (New York, 2001).

12  D. Birmingham, *Trade and Conflict in Angola: The Mbundu and Their Neighbours under the Influence of the Portuguese, 1483–1790* (Oxford, 1966); P. Manning, *Slavery and African Life: Occidental, Oriental and African Slave Trades* (Cambridge, 1990); J. K. Thornton, *Africa and Africans in the Making of the Atlantic World, 1400–1680* (Cambridge, 1992).

13  Véasa D. Henige, *Numbers from Nowhere: The American Indian Contact Population Debate* (Norman, Okla., 1998); on sub-Saharan Africa, see J. Inikori and S. Engerman, eds., *The Atlantic Slave Trade: Effects on Economics, Society and Peoples in Africa, the Americas and Europe* (Durham, N.C., 1997).

14  D. Ringrose, *Expansion and Global Inter-Action, 1200–1700* (New York, 2001), is the best introduction. In recent years, several different approaches have been offered. On the global system, see F. Braudel, *Civilisation matérielle: Économie et capitalisme, xve–xviiie siècles,* 3 vols. (Paris, 1979), and I. Wallerstein, *The Modern World-System*, 3 vols. (New York, 1974–1989); on the boom of the West, see W. McNeill, *The Rise of the West* (New York, 1972); E. L. Jones, *The European Miracle: Environments, Economies and Geopolitics in the History of Europe and Asia* (Cambridge, 1981); J. Roberts, *The Triumph of the West* (London, 1985); G. Parker, ed., *The Times Atlas of World History,* 4th ed. (Londres, 1993); and D. Landes, *The Wealth and Poverty of Nations* (New York, 1998); on the readjustment in favor of other cultures, see the following pioneering works: J. Needham, *Science and Civilization in China*, 12 vols. (Cambridge, 1956–); D. F. Lach, *Asia in the Making of Europe,* 9 vols. (Chicago, 1965–); J. R. Levenson, *European Expansion and the Counter-Example of Asia* (Englewood Cliffs, N.J., 1967); and M. Hodgson, *The Venture of Islam,* 3 vols. (Chicago, 1974). In the 1990s came, among others, F. Fernández-Armesto, *Millennium: A History of the Last Thousand Years* (New York, 1995, última ed. *Millennium: A History of*

*Our Last Thousand Years* [London, 1999]); J. Goody, *The East in the West* (London, 1996); A. Gunder Frank, *ReOrient: Global Economy in the Asian Age* (Berkeley, Calif., 1998); and E. L. Jones, *Growth Recurring: Economic Change in World History* (Ann Arbor, Mich., 2000). K. Pomeranz, *The Great Divergence: China, Europe and the Making of the Modern World System* (Princeton, N.J., 2000) is an impressive attempt to reach a synthesis. Ultimately, it outlines a union of comparative studies. See, for example, P. D. Curtin, *The World and the West: The European Challenge and the Overseas Response in the Age of Empire* (Cambridge, 2000).

15  C. Verlinden, "European Participation in the Portuguese Discovery Era," in *Portugal the Pathfinder*, ed. G. Winius (Madison, Wis., 1995), 71–80.

16  A. W. Mair, trans., *Works and Days* (Oxford, 1908), 11.

17  F. Fernández-Armesto, *Civilizations: Culture, Ambition and the Transformation of Nature* (New York, 2001), 302–7, 323–45.

18  B. Cunliffe, *Facing the Ocean: The Atlantic and Its Peoples* (Oxford, 2001).

19  A. V. Berkis, *The History of the Duchy of Courland, 1561–1765* (Towson, Md., 1969), 75–79, 144–57, 191–95.

20  Fernandez-Armesto, *Civilizations,* 337–44.

21  F. Fernández-Armesto, "The Sea and Chivalry in Late Medieval Spain," in Hattendorf, *Maritime History,* 137–48; F. Fernández-Armesto, "Exploration and Discovery," in *The New Cambridge Medieval History,* vol. 7, ed. C. Allmand (Cambridge, 1998), 175–201; F. Fernández-Armesto, "England and the Atlantic in the Early Middle Ages," in *England and the Canary Islands throughout History,* A. Béthencourt Massieu et al. (Las Palmas, 1995), 11–28; F. Fernández-Armesto, "The Contexts of Columbus: Myth, Reality and Self-Perception," in *Columbus and the Consequences of 1492,* ed. A. Disney (Melbourne, 1994), 7–19; J. Goodman, *Chivalry and Exploration, 1298–1630* (Woodbridge, Conn., 1998).

22  E. L. Dreyer, *Early Ming China* (Stanford, Calif., 1982), 120.

23  L. F. F. R. Thomaz, "The Economic Policy of the Sultanate of Malacca (XVth–XVIth Centuries)," *Moyen-orient et Océan Indien* 7: 1–12.

24  F. Fernández-Armesto, "The Indian Ocean in World History," in *Vasco da Gama and the Linking of Europe and Asia,* ed. A. Disney and E. Booth (New Delhi, 2000), 11–29.

25  R. Cormack and D. Glaser, eds., *Art of Holy Russia* (London, 1998), 180.

26  T. Armstrong, ed., *Yermack's Campaigns in Siberia* (London, 1975), 38, 41, 43–44, 49–50, 60, 65, 69.

27  Ibid., 40, 46, 108, 138, 290–93; R. H. Fisher, *The Russian Fur Trade, 1550–1700* (Berkeley, Calif., 1943), 21.

28  B. Bobrick, *East of the Sun: The Conquest and Settlement of Siberia* (London, 1993), 43; compare the version in Armstrong, *Yermack's Campaigns in Siberia,* 163: "Unclean son of the dark demon, Bakhunet, leave this land, for the land and its fullness is the Lord's."

29  P. J. D'Orleans, *History of the Tartar Conquerors of China*, ed. The Earl of Ellesmere (London, 1854), 132.

30  C. Varela, ed., *Cristóbal Colón: Textos y documentos* (Madrid, 1984), 142, 145.

31  F. Mauro, *Le Portugal et l'Atlantique au XVIIe siècle, 1570–1670* (Paris, 1960), 113–257.

32  A. Disney, "The Portuguese Empire in India, c. 1550–1650: Some Suggestions for a Less Seaborne, More Landbound Approach to Its Socio-Economic History," in *Indo-Portuguese History: Sources and Problems,* ed. J. Correia-Afonso (Bombay, 1981), 148–62.

33  A. Reid, *Southeast Asia in the Age of Commerce*, 2 vols. (New Haven, Conn., 1988–1993), 2:277–303.

34  B. Bailyn, *Voyagers to the West: Emigration from Britain to America on the Eve of the Revolution* (New York, 1987), 8–20.

35   S. Marzagalli, "The French Atlantic," *Itinerario* 23, no. 2 (1999): 70–83, at 73.

36   J. Carvajal et al., *La aventura de Amazonas* (Madrid, 1992); Mauro, *Le Portugal et l'Atlantique au XVIIe siècle,* 139–40.

37   J. A. von Mandelslo, *Voyages célèbres et remarquables faits de Perse aux Indes orientales* (Amsterdam, 1728).

38   F. Fernández-Armesto, *Millennium* (Barcelona, 1995), 430–31.

39   F. Fernández-Armesto, *Philip II's Empire: A Decade at the Edge* (London, 1999), 3–5.

40   F. Fernández-Armesto, "The Stranger-Effect in Early Modern Asia," *Itinerario* 24, no. 2 (2000): 80–103.

41   M. Restall, *Maya Conquistador* (Boston, 1998).

42   H. E. Cross, "South American Bullion Production and Export, 1550–1750," in *Precious Metals in the Later Medieval and Early Modern Worlds,* ed. J. F. Richards (Durham, N.C., 1983), 397–423; A. Attman, *American Bullion in the European World Trade, 1600–1800* (Göteborg 1986); Frank, *ReOrient,* 131–64, 278–83; V. Magalhães Godinho, *Os descubrimentos e a economia mundial,* 2 vols. (Lisbon, 1963–1965), 1:160–233, 327–47, 379–89. L. Dermigny, *La Chine et l'occident: Le commerce à Canton au XVIIIe siècle*, 3 vols. (Paris, 1964), made an enormous contribution. Pomeranz, *The Great Divergence,* addresses the question of resources in general and the contribution of the New World; about this, see also Fernández-Armesto, *Millennium,* 345–63.

43   Attman, *American Bullion,* 27–29; C. R. Phillips, "Trade in the Iberian Empires," in James D. Tracy, *The Rise of Merchant Empires: Long-Distance Trade in the Early Modern World* (New York, 1990), 34–101, esp. 65.

44   A. Smith, *The Wealth of Nations*, IV.vii.b.61 (1937), 590.

*As in the chapter by Fernández-Armesto, the Atlantic is too small a container to hold the story that Peter A. Coclanis tells, in this case about the history of the rice trade. Coclanis crosses national and oceanic boundaries with abandon because that is precisely what the trade in rice did—and does.*

*It may be clear that any account of today's rice trade, when Arkansas competes for market share with Myanmar (formerly Burma), must be set against a global backdrop. But Coclanis's move is more fundamental than that: he argues that as far back as the Age of Discovery, the rice trade had global dimensions. Even a unit of analysis as capacious as the Atlantic leads to a "truncation problem" when trying to understand the history of the rice trade. An Atlantic analysis of the eighteenth-century rice trade would leave out important connections between the African slave trade, the rice-producing areas of South Carolina and Georgia, and the emergent rice trade between Great Britain and Bengal. In this way, Coclanis's chapter parallels recent work on the global circulation of silver in the early modern period, a flow of specie that connected China, the Philippines, Mexico, and Spain. Coclanis thus joins a nascent historiographical trend that challenges Atlanticists to broaden their oceanic horizons when their subjects warrant such an approach. The question then becomes, What subjects warrant a global approach? Is Coclanis's model better suited to commodities than to peoples?*

# ReOrienting Atlantic History: The Global Dimensions of the "Western" Rice Trade

## Peter A. Coclanis

Let us begin with the credit crisis in the Tharrawaddy District of Lower Burma in 1908. In that year, peasant rice producers all over the district—situated along the Irrawaddy at the head of the Burma delta—found it extremely difficult to get the loans needed to finance their crops. They were accustomed to getting financing from rural moneylenders, particularly Chettiar moneylenders, who were members of a banking caste originating in southern India. But the Chettiar moneylenders in the Tharrawaddy District and in other parts of rural Burma were short on funds that year. Their own sources of capital—their caste compatriots in southern India—were strapped, it seems, and hadn't been able to spare much capital for lending abroad. Why were they so strapped? Because both the Imperial Bank of India and the big Indian banks in Madras—key sources of capital for the Chettiars of southern India—were themselves pinched. The problems these banks faced had originated not in India, however, but with banks headquartered thousands of miles away in Britain—the National Bank, the Mercantile Bank, the Chartered Bank, the P. and O. Bank, and the Lloyds Bank, among others—which at the time were tottering because of liquidity problems of their own, problems that those of us in the "Atlantic World" have come to call the Financial Panic of 1907.[1]

On the surface, the fact that Burmese peasants were implicated in the panic—and were in a sense "saved" a bit later in a deal famously brokered by J. P. Morgan—may seem surprising, for we in the West are used to thinking of the panic as a story largely about New York and London. To be sure, *some* agriculturalists may also have been affected, but we're talking here about bonanza wheat farmers on the Great Plains and large-scale ranchers on the Argentine pampas, right? And why should we in the West care about Burmese rice producers anyway, what with Italy and Spain, and Brazil, and the United States, didn't we have our own sources of rice?

Well, we *did* have our own sources of rice, but by 1908, Burma, long the world's greatest rice exporter, had been the West's leading supplier for over half a century.[2] Moreover, when Burma assumed supremacy in the Western rice trade in the 1850s, it took the lead not from Italy or the United States but from India, which had itself superseded Java not long before. And, really, from the 1790s or early 1800s on—that is to say, from the time it became possible profitably to ship bulk commodities from Asia to Europe—the handwriting was on the wall for Western rice exporters. But few scholars in the West realize this, concerned as they've been with their own little paddies of history. Indeed, but for a few exceptions—most notably, the great economists Arthur H. Cole and W. Arthur Lewis—students of the Western rice trade have seldom factored the East into their interpretive frames, particularly prior to the late nineteenth century.[3] And, unfortunately, this problem is unlikely to be remedied completely through recourse to the Atlantic World gambit, historians' analytical flavor of the decade.

\*\*\*

Over the past thirty-odd years, the historical profession has seen its share of scholarly trends, fashions, and fads—a series of new new things, to use journalist Michael Lewis's terminology. Any short list of "new historical things" would perforce include quantification, the *Annales* paradigm, history from the bottom up, republicanism, and the so-called cultural turn. If each of these new things, in retrospect, was oversold, if each, again in retrospect, can readily be parodied, each was responsible for or at least associated with some positive historical/historiographical developments. I'm all for multiple regression equations, tree-ring analyses, female factory workers, Commonwealth men, and Michel Foucault, then, albeit each in its proper place.

And now, it seems, it's the Atlantic World's turn at the plate. Such is the traction of this conceit among certain (ahem) discursive communities in recent years that it has become rather quaint if not downright parochial to refer to oneself as a mere historian of Habsburg Spain, Stuart England, or eighteenth-century British North America. Much better to be viewed as an Atlanticist, as being "trans" something or other, or, at least, to be frequenting liminal areas, breaching imperial boundaries, or slouching toward the interstitial.

Why? What is it about the Atlantic that has rocked historians' worlds? Before answering these questions, it might be a good idea to lay out if not a definition of at least an approach to our assumptions about the subject. This task is not as easy as it appears to be at first glance. Even before the concept had its sea legs, so to speak, scholars were fighting over its origins and trajectory, not to mention its purview and meaning. I've touched on such debates elsewhere and won't repeat myself here.[4] Suffice it to say that scholars differ sharply over the genealogy of "Atlantic history," finding its roots in traditions ranging from classical Marxism to imperial history to Catholic universalism. Some believe the concept is most applicable to—or at least resonates best in—the period between about 1500 and 1800 C.E., while others (including the editors of this volume) extend Atlantic history's bounds backward or forward by a century or two. Some scholars believe the concept makes most sense as an organizational scheme when considering biological, economic, or demographic themes, while others privilege cultural concerns, particularly institutions and the circulation of ideas. Still others, proponents of a "big tent" approach, would include all the above considerations.[5]

One overriding assumption—or "covering idea," as Bernard Bailyn puts it—seems to be shared by all proponents of Atlantic history, however: during a significant chunk of time, extending at least from 1500 through 1800, the Atlantic World—which is to say, western Europe, the Americas, and West Africa—was sufficiently integrated as to invite if not require treatment in a relatively unitary manner. To this simple expression must be added the usual scholarly caveats and qualifications, and various and sundry nits can be—and will be—picked by tweedy academics. Not here, but there, not yet, what about this, and so on. Nonetheless, the central interpretive point of the "Atlantic" approach or perspective seems to be captured in this expression.[6]

Now I'll be the first to acknowledge that in many ways an integrated approach to the history of the Atlantic basin makes greater sense than more fragmented alternatives. Moreover, I do not doubt that what David Armitage calls trans-, circum-, and cis-Atlantic approaches can enhance our understanding of many types of historical problems, most notably those relating to bodies and constellations of ideas.[7] Nonetheless, I am not convinced that this "covering idea" covers enough, and my problems with the Atlantic approach/perspective transcend caveat, qualification, or nit. Rather, my problems are global in nature, as is the solution, at least in my view.

In the remainder of this chapter—a case study of the "Western" rice trade—I shall argue for the efficacy of a "global history" approach, that is, a more embracive covering idea still. This approach seems particularly efficacious when dealing with issues relating to the material world—commodity and capital flows, biological exchanges, and the like—but, as Jerry Bentley among others have shown, it may in certain cases prove useful in other realms as well.[8] In the case of the rice trade, a global approach clearly reduces if not eliminates the fatal flaw of Atlantic approaches: the problem of evidentiary and analytical truncation.

For just as geometric truncation of a figure or a solid means that the apex, vortex, or end is cut off by a plane, just as truncation in prose means that a line of verse lacks at the beginning or end one or more unstressed syllables needed to fill out the metrical pattern, truncation in the history of the rice trade—lopping off the "world" beyond the African Cape—renders inexplicable that which would be explained.

***

Marxism, the old, old thing, is not much in vogue in academic circles today, probably for good reason. Not to get misty eyed here, but I always found two things about Marxism, particularly Marxist sociology, to be very instructive: first, the idea that everything is related and that social phenomena should perforce be considered in toto and, second, the belief that, ceteris paribus, material forces ultimately rule. (Or as one of Mark Twain's characters—a black slave preacher— put the latter point in Twain's essay *Corn-pone Opinions*, "You tell me whar a man gets his corn pone, en I'll tell you what his 'pinions is.")[9] These two ideas—the relational and the material, as it were—have guided much of my scholarship over the years and helped trigger my ongoing interest in global economic history.

***

There's a neat children's book by Norah Dooley called *Everybody Cooks Rice*, which relates the story of a girl in an immigrant neighborhood of a modern American city who is asked to fetch her little brother for dinner. The girl goes up and down her street in search of her brother, stopping on the way at houses resided in by Barbadians, Puerto Ricans, Vietnamese, Indians, Chinese, and Haitians, respectively, to inquire about her brother's whereabouts. In each case, the residents were cooking rice, for, as the book's title states, *everybody* cooks rice![10] Almost everybody in any case.

It wasn't always that way, for rice is an "Old World" cultigen with a venerable and complicated genealogy. There are two main species of rice grown today: *Oryza sativa* and *Oryza glaberrima*.The former originated in Asia, the latter in West Africa. *Oryza sativa* is the older and by far the more important of the two, and the world rice trade has been completely dominated by this species for as long back as records exist. Cultivation of *Oryza sativa* began in southern China or perhaps in parts of mainland Southeast Asia almost 10,000 years ago. It spread gradually through much of Asia, and between about 700 and 1100 C.E., via a remarkable process of biological and technological diffusion, rice was transferred by Arab traders—or by those they conquered—from India throughout the Middle East, around the Mediterranean, to the savanna lands contiguous to the Sahara, to West Africa, and to the coastal zones of East Africa, among other places. That rice was already grown in certain *parts* of the Middle East, the Mediterranean littoral, and Africa prior to this diffusion—in Persia, Egypt, and Sicily, for example—does not diminish the magnitude of the transformation in rice geography attending the spread of Islam. *Oryza sativa* (and to a lesser degree *Oryza glaberrima*) spread to the Americas in the late fifteenth or early sixteenth century as part of the so-called Columbian exchange, and rice cultivation became relatively widespread through various tropical and semi-tropical areas in the Western Hemisphere over the next few centuries. During the so-called early modern period, then, rice was grown in huge quantities in many parts of Asia and in significant quantities in certain parts of Africa, Europe, and the Americas as well.[11]

Earlier in this chapter, I mused a bit on the relational and the material. Before moving on to the relational aspects of rice, that is, its trade and exchange, let me say something about matters material, that is, about the nature—and uses—of the grain. In this regard, it is not merely plausible but strongly defensible to argue, first of all, that rice has long been and is still today the world's most important cereal, with maize and wheat being its only serious rivals. Eaten by about half the earth's population today, rice is the leading staple in the world, and rice farming constitutes the single largest use of land for food production. (That roughly 9 percent of the earth's arable land—about 125 million hectares—is currently devoted to rice testifies powerfully to this last point.) Moreover, it is today—again, as it has long been—the single greatest food source for the world's poor, and rice farming constitutes the single greatest source of employment for the world's poor. At between 354 and 362 kilocalories per 100 grams (almost all small grains run somewhere between 320 and 365), rice continues to account for a very substantial proportion of the total caloric intake of the entire world population even today. Just do the numbers.[12]

From the previous discussion, it should be clear that rice maintains a hugely prominent place in the world food system, but what about the *place* of rice in a literal sense? That is to say, what about its economic and cultural geography? First of all, it is important to note that rice is consumed in situ or near to the site of its production to a far greater degree than is the case with the world's other great cereals. Given this fact, it is not surprising to learn that a far smaller proportion of the world's rice crop ends up being exported than is the case with wheat, for example. Moreover, despite its huge role in the *world* food system, rice is not produced or consumed to the same extent, much less in the same way or with the same cultural resonance, everywhere. Indeed, on disaggregation, rice production and consumption patterns are marked by extreme variation.[13]

In Asia, of course, the role of rice—economically, socially, culturally, and cosmically—is difficult to exaggerate. At this juncture, scholars trying to demonstrate this point typically provide a few linguistic or cultural examples—the Hindi word for rice, *dhanya*, means "sustainer of the human race"; in traditional Chinese society the idiomatic expression "Have you eaten your rice today?" was a polite way of saying hello; and so on—or make mention of iron rice bowls or go psychoanalytic by discoursing on "rice as self." Let me use some blunter instruments to get to the same place: "Toyota" means "bountiful rice field" in Japanese, and "Honda" means the "main rice field." Bangladeshis and Cambodians even today get 76 percent of their daily calories from rice, Burmese 73 percent, Laotians 70 percent, Vietnamese 65 percent, and Indonesians 52 percent. By way of contrast, Americans get 3 percent of theirs from rice. Rice is not just *self* in much of Asia, then, but nearly everything else as well.[14]

The situation differs dramatically in most of the West. To be sure, Asia is not "all rice all the time," as is sometimes assumed. Some parts of the region have long been linked to other staples: wheat and sorghum in northern China and gram and lentils in some areas of India, for example. But unlike the case in Asia, such cultigens—particularly small grains, maize, and manioc/cassava—dominate by a huge margin in Europe, Africa, and the Americas. Breadwinners rather than rice winners, westerners, by and large, pray for their daily bread, not their daily bowl of rice (iron or otherwise!).

The limited role of rice in the West is suggested as well by its slippery and fugitive status in the marketplace. If rice is grown in many different places in the West and is vendible in more, it is considered indispensable in only a few. The Western rice trade has always been quite variable as a result, particularly at the margin. The center of this trade has generally been in northern Europe—primarily Germany and the Netherlands, which over time developed considerable milling complexes—but the ultimate consumers of the rice entering this area have often resided elsewhere, whether far down the Rhine or Danube or in the Americas or even West Africa.[15]

Despite its market limitations, rice has long had a variety of uses in the West. Indeed, the cereal's versatility helps explain the persistence, pervasiveness, and elusiveness of the Western rice trade over the centuries. For example, rice has long served certain ceremonial functions in many parts of the West—at weddings, for example—and it often cropped up in past times in Western pharmacopoeia/materia medica. At times, it seems to have been treated as a luxury item, even as a superior good, the demand for which rose with price. At the end of the day, though, it wasn't ceremony, pharmacy, or luxury that explains rice's importance in the West. Rather, the interest in and demand for the cereal derived principally from its transformation during the latter half of the early modern period—the heyday of the alleged Atlantic economy—into a cheap everyday *commodity* with multiple alimentary, intermediate, and industrial usages, a number of them murky and inconspicuous if not invisible.[16]

Rice and its by-products found employment in the starch and paper industries, for example, and were used extensively for animal feed (particularly in what later would be called Germany). In the eighteenth century, liqueurs such as brandies and arrack often included rice among their ingredients, and later rice became a standard input in the brewing industry. Middle-class consumers often purchased rice as a nutritional complement or supplement—with or instead of pulses or potatoes, for example. Over the course of the eighteenth century and increasingly in the nineteenth, rice came to be viewed (and utilized) as a relatively cheap dietary staple, especially useful for feeding commoners and *lumpen* groups—laborers, soldiers, sailors, inmates, orphans, and those on the dole—in the absence of or instead of other cereals. No longer a supplement or complement, rice, at least for certain groups, had thus become a substitute for other, pricier staples.[17]

Again, however, let me reiterate that one must nonetheless proceed with caution when speaking of demand for rice in the West. As I said earlier, this subject is murky—and complicated. For example, because rice, like most cereals, has generally been found to be a highly income-inelastic foodstuff, it seems reasonable to focus on commoners and *lumpen* groups when studying human consumption, right? Maybe, maybe not. One should note that rice demand was general rather than class specific during periods of harvest failures and shortfalls in the West, and rice, as we have seen, was used in a number of foods, medicines, and beverages and in a number of industrial products, the demand for which in numerous cases was much more income elastic.[18] Finally, as the rich work of Thomas Haskell, among others, suggests, much of what is viewed (and interpreted) as "*lumpen*" demand for rice actually sprung from a new sensibility among other wealthier social groups and constellations. That is to say, a new or at least enhanced social preference for feeding the "dregs of society" (sometimes with rice) rather than letting them suffer malnutrition if not starve outright can itself be treated as a kind of income-elastic psychic good or commodity.[19]

Enough here about the demand for rice in the West. Let us move to an equally thorny problem: the manner in which said demand was met. As mentioned earlier, cultivation of *Oryza sativa* in the West was due primarily to transmission mechanisms initiated or fostered, directly or indirectly, by Arabs. Saracens, Turks, Moors, Malays, Indians, and others are thus credited with introducing the cultivation of *Oryza sativa* to various parts of Africa and Europe, particularly in the latter part of the first millennium C.E. As suggested earlier, however, even before the Arabic diffusion the great classical civilizations—Egypt, Greece, and Rome—were familiar with *Oryza sativa* from their contacts/conquests in the East.[20]

Both the Greeks and the Romans often imported rice from India and the Middle East, and during the medieval period European merchants, primarily Italians, imported rice via the Levant for distribution to various parts of the Continent. During the same period, rice was traded in significant quantities along the east coast of Africa, on Madagascar, and on other East African islands by merchants of diverse origins involved in the robust Indian Ocean trade. Although small amounts of rice were already being grown along the Mediterranean littoral, European cultivation began in earnest only with the Moors' incursion into Spain in the eighth century and the concomitant thrust by the Turks into southeastern Europe and the Balkans. Both Spain and southeastern Europe have remained rice-producing areas ever since, but beginning in the late fifteenth century, populations on another part of the Continent, Italy, commenced rice production, and Italy quickly became the center of European production and trade.[21]

While rice was grown on the island of Sicily since antique times, it was not Sicily but northern Italy—particularly present-day Piedmont and Lombardy—that proved most congenial to rice cultivation. Once the cereal was introduced to northern Italy by the Spanish—the first direct reference to production in the region dates from 1475—rice quickly gained a foothold, especially in the rich alluvial valleys of the upper Po. By the sixteenth century, rice from the region was being traded along the Italian peninsula and to other parts of Europe, where it competed with rice imported via the Levant by Venetian traders. This was the status of the "Western" rice trade around the time that the so-called Age of Exploration—and, according to some, the Atlantic economy—began.[22]

The Age of Exploration is, of course, one of the most complex, controversial, and historically charged conceptual schemes in modern historiography. Without getting bogged down in complexity or controversy—I'll skip over moral outrage altogether—let me just say in passing that the onset (intensification?) of said exploration was at once related to and a function of Europe's economic dynamism during the long sixteenth century. Whether one prefers to interpret such dynamism as a manifestation of the simultaneous birth of European capitalism or as a result or concomitant of that system's gradual development over the course of several centuries, it is clear that such dynamism expressed itself in outward economic thrusts by organized collectivities of Europeans—public, public/private, and private—both to the West and to the East. Indeed, early on in the period it seems anachronistic even to attempt to distinguish between discrete "Atlantic" and other—what shall we call them, "non-Atlantic" or "extra-Atlantic"?—thrusts, particularly when most "thrusters," Atlantic or otherwise, were certainly searching for the East.

This is not to say that in the centuries that followed differences did not emerge between the so-called Atlantic World and other outlets for European expansion. Differential structures of opportunity channeled European labor and capital, energy, and entrepreneurship down different paths with differential outcomes. Even so, the degree of separation between the "Atlantic World" and the rest of the world is chronically overstated, as the rich work on silver, China, and the Manila Galleon by Dennis O. Flynn and Arturo Giráldez has shown, as close analyses of "European" treaties during the early modern period demonstrate (almost all these treaties, such as Breda, Ryswick, Utrecht, Aix-la-Chapelle, and Paris, have important provisions relating to Asia), and as the following examination of the "Western" rice trade will corroborate.[23]

Soon after rice production began in Piedmont and Lombardy, northern Italy became the key producing area in Europe, which status it has retained for the past 500 years. And Italian rice, as we have seen, quickly began to trade in European markets, often via the offices of Rhineland traders as well as the German Hanse. During the sixteenth and seventeenth centuries, surplus rice from Italy, supplemented by small quantities of rice originating in Spain, the Middle East, and India (in the latter two cases, Venetian merchants continued to serve as the principal conduits), accounted for pretty much all the rice traded in extraregional and export markets in the West. The total value of this trade was small, for, as we have seen, relatively few European *breadwinners* at the time thought about—much less prayed for or, the bottom-line consideration here, *consumed*—rice on a daily basis.[24]

Things gradually began to change, however. Although rice has never become the "staff of life" for westerners, in the late seventeenth century and increasingly in the eighteenth, as suggested earlier, its uses began to multiply, and its usefulness became more and more apparent. Why? In retrospect it seems clear that rising population and income in parts of Europe, northern Europe in particular, had led to an increase in aggregate demand necessary and sufficient to broaden and deepen considerably the Western market for a wide range of goods, including rice, which, as we have seen, fulfilled a variety of alimentary and industrial needs. Whether because of pigs, paste, or the poor, as it were, demand for rice grew, and Western capital and capitalists, already in dazzling motion, were not slow to pick up on this.[25] The expansion of the northern Italian rice complex was one result.[26] The search for or, less insistently, the openness toward the possibility of new supply platforms was another.

In some ways, of course, the story of rice is the story, writ *small*, of the so-called Age of Discovery. That is to say, rising income and output per capita in Europe during the early modern period (achieved via a multiplicity of factors ranging from increased agricultural productivity to a secular decline in transactions costs) sparked changes in the schedules of both demand and supply, which changes encouraged and facilitated expanded economic contacts with other parts of the world. At a certain level of abstraction, Europe's outward thrust can thus be read as a rational market response to perceived economic opportunities.

This led in the East to the establishment—via invitation or compulsion—of European trading factories and to the rerouting to some degree of intra-Asian trade and, in the West, to direct European involvement in or at least supervision of production itself. Indeed, in this effort, one can see, however faintly, the beginnings of a Western-inspired "global" economy. To be sure, long-distance, intercontinental trade pre-dated the era of the English East India Company and the Dutch East India Company by a millennium or two and was especially well developed, apparently, in the Indian Ocean and South China Sea. But prior to the European thrust outward, no social formations, economic classes, or political constellations—anywhere (pace Andre Gunder Frank)—attempted, even rudimentarily, to integrate factor and product markets on a global basis.[27]

Not that the Europeans achieved overnight success in this endeavor. Globalization, such as it was, proved a halting process, two steps forward, one step back. Prior to the late seventeenth or even the early eighteenth century, Western-inspired global trade, generally speaking, was quantitatively insignificant, often entailing the intermittent or, at most, periodic exchange of precious metals, spices, luxury goods, and so-called preciosities of relatively limited market purview: silver for porcelain, silk, nutmeg, and edible bird's-nests.

But in the eighteenth century—even a bit earlier in some places—European merchant capital, supported when necessary by state power, succeeded in regularizing and routinizing such trade. In many cases, it did so only after regularizing and routinizing or even initiating production itself. And over time, it succeeded as well in shifting the emphasis of world trade from precious metals and preciosities, so to speak, to bulk commodities, of which rice was one: not the major one by any means—not when the list of such commodities included sugar, coffee, tea, tobacco, cotton, and later tin and rubber as well—but an interesting and revealing commodity nonetheless. Moreover, this was a commodity that played an important intermediary role in the production and exchange of other, higher-profile trades.[28]

The obvious place for Europeans to get additional (and cheaper) rice during the early modern period was Asia. At the time, Asia was producing at least 95 percent of the world's rice, and the cereal had been trading in significant quantities—as Europeans well knew—around the Indian Ocean basin and the South China Sea for centuries, typically to deficit areas during times of harvest failure and after the types of catastrophic weather "events" to which, as Eric Jones has demonstrated, large swaths of Asia were prone. Europeans and West Africans weren't dummies, then, and, not surprisingly, modest amounts of Asian rice did in fact flow into both areas throughout this period. The limited size of the market for imported rice in Europe (and Africa), the cereal's value-to-weight ratio, and time and distance concerns held back the tide of Asian rice at least for a time. In retrospect, it is clear that the "world" market that European merchant capital (and its legatees) was creating was not yet sufficiently integrated, demand for rice in the West was not sufficiently large, Asia–Europe transactions costs were still too high, and the opportunity costs of shifting over to the cereal were too great to justify the trouble and expense of rerouting systematically the intra-Asian rice trade to the West.

What other options were out there? There were existing producing areas in Europe, the Levant, and West Africa, but these areas posed various problems: high production costs, inelastic supply possibilities, weak institutional/political supports, and, in the case of West Africa in particular, a prohibitively morbid and mortal disease environment, to name but a few. Better perhaps to seek out, encourage, support, and finance—directly or indirectly—new production complexes in other, less distant locales, which is exactly what European merchant capital did. And so, rice—a plant that can be grown almost anywhere—was tried on an experimental basis in various and sundry European staging areas, that is, colonies in the Western Hemisphere. Rice was tried in the central Andes, in the West Indies, along the eastern coast of Mexico, and in the tidewater of Virginia, for example. By the early eighteenth century, however, two areas became the focal points of rice production in the "New World," northeastern Brazil, and the youthful British colony of South Carolina. By the middle of the eighteenth century, the latter had in all likelihood already surpassed Italy to become the West's leading rice supplier, and one must perforce ask why.[29]

Not surprisingly, South Carolina, along with neighboring Georgia, which soon became a major exporter as well, possessed a number of attributes that help explain why rice proved so successful there *at that time*. First of all, the physical environment of the coastal plain of both South Carolina and Georgia—although highly morbid and highly mortal—was also highly conducive to rice production. Both the region's human and nonhuman capital resources and its market position by the mid-eighteenth century were equally propitious.

By the middle of the eighteenth century, an ample, cost-efficient, disciplined, and technologically skilled African and Creole labor force was available, at least some members of which had cultivated rice in West Africa.[30] In light of this chapter's theme, it is extremely interesting to note that the trade that brought African labor—and its knowledge regarding risiculture—to South Carolina and Georgia was closely tied to Asia, for cowry shells from the Maldive Islands and Indian cotton textiles ("long cloths," "Guinea cloths," allijars, salemporis, and the like) were among the items most sought after on the African side of things.[31] While on matters of human capital, let me stress that it would be a mistake—one historians today often make—to forget the vigorous and aggressive behavior of the European and Euro-American entrepreneurs who rendered possibilities into reality, that is, who organized and financed production and long-distance trade and, in so doing, created a rice *industry*. Without the same, African knowledge about rice wouldn't have mattered nearly so much. Think sorghum here, another African transplant, but one that didn't command similar interest among the European and Euro-American entrepreneurial communities. In any case, the physical environment, African knowledge, and European and Euro-American entrepreneurship—along with transport costs, market information, and the degree of integration of what was still a rudimentary global economy—favored this region over other rice-producing alternatives, including both Asian alternatives and "Atlantic World" alternatives such as Maranhão and Pará in northeastern Brazil.[32]

In world-historical terms, North American supremacy in the "Western" rice trade did not last long. During the first half of the nineteenth century, the South Carolina–Georgia rice region, despite producing more rice than ever before, saw itself surpassed as a supply source for the principal Western markets. The region fell behind for a variety of reasons, some more important than others. The amount of land suitable for rice cultivation—cultivation increasingly dependent on tidal irrigation technology—was limited by geography. At its peak in 1859, roughly 175,000 to 200,000 acres (71,000 to 81,000 hectares) were in production in this region, and by then some of the best land in the tidal zone was losing fertility. Moreover, the simultaneous expansion westward of the U.S. cotton industry hurt the coastal rice region in two significant ways: first, such expansion forced coastal rice planters to compete for outside capital—northern, British, and Dutch mainly—with a more dynamic industry, and, second, profit possibilities in what Sven Beckert calls the "empire of cotton" actually led to the siphoning off of a good part of indigenous entrepreneurship and capital (including capitalized labor, i.e., slaves) from the rice region itself.[33]

This said, it would nonetheless be a mistake to focus primarily much less solely on internal constraints in explaining the relative decline of the South Carolina–Georgia rice region, for the economic geography of international rice supply was being drastically transformed at precisely the same time. There were, for example, some developments in the West that adversely affected the South Carolina–Georgia rice region: the Portuguese market was "lost" to Brazil as early as the 1790s, Spanish needs were increasingly met by domestic producers in Valencia, and Italian rice continued to claim segments of the European market. The stagnation and ultimate demise of the South Carolina–Georgia rice industry was not due chiefly to competition from these areas or, for that matter, to competition from other official, dues-paying, card-carrying members of the "Atlantic economy." Rather, the region's fate was determined by and large by competition from the other side of the world, from Bengal, then Java, then a bit later from Lower Burma, Siam, and Cochin China (map 1).[34]

If Asian suppliers emerged as a viable threat *in this particular industry* only in the 1790s, other industries in the West—industries ranging from textiles to ceramics to saltpeter—had long known what competition from Asia was all about. Indeed, all the major "Atlantic" powers—England/Britain, the Netherlands, Portugal, Spain, and France—were *directly* engaged commercially in Asia from the sixteenth century on (England/Britain, the Netherlands, and Portugal deeply so), and almost from the start various observers in the West wrote on, expected, hoped for, and feared Asian economic rivals. Until the late eighteenth century, Western suppliers of rice had little to fear, but by that time global market integration had proceeded sufficiently as to allow Asian rice entrée into Western markets.[35] In a proximate way, all it would take was a harvest failure or two—failures such as those in Britain in the mid-1790s—to render Asian competition in rice a reality. In a deeper sense, though, it should be noted that such failures happened just as time and distance were being shrunk by technology and, in the specific case of Britain, for example, just as policymakers were both looking East and articulating and promoting a strategy of economic globalization or, as some (in my view, erroneously) would have it, moving from British Empire I to British Empire II. Just as this imperial two-step will not do, one cannot understand the huge flow of Asian rice into the West in the nineteenth century without cognizance of the long-running East–West pas de deux.[36]

Although (as we have seen) small amounts of Asian rice had long been arriving in Europe both via the Levant and via the route around the African Cape, the entire context changed as a result of Clive's victory at Plassey in 1757. In the generation after this victory, Bengali raw materials—indigo, cotton, saltpeter, sugar, flax, and spices—began

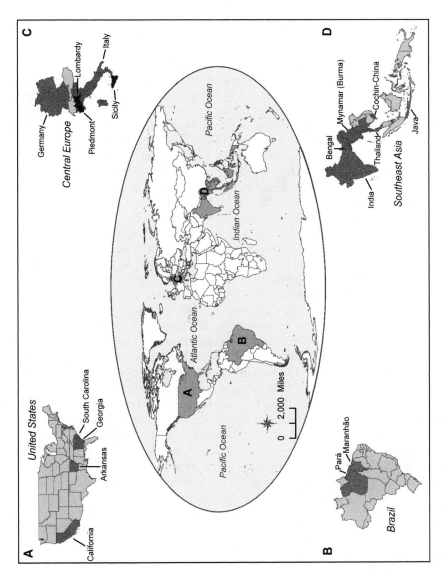

**Map 1**   Global Rice Production.

to pour into Europe. As a result of bad harvests in Britain in 1795 and 1800, rice imports surged as well, and by the 1820s rice produced by Bengali peasants was cutting significantly into South Carolina and Georgia's principal markets in northern Europe (indeed, into Italy's markets as well). Given what I said earlier about the uses to which rice was put in the West, it is important—and revealing—to note that political economist David MacPherson, writing in 1795, pointed out that rice was the first "necessary" sent in significant quantities to the West from Asia, all previous trade consisting of articles and products "rather of ornament and luxury than of use."[37]

The fact that India began to serve as a key source of rice was clearly related as well to a strategic shift on the part of British statesmen in the last third of the eighteenth century. As a result of said shift or reprioritization, potential trading partners in both the Indian Ocean and the Pacific were (depending on one's point of view) either coerced into or encouraged to reroute existing trade or establish new trade connections with Western partners. This shift was viewed by men such as Pitt the Younger, the Earl of Shelburne, Henry Dundas, and William Grenville as part of a broader initiative to create a truly global commercial order involving Europe, Asia, and the Americas, an order that would be organized and controlled by Britain operating in a titular sense at least under the premises and ideology of "free trade."[38]

From this jumping-off point in Bengal in the 1790s, it was but a small step for European (and Asian) merchant capitalists either to set up rice export platforms or to reconfigure existing platforms in adjacent areas of Southeast Asia: first on Java, then in Tenasserim and Arakan ("the granary of the Bay of Bengal"), and a bit later in Lower Burma more generally and Siam and Cochin China. Within decades—well before the American Civil War, U.S. historians should note—South and Southeast Asian exporting areas had knocked the South Carolina–Georgia rice region out of its most important markets, beginning the long-term, spiraling fall of the region into economic oblivion. At the same time, other Western exporters—Italy most notably—were rendered irrelevant even as the Western rice market grew exponentially as a result of a complicated (and intercorrelated) mélange of factors—rising income per capita, urbanization, and industrialization among them. Indeed, given the uses to which rice was put in the West, the proletarianization of much of the European labor force as well as the expansion of the slave labor force in parts of the Americas (Cuba, for example) helps explain the surge in demand for rice as well. Interestingly enough, in a way the "Western" market for rice was growing dramatically *in Asia* at the same time as European interests (particularly British and Dutch) established mining and plantation-crop zones in places such as Malaya and Sumatra, zones that quickly became heavily dependent on imported rice.[39]

By the late nineteenth century, the domination of world rice markets by Asian suppliers was virtually complete, as several powerful developments in transport and communications—the rise of steamshipping, the opening of the Suez Canal, and the laying of the transoceanic cable, most notably—rendered the region's significant competitive advantages greater still. Not surprisingly, the challenge posed by Asian exports wreaked havoc on Western rice suppliers even as cheap Asian rice helped keep Western factories humming and Western bellies full. This is not to say that Western rice interests sat on their hands, though. The rise of the West had not been achieved through inertia and inaction, and, when confronted with what must have seemed to some an inexorable, perhaps inevitable process and to others as a cataclysmic shock, rice interests mobilized and for the most part responded robustly, if with only mixed success, at least at first. Tariff barriers against Asian imports were erected virtually everywhere, and the geography of rice production shifted dramatically: in the United States from the Southeast to Louisiana, Texas, Arkansas, and, a bit later, California and in Brazil from the northeast southward to Rio, São Paulo, and eventually Rio Grande do Sul, for example. The geographic shift coincided with—indeed, in large part was driven by—new production technology as producers strove furiously to find a way to drive down costs or, failing at that, to find other ways to survive the Asian onslaught. Over time, producers in some parts of the West were able to do just that, and by the 1920s a radically different rice industry had emerged in such areas. This new industry—the epicenters of which in the United States were east-central Arkansas and the Sacramento Valley of California and in Brazil the Rio Grande do Sul—was predicated on "high modernist" assumptions: virtuosic forms of hydraulic engineering, the substitution of capital for labor, the government-sanctioned union of science and industry, and, not least, a "supportive" environment created by a developmentally minded state. (To some extent, the rice industries of Italy and Spain began to partake of some of these same characteristics, too.) Operating in this climate, "new rice" not only survived but sometimes flourished, florescence signified by retention or recapture of segments of domestic markets and the return to certain targeted export markets as well.[40]

If this chapter were concerned mainly with shifting comparative advantage/competitive superiority in the world rice trade, I would now explain in detail—and demonstrate both empirically and statistically—how and why Asia rose to dominance when it did and then detail the differential supply responses on the part of Western producers/producing areas. If, instead, this were a technical work, focused, let us say, around the integration of hitherto discrete, nonintegrated markets, I would produce price series as well as evidence of both price convergence and the "law of one price" gaining sway worldwide.[41] As I have been working on rice for some time, I can point interested readers to places where I have in fact written on precisely these themes. Rather, this chapter is concerned with something harder to "prove" but no less important: the relationship between Asia and the West and the danger of downplaying if not severing the connections between the two. If the Atlantic approach represents an improvement over narrow national approaches to analyzing the history of the "Western" rice trade, this approach still suffers from a truncation problem, leaving students and scholars alike unappreciative if not unaware of the big picture in the early modern period and, as a result, unprepared adequately to explain the hegemonic position Asian rice achieved in Western markets in the nineteenth century.

***

In June 1995, I spent a few weeks in Arkansas doing archival and field research on the U.S. rice industry. While there, I spent a week in the Grand Prairie region of east-central Arkansas—the focal point of the American rice industry today—at places like De Wit, Forest City, and especially Stuttgart (pronounced as in the word *strut*), where a famous rice experiment station is located. At Stuttgart, I talked to a lot of soil scientists, plan geneticists, breeders, and so on and spent a good bit of time with Stewart Jessup, former president of Riceland Foods, the largest rice co-op in the United States. I visited the unassuming and, in many ways, charming Stuttgart Agricultural Museum and visited some implement dealers. I learned a lot from all this, but I learned even more from spending some time in the fields. For Stuttgart is the site of the most advanced, capital-intensive "hydraulic agricultural system" in the world. It is a world of massive irrigation works and seeding and spraying by air (the 1996 GTE telephone directory for Stuttgart listed twenty-seven separate aerial-dusting services, for example) and a world of self-propelled tractor/cultivator/combines that are satellite guided and employ Global Positioning System (GPS) technology, mounted computers, and laser-directed delivery systems developed by the U.S. Department of Agriculture's National Soil Tilth Labs in Ames, Iowa, to regulate and vary the amount and composition of fertilizer dropped every couple of inches based on soil needs, past yields, and future potential. Most of all, it is an agricultural world virtually devoid of people—that is, vast irrigated prairies where two workers can easily cultivate 750 acres (303.6 hectares) with yields of 5,500 pounds of clean rice per acre. Indeed, but for an aluminum shed here, a pumping station there, there were few signs of life at all, producing a curiously disembodied alienating cultural landscape, less like that evoked by the writer Wendell Berry than that suggested by the novelist Don Delillo or, better yet, Frederick Barthelme. I learned a lot in Stuttgart on that trip.[42]

Cut to Southeast Asia, January 1996. I'm in Myanmar, the country formerly known as Burma, for the fourth time since 1993. This is the second time I've actually been allowed into an archive there—namely, special collections at the Universities' Central Library in Yangon (Rangoon)—but more important is the time I spend outside the village of Go Pin Chauk, two hours south of Pyi (Prome) in Bago District, Lower Division, an area that was once included in the Tharrawaddy District, with which district I began this chapter. At Go Pin Chauk, I meet with the village headman—a cart maker—who takes me to meet a dozen rice farmers underneath a thatch-and-atap hut, which is up on stilts adjacent to the village rice fields. Along with two Burmese translators, I sit on a rough-hewn bench underneath the house, among various and sundry children, a horse, chickens, two cows, and a water buffalo. I ask questions and listen to the assembled farmers, ranging in age from their late twenties to early eighties, as they answer them.

Go Pin Chauk is as far from Stuttgart as can be imagined. Much of rural Burma has no electricity (let alone GPS technology), few paved roads, little agricultural mechanization, and only rudimentary water control. The "Green Revolution" package—HYVs (high-yielding varieties), commercial fertilizers, mechanized equipment, and so on—has been intermittently tried, but for the most part risiculture in Go Pin Chauk is still about hand implements, the water buffalo, and the monsoon.[43]

A decade later, not much has changed. Despite the vast difference, literally and figuratively, between Stuttgart and Go Pin Chauk—between Arkansas and Burma, as it were—the areas share certain things in common: they are still economic rivals, and they are both among the leading rice-exporting areas in the world and have been competing against each other for a long, long time. This said, the histories of Arkansas and Burma are *never* connected by historians of the West or by historians of the East for that matter, to the detriment of scholarship on each of these arenas. The manner in which Stuttgart and Go Pin Chauk—and other rice-exporting areas around the world—were brought together and the analytics of their links is an interesting and suggestive story with huge implications, however, which is why I have attempted to tell it here. If readers, whether East or West, would take away from this chapter just *one* point, I'd be gratified, that point being, as William Carlos Williams put it in opening book 2 of his great poem *Paterson*, "outside, outside myself, there is a world . . . "[44]

## Notes

1   See *Burma Gazetteer: Tharrawaddy District, Volume A* (Rangoon, 1959); *Report of the Burma Provincial Banking Enquiry Committee, 1929–1930*, 3 vols. (Rangoon, 1930); and Cheng Siok-Hwa, *The Rice Industry of Burma 1852–1940* (Singapore, 1968), 137–97. On the role of the Chettiars in British Burma, see Cheng, *The Rice Industry*, 187–90; Michael Adas, "Immigrant Asians and the Economic Impact of European Imperialism: The Role of the South Indian Chettiars in British Burma," *Journal of Asian Studies* 33 (1974): 385–401; and David West Rudner, *Caste and Capitalism in Colonial India: The Nattukottai Chettiars* (Berkeley, Calif., 1994), 79–85.

2   Peter A. Coclanis, "Southeast Asia's Incorporation into the World Rice Market: A Revisionist View," *Journal of Southeast Asian Studies* 24 (1993): 251–67.

3   Arthur H. Cole, "The American Rice-Growing Industry: A Study of Comparative Advantage," *Quarterly Journal of Economics* 41 (1927): 595–643; W. Arthur Lewis, *Growth and Fluctuations, 1870–1913* (London, 1978), 201–2 and passim. See also A. J. H. Latham, *Rice: The Primary Commodity* (London, 1998).

4   Peter A. Coclanis, "*Drang Nach Osten:* Bernard Bailyn, the World-Island, and the Idea of Atlantic History," *Journal of World History* 13 (2002): 169–82.

5   On the various genealogies, conceptualizations, and chronologies of Atlantic history, see, for example, Coclanis, "*Drang Nach Osten*"; Bernard Bailyn, "The Idea of Atlantic History," *Itinerario* 20 (1996): 19–44; Felipe Fernández-Armesto, "The Origins of the European Atlantic," *Itinerario* 24 (2000): 111–28; David Armitage, "Three Concepts of Atlantic History," in *The British Atlantic World, 1500–1800*, ed. David Armitage and Michael J. Braddick (New York, 2002), 11–27; and J. H. Elliott, "Atlantic History: A Circumnavigation," in Armitage and Braddick, *The British Atlantic World*, 233–49.

6   Bailyn, "The Idea of Atlantic History"; Peter A. Coclanis, "Introduction," in *The Atlantic Economy during the Seventeenth and Eighteenth Centuries: Organization, Operation, Practice, and Personnel*, ed. Peter A. Coclanis (Columbia, S.C., 2005), xi–xix.

7   Armitage, "Three Concepts of Atlantic History," 15–27.

8   Jerry H. Bentley, *Old World Encounters: Cross-Cultural Contacts and Exchanges in Pre-Modern Times* (New York, 1993).

9   Mark Twain, "Corn-pone Opinions," in Twain, *The Complete Essays of Mark Twain*, ed. Charles Neider (Garden City, N.Y., 1963), 583.

10  Norah Dooley, *Everybody Cooks Rice* (Minneapolis, 1991).

11  D. H. Grist, *Rice*, 3rd ed. (London, 1959), 3–7; Andrew M. Watson, "The Arab Agricultural Revolution and Its Diffusion, 700–1100," *Journal of Economic History* 34 (1974) 8–35, and *Agricultural Innovation in the Early Islamic World: The Diffusion of Crops and Farming Techniques, 700–1100* (Cambridge, 1983); Peter A. Coclanis, "Distant Thunder: The Creation of a World Market in Rice and the Transformations It Wrought," *American Historical Review* 98 (1993): 1050–78, esp. 1050–55; J. L. Maclean, D. C. Dawe, B. Hardy, and G. P. Hettel, eds., *Rice Almanac*, 3rd ed. (Los Baños, 2002), 1–2.

12  Maclean et al., *Rice Almanac*, vii, erratum vii, 4–8; Coclanis, "Distant Thunder," 1051.

13  Grist, *Rice*, 348–75; Maclean et al., *Rice Almanac*, vii, 4–8. Today the global trade in rice amounts to about 25 million tons (in milled-rice equivalents). Total world rice production is about 400 million tons, so the international rice trade constitutes only about 6.25 percent of world production. This percentage is considerably smaller than the figure for wheat. See *The Economist*, November 20, 2004, 67.

14  Grist, *Rice*, 3–7; E. J. Kahn Jr., *The Staffs of Life* (Boston, 1985), 210, 212, 219; Coclanis, "Distant Thunder," 1050; Maclean et al., *Rice Almanac*, vii, 6–8.

15  On the production/consumption of other staples in parts of Asia, see V. D. Wickizer and M. K. Bennett, *The Rice Economy of Monsoon Asia* (Stanford, Calif., 1941), 113–21, and Latham, *Rice*, 32–34. On the main contours of the Western rice trade, see Coclanis, "Distant Thunder."

16  Coclanis, "Distant Thunder," 1051–55; Peter A. Coclanis, "The Globalization of Agriculture: A Cautionary Note from the Rice Trade," *Shixue Lilun* [*Historiography Quarterly*], no. 1 (2001): 112–20 (in Chinese).

17  Coclanis, "Distant Thunder," 1051–53; R. C. Nash, "South Carolina and the Atlantic Economy in the Late Seventeenth and Eighteenth Centuries," *Economic History Review* 45 (1992): 677–702, esp. 681–82; Kenneth Morgan, "The Organization of the Colonial American Rice Trade," *William and Mary Quarterly* 52 (1995): 433–52, esp. 434–35.

18  Income elasticity of demand measures the rate of response in the demand for a particular good or product in relation to a change in income. To compute income elasticity of demand, one divides the percentage change in quantity demanded of good X by the percentage change in income of consumer (or consumer group) Y. Goods and products vary a great deal in the degree to which demand for them changes with changes in income. Generally speaking, demand for basic necessities such as rice does not rise at a proportionate rate with income—after income rises beyond a certain minimal level.

19  Coclanis, "Distant Thunder," 1052; Thomas L. Haskell, "Capitalism and the Origins of the Humanitarian Sensibility," *American Historical Review* 90 (April 1985): 339–61 and (June 1985): 547–66.

20  Grist, *Rice*, 6–7; Watson, "The Arab Agricultural Revolution and Its Diffusion."

21  Grist, *Rice*, 6–7; Watson, "The Arab Agricultural Revolution and Its Diffusion"; "Riso," in *Enciclopedia italiana di scienze, lettere ed arti*, 36 vols. (Rome, 1929–1952), 29:424–31; Coclanis, "Distant Thunder," 1054.

22  "Riso"; Grist, *Rice*, 6–7; Coclanis, "Distant Thunder," 1054.

23  See Dennis O. Flynn and Arturo Giráldez, "Born with a 'Silver Spoon': The Origin of World Trade in 1571," *Journal of World History* 6 (1995): 201–21, and "Cycles of Silver: Global Economic Unity through the Mid-Eighteenth Century," *Journal of World History* 13 (2002): 391–427. One can get some sense of the Asian dimensions of "European" treaties from the treaties themselves. Many of the treaties have been brought together as part of the Avalon Project at Yale Law School. See http://www.yale.edu/lawweb/avalon/.

24  Coclanis, "Distant Thunder," 1053–56.

25  Ibid., 1051–55.

26  Domenico Sella, *The Economy of Spanish Lombardy in the Seventeenth Century* (Cambridge, Mass., 1979); Liugi Faccini, *L'economia risicola lombarda dagli inizi del XVIII secolo all'Unità* (Milan, 1976).

27  Coclanis, "Distant Thunder," 1055–57; Andre Gunder Frank and Barry Gills, eds., *The World System: Five Hundred Years or Five Thousand?* (London, 1993).

28  Coclanis,"Distant Thunder," 1054–55; Peter A. Coclanis, "Home and the World: The Creation of an Integrated World Market for Rice," *Proceedings, XIII Economic History Congress . . .* (Buenos Aires, 2002), session 64, 26–31 [CD-ROM].

29  Eric L. Jones, *The European Miracle: Environments, Economies, and Geopolitics in the History of Europe and Asia*, 3rd ed. (Cambridge, 2003); Coclanis, "Distant Thunder," 1055–56; Paul I. Mandell, "The Rise of the Modern Brazilian Rice Industry: Demand Expansion in a Dynamic Economy," *Stanford Food Research Institute Studies* 10 (1971): 161–219; José Almeida Pereira, *Cultura do Arroz no Brasil: subsídios para a sua história* (Teresina, 2002), 27–37, 39–57, 59–106; Peter A. Coclanis, *The Shadow of a Dream: Economic Life and Death in the South Carolina Low Country, 1670–1920* (New York, 1989).

30  Coclanis, *The Shadow of a Dream*, 96–98, 140–57; Peter A. Coclanis, "How the Low Country Was Taken to Task: Slave-Labor Organization in Coastal South Carolina and Georgia," in *Slavery, Secession, and Southern History*, ed. Robert Louis Paquette and Louis Ferleger (Charlottesville, Va., 2000), 59–78. A number of scholars—Peter H. Wood, Daniel C. Littlefield, Philip D. Morgan, and Judith A. Carney, most notably—have written extensively on the role of African rice technology and knowledge systems in the rice economy of South Carolina and Georgia.

31  The role of Asian imports into Africa in the Atlantic slave trade is captured vividly in British customs records, particularly the famous "Customs 3" series. See Customs 3/1–82, Customs Office Records, Public Record Office, London. In any given year, significant quantities of cowries, beads, Indian textiles, spices, and so on were imported into West African ports by British traders in exchange for slaves and other "goods." The same was true in parts of West Africa frequented by traders from other European powers. See, for example, Joseph C. Miller, "A Marginal Institution on the Margin of the Atlantic System: The Portuguese Southern Atlantic Slave Trade in the Eighteenth Century," in *Slavery and the Rise of the Atlantic System*, ed. Barbara L. Solow (New York, 1991), 120–50; Robin Law, *The Slave Coast of West Africa 1550–1750: The Impact of the Atlantic Slave Trade on an African Society* (Oxford, 1991), 199–206; and Joseph E. Inikori, "Slavery and the Revolution in Cotton Textile Production in England," in *The Atlantic Slave Trade: Effects on Economies, Societies, and Peoples in Africa, the Americas, and Europe*, ed. Joseph E. Inikori and Stanley L. Engerman (Durham, N.C., 1992), 145–81, esp. 175–76.

32  Coclanis, *The Shadow of a Dream*, 130–35; Coclanis, "Distant Thunder," 1055–57.

33  Coclanis, *The Shadow of a Dream*, 130–39. On estimated total rice acreage in the South Atlantic region, see Coclanis, *The Shadow of a Dream*, 255–56, and Peter A. Coclanis, "Rice," in *The New Georgia Encyclopedia*, ed. John C. Inscoe (Athens, Ga., 2004) [online], and "Rice," in the *Handbook of North Carolina History*, ed. William S. Powell (Chapel Hill, N.C., in press).

34  See Coclanis, "Southeast Asia's Incorporation in the World Rice Market."

35  Ibid.

36  See Alan Frost, *The Global Reach of Empire: Britain's Maritime Expansion in the Indian and Pacific Oceans, 1764–1815* (Carlton, 2003).

37  Coclanis, "Distant Thunder," 1056–57.

38  Coclanis, "Southeast Asia's Incorporation into the World Rice Market"; Frost, *The Global Reach of Empire*.

39  Coclanis, "Southeast Asia's Incorporation into the World Rice Market"; Coclanis, "The Globalization of Agriculture."

40  Coclanis, "Southeast Asia's Incorporation into the World Rice Market"; Peter A. Coclanis, "The Poetics of American Agriculture: The U.S. Rice Industry in International Perspective," *Agricultural History* 69 (1995): 140–62. On "high modernism" as used here, see James C. Scott, *Seeing Like a State: How Certain Schemes to Improve the Human Condition Have Failed* (New Haven, Conn., 1998), esp. 4–6.

41  Coclanis, "Distant Thunder," 1072–75.

42  Peter A. Coclanis, "Lessons from the Past? The Globalization of Agriculture in Historical Context," *Studies of Modernization: Theories and Process* 3 (Feb. 2005): 69–81 (in Chinese), and "Breaking New Ground: From the History of Agriculture to the History of Food Systems," *Historical Methods* 38 (Winter 2005): 5–13.

43  Field notes, Go Pin Chauk, Bago District, Lower Division, Union of Myanmar, January 1996.

44  William Carlos Williams, *Paterson* (New York, 1963), bk. 2.

*In making his case that the Atlantic can be too confining a unit of analysis, Pier M. Larson takes as his subject a topic that is quintessentially Atlantic: the African diaspora. Many historians agree that the Black Atlantic provides the most successful example of a truly Atlantic history. For decades, historians (and anthropologists, art historians, and literary critics) have traced the forced movement of Africans into the New World. These studies have been admirably transnational: just as the use of slaves knew no national boundaries, so too has the historiography of the Black Atlantic moved beyond the nation-state as its fundamental organizing principle.*

*Yet Larson shows that, though noteworthy for their energy and breadth of vision, scholars of the African diaspora in the Atlantic have not gone far enough. By using the Atlantic as their unit of analysis, they have encountered a truncation problem of the sort diagnosed by Coclanis. They have neglected the enormous and tragic forced migrations of Africans to areas other than the Atlantic and to areas within Africa itself. Bringing together statistics on these other African diasporas for the first time, Larson shows how the Atlantic slave trade was part of a longer and larger slave-trading process. Thus, while Atlanticists are well aware of the estimate that 11.3 million Africans were forced onto European ships bound for Atlantic slavery, they are generally not aware that another 11.6 million were transported as slaves across the Sahara or into the Indian Ocean in the period 650–1900. Nor are most Atlanticists aware that in the same period a staggering 20 million more Africans were removed from their homelands to become slaves elsewhere in Africa. Thus a global perspective is necessary if one wants to fully understand the many African diasporas. How will Larson's insights alter scholarly assessments of the Black Atlantic?*

# African Diasporas and the Atlantic

## Pier M. Larson

## THE PROBLEM OF DIASPORA

As a cursory consultation of any library catalog quickly confirms, the African diaspora as both concept and field of study is overwhelmingly defined by Atlantic scholarship. This is paradoxical in two respects. The Atlantic is one of three broad regions of African dispersion outside the continent. Between 650 and 1900 C.E., a comparable number of sub-Saharan Africans left their homes for destinations in the Mediterranean and the Indian Ocean as they did into the Atlantic (see table 1).[1] Second, African diaspora, a relatively new concept, is widely thought to have been introduced into academic discourse through a conference paper delivered in 1965 by George Shepperson.[2] The conference in question united scholars of African history to consider intellectual problems in their fledgling field. It was held at the University of Dar es Salaam, Tanzania, a port on the Swahili coast of the Indian Ocean (map 1). From antiquity to the nineteenth century, Africans entered the Indian Ocean and its Red Sea extension as slaves from the continent's eastern seaboard. First articulated at an African center of research and among scholars who taught about the departure of slaves into the Indian Ocean from their own shores, Shepperson's notion of African diaspora found its intellectual home an ocean away, in Atlantic America.

Although this paradox is curious, the reasons for it are apparent. In his disquisition on the African diaspora, Shepperson had the Atlantic foremost in mind. "From 1511, when the first fifty negroes were brought to the West Indian islands, to 1888 and the total abolition of slavery in Brazil," he wrote, "this dark-skinned diaspora, due to the slave trade, has chequered the Caribbean and North, South and Central America with peoples of African origin." Shepperson was not incognizant of sub-Saharan Africa's trades across the Indian Ocean and Sahara; rather, he discounted them as essential to thinking about African diaspora. One important reason for this was his perception of the differential treatment of slaves in Africa's dispersions. "Arab slavery was often felt less harshly by the negro than the European slave trade across the Atlantic," he reasoned, "especially in the days of the 'Cotton Kingdom' in the United States of America. . . . Whatever conclusions are ultimately reached . . . the period of almost four hundred years of the European enslavement of Africans remains the heart of the African diaspora."[3]

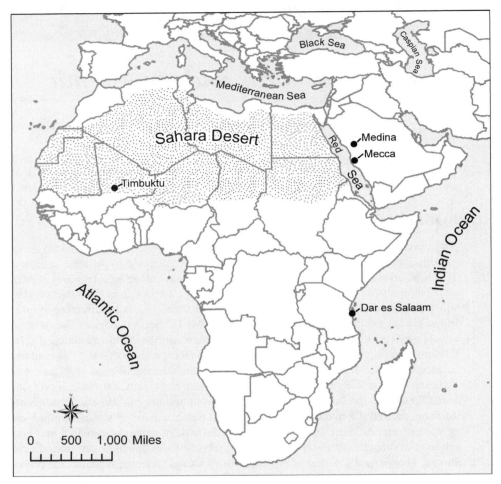

**Map 1**   Africa

Writing in the 1960s, Shepperson and his colleagues may also have privileged Atlantic dispersion because of the pressing importance of struggles over civil rights. For many, engagement in American racial politics focused intellectual efforts on the unique-ness of Africans' experiences in the Americas, qualifying Atlantic dispersion for primary diasporic status. Scholars had Georgia on their minds. By contrast, the dispersion of sub-Saharan Africans into the Mediterranean and the Indian Ocean has been "known and ignored, dismissed and described," by those interested in African dispersion.[4] From its earliest expression and shaped by American politics and dubious reasoning about treatment, the African diaspora was to favor Atlantic flows of African people, narrowing theories of diasporic experience to Africans and their descendants in the Americas.

That the Mediterranean and the Indian Ocean are poorly represented in recent writing on the African diaspora can also be attributed to the varying demographic legacies of global African slavery. Comparatively speaking, there are today few populations of identifiable sub-Saharan descent and culture in the Mediterranean to account for the flow of Africans into that region over many centuries. Some such communities are to be found, though in very modest numbers, inhabiting "virtually all the countries of the western Indian Ocean littoral," principally Iraq, Iran, Pakistan, India, and the Mascarene islands (Mauritius and Réunion).[5] Where such populations do exist, intellectuals of self-identifying African derivation who would publicly interpret African histories and identities in dispersion or press political claims on behalf of ex-slaves and their descendants—as they have in the Americas—are either practically nonexistent (the Middle East) or merely inchoate (India and the Mascarenes).[6]

Where the descendants of Africans are found today in Africa's diasporas beyond the Atlantic, as in Iran, their political and racial consciousness is strikingly different from that of their counterparts in the Americas. "Hence, there are no active 'constituencies' that create a demand to have their slave or slaveholding past investigated, so that they can come to terms with it."[7] Given the relative invisibility of contemporary diasporic communities beyond the Atlantic and a lackluster scholarly interest in African dispersion there, Atlantic patterns of forced migration, demography in host societies, and racial consciousness have been accepted as a standard for African diaspora. Atlantic scholars of dispersion have tended to take as their starting point the abundant modern diasporic populations of the Atlantic and pursue their experiences back in time, inappropriately claiming those experiences as *the* history of African diaspora. Including the experiences of Africans in sites of exile beyond the Atlantic will permit an understanding of African diaspora in its full diversity, contextualizing Atlantic-centered paradigms.

In part, however, the African diaspora remains primarily a matter of Atlantic concern because scholars of Africa in North America and in much of Europe and Africa eschewed a global approach to the study of the African continent. In the United States, intellectual developments in the study of Africa at historically white institutions were shaped in response to Cold War struggles over global influence and manifested in the creation of Title VI National Resource Centers for African studies at more than fifteen universities nationwide. Postwar intellectual directions in African history in the United States and beyond developed in response to the Atlantic-focused work of scholars such as W. E. B. Du Bois and Melville Herskovits. As Africa emerged from colonial rule, African scholars and many of their European and American colleagues sought to create an autonomous history for the continent uninfluenced by external constituencies. Many felt global approaches were overly diffuse and premised on research in European languages. As a result, the characteristic intellectual emphases of the period were inward looking, with a concern for basic research in Africa, on continental African subjects, and employing African languages. African history was to center on the continent, not stray outside its borders.[8]

In particular, most researchers shied away from engagement with slavery or the external slave trades in which Europeans were not implicated. Slavery became a contentious and difficult topic.[9] Despite notable exceptions, among which is the work of Joseph Harris and Philip Curtin, African history both focused and narrowed the research agendas of many scholars, impeding an earlier examination of the role of Africans in global diasporas.[10] Scholars of the Atlantic slave trade, among others, have criticized these developments.[11] For his part, George Shepperson viewed the study of African diaspora as a necessary antidote to "tendencies towards the isolationist, restricted spirit in African historical study."[12] Unsurprisingly, the history of slavery and African dispersion in the Atlantic are today among the chief intellectual forces broadening the scope of African history.

Other reasons for the dominance of the Atlantic in African diaspora studies suggest themselves. The sustained outpouring during the past thirty years of research on the Atlantic as an arena of transnational history has little parallel in either the Sahara or the Indian Ocean. Early synthetic works on these regions, like Braudel's *La Méditerranée et le monde méditerranéen* or Auber, Toussaint, and Chaudhuri's early histories of the Indian Ocean, offered little regarding Africa or its slave trades.[13] Despite a recent and exciting outburst of research on slaving and African diaspora in the Indian Ocean, the same problem remains true of most new syntheses in both regions.[14] "Slavery in Muslim societies has figured only marginally in comparative studies on slavery," notes Ehud Toledano, one of the few to tackle the "sensitive topic" of slavery in Ottoman history. One of the reasons for the relative invisibility of servile histories in Islamic societies, he suggests, is the complexity of slavery in the area.[15]

Two others are academic boundaries and embarrassment about slavery. The trans-Sahara trade spanned West Africa, North Africa, and the Middle East, overlapping regions that have developed disparate modern historiographies and methods of graduate training. John Hunwick writes of a persistent propensity in the Mediterranean Islamic countries not to lay claim to slavery as a heritage. European slaving is seen as a more appropriate subject for inquiry. Silence on slavery serves to preserve the Arab world's diplomatic, cultural, and religious relationships with the modern countries of Africa from within whose borders slaves once derived.[16] But the Middle East's tradition of circumventing discussions of African slavery also arises from a reluctance on the part of descendants of slaves to identify with African ancestry. Africans have long been associated in Middle Eastern thought with unbelief (*kufr*), the primary Islamic justification for enslavement. To locate one's ancestry in infidelity and the related stain of slavery can result in profound shame.[17] The "history of silence" that Hubert Gerbeau once wrote characterized slaving in the Indian Ocean describes with equal accuracy the trans-Sahara trade into the Mediterranean lands of Islam.[18]

## THE DISPERSIONS

The dispersion of sub-Saharan Africans about the oceans bounding their continent over the past 1,500 years is a legacy chiefly of forced migration. Until the abolition of Africa's external slave trades, only a small proportion of Africans voluntarily traveled the oceans and the Sahara to settle *permanently* in North Africa and lands beyond the continent. That "most migration before 1500 was voluntary in a fundamental way," as David Eltis has argued, does not reflect specifically African experiences.[19] The many *temporary* migrations of Africans as merchants, seafarers, scholars, and pilgrims over the centuries do not modify this proposition. Africa may be unique among the continents in its sustained history of forced migrations. To assess the volume, locations, and significance of African dispersions in history is to track each of Africa's external slave trades and to examine the conditions of life and labor that Africans encountered in their many places of exile.

Both the Indian Ocean and the Sahara were important corridors of trade and communication well before Europe's maritime revolution. Trade in slaves along the coasts of the Red Sea between the Horn of Africa and Egypt dates to at least 5,000 years ago. Knowledge of how to navigate the seasonally alternating monsoon winds of the Indian Ocean developed shortly thereafter. By at least 2,000 years ago, ships laden with goods, people, and ideas utilized the monsoons to travel between the east coast of Africa and the Arabian Peninsula, Persian Gulf, and Indian subcontinent. The first-century C.E. author of the *Periplus of the Erythraen Sea* reported a trade in African slaves from Red Sea shores into surrounding regions of the Indian Ocean. A century later, Mediterranean merchants had learned enough of the western Indian Ocean and its trade in slaves that Alexandrian astronomer Claudius Ptolemy set out the contours and major ports of the East African coast to the Ruvuma River. Evidence for the earliest export of slaves from the Swahili coast dates to the eighth century.[20]

Despite indications of horse and chariot traffic across the Sahara more than two thousand years ago, it was not until widespread use of the domesticated Arabian camel early in the fourth century C.E. that trade became practical and significant. Camels transformed the desert into a "sea" capable of supporting regular "navigation" and commerce. "The caravan routes which crisscrossed the deserts like so many slow sea-passages across the stony and sandy wastes of Africa," Fernand Braudel wrote poetically, "created a fantastic network of connections."[21] The revolution of camel-borne trade in gold, salt, and other products fostered the rise of states along the southern fringe of the Sahara Desert. Slaves figured in this commerce from its earliest periods but became especially important as West African states from about the tenth century C.E. sent out armies to capture or extract captives as tribute from subjected provinces. Those not set to labor locally were marched northward across the desert in caravans guarded by camel-riding merchants. Some slaves were exchanged at oases along the way. Captives who survived the hazardous journey to the northern edge of the desert were either sold in North Africa or set aboard boats bound for more distant Mediterranean markets. For many Africans forcibly crossing the Sahara and entering the Indian Ocean, the journey out of sub-Saharan Africa entailed a Middle Passage by both land and sea (this was true also in the Atlantic).

While commerce and slaving across the Indian Ocean and Sahara increased significantly during the Islamic era—and especially after 1000 C.E.—each system pre-dated Muhammad's flight to Medina in the early seventh century.[22] The Prophet's birthplace at Mecca lay near the crossroads of the Sahara and Indian Ocean systems of trade, and slaves were a common and accepted feature of Arabian life at the time of Muhammad's revelations. By conquest and persuasion, Islam spread outward from the Hijaz along prevailing commercial routes. The rise and spread of the Islamic empire spurred economic integration and expansion in the areas of its conquests. As a result, new uses for slaves were added to old ones.[23] Most demand in the Mediterranean after Arab conquest was from Islamized areas, though a certain percentage of African slaves crossing the Sahara entered Italy and Provence as well as Islamic Spain.[24] While demand from the world of Islam was not always responsible for Indian Ocean trade (some slaves went to the Mascarenes, Hindu India, China, and Southeast Asia), most slaves from about 1000 C.E. to the end of the trade were conveyed across the Sahara and Indian "oceans" by Muslim merchants, marketed to Muslims, and employed in societies where Islam was a key force.[25]

**TABLE 1    The External Slave Trades of Sub-Saharan Africa, 650–1900**
(volumes in thousands)

| Period | Atlantic | Sahara | Indian Ocean[a] | Total | Annual average volume | Atlantic as % of total |
|---|---|---|---|---|---|---|
| 650–1000 | | 1,320 | 600 | 1,920 | 5.5 | |
| 1001–1400 | | 2,520 | 1,200 | 3,720 | 9.3 | |
| 1401–1500 | 81 | 430 | 300 | 811 | 8.1 | 10 |
| 1501–1600 | 328 | 550 | 300 | 1,178 | 11.8 | 28 |
| 1601–1700 | 1,348 | 710 | 300 | 2,358 | 23.6 | 57 |
| 1701–1800 | 6,090 | 715 | 600 | 7,405 | 74.0 | 82 |
| 1801–1900 | 3,466 | 1,205 | 900 | 5,571 | 55.7 | 62 |
| 650–1900 | 11,313 | 7,450 | 4,200 | 22,963 | 18.4 | 49 |
| 1401–1900 | 11,313 | 3,610 | 2,400 | 17,323 | 34.6 | 65 |

[a]Red Sea and East African external trades combined.

*Sources*: Trans-Atlantic: Paul Lovejoy, *Transformations in Slavery: A History of Slavery in Africa*, 2nd ed. (Cambridge, 2000), table 1.1, 19, and table 3.1, 47. Trans-Sahara: Ralph A. Austen, "The Trans-Saharan Slave Trade: A Tentative Census," in *The Uncommon Market: Essays in the Economic History of the Atlantic Slave Trade*, ed. Jan S. Hogendorn (New York, 1979), table 2.8, 66. Red Sea and East African trades are combined as the "Indian Ocean" in this table, but I cite the sources separately. Red Sea: For data to 1800, Austen, "The Trans-Saharan Slave Trade," table 2.9, 68. For the nineteenth century, Ralph A. Austen, "The 19th Century Islamic Slave Trade from East Africa (Swahili and Red Sea Coasts): A Tentative Census," *Slavery and Abolition* 9 (1988): 33. Indian Ocean: For estimates to 1700, Austen, "The Trans-Saharan Slave Trade," table 2.9, 68. For the eighteenth century, Lovejoy, *Transformations*, table 3.7, 62. For the nineteenth century, Edmond Martin and T. C. Ryan, "A Quantitative Assessment of the Arab Slave Trade of East Africa," *Kenya Historical Review* 5 (1977), table 4, 79; Austen, "The 19th Century Islamic Slave Trade from East Africa," 29; Lovejoy, *Transformations*.

Table 1 sets out currently accepted estimates for the volume of sub-Saharan Africa's external slave trades from 650 to 1900 C.E. No scholar has ventured to quantify the slave trades prior to 650, although, as I have mentioned, some Africans forcibly departed the continent in antiquity.[26] Readers should note that this is the first time figures for all three trades have been assembled in a single table, for scholars are reticent to imply that estimates for the trans-Sahara and Indian Ocean trades are equivalent in margin of error to those for the Atlantic. They are not. Whereas the volume of the Atlantic slave trade is estimated from a comprehensive collection of direct evidence consisting of ship-by-ship data on the number and demographic mix of captives carried on 27,233 slaving voyages, trans-Sahara and Indian Ocean estimates are "based mainly on observations by European travelers and diplomats which are concentrated in the period after 1700" and on projections from slave censuses, as is the case for the Mascarenes.[27] For periods before 1600, after which estimates become more accurate, Paul Lovejoy suggests we consider both the trans-Sahara and the Indian Ocean figures "a convenient measure," as midpoints in a possible range extending both appreciably higher and significantly lower.[28]

Estimates for the trans-Sahara trade are based on the work of economic historian Ralph Austen. While some components of this commerce are being examined, relatively little new work has been published on its overall volume. Much unexploited documentation concerning trade across the Sahara is waiting for researchers literate in Arabic, Turkish, and vernaculars and willing to tackle the abundant but widely scattered manuscripts pertaining to it, including those in private collections and libraries in desert-edge towns like Timbuktu, Mali, or in locations across the former Ottoman

Empire.[29] The trans-Sahara slave trade is the least-studied component of Africa's external traffic and the subject of considerable debate. Future research in primary materials may revise the estimates for its volume either upward or downward.

The Indian Ocean figures derive from the work of multiple scholars and are probably more reliable. Voyage-based data on the number and port origins of slaves as have been compiled for the Atlantic are not available for the Indian Ocean. Census, tax, and customs records for studying the slave trade into the colonial Mascarenes from the late seventeenth century do exist but are far less complete than those for the Atlantic. In part, and especially for the island of Réunion, some public records relating to slavery have been deliberately destroyed.[30] Even so, it may be possible in the future to assemble volume, sex, age, and ethnic data for some voyages to the Mascarene islands. In the case of slaves transported about the Indian Ocean by crews and captains indigenous to the area (the so-called *dhow* trade, which preponderated by volume), few documents are likely ever to come to hand. Despite these impediments, there is currently much new research being undertaken on the volume and directions of slave trades into and around the Indian Ocean. When final results are tabulated together, the new aggregate numbers will almost certainly revise those in table 1 upward, at least from the sixteenth century on.[31]

Of all Africa's external slave trades, the Atlantic is the most widely researched and best documented.[32] Unlike the others, it operated during a relatively short period from the fifteenth to the mid-nineteenth century, opening well after and closing significantly before both the trans-Sahara and Indian Ocean trades. In fact, 85 percent of the transatlantic slave trade by volume occurred between 1700 and 1867, just over a century and a half. During more than 1,200 years, by contrast, the trans-Sahara and Indian Ocean trades together delivered over 11 million persons beyond sub-Saharan Africa, roughly equaling the Atlantic commerce in volume. Relatively few slaves annually entered the trans-Sahara and Indian Ocean systems during the earliest times of their operation, but a steady stream over an extended period belies substantial growth in their final centuries. Taken together, the two slave trades beyond the Atlantic nearly tripled in volume from the fifteenth to the nineteenth century, rising from an estimated 730,000 to over 2.1 million in this interval (see fig. 1).

During the five centuries over which the Atlantic slave trade operated, that trade represented 65 percent of sub-Saharan Africa's external exchange of slaves, with the trans-Sahara and Indian Ocean trades together making up the other 35 percent. Put in different figures, for every 100 persons removed from Africa by the Atlantic slave trade from the fifteenth to the nineteenth century, fifty-three left sub-Saharan Africa into the Mediterranean and the Indian Ocean during the same period. The volume and diverse patterns of Africa's dispersions beyond the Atlantic are often eclipsed by an exclusive preoccupation with the Americas. Viewing the Atlantic within the global dispersion of Africans will help delimit the unique dimensions of African diaspora there.

## DIASPORIC EXPERIENCES

If the principal themes in Atlantic dispersion are community formation and race consciousness, a more inclusive interpretive framework will emerge from a focus on diasporic experience in its several varieties. The way slaves were employed in host

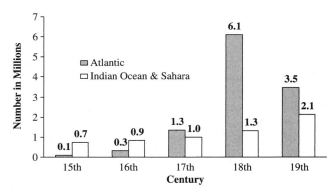

**Figure 1** Atlantic and Other Slave Trades from Africa, Fifteenth to Nineteenth Centuries. *Source:* Table 1.

societies influenced the sorts of diasporic communities they forged or whether they were able to create communities at all. A distinguishing characteristic of slavery in the western Atlantic was the extent to which masters exploited the economic potential of their African captives. Almost as a rule, slaves were set to the production of staple crops on rural estates or to hard labor in mines and other profit-generating enterprises. Above all, slaves were factors of production, though they also brought social and political prestige. In the Mediterranean and the Indian Ocean, slaves were directed chiefly to urban locations where they entered domestic units as wives, concubines, household helpers, and laborers, or government service as administrators, servants, and soldiers. Relatively few captives were set to agriculture. Slavery in the Mediterranean and the Indian Ocean was more a form of conspicuous consumption and an extension of government than an investment in production. During the seventeenth century, the wealthiest masters rarely owned more than 100 slaves.[33] Subsequent centuries evinced a tendency toward enlargement, but slaveholding in Africa's diasporas beyond the Atlantic was roughly comparable to that in the early colonial Chesapeake: slaves were unevenly distributed, and the majority of slaveholdings were small.

Large units of government (*kul*) slaves defied the slaveholding norm, particularly in the servile armies that supported central governments from Morocco to Mogul India.[34] In India, such military and administrative duties were common for African captives, while elsewhere they were merely one employment among a broader range of servile occupations.[35] Theoretically kinless and without vested interests, slave soldiers, servants, and administrators were renowned for loyalty to their political masters. Born about 1550 in Ethiopia, Shambu was enslaved and exchanged several times, serving in Yemen for a period and ending his life in India, where he was known as Malik Ambar. Shambu-Ambar loyally served two leaders in the Deccan and became widely known there as a heroic resister against Mogul encroachment.[36] There are many such tales of elite slaves' individual success in military or administrative positions across the Islamic world. Among the trusted slaves who managed extended court households (*harems*), African eunuchs were highly valued and extremely expensive.[37] African slaves in the Islamic world mingled among the free citizens of towns and cities, creating for themselves lives of relative autonomy that typify urban servitude. Yet most slaves, unlike Shambu-Ambar, never rose from their lowly social positions.

The most notable exception to the patterns outlined in the preceding paragraphs was slavery in the salt marshes of southern Mesopotamia during the eighth and ninth centuries C.E., where gangs of African captives and other servile laborers were set to land reclamation and the construction of irrigation canals. These slaves were once thought to have derived primarily from the Swahili coast, but many hailed from lands farther north instead. They were known as the Zanj and arrived in large numbers, living separately from their masters. As is typical of large concentrations of new captives, the population was not self-reproducing, and many did not speak Arabic. The Mesopotamian Zanj joined with other slave and nonslave laborers in a Kharijite-inspired revolt of social dimensions that resulted in the occupation of Basra and a fundamental challenge to the rulers of the 'Abbasid caliphate. Some thereby gained their freedom. During the eleventh century, up to 30,000 African slaves were employed in agricultural pursuits along the coast of what is now Bahrain.[38] Beyond the Persian Gulf, African slaves were among those laboring the medieval sugar estates of the Mediterranean and tending the coastal date plantations of the Batinah in Oman from at least the ninth century to the nineteenth.[39] The Mascarene islands with their slave majorities, commercial agriculture, diverse set of staples, resident Francophone planters, broadly dispersed slave owning, and task systems of labor were a curious hybrid of the colonial Caribbean and Chesapeake.[40]

The differing age and gender compositions of African populations entering the external slave trades are essential to assessing the subsequent experience and consciousness of Africans in the regions of their arrival. For the Atlantic slave trade (between 1663 and 1864), a major database reveals that 64.6 percent of forced migrants were male and 25.1 percent children.[41] Although males clearly predominated, Africans came westward across the Atlantic in proportions more resembling free migrant families than indentured laborers (who were overwhelmingly adult males). Comparable gender and age data for the trans-Sahara and Indian Ocean trades are not available, but narrative accounts consistently report a majority of females in each. Most scholars writing on the flow of Africans into Islamic regions assume that at least two females arrived for every male, but this is likely an overstatement.[42] However, the proportion of children entering Africa's slave trades into the Mediterranean and the Indian Ocean was clearly higher than that of victims in the Atlantic commerce. Although the proportion of children in all of Africa's trades tended to rise over time, the gender structure of the slave trade into the Atlantic was generally the converse of that into other regions.[43]

Judging by these divergences in demography, one might hypothesize that slave populations in Islamic regions experienced growth and were able to form stable communities (rates of natural reproduction are directly related to the proportion of women in a population). The social roles and legal rights of servile women in much of the Mediterranean and the Indian Ocean, however, produced an altogether singular outcome. The laws and customs relating to slavery as interpreted from the Koran produced analogous results in lands as dispersed as the Hijaz, the Maghreb, Oman, the Persian Gulf, and North India. In all these regions, slave women were prized by free men as wives and concubines, while free women sought female slaves as attendants and household laborers. In Islamic practice, the wedlock of any free man with a slave he owned was prohibited; he was first required to manumit her. Children resulting from such marriages were born free, for offspring acquired the status of their mothers. Children issuing from unions between slave concubines and free men were also considered free. At the same time, slave concubines who bore children to free men were themselves to be manumitted on the death of the child's father. In the Americas, equivalent practices of marriage and manumission were usually publicly shunned or disallowed by law.

Additional manumission practices reinforced these widespread marital and childbearing patterns. Manumitting one's slaves was considered a pious act and encouraged by the Koran. On their deathbeds, slaveholders frequently manumitted slaves but sometimes also granted the favor while still alive. As a result, rates of manumission in the Islamic world were comparatively high by Atlantic standards. The incessant drain on the slave population through marriage, concubinage, and selective manumission annually brought many Africans into the free population. Their modes of exit from slavery linked them into the culture, religion, and kin structures of their masters. African slaves in towns and cities of the Islamic world sought one another out and formed loose associations, but communities fashioned by such informal means rarely persisted beyond the first generation—they were sustained primarily by the influx of new slaves.[44] Rather than forming separate diasporic communities that persisted through time, Africans brought their practices and customs into the dominant culture. In such cases, it is compelling to think of the lasting influence of African diaspora in terms of cultural transmission rather than community formation and racial consciousness.

Under domestic-Islamic regimes of slavery, free and slave men of African origin found it difficult to acquire African wives; children born to African women tended to be of mixed race, free, and oriented to the slave-owning society. A cultural breach opened between African men on the one hand and African women and their children on the other, as their age and gender linked them to masters' households and social groups in contrasting ways. Whether through incorporation (women and children) or through exclusion and the withering away of separate communities (men), over a generation or two slaves and their descendants in most Islamic lands shed much that was distinctively African about their culture and modes of life. Traces remain, and scholars have much yet to learn about the dynamic between diasporic cultural forms and the incorporative mechanisms of Islamic societies. If both Atlantic slave systems and those in the Islamic regions were constrained continually to import slaves to sustain their servile populations, they did so for entirely different reasons (such as death in the Atlantic or manumission elsewhere).

Exceptions to the norms guiding diasporic demography set out here could be found about the Islamic world. In Iran's province of Baluchistan, for example, local practices discouraged marriage with Africans. Ethnically endogamous practices tended to favor the development of identifiable and enduring diasporic African communities consisting of both men and women.[45] Such numerically anomalous pockets of African communities could be found scattered from India to Morocco but mostly in the hinterland and away from cities. In the countryside and out of the limelight, African captives often grew grains and tree crops (dates and olives) or were involved in other productive enterprises. In certain rural areas, they were forced into a stratum of servile laborers, housed separately from masters, and retained their phenotypic and cultural distinctiveness as Africans, as in the case of Iranian Baluchistan or 'Abbasid Mesopotamia. Here, Atlantic-type patterns of dispersion and community could be found but without a pronounced racial consciousness and African identification.

Where slaves provided labor for profit-making enterprises, such as on Omani date plantations, their chances of maintaining African practices and a distinct identity were also strong. William Palgrave noted in the mid-nineteenth century that one-quarter of the population of Oman consisted of freed African slaves and their descendants who lived in distinct communities of African culture.[46] Traces of such communities can be found today in Muscat (Oman) and other regions where Africans were employed as productive labor.[47] If African diasporic communities tended to be fragile and short lived in the cities and ports of the Islamic world, they were more enduring in the smaller towns and rural settings of agricultural labor.

In the Americas, by comparison, lower rates of manumission and comparatively effective ideologies of exclusion based on notions of race emphasized the foreignness of African captives. Here, and especially in the British Atlantic, even where interracial sexual contact was common slaves tended to be barred from their masters' kin groups and social institutions, except at the outset or on frontiers. Offspring resulting from the often predatory unions between slave women and free men remained slaves, for children always followed the status of their mothers. Slaves in the Americas were usually housed separately from their masters and sought sexual partners among fellow captives. A potent impediment to sociopolitical advancement by comparison to the Mediterranean and the Indian Ocean (excepting the Mascarenes), exclusion in the Atlantic generally fostered development of distinctive and lasting diasporic communities. There were exceptions to this norm, particularly in Spanish America and to a lesser extent in the French Caribbean. In Argentina, for example, the African American communities of Buenos Aires "disappeared" in the nineteenth century, reproducing a typically Islamic pattern but by different mechanisms.[48] The important point is that while the Black Atlantic was the peculiar outcome of American racisms in their various forms, both community formation and dissolution were typical of African diasporic experiences from one end of the dispersion to another.

It is true that slaves and ex-slaves in the Islamic world were generally dishonored and subject to much prejudice based on the hue of their skin.[49] For the Maghreb, John Hunwick argues that much Islamic law respecting capture of slaves was disregarded, for darkness of skin became synonymous with enslaveability.[50] But even if at times and places Africans in dispersion beyond the Atlantic were the target of race ideologies that linked status to genealogy, these ideologies seldom effectively excluded them from the societies of their masters by means of systematic practice or homespun legislation, for the basis of law and practice everywhere—at least in principle—was the Koran. Ideologies of exclusion were weaker in the Mediterranean and the Indian Ocean as compared to the Americas; they were unstable and more prone to breakdown over time precisely because slaves were sought primarily for intimate and domestic roles. Although frequently opposed by masters, slaves' quests for personal advancement through the social and religious institutions of the dominant society were seldom successfully blocked.

Consider Islam itself. Enslavement of non-Muslims was justified by unbelief and generally regarded as a religious apprenticeship, the introduction of infidels to the community of believers. Islamic masters seldom sought to prevent slaves from adopting their religion, even sending some to Koranic schools where they learned to read. Many slaves had converted even before their arrival at Islamic destinations. The practice of baptizing captives entering Catholic colonies, where masters early conceived of slavery as a means for saving the heathen, resonates with the Islamic ideal of slavery as conversion. In the Protestant Atlantic, by contrast, masters were generally hostile to evangelization among slaves, at least until the nineteenth century. In principle, slaves and ex-slaves were to be admitted to Islam as spiritual equals of their masters. In practice, bondsmen and freed Africans often had to struggle to claim their place in the mosques and the social institutions of the towns.[51] Despite the principle, Islam was not *equally* open to masters and slaves.

## THE AFRICAN DIASPORA IN AFRICA

Up to now, I have discussed only the scattering of Africans beyond sub-Saharan Africa. Yet Africa's three external slave trades were linked to the employment of slaves within the continent. Because they possessed a "well-developed system of slavery, slave marketing, and slave delivery that preexisted any European contact," writes John Thornton, Africans responded to the earliest Portuguese demands for slaves with alacrity. "The Atlantic slave trade," he concludes, "was the outgrowth of this internal slavery."[52] The preexistence of the Indian Ocean, trans-Sahara, and domestic African trades made the Atlantic commerce possible, and each in turn contributed to the rising importance of slavery within Africa. Not all captives were sent into external exile. "Wherever slaves were exported," Paul Lovejoy has argued convincingly of the fifteenth and sixteenth centuries, "they were often used domestically in large numbers." By the seventeenth century, when it first exceeded Africa's other external slave trades in volume, the Atlantic commerce required a significant number of new enslavements within Africa to sustain it.[53] Similar linkages characterize Africa's other external trades.

The connection between internal and external slave trades presents scholars of the African diaspora with two challenges. The first is conceptual. The full title of George Shepperson's foundational essay on the African diaspora was "The African Diaspora or the African Abroad." By "abroad" Shepperson meant outside continental Africa, eliminating "internal" forced migrations from the diaspora he sought to define. Since the publication of Shepperson's paper, as I have argued, historians of the African diaspora have hewed closely to this restricted and flawed definition: a continental identity did not emerge in Africa until the late nineteenth century at the earliest. During the slave trades, Africans were "abroad" whenever they departed from their place of nativity. Despite the rise of a continental identity in the modern period, the same remains largely true today.

The second challenge is an empirical one. As virtually all experts agree, as many or more captives as were ejected from the continent were retained within sub-Saharan Africa itself.[54] In his study of the demography of enslavement, Patrick Manning, for example, found that "the slave population in Africa was roughly equal in size to the New World slave population from the seventeenth to the early nineteenth centuries. . . . After about 1850, there were more slaves in Africa than in the New World."[55] Herbert Klein has similarly written that the number of slaves held in Africa during the early eighteenth century was on the order of 3 to 5 million. "By 1850" he notes, "there were more slaves in Africa than there were in America—probably now numbering close to 10 million."[56] The combined volume of sub-Saharan Africa's external slave trades can be taken as a rough approximation of the number of new slaves captured and retained within Africa

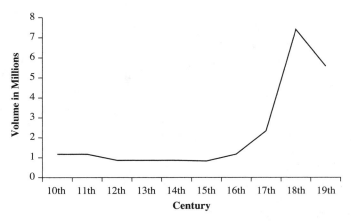

**Figure 2**  Volume Trend of Africa's Combined External Slave Trades, Tenth through Nineteenth Centuries. *Source:* Table 1.

(see fig. 2). The sum total of Africa's internal and external slave trades, then, is likely double that of its external commerce, on the order of 40 million or more (more than 20 million exported, as shown in table 1; a comparable number retained). Taken together with those killed in the process of capture and transportation, the numbers are staggering.

As in all systems of slavery, captives in Africa were moved from kin, nation, or state to place of servitude. The value of slaves was determined not solely by age, gender, physical condition, intrinsic abilities, and training but also by distance traveled. This could be hundreds of miles. Slaves must be "natally alienated" and are strangers in the societies of their masters.[57] Africa is no exception. As all slavers knew, the best way to crush a captive's spirit was to remove him or her as far from home as possible. Persons captured in the interior might equally likely be sent off into external as internal exile; the process of capture and natal alienation were similar for those departing the continent or remaining in sub-Saharan Africa. Many captives served months, even years, in African slavery before being sold by design or a twist of ill fate into an external trade. The rest never departed sub-Saharan Africa.

Patterns of capture varied by place, method, interaction with external slave trades, and sex of the victim, but despite regional variations, most captives retained within sub-Saharan Africa were female. In some places, the number of slave women was on a parity with slave men; in others, women outnumbered enslaved men by more than two to one.[58] Typical sex ratios of African slave populations probably lay somewhere between these two examples. Many men were killed in the violent confrontations that resulted in enslavement. In more "peaceful" forms of capture, such as kidnapping and enslavement for debt, men were less frequently targeted and generally not as vulnerable as women and children. Female slaves, too, were valued for their roles in farming and household economies and as wives and bearers of children.[59]

At Africa's west coast, Europeans seeking captives for transportation to the Americas demanded more men than women. Although they generally achieved this goal, they were constrained by their African suppliers to accept more women than they preferred, particularly along the Gold Coast and the Bight of Biafra. In these regions, nearly as many females as males entered the Atlantic slave trade. Senegambia lay at the other extreme. From its shores, nearly three-quarters of slaves entering the Atlantic were male. Senegambia supplied both the trans-Sahara and Atlantic slave trades; its merchants solved the double demand by conveying many of its servile women northward into the Mediterranean and most of its men into the Atlantic.[60] Similar interactions between Atlantic and trans-Sahara trades endured into the nineteenth century.[61]

More than any other region of dispersion, Africa was a land of diversity in slavery and diasporic experience. There were nearly as many types of slavery in Africa as languages. In many societies, captives entered individual households as supplemental kin, participating in the labor of cultivation, in domestic industry, and in local politics. This "lineage" or "kinship" slavery, as it has been called, enlarged social groups through the incorporation of dependent foreigners. Lineage slavery could be found in both Islamic and non-Islamic African societies. Ideologies of exclusion were particularly weak in lineage slaveries, for one of the purposes of acquiring strangers was to make them kin.[62]

From about the tenth century, the West African savanna and the East African littoral from the Red Sea to northern Mozambique entered the Islamic world. In sub-Saharan Africa's Islamic regions, however, slaves were far more involved in commercial agriculture than they were in other areas of the *dar al-Islam*. Slaves were positioned on agricultural estates as early as the twelfth century by rulers and military leaders of medieval sudanic kingdoms. But not all productive African slavery was Islamic. Commercial agricultural systems employing slaves proliferated during the era of the Atlantic slave trade, especially during the nineteenth century, when slaves cultivated staple commodities for sale on domestic and international markets in disparate regions of the continent. There were plantations of cloves, millet, sesame, and coconuts in Zanzibar and along the East African coast; of grains in the Sokoto caliphate of the West African savanna; of groundnuts in parts of Senegambia; and of oil palms in the Niger River delta. The markets served by these plantations reached from India to the Americas.[63]

From the incorporative ethos of kinship slavery to the opposing tendencies of labor, exploitation, and exclusion in plantation agriculture, Africa was a laboratory for different forms of slavery. In the most general sense, Africa's diverse forms of slavery lay at several intermediate locations on a continuum of forms of servitude between the Middle East and Indian Ocean's domestic slaveries at one end and the western Atlantic's economically rationalized slave plantation regimes and exclusionary ideologies of race at the other.[64] The exception to this geographic model would be African lineage slavery, which was probably even more incorporative than that found in most of the Islamic world. Africa belonged to the Atlantic Ocean, the Mediterranean, and the Indian Ocean; its internal slaveries were informed by the uses to which captives were put in each of the broader systems that bordered and overlapped it.

If we turn to the principal variables affecting diasporic experience in host societies, sub-Saharan Africa again demonstrates a wide diversity. Ideologies of exclusion that mark slaves as foreigners varied from the weak to the strong. Race was seldom a tool successfully wielded by African masters (there were exceptions), but exclusion could be signaled by language, dialect, body scarification, hairstyles, cultural practices, and hues of skin. In systems of kinship slavery or where the function of enslavement was the expansion of a lineage through the incorporation of strangers, markers of exclusion could fall away quickly. The societies in which slaves were employed in production tended to throw up the most exclusionary ideologies, such as the plantation systems of Zanzibar or those of the Sokoto caliphate. In parts of these regions, distinct communities descending from former slaves and masters exist today.[65] Such African systems most closely resemble Atlantic societies, where ex-masters and ex-slaves remain separated culturally and politically. But even where slaves were not employed in large-scale production, such as along the rivers of southern Somalia, contemporary communities of ex-slaves whose culture and consciousness differ markedly from those of the dominant society remain.[66]

The residential disposition of servile groups within Africa exerted a significant influence on if or how diasporic communities and consciousness developed. When they were newly captured or labored on plantations and mines, slaves tended to form an economic class distinct from that of their masters and were housed in separate quarters. The slave villages of nineteenth-century West Africa are a classic example. As French forces conquered much of the West African interior during the early years of the twentieth century, more than a million slaves fled their places of confinement.[67] Most escapees had been captured in their lifetimes and sought to return home, but only some were successful. In many locations across the continent, on the other hand, the lines between former masters and slaves have blurred, depositing a fuzzy memory of slavery into the new society that resulted and creating hybrid communities. Historians of African dispersion must take account of all these variant forms of diasporic experience.

## A MULTIFACETED DIASPORA

The problem of the African diaspora in contemporary thought is the problem of exclusion. Taking the part (the Atlantic dispersion) for the whole (the African diaspora) not only privileges certain diasporic experiences and structures over others but also renders the diasporic lives of Africans in Africa, the Mediterranean, and the Indian Ocean invisible in the rich and varied global drama of African captives' dispersion and social rebirth. Atlantic forms of diasporic experience (distinct and lasting communities, racial consciousness, identification with Africa, intellectual elites, and Africa as imagined and claimed origin) are one manifestation of the African diaspora, an important one to be sure. To broaden our vision from this variant, we need to focus on the diversity of experiences— community formation, dissolution, and amalgamation—in Africa's many dispersions. Looking at African diaspora beyond the Atlantic helps set the Atlantic diaspora in context and recognize its unique characteristics. It also serves as a corrective to myopic vision. A comparative approach reminds us that whatever our primary focus, new perspectives can be gained through broader thinking.

In this chapter, I have identified different streams of African forced migration and modes of social rebirth. Much remains to be done. And although slavery accounts for most flows of Africans to 1850, other voluntary and refugee migrant streams have become important since then and should be taken into account.[68] More Africans have been killed and displaced in the past thirty years as a result of regional wars on the continent, for example, as ever departed sub-Saharan Africa into external trades. According to major news organizations, the conflicts in Algeria, Angola, Congo, Rwanda, Somalia, Sudan, and Uganda have resulted in 8 million deaths and 17 million displaced since about 1975. New dispersions are continually in the making. Whatever their particular manifestations over time, all African dispersions have a diasporic component consisting of demographic structure, interaction with host society, and cultural expression. And each, in its uniqueness, informs the legacy of Africa on the move in good circumstances and in bad, each diasporic in its own characteristics and each demanding the attention and respect that the uprooting and rerooting of Africans in our time merits.

## Notes

1   François Renault estimates the Sahara and Indian Ocean trades at 14 million, some 3 million higher than that of the Atlantic. François Renault, "Essai synthèse sur la traite transsaharienne et orientale des esclaves en Afrique," in *La dernière trait*, ed. Eric Saugera (Paris, 1994), 23.

2   The paper was subsequently published as George Shepperson, "The African Abroad or the African Diaspora," in *Emerging Themes of African History*, ed. Terence O. Ranger (Nairobi, 1968), 152–76.

3   Ibid., 152, 157.

4   Michael Naylor Pearson, *The Indian Ocean* (London, 2003), 3.

5   Edward Alpers, "Recollecting Africa: Diasporic Memory in the Indian Ocean World," *African Studies Review* 43 (2000), quotation at 84; Joseph Harris, "The African Diaspora in World History and Politics," in *African Roots/American Cultures: Africa in the Creation of the Americas*, ed. Sheila Walker (Lanham, Md., 2001), 105–6.

6   For India, see Vijay Prashad, "Afro-Dalits of the Earth, Unite!," *African Studies Review* 43 (2000): 189–201.

7   Ehud Toledano, "The Concept of Slavery in Ottoman and Other Muslim Societies: Dichotomy or Continuum," in *Slave Elites in the Middle East and Africa*, ed. Edward Philips (London, 2000), 162.

8   Jane Guyer, *African Studies in the United States* (Atlanta, 1996); William G. Martin and Michael O. West, "The Ascent, Triumph, and Disintegration of the Africanist Enterprise, USA," in *Out of One, Many Africas: Reconstructing the Study and Meaning of Africa*, ed. William G. Martin and Michael O. West (Urbana, Ill., 1999), esp. 85–97.

9   Frederick Cooper, "The Problem of Slavery in African Studies," *Journal of African History* 20 (1979): 103–25.

10  Philip Curtin, *The Atlantic Slave Trade: A Census* (Madison, Wis., 1969); Joseph Harris, *The African Presence in Asia: Consequences of the East African Slave Trade* (Evanston, Ill., 1971).

11  Most notably Paul Lovejoy, "The African Diaspora: Revisionist Interpretations of Ethnicity, Culture and Religion under Slavery," *Studies in the World History of Slavery, Abolition, and Emancipation [Electronic Web Journal]* 2, no. 1 (1997), not paginated. The criticism is implicit in Joseph Miller, *Way of Death: Merchant Capitalism and the Angolan Slave Trade, 1730–1830* (Madison, Wis., 1988).

12  Shepperson, "The African Abroad," 173.

13  J. Auber, *Histoire de l'océan Indien* (Tananarive, 1955); Auguste Toussaint, *Histoire de l'océan Indien* (Paris, 1961); K. N. Chaudhuri, *Trade and Civilisation in the Indian Ocean: An Economic History from the Rise of Islam to 1750* (Cambridge, 1985).

14  Kenneth McPherson, *The Indian Ocean: A History of People and the Sea* (Delhi, 1998); Predrag Matvejevic, *Mediterranean: A Cultural Landscape*, trans. Michael Henry Heim (Berkeley, Calif., 1999); Peregrine Horden and Nicholas Purcell, *The Corrupting Sea: A Study of Mediterranean History* (Oxford, 2000); Pearson, *The Indian Ocean*.

15  Toledano, "The Concept of Slavery," 159.

16 For an example of this silence in print, see Ministry of Information, Sultanate of Oman, *Oman in History* (London, 1995), 491–509.

17 John Hunwick, "The Same but Different: Africans in Slavery in the Mediterranean Muslim World," in *The African Diaspora in the Mediterranean Lands of Islam*, ed. Eve Troutt Powell (Princeton, N.J., 2002), xi–xiii.

18 Hubert Gerbeau, *Les esclaves noirs: Pour une histoire du silence* (Paris, 1970).

19 David Eltis, "Introduction: Migration and Agency in Global History," in *Coerced and Free Migration: Global Perspectives*, ed. David Eltis (Stanford, Calif., 2002), 5.

20 Yu M. Kobishanow, "On the Problem of the Sea Voyages of Ancient Africans in the Indian Ocean," *Journal of African History* 6 (1965): 137–41; Lionel Casson, ed., *The Periplus Maris Erythraei: Text with Introduction, Translation, and Commentary* (Princeton, N.J., 1989); Claudius Ptolemy, *The Geography*, trans. Edward Luther Stevenson (New York, 1991); Mark Horton, "Early Maritime Trade and Settlement along the Coasts of Eastern Africa," in *The Indian Ocean in Antiquity*, ed. Julian Reade (London, 1996), 454.

21 Fernand Braudel, *Memory and the Mediterranean*, trans. Siân Reynolds (New York, 2001), 8.

22 Olivier Pétré-Grenouilleau dates the "invention" of the trade to the Islamic era: Pétré-Grenouilleau, *Les traites négrières: essai d'histoire globale* (Paris, 2004), 26.

23 William D. Phillips, *Slavery from Roman Times to the Early Transatlantic Trade* (Minneapolis, 1985), 71.

24 Charles Verlinden, *L'esclavage dans l'Europe médiévale*, 2 vols. (Brugge, 1955, 1977), 1:358–62, 762–65, 2:208–20, 319–32, 657–62; Jacques Heers, *Esclaves et domestiques au Moyen Age dans le monde méditerranéen* (Paris, 1981), 89–93.

25 For African slaves in China, see Chang Hsing-lang, "The Importation of Negro Slaves to China under the T'ang Dynasty (A.D. 618–907)," *Bulletin of the Catholic University of Peking* 7 (1930): 37–59, and C. Martin Wilbur, *Slavery in China during the Former Han Dynasty, 206 B.C.–A.D. 25* (Chicago, 1943). A limited number of African slaves entered Indonesia during the Dutch colonial period.

26 Frank Snowden, *Before Color Prejudice: The Ancient View of Blacks* (Cambridge, Mass., 1983), 31–34, 65–71; Pétré-Grenouilleau, *Les traites négrières*, 22–26.

27 Ralph Austen, "Slave Trade: The Sahara Desert and Red Sea Region," in *Encyclopedia of Africa South of the Sahara*, ed. John Middleton (New York, 1997), iv, quotation at 103; David Eltis et al., eds., *The Trans-Atlantic Slave Trade: A Database on CD-ROM* (Cambridge, 1999); Richard Allen, "The Mascarene Slave-Trade and Labour Migration in the Indian Ocean during the Eighteenth and Nineteenth Centuries," *Slavery and Abolition* 24 (2003): 33–50.

28 Paul Lovejoy, *Transformations in Slavery: A History of Slavery in Africa*, 2nd ed. (Cambridge, 2000), 25.

29 John Hunwick, "CEDRAB: The Centre de Documentation et de Recherches Ahmad Baba at Timbuktu," *Sudanic Africa* 3 (1992): 179–81; Hunwick, "The Same but Different," xiii; Paul E. Lovejoy, ed., *Slavery on the Frontiers of Islam* (Princeton, N.J., 2004).

30 Hubert Gerbeau, "L'Océan Indien n'est pas l'Atlantique: La traite illégale à Bourbon au XIX$^e$ siècle," *Outre-Mers: Revue d'Histoire* 336–337 (2002): 80–83.

31 See especially ibid.; Allen, "The Mascarene Slave-Trade"; Pedro Machado, "A Forgotten Corner of the Indian Ocean: Gujarati Merchants, Portuguese India and the Mozambique Slave-Trade, c.1730–1830," *Slavery and Abolition* 24 (2003): 17–32; Thomas Vernet, "Le commerce des esclaves sur la côte swahili, 1500–1750," *Azania* 38 (2003): 69–97.

32 See Eltis et al., *The Trans-Atlantic Slave Trade*, Herbert S. Klein, *The Atlantic Slave Trade* (Cambridge, 1999); David Eltis, *The Rise of African Slavery in the Americas* (Cambridge, 2000); Lovejoy, *Transformations*.

33 Markus Vink, "'The World's Oldest Trade': Dutch Slavery and Slave Trade in the Indian Ocean in the Seventeenth Century," *Journal of World History* 14 (2003): 169.

34    Patricia Crone, *Slaves on Horses* (Cambridge, 1980); Daniel Pipes, *Slave Soldiers and Islam* (New Haven, Conn., 1981).

35    Simon Digby, "The Maritime Trade of India [1200–1500]," in *The Cambridge Economic History of India, vol. i, c. 1200–c.1750*, ed. Tapan Raychaudhuri and Irfan Habib (Cambridge, 1982), 149–50, 152.

36    Harris, *The African Presence*, 91–98.

37    François Renault, *La traite des noirs au Proche-Orient médiéval: VIIᵉ–XIVᵉ siècles* (Paris, 1989), 55–57; Ehud Toledano, *Slavery and Abolition in the Ottoman Middle East* (Seattle, 1998), 20–80; Jan Hogendorn, "The Location of the 'Manufacture' of Eunuchs," in Philips, *Slave Elites*, 41–68.

38    J. Spencer Trimmingham, "The Arab Geographers and the East African Coast," in *East Africa and the Orient: Cultural Syntheses in Pre-Colonial Times*, ed. Robert Rotberg (New York, 1975), 116–22; Ghada Talhami, "The Zanj Rebellion Reconsidered," *International Journal of African Historical Studies* 10 (1977): 443–61; Phillips, *Slavery*, 76–77; Renault, *La traite des noirs*, 44–49, 60–63; Alexandre Popovic, *The Revolt of African Slaves in Iraq in the 3rd/9th Century*, trans. Léon King (Princeton, N.J., 1999).

39    Mediterranean: Verlinden, *L'esclavage;* Phillips, *Slavery*, 98–113; Philip Curtin, *The Rise and Fall of the Plantation Complex: Essays in Atlantic History* (Cambridge, 1990), 8–11. Oman: Frederick Cooper, *Plantation Slavery on the East Coast of Africa* (New Haven, Conn., 1977), 35–37; Patricia Risso, *Oman and Muscat: An Early Modern History* (New York, 1986), 13–14; Isam Al-Rawas, *Oman in Early Islamic History* (Reading, 2000), 156–57.

40    Moses Nwulia, *The History of Slavery in Mauritius and the Seychelles, 1810–1875* (East Brunswick, N.J., 1981); J. V. Payet, *Histoire de l'esclavage à l'île Bourbon* (Paris, 1990); Sudel Fuma, *L'esclavagisme à la Réunion, 1794–1848* (Paris, 1992); Vijaya Teelock, *Bitter Sugar: Sugar and Slavery in 19th Century Mauritius* (Moka, 1998).

41    David Eltis and Stanley Engerman, "Was the Slave Trade Dominated by Men?," *Journal of Interdisciplinary History* 23 (1992), table 1, 241.

42    Verlinden, *L'esclavage*, 2:208–20; Behnaz Mirzai, "African Presence in Iran: Identity and Its Reconstruction in the 19th and 20th Centuries," *Outre-Mers: Revue d'Histoire* 336–337 (2002): 234.

43    Harris, *The African Presence*, 35; Patrick Manning, *Slavery and African Life: Occidental, Oriental, and African Slave Trades* (Cambridge, 1990), 22–23, 41, 45–46; Toledano, *Slavery and Abolition*, 13–14; Lovejoy, *Transformations*, 64.

44    John Hunwick, "The Religious Practices of Black Slaves in the Mediterranean Islamic World," in Lovejoy, *Slavery on the Frontiers of Islam*, 156.

45    Mirzai, "African Presence," 236–37.

46    William Gifford Palgrave, *Narrative of a Year's Journey through Central and Eastern Arabia, 1862–1863*, 2 vols. (London, 1865), 2:271–73.

47    Edward Alpers, "The African Diaspora in the Northwestern Indian Ocean: Reconsideration of an Old Problem, New Directions for Research," *Comparative Studies of South Asia, Africa and the Middle East* 17 (1997): 62–81; Edward Alpers, "The African Diaspora in the Indian Ocean: A Comparative Perspective," in *The African Diaspora in the Indian Ocean*, ed. Shihan de Silva Jayasuriya and Richard Pankhurst (Trenton, N.J., 2003), 19–50.

48    George Reid Andrews, *The Afro-Argentines of Buenos Aires, 1800–1900* (Madison, Wis., 1980).

49    Bernard Lewis, *Race and Slavery in the Middle East* (New York, 1990).

50    John Hunwick, "Islamic Law and Polemics over Race and Slavery in North and West Africa, 16th–19th Century," in *Slavery in the Islamic Middle East*, ed. Shaun Marmon (Princeton, N.J., 1999), 52–63.

51   Jonathon Glassman, *Feasts and Riot: Revelry, Rebellion, and Popular Consciousness on the Swahili Coast, 1856–1888* (Portsmouth, N.H.., 1995), 117–74.

52   John Thornton, *Africa and Africans in the Making of the Atlantic World, 1400–1680* (Cambridge, 1992), 74, 97.

53   Also known as the "transformation thesis," this position has been most extensively argued in Lovejoy, *Transformations*. Its foremost critic (though only for the period before 1600) is Thornton, *Africa and Africans*.

54   See Pier M. Larson, *History and Memory in the Age of Enslavement: Becoming Merina in Highland Madagascar, 1770–1822* (Portsmouth, N.H., 2000), 271 n.44.

55   Manning, *Slavery*, 23.

56   Klein, *The Atlantic Slave Trade*, 129.

57   Orlando Patterson, *Slavery and Social Death: A Comparative Study* (Cambridge, Mass., 1982), 35–76.

58   John Thornton, "The Slave Trade in Eighteenth Century Angola: Effects on Demographic Structures," *Canadian Journal of African Studies* 14 (1980): 417–27; Claire Robertson and Martin Klein, "Women's Importance in African Slave Systems," in *Women and Slavery in Africa*, ed. Claire Robertson and Martin Klein (Madison, Wis., 1983), 5.

59   Robertson and Klein, "Women's Importance," 3–25.

60   Ibid., 4–5; Paul Lovejoy and David Richardson, "Competing Markets for Male and Female Slaves: Prices in the Interior of West Africa, 1780–1850," *International Journal of African Historical Studies* 28 (1995): 261–93; Eltis, *The Rise*, 85–113.

61   Paul Lovejoy, "The Central Sudan and the Atlantic Slave Trade," in *Paths to the Past: African Historical Essays in Honor of Jan Vansina*, ed. Robert Harms et al. (Atlanta, 1994), 345–70; E. Ann McDougall, "In Search of a Desert-Edge Perspective: The Sahara-Sahel and the Atlantic Trade, c. 1815–1890," in *From Slave Trade to "Legitimate" Commerce: The Commercial Transition in Nineteenth-Century West Africa*, ed. Robin Law (Cambridge, 1996), 215–39.

62   Igor Kopytoff and Suzanne Miers, "African 'Slavery' as an Institution of Marginality," in *Slavery in Africa: Historical and Anthropological Perspectives*, ed. Igor Kopytoff and Suzanne Miers (Madison, Wis., 1977), 3–81.

63   George Brooks, "Peanuts and Colonialism: Consequences of the Commercialization of Peanuts in West Africa, 1830–70," *Journal of African History* 16 (1975): 29–54; Cooper, *Plantation Slavery;* Paul Lovejoy, "The Characteristics of Plantations in the Nineteenth-Century Sokoto Caliphate," *American Historical Review* 85 (1979): 1267–92; Ken Swindell, "Serawoollies, Tillibunkas and Strange Farmers: The Development of Migrant Groundnut Farming along the Gambia River, 1848–95," *Journal of African History* 21 (1980): 93–104; Law, *From Slave Trade to "Legitimate" Commerce;* Martin Lynn, *Commerce and Economic Change in West Africa: The Palm Oil Trade in the Nineteenth Century* (Cambridge, 1998).

64   See Cooper, *Plantation Slavery*, 253.

65   Jean-Pierre Olivier de Sardan, ed., *Quand nos pères étaient captifs: récits paysans du Niger* (Paris, 1976).

66   Lee Cassanelli, "Social Construction on the Somali Frontier: Bantu Former Slave Communities in the Nineteenth Century," in *The African Frontier*, ed. Igor Kopytoff (Bloomington, Ind., 1987), 216–38; Francesca Declich, "'Gendered Narratives,' History, and Identity: Two Centuries along the Juba River among the Zigula and Shanbara," *History in Africa* 22 (1995): 93–122; David Finkel, "For Chosen Few, First Steps to a New Life," *Washington Post*, 18 August 2002.

67   Martin Klein, *Slavery and Colonial Rule in French West Africa* (Cambridge, 1998), 170–73.

68   Liisa Malkki, "Refugees and Exile: From 'Refugee Studies' to the National Order of Things," *Annual Review of Anthropology* 24 (1995): 495–523; Emmanuel Akyeampong, "Africans in the Diaspora: The Diaspora and Africa," *African Affairs* 99 (2000): 183–215.

*Like Larson, Claire S. Schen takes a topic dear to the hearts of many Atlanticists—pirates—and shows how broadening one's geographical focus leads to new and unexpected insights. Schen calls on scholars to turn their attention to an area peripheral to Atlantic studies but, ironically, central to the work of a previous generation of transnational historians: the Mediterranean.*

*Focusing on the connections between Atlantic and Mediterranean piracy helps establish a valuable comparative dimension to our understanding of English imperial expansion. Whereas the successful expansion of the English empire in the Atlantic can seem almost inevitable, the English found themselves chastened by their experiences in the Mediterranean. For example, the Stuart monarchs were able to do precious little to aid the hundreds of English captives taken by North African pirates in the early seventeenth century. And while scholars have assiduously examined English images of and ideas about American Indians, they have paid far less attention to English ideas about the "other" formed in contact with what they referred to variously as "Turks" and "Mahometans." Nothing could be more timely than a study—executed on a broad geographical canvas—of the history of relations between Muslims and "the West." Are there hints in Schen's story of some of the later conflicts that would develop between Muslims and Christians?*

# Piracy in the Atlantic and the Mediterranean

## Claire S. Schen

The "Atlantic World" encapsulates a geographic unit that stretches across an ocean and a mental construct that brings together Europe, the Americas, and western, sub-Saharan Africa. The school of historical writing it represents seeks to ask new questions about the flow and exchange of people, goods, and ideas. Despite the fruits of those intellectual labors, modern historians should not overlook the significance of the Mediterranean in the context of global trade, early empire, and cultural contact or the importance of early modern connections between the Mediterranean Sea and the Atlantic Ocean. Early modern Europeans and early historians were well aware of the economic and cultural significance of the Mediterranean. The connections among Atlantic Ocean schemes and endeavors and those undertaken in the Mediterranean Sea need to be revisited in light of recent scholarship on the Atlantic World. At the same time, teasing out the webs of cultural expectations, trade, and people cannot deny the independence of developments in the ocean and the sea.

The ambitions and policies of the early modern British serve as but one case study for the interplay of Atlantic and Mediterranean experiences and the ongoing importance of the Mediterranean alongside Atlantic exploration. This particular case study provides a rich example of the economic, social, and cultural consequences of the movement in the Atlantic and Mediterranean. Legal and illicit trade, including piracy and privateering, impacted colonial ventures and trade ambitions. The exchange of goods, while valued and encouraged by government policy and private initiative, nevertheless wrought suffering for individuals and their families, especially those who experienced attack or captivity through trade or as a result of disputes arising over the nature of trade and depredations on shipping. The social costs of trade were matched by the cultural lessons learned through contact with different societies and religions. Historians' discussion of European impressions of the "other," which has focused largely on Indians and Africans in the Atlantic World, cannot be properly understood without further study of the multivalent impressions of Arabs, Muslims, Turks, and the Maghribi.

Perhaps most significantly, comparing the British experience in the Mediterranean and in the countries surrounding it with that of the Atlantic recasts our understanding of Britain's trade and empire. The contrast between imperial strengths in one area (the Atlantic) and weaknesses in another (the Mediterranean) is an enlightening one, not visible if one looks only at the Atlantic. Britain's North American and Caribbean ventures yielded profits and ultimately produced permanent settlements; its attempts to profit from Mediterranean trade brought Britons into contact with stronger republics, states, and empires that challenged British diplomatic and military skills and tested their religious and cultural identities.

Querying the cultural exchange in these bodies of water necessitates tackling the problem of "identity" in past times. People in past times identified themselves differently than many modern peoples, particularly those in the West, who might highlight ethnicity, nation, or more personal self-identifiers to describe themselves and others. In this case, I will use "British" to include those inhabiting England, Scotland, and those parts of Ireland under (greater) control by the Tudor and Stuart monarchs. This is a modern understanding of an early modern problem of identity and does not preclude other, more local identities of smaller kingdom or of county, village, or town. When the British turned to identify others in the sixteenth and seventeenth centuries, the labels they used often confused ethnicity and religion, as when the word "Turk" stood to mean "Muslim." The traveler and delegate Ahmad bin Qasim was asked by a French woman if he was a Turk; "'A Muslim, praise be to God,' I said to her."[1] Other documents from the time referred to "Mahometans," demonstrating European misunderstanding and/or denigration of Islam as a religion that taught submission to Muhammad rather than to Allah. Imprecision about identities or allegiances was exaggerated by the complex political affiliations in the Maghrib (northern and northwestern Africa, between the Atlantic Ocean and Egypt), with independent Moroccans, inhabitants of Sallee forming an independent republic in the 1620s, and Algerians and Tunisians living in client states of the Ottoman Empire.[2] Even those identified as "Turks" when the context points to an Ottoman connection are of uncertain ethnic or racial background. At least some of the Muslims of the early modern world understood not only Christianity but also the doctrinal differences between Protestantism and Catholicism more broadly, as when Qasim described Martin Luther, John Calvin, and the reformers' objections to the papacy.[3] The early modern European sources that spoke broadly of Muslims did not to take into account different sects or strains within Islam (Map 1).

To turn to connections between the Atlantic and the Mediterranean is to return to Fernand Braudel and even to some nineteenth-century historians. In Braudel's sweeping and truly grand history of the Mediterranean, he rescued the Sea from its "role of a picturesque background."[4] His analysis of the Mediterranean was more than a historical study: it was part of a historiographical struggle to "create a history that would be different from the history our masters taught us."[5] Braudel attempted "to encompass the history of the Mediterranean in its complex totality," from the history of the environment and geography through the history of events. Although the focus of his work was the Sea, he paid careful attention to developments in the Atlantic. The histories of the bodies of water had been intertwined. For instance, Mediterranean sailors of the fourteenth century, Braudel wrote, led the way in sailing the Atlantic coast of Europe. They were, however, overtaken by sailors of northern Europe and the Atlantic in the "struggle for world domination" begun at the end of the fifteenth century.[6]

Thus, one theme emerged in his study these bodies of water: that of the decline of the Mediterranean in relation to the Atlantic. The notion is not without its critics or contrary evidence, however. Braudel posited decline, noting the "invasion" of northern European ships and sailors, especially Dutch and English ones, in the Mediterranean after 1590.[7] He ended his study in 1598, when he believed that the rise in Atlantic seafaring and empires diminished the Mediterranean's role. "Economic upheaval"

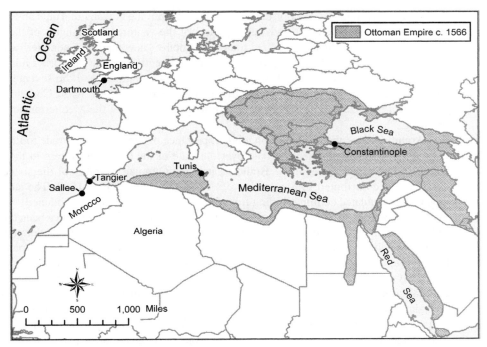

**Map 1**   Ottoman Empire

followed the opening of the Atlantic and the greater importance of long-distance connections in the seventeenth century and later.[8] By contrast, Linda Colley argues for the ongoing significance of the Mediterranean in the seventeenth century, as demonstrated by the English occupation of Tangier (1662–1684). "Tangier guarded the entrance of what one contemporary called 'the greatest thoroughfare of commerce in the world,'" she writes, "by which he meant not the Atlantic Ocean, but the Mediterranean, at this stage still the most profitable arena by far for English imports and exports."[9] Commercial ambitions preserved the Mediterranean as a "major zone of activity for the British and other maritime powers long after the mid-seventeenth century."[10] In 1700, the value of the trade in India and North America equaled that of trade with southern Europe and the Mediterranean, and at the end of the century "there were probably as many British ships and crews active in the Mediterranean as there were in the Atlantic."[11]

Indeed, early historians noted the significance of the Mediterranean to European trade and competition through the sixteenth and seventeenth centuries. Nationalistic lectures delivered by James Anthony Froude at Oxford in 1893–1894 on "English Seamen in the Sixteenth Century" celebrated the growth of the British navy, incidentally at a moment when British concern about German naval power was on the rise. Not surprisingly for a man who had inspired Victorian celebration of Sir Walter Raleigh and other "sea dogs," greatness began with the defeat of the Spanish Armada in 1588.[12] Modern historians, like David Armitage, have instead argued that maritime supremacy only followed the Napoleonic Wars.[13] Froude acknowledged Spanish accomplishments prior to 1588 in Mexico, Peru, and "Spanish America," while "with the other [hand] they were fighting Moors and

Turks and protecting the coast of the Mediterranean from the corsairs of Tunis and Constantinople."[14] This late nineteenth-century view of the ventures and dangers of the sixteenth century saw a dual approach to trade and empire: "new worlds to conquer" across the Atlantic and the old world to protect.[15] The early twentieth-century historian Julian S. Corbett distinguished between Elizabethan transatlantic ventures and the seventeenth-century focus on the Mediterranean. "With Raleigh's death [in 1618]," wrote Corbett, "the oceanic era of Elizabeth passed away, and in its place the era of the Mediterranean was dawning."[16]

Argument over the decline or ongoing importance of Mediterranean trade to Europe is linked to another significant debate over the state of the Ottoman Empire in the sixteenth and seventeenth centuries. Braudel cataloged Ottoman mistakes of the sixteenth century that contributed to the decline of the Mediterranean after 1598. The sultans engaged in "outdated conflicts, hiding from them the true problems," he explained, "wasting their substance in futile wars in the Mediterranean when they should have been trying to break out of that charmed circle: lost opportunities, every one."[17] Reconsideration of Ottoman decline has instead emphasized difference—economic growth in some parts of the empire, innovation leading to greater political stability, and military victories.[18]

Early modern Europeans figured the Ottoman Empire into their plans at sea and drew cultural comparisons and contrasts with it, while modern historians have tended not to consider fully the importance of it to Europeans. Embedded within Froude's anti-Spanish and anti-Catholic polemic is a reference to Spanish preoccupation with "Moors and Turks" and the defense of the Mediterranean from them. Even in his paradigm-shifting work *The Ideological Origins of the British Empire*, David Armitage focuses on examples of British imperial and maritime or commercial ventures largely in relation to the Atlantic and other western European powers, making some reference to India but leaving out the Ottoman Empire. Anthony Pagden, on the other hand, points to the comparisons drawn by the British and French between the Spanish and the Ottomans, a jealous commentary on the galling inferiority of their own empires and claims to "world," as distinct from global, power. According to Pagden, Spain's European rivals saw it as an "aspirant to Universal Monarchy" and a "tyrant" and likened it to the Ottoman Empire.[19]

The Islamic states and empires that bordered the Mediterranean also suggest the need to rethink notions of imperial ideology and to include the Maghrib in discussions of exploration and expansion beyond an Atlantic focus. Nabil Matar has written a stinging indictment of shortcomings in the historiography on Europe and the "world." For example, he cites Anthony Pagden's *Facing Each Other: The World's Perception of Europe and Europe's Perception of the World*, where no entries of Islamic civilizations are given in two volumes. "It is as if," Matar muses, "Arabic and Ottoman Islam, with which Europe had been interacting since the Crusades, did not exist at all."[20] Not simply the Ottoman Empire wielded power in the Mediterranean: North African Islamic states and republics, not all of them under the sultan's dominion, also sailed the Mediterranean and the Atlantic coast of Europe. Colley strives in *Captives* to reinsert the Maghrib into our picture of the origins of the British Empire. Colley moves beyond trade to discuss the influence of the "rivalries and insecurities of the major European powers" on Mediterranean ventures. Although Tangier was ultimately a failure, it provided the "prototype for a succession of similar and more enduring Mediterranean strongholds" that gained significance with the seizure of India and the Suez Canal.[21]

Study of the Mediterranean, in conjunction with the Atlantic, offers a broader context for understanding empire, especially in relation to the powerful Ottoman Empire and the resilient client and independent states of the Maghrib. For the British in the sixteenth and early seventeenth centuries, their Mediterranean experience was difficult to cast as a success, as a sign of providential favor on the nation. The inability to counter piracy by North Africans and "Turks" and to end the captivity of British and Irish peoples in Tunis, Algiers, and Sallee undermines a clear narrative of success, of imperial "progress" in the Atlantic. The lectures by Froude, given before the sun set on the British Empire, mentions corsairs but neglects the issue of British captivity in North Africa, in ignorance or in denial of "white" enslavement. Instead, he continues his anti-Catholic themes, noting that Inquisitors took British seamen in Spanish ports, torturing and starving them in dungeons, forcing them to row in galleys, or burning them in an auto-da-fé, some of the central features of British anti-Spanish sentiment and propaganda.

"If the Mediterranean has done no more than force us out of our old habits," wrote Braudel, "it will already have done us a service."[22] We might wonder, however, about newer "old habits" that limit our understanding of the early modern world and separate the history of the Atlantic from the history of trade through the Mediterranean and into the Levant (that is, the eastern Mediterranean). Braudel devoted sections to historical developments in the Atlantic, but, as Colley points out, the recently published *Oxford History of the British Empire* shows its "Atlanticist bias," spending little ink on the Mediterranean and early British imperial actions in North Africa.[23]

*** 

The Tudors and Stuarts aspired to create a "Great Britain" in politics and religion and strived to develop trade and an empire abroad. The Tudor monarchs of the sixteenth century labored to create a domestic empire. Bloody fighting in Ireland and battles with Scotland marked Elizabeth's reign.[24] For the English monarch, Scotland had been a source of anxiety, home to a rival claimant to the throne, Mary, Queen of Scots. The ascension of the Scottish James VI to the throne as James I unified Scotland and England in name and geography but not as a nation. As the experience of James's son Charles would demonstrate, Scotland remained a hotbed of unrest and disunion in politics and religion.

Paralleling attempts to bring three kingdoms into one, trade around the Mediterranean and the connection of Mediterranean ports to the trade routes and commodities of Africa and the East determined foreign policy. Atlantic settlements and trade routes were developed, often despite enormous setbacks. Participation in the slave trade in Africa and ongoing trade in the Mediterranean figured highly in Tudor and Stuart policies.[25] Queen Elizabeth I supported expeditions to North America, privateers in the Atlantic and Caribbean, and forays into the slave trade in Africa. Yet signs of special interest in the Mediterranean are apparent. Elizabeth negotiated with the Ottoman Empire and supplied it with iron, steel, lead, copper, arquebuses, muskets, sword blades, brimstone, saltpeter, and gunpowder. The supply of munitions and attempt to circumvent Catholic countries and republics, especially France and Venice, that dominated trade in the Mediterranean Sea earned the English the reputation of traitors to Christianity.[26] Queen Elizabeth exchanged gifts with the *valide sultan* (the royal mother, Safiye), a powerful person in the harem and in the "reproductive politics" of the Ottoman Empire.[27]

The Stuarts, James I and Charles I, continued to forge alliances with the Ottomans, for economic and even religious reasons, and to foster Mediterranean trade. The monarchs treated with the Ottomans, exchanging promises and threats with the sultans to foster trade and protect merchants and sailors. Charles I apologized for the delay in writing back to the Sultan Murãd IV in 1642, explaining that the "dangerous troubles" infecting the kingdom had distracted him.[28] Cultural opportunities were taken, as Charles mandated that ships traveling east bring back Arabic and Persian books, though not so many "Alkarons," already common in Britain.[29] Presumably, Charles sought to provide texts to the new chairs in Arabic languages and culture at Oxford and Cambridge.[30] Further, the Ottomans protected British religious interests in Constantinople against the Jesuits in the 1620s, when that order attempted to disrupt Stuart attempts to forge a special relationship between Greek Orthodox believers and English Protestants.[31]

The British Mediterranean experience shaped domestic politics leading up to the civil wars in ways contemporaries might not have fully grasped. Better-connected captains, merchants, and trade "factors" and ordinary British seamen risked captivity and exposure to piracy when trading or fishing, as did Muslim sailors and merchants. Arguments in favor of better naval and coastal defense spoke to these problems of trade but highlighted the government's lack of funds to create it. "Ship money" provided for the defense of the country by sea and the defense of its ports, but as an innovation it foreshadowed battles between king and Parliament.[32] When the Stuarts attempted to force each town to pay ship money, not just the coastal communities, they raised the ire of the country. Yet, through the petitions of families asking the King, Lord Admiral, and Privy Council to ransom or rescue loved ones, we can see why the King might have thought ship money a good idea for the entire country. Depredations at sea took men, women, and children but also disrupted the livelihoods of those selling wool or finished cloth or fish and those importing goods from around the world to be sold throughout Great Britain. David Hebb estimates national costs, for lost ships and the redemption of captives, at more than £1,000,000, in the roughly twenty years before the outbreak of civil war in 1642.[33] The issue of "ship money" was once seen as a major factor in the civil wars and revolution of the 1640s; although it is far less simple cause and effect than that, ship money was deeply unpopular and demonstrates the crown's difficulty in raising revenues and defining national interests.[34]

The state was but one party to the development of trade and empire; private interests made up the other. The fleet that defeated the Armada in 1588, with the help of providential bad weather, was comprised of twenty-three royal ships and seventy-nine private merchantmen; the fleet that sailed to Lisbon the following year was even more dependent on private ships.[35] Sea power and trade depended on private enterprise working with a state in its formative stages. Michael Braddick demonstrates how the expansion of overseas settlement and trade began with private interests nudging the state. "Mercantile interests" developed new opportunities, described them in terms that coalesced with other state interests, and thereby fostered territorial expansion undertaken by the state.[36] Trading companies allowed the government to encourage trade without incurring much cost, and joint-stock ventures allowed risk sharing, especially in "exotic trades."[37] Even privateering and "contraband trade" helped to create and pay for permanent settlements.[38]

Thus, merchants and investors played a role in shaping government policies and diplomacy with foreign kingdoms and states. Communications between Anzolo Corter, the Venetian ambassador to England, and the doge and senate illustrate how merchants' interests factored into negotiations. Gaudar ben Abdala, representing the king of Morocco, came on an embassy to England in November 1637. A possible alliance between the kings against the Spanish was discussed but not finalized.[39] The embassy also celebrated an English victory against the independent republic of Sallee, feared by many for its far-reaching corsairs.[40] Yet the embassy highlighted contradictory impulses in British diplomacy. The British treated with the sultan to curb Tunisian or Algerian pirates, his "slaves," according to the British, to allow the British to trade and travel freely. British intervention in the Maghrib, however, complicated relations with the Ottoman Empire. After all, kingdoms and communities, like Morocco, that "feared Ottoman encroachment or sought assistance against Ottoman hegemony sent envoys and delegations to European Christendom."[41]

When Gaudar ben Abdala prepared to leave in April 1638, Charles I provided him with a man-of-war escort to protect him from Algerian pirates and "gave him various cloths, worth some 4000 crowns and a chain worth 500 to his English companion. The merchant's [*sic*] who trade in Africa are preparing another very rich one, to keep his master in good humour, as he has renewed the articles for trade in cloth between this kingdom and his own, which existed in the time of Queen Elizabeth and was interrupted by the rebellion of the pirates of Sale [*sic*], who have recently been subdued with the help of English ships. They hope to obtain many favours from this ambassador and great profit from the trade."[42] The presence of merchants was frequently noted by Correr, reflecting the importance of Mediterranean trade to the Venetian republic and suspicion of British actions. He remarked in November that "besides a numerous escort of aldermen and merchants, on horseback, he was accompanied at both functions by an earl." The latter's presence indicated a diplomatic slight to Venice, being a level of honor not accorded to representatives of the doge and senate. Correr urged the doge to "assert your rights, as it is not possible that they can pretend to treat your ambassadors with less respect than those of a barbarous prince, with whom they have not and can never have any great interest."[43]

Human costs, however, balanced the promise of great returns from Mediterranean trade. One hundred and fifty sail were taken between about 1614 and 1620. Contemporary documents estimated between 500 and 2,000 British captives in North Africa, many in Algiers, at any time in the 1620s and 1630s.[44] By way of comparison, survivors of disease and massacre in Virginia numbered 1,700 in 1622.[45] Some victims of piracy saw merchants as an obstacle to their relief. Petitioners, captives under the king of Morocco in 1628, urged the king to consider the "lives and liberties of so many of your distressed subjects" and not the "private benefit of a few merchants," precisely those who ten years later attended the embassy from the king of Morocco.[46] The distress led "many poore weomen" to petition Charles I about their 500 husbands, sons, and friends who were held captive in Algiers and Tunis, another foreshadowing of the popular politics and petitioning by women that would play a key role in the civil wars and revolution.[47]

In response to plaintive petitioners, the King appointed a commission in 1633 to study the problem of piracy and captivity in Barbary and to formulate a plan of action. The original charge to the commission was to determine how to redeem these captives and an estimated 500 more. The sheer cost of redemption, however, and the potential to encourage further profitable slave taking by paying ransoms instead led the commissioners to advocate attacking the root problem of piracy. Piracy, reasoned the members, "will like a Consumption weaken and ruin the whole body of trade insensibly, but as surely and mortally as the force of any just enemy in a lawful war." The commission identified three options: a peace treaty, war on the pirates, or the withdrawal of trade from the Grand Signor's dominions and subsequent attacks on pirate strongholds. The first two were discounted. First, treaties had been broken before. The commissioners asked if past actions could lead the King to depend on "Treatye or ye faith of Mahumetans," the use of "faith" here implying that Muslims could not be trusted to keep their word, that obligations would be broken. Second, war had "been tried at great charge w[i]thout effect, their ships are light, always clean and fitted as well to fly as to fight, so that they can (except surprised in a straight) choose their party." British ships were inadequate for fighting these enemies, being too heavy and concentrated on firepower. The foreign pirates had quicker ships that could escape into shallow waters. In addition, they estimated yearly war costs of £50,000.

The commission therefore settled on the last option: a temporary halt to trade, the withdrawal of ambassadors, and the provision of letters of marque for reprisals and the exchange of prisoners. The commissioners expected that those who had lost by piracy would seek reprisals at their own costs. After all, they argued, the Mediterranean trade was more lucrative than that in the West or East Indies. "One year's forbearance" would be "recompenced sevenfold" to the merchants; the Grand Signor would bring his "slaves of Tunis and Algiers" into line in order to preserve the flow of food from the White Sea and to maintain the trade with Constantinople.

The commissioners' acknowledgment of the greater value in Mediterranean than Atlantic or Asian trade hinted at the futility of the plan. Even their anticipation of and rejection of possible objections showed the primacy of trade in policies and the nature of merchants' counterarguments: the loss of customs revenues, the end to the trade and vending of cloth, and the difficulties in reestablishing merchants after a new peace. The members tried to answer the objections with calls to patience and promises of greater future returns. In return for temporary losses, the decay of trade and fishing in the west of England would be lessened. Trade might faint but never die. To sustain production for future trade, the Turkey, East India, and "East Land" companies should buy up the cloth that would have been sent to closed areas. The limitations of the state, so thoughtfully analyzed by Braddick, explain why the commissioners expected private subsidies and private patience for the plan to work.[48] Calls for private sacrifice to halt trade yet purchase goods from suppliers were not heeded. The trade did not end, nor did the problem of piracy. In fact, in the mid-1630s, merchants continued to trade with the sultan's enemies in North Africa, those who were "rebels to him." Contemporaries blamed this trade, which broke promises made to the sultan, for more English being made captive.

Although some voiced suspicions that merchants endangered sailors by violating agreements and served their own interests in influencing the government, the merchants might nevertheless play crucial roles in redeeming captives. Merchants served as interpreters and cultural mediators to help ransom captives, for instance, by explaining that gifts had to accompany ransom money, an exchange observed by the French and Spanish and only belatedly adopted by the British. The wealthy London merchant Sir William Curteen participated in the collection of £1,000 to redeem captives in the 1630s. His extensive trading ties with Morocco and his prior audience with the King emboldened him to intervene. He was frustrated by the gifts assembled to accompany a ransom, impatiently decreeing them "altogether improper and not fitt to be sent."[49] He complained about the English horses, markedly inferior to Arabian ones. The iron chest was useless to a king who had recently broken up all his gilt ones. The helmets "neither are nor can be worn in that country by reason they wear turbans, neither will the heat of the country permit it." Despite travel narratives and extensive contact over many years, those who prepared the payment seemed unaware of the climate, let alone the culture. Curteen, like other merchants, could use his personal experience in North Africa and the Levant to minimize English embarrassment or even the failure of an attempt to redeem captives.

The consequences of the interactions of pirates, merchants, and passengers from Christian and Islamic lands reached far beyond the money in trade or in ransoms, as the allusions to mutual distrust and fear suggest. British sources of the early seventeenth century reveal the anxiety and anger provoked by Turkish and North African pirates and the costs paid by ordinary seamen and their families. European fear of Muslims at sea and in land battles, however, was mirrored by Muslim fear of Christians. Muslim travelers to Europe lacked religious space and lodgings or neighborhoods specifically intended for Muslim visitors, versions of which did exist in Islamic cities for European visitors. Moriscos who settled in Tunisia, Algeria, and Morocco after the 1609 expulsion from Spain shared their graphic accounts of robbery, atrocities, and autos-da-fé in Spain, demonstrating that not only Protestant nations like Britain told anti-Spanish narratives that fed the "Black Legend."[50] British occupation of Tangier and attacks on Maghrib ports by European forces through the seventeenth century "revealed the vulnerability of coastal cities, which forced Moroccan rulers to move their capitals inland."[51] Nabil Matar pointedly uses "corsair" to describe both European and Barbary pirates and privateers, for instance, to demonstrate the ferocity of the European *nasara* (Christians) who attacked independent polities and client states of the Ottoman Empire. Matar blames the "relentless captivity" of Maghribi seamen by European corsairs for the manpower shortage that ultimately undermined the Maghribi naval capacity by the eighteenth century.[52] The impact on Mediterranean sailors provides another angle on the problem of "decline," as raised by Braudel.

***

The previous examples suggest the separateness of projects in the Mediterranean and Atlantic in the sixteenth and seventeenth centuries. The growth in trade across the Atlantic and the settlements attempted in that part of the world did, however, impact the Mediterranean system. The British government, confronted with piracy, acknowledged the connections before many towns did. In the 1610s, the mayor and civic leaders of Totnes, one of the boroughs whose trade passed through Dartmouth near the mouth of the River Dart, resisted contributing to a proposed levy of £1,000 to attack the pirates of Tunis and Algiers. Although the Privy Council argued the West Country of England had "receaved inestimable damage" from North African pirates, Totnes's merchants and leaders countered that they traded principally with Normandy and Brittany.[53] By the 1630s, however, these towns had become far less tolerant of the disruption of their trade because of piracy and more interested in defense, particularly because of Atlantic fishing. The counties in this region of England enjoyed a monopoly over the Newfoundland fishing banks and the trade in fish. As a consequence, the commodities and fishermen of these counties were frequently the targets of pirates, foreign and English.

Small coastal towns in the West Country, like Dartmouth and surrounding boroughs, were arguably disproportionately affected by piracy and captivity in the Atlantic and Mediterranean, even though London was a "hub" of "commercial and cultural developments," to borrow from Michael Braddick.[54] Petitioners to the Privy Council in 1636 sounded a far different note than had leaders in the 1610s. These petitioners estimated that £35,000 had been lost in twelve months, 2,000 captives could be counted in North Africa, and forty ships and barks from western ports had been taken.[55] A list of 343 captives in Sallee in 1637 similarly demonstrated the impact on communities in the West Country. Captain William Rainborow sailed the *Leopard* and led a naval expedition in 1636–1637 with two main goals: the redemption of captives and the destruction of "Turkish pirates" to Sallee. His list of captives included twenty-two people from Dartmouth, a number equal to those from London but less than the numbers from Plymouth (thirty-eight) and from Dungarven in Ireland (twenty-seven).[56]

Settlement in Virginia and the development of a lucrative fishery in Newfoundland exemplify the connections between the newer Atlantic trade and the established Mediterranean one. In the 1630s and 1640s, numerous ships bearing aspiring British colonists to Maryland, Virginia, and Providence Island were taken by Barbary or "Turkish" pirates.[57] For Dartmouth, experiencing the height of its economic prosperity in the 1630s, the vulnerability of cargoes, from Atlantic fishing grounds and from Virginia, to North African piracy was tangible. In 1636, inhabitants of the towns and boroughs sailing out of Dartmouth joined together in complaining that the Sallee pirates—and their old nemeses from Algiers and Tunis—severely limited trade. "Seamen will not be p[er]suaded to goe to sea, saying they had rather suffer the worst of miseries at home, then to be taken and made slaues by the Turks," thus putting an end to adventuring. "The petitioners allso present to y[ou]r Ma[jes]ties Princelie considerac[i]on the great dangers unto w[hi]ch the Virginia and Newfoundland flete and divers other m[er]chants shipps abroad in forraine p[ar]ts being about three hundred saile and are to come home scattered in the moneths of September and October, wilbe subiecte unles tymely prevenc[i]on be used."[58] The petitioners warned of an inability to expand their trade because of their difficulty finding enough men to sail, and they warned of the possible enormous losses to be suffered by 300 vulnerable ships.

Dartmouth's concern for ships from Virginia shows that Newfoundland cod was not the only valuable commodity brought across the Atlantic. Tobacco was traded in European centers in North Africa and in European ports and was similarly vulnerable to well-established piracy in the English Channel, along the "old" European and African Atlantic coasts, and in the Mediterranean. One historian who discusses Virginia's "tobacco-producing frenzy" mentions the demand in Europe but not in the Ottoman Empire or in North Africa.[59] Early modernists and early American historians are familiar with King James's "counterblast to tobacco," an herb used by "pocky Indian slaves." Muslim writers similarly decried the importation of a foreign herb, one from the "lands of the infidels," that had so easily caught on among Muslims. Mulay Ahmad ordered all the tobacco in New Fez burnt. One writer, Abu Salim Ibrahim al-Kallali, noted that European ships carried nothing but tobacco and entire cargoes were sold rapidly, paid for with "pure gold."[60] No country desired to see gold or silver move out of their domains in such quantities.

Scholars have only begun to explore how ongoing contact with Islamic civilizations may have shaped British contact with peoples in North America and the Caribbean. Wildness marks the experience with the environment and the people for the British making a westward crossing of the Atlantic. Colley contrasts the urbanized Islamic cultures with the settlement patterns of Native Americans, at least in the regions settled by the British. The dissimilarity between what the British encountered in the Maghrib and Levant and in their Atlantic forays and the denigration of the less urban, even nomadic societies for being less or un-"civilized" suggests the connections between the Atlantic and the Mediterranean experiences.[61] To the lack of native towns found in British regions of America and the paucity of colonial ones before the 1630s, Matar adds the dangers of transatlantic crossings and terrible weather. He quotes Sir Thomas Gates on Caribbean hurricanes: "Windes and Seas were as mad, as fury and rage could make them," worse than any storm in North Africa or the Levant he had ever experienced.[62] Similarly, in exploring racial communities, Pagden points out the British abhorrence of intermarriage, in contrast to (initial) Spanish intermarriage with what they saw as a "native aristocracy." The English saw wilderness and wildness, not cities and plantations and an aristocratic parallel.[63]

The British experiences in the Mediterranean, with Muslims and with the other European powers in that sea, and in the colonial ventures in North America and the Caribbean call for comparisons. The British felt a mixture of awe and fear of Islamic wealth, power, and "civilization" that contrasted with their perceptions of Indians. The British may have "yoked" together the Indians and Muslims, as Matar notes, but "their colonial ideology was winning against the Indians but losing against the Muslims."[64] The Indian–Muslim connection was not the only one that informed British ideology, however. The Spanish, with their colonial ideology, had success against Muslims and Indians and often against the English, too. Their conquest of highly urbanized civilizations in Central America casts doubt on a simple dichotomy of "urban" versus "nonurban" and therefore "uncivilized." British Protestants and Muslims shared the experience of captivity in Spanish prisons, and each developed a narrative of religious persecution around that experience. In London in the mid-1610s, when rhetoric about Barbary corsairs was well established, churchwardens and the Court of Aldermen nevertheless helped "barbarryens" return home, especially noting their capture by Spaniards. The elusiveness of the status of "deserving" of charity for many native-born English makes the donations to "strangers," particularly those so strongly associated with piracy and the misery of many English, all the more remarkable.[65]

***

Lewes Roberts's *The Merchants Mappe of Commerce*, published in 1638, included maps of trading cities around the world and lists of their commodities. The work celebrated trade and condemned any effort to restrict trade in dangerous places, including regions surrounding the Mediterranean, because of threats of piracy or loss. Algiers, for instance, traded Barbary horses, ostrich feathers, honey, wax, raisins, figs, dates, oils, castile soap, brass, copper, drugs, "and lastly, excellent piratical Rascalls in great quantitie, and poore miserable Christian captives of all Nations too too many."[66] The long list of commodities, finished by an almost jocular mention of pirates and captives, explained why trade was not halted in the Mediterranean despite the pressures of piracy and the development of Atlantic trade. National and personal risks and consequences were great, but trade and travel continued to the Maghrib and around the Mediterranean and to the rich fishing banks of the Atlantic. The trade in the Atlantic and Mediterranean followed independent routes, yet many of the commodities and the people involved reached both bodies of water.

For England, Great Britain in name, undergoing uneven state formation and lacking an "imperial identity," moving between Mediterranean and Atlantic ventures allowed diplomatic and trade ventures across religious boundaries that tested extra-European locales and alliances. The unevenness of British imperialism, marked by strengths and weaknesses in different parts of the world, attests to the uncertainty of empire. Ultimately, the picture revealed by the comparison of British experience in the Mediterranean and the Atlantic testifies to the need to place the Atlantic World within a more global context.

## Notes

1   Ahmad bin Qasim, "Selections from *Kitab Nasir al-Din ala al-Qawm al-Kafirin (The Book of the Protector of Religion against the Unbelievers)*," in *In the Lands of the Christians: Arabic Travel Writing in the Seventeenth Century*, ed. Nabil Matar (New York, 2003), 17.

2   I have chosen to use the spelling "Sallee," as this is most often used in these British sources.

3   Qasim, "Selections," 32–33.

4   Fernand Braudel, *The Mediterranean and the Mediterranean World in the Age of Philip II*, trans. Siân Reynolds, 2 vols. (1949; reprint, New York, 1972), 1:20.

5   Ibid.

6   Ibid., 1:140.

7   Ibid., 1:119.

8   Ibid., 1:137, 170.

9   Linda Colley, *Captives* (New York, 2002), 25.

10  Ibid., 34.

11  Ibid.

12  See David Armitage, *The Ideological Origins of the British Empire* (Cambridge, 2000), 6.

13  Ibid., 100.

14  James Anthony Froude, *English Seamen in the Sixteenth Century: Lectures Delivered at Oxford Easter Terms 1893–1894* (London, 1895), 2–3.

15  Ibid., 3.

16  Julian S. Corbett, *England in the Mediterranean: A Study of the Rise and Influence of British Power within the Straits* (1904; reprint, Westport, Conn., 1987), 82.

17  Braudel, *The Mediterranean*, 1:188.

18  Daniel Goffman, *The Ottoman Empire and Early Modern Europe* (Cambridge, 2002), 192.

19  Anthony Pagden, *Lords of All the World: Ideologies of Empire in Spain, Britain and France c. 1500–c. 1800* (New Haven, Conn., 1995), 87–88.

20  Matar, *In the Lands of the Christians*, xiii–xiv.

21  Colley, *Captives*, 35.

22  Braudel, *The Mediterranean*, 1:20.

23  Colley, *Captives*, 33 n.13.

24  Susan Brigden, *New Worlds, Lost Worlds: The Rule of the Tudors* (London, 2000), 228–31.

25  On empire within Europe, see Colley, *Captives*, 35.

26  *The New Cambridge Modern History, Vol. III, The Counter-Reformation and Price Revolution, 1559–1610* (Cambridge, 1968), 367–69.

27  Lesley L. Peirce, *The Imperial Harem: Women and Sovereignty in the Ottoman Empire* (Oxford, 1993), 227–28.

28  *King Charles His Letter to the Great Turk* (London, 1642), q. 2v-4. Thomason Tracts, E.110[10].

29  Meaning the Koran, or al-Quran; *Calendar of State Papers Domestic*, Charles I, vol. 260, 116, pp. 476–77.

30  P. M. Holt, "The Study of Islam in Seventeenth- and Eighteenth-Century England," *Journal of Early Modern History* 2 (1998): 113–23; Holt, "Edward Pococke (1604–1691), the First Laudian Professor of Arabic at Oxford," *Oxoniensia* 56 (1991): 119–30.

31  V. J. Parry, "The Period of Murād IV, 1617–48," in *A History of the Ottoman Empire to 1730*, ed. Parry, H. Înalcik, A. N. Kurat, and J. S. Bromley (Cambridge, 1976), 151. See also Claire Schen, "Constructing the Poor in Early Seventeenth Century London," *Albion* 32 (2000): 456.

32  See also Colley, *Captives*, 50; David Hebb, *Piracy and the English Government, 1616–1642* (Aldershot, 1994), 26–28; Hebb, "Profiting from Misfortune: Corruption and the Admiralty under the Early Stuarts," in *Politics, Religion and Popularity: Early Stuart Essays in Honour*

*of Conrad Russell*, ed. Thomas Cogswell, Richard Cust, and Peter Lake (Cambridge, 2002), 103–23.

33  As related in Todd Gray, "Turkish Piracy and Early Stuart Devon," *Report and Transactions of the Devonshire Association for the Advancement of Science, Literature and Art* 121 (1989): 168; Colley, *Captives*, 49–50.

34  On ship money, see also Conrad Russell, *Causes of the English Civil War* (Oxford, 1990), 183, 192; Armitage, *The Ideological Origins*, 115–16.

35  Michael Braddick, *State Formation in Early Modern England c. 1550–1700* (Cambridge, Eng., 2000), 205.

36  Ibid., 401.

37  Ibid., 398–99.

38  Ibid., 402.

39  *Calendar of State Papers Venetian* (CSPV), vol. 24 (1636–1639), 356, p. 332.

40  CSPV, 336, p. 316.

41  Matar, *In the Lands of the Christians*, xvi.

42  CSPV, 427, p. 400.

43  CSPV, 346, pp. 322–23.

44  On numbers in captivity, see Robert C. Davis, *Christian Slaves, Muslim Masters: White Slavery in the Mediterranean, the Barbary Coast, and Italy, 1500–1800* (Basingstoke, 2003), 3–26. On captivity, see also Daniel Vitkus, ed., *Piracy, Slavery, and Redemption: Barbary Captivity Narratives from Early Modern England* (New York, 2001).

45  Virginia figures from Susan M. Kingsbury, *The Records of the Virginia Company of London*, 4 vols. (Washington, D.C., 1906–1935), 3:536–37.

46  The National Archives: Public Record Office State Papers (TNA: PRO SP) 71/12, part 1, fol. 113.

47  TNA: PRO SP 71/1, part 2, fols. 130–132v.

48  Braddick, *State Formation*, 398–402.

49  TNA: PRO SP 71/12, part 2, fol. 234; *Dictionary of National Biography* (DNB): Sir William Courten or Curteene (1572–1636).

50  Matar, *In the Lands of the Christians*, xxvii.

51  Ibid., xxvi.

52  Ibid. Please note that "corsair" may refer to a pirate or privateer *or* a vessel.

53  Devon Record Office (DRO) 1579A/16/37–41.

54  Braddick, *State Formation*, 338.

55  DRO 1579/16/45 (3), fol. 2.

56  TNA: PRO SP 71/13, part 1, fols. 34r–35v. DNB: William Rainborow (d. 1642), one of whose daughters incidentally married Governor John Winthrop.

57  As related in Nabil Matar, *Turks, Moors and Englishmen in the Age of Discovery* (New York, 1999), 94.

58  DRO 1579/16/45 (3), fol. 1.

59  Betty Wood, *The Origins of American Slavery: Freedom and Bondage in the English Colonies* (New York, 1997), 71.

60  Matar, *In the Lands of the Christians*, xix–xx.

61  Colley, *Captives*, 106. See also Karen Ordahl Kupperman, *Indians and English: Facing Off in Early America* (Ithaca, N.Y., 2000), 138.

62  Matar, *Turks, Moors, and Englishmen*, 88–89.

63  Pagden, *Lords of All the World*, 150.

64  Matar, *Turks, Moors, and Englishmen*, 103.

65  Schen, "Constructing the Poor," 461.

66  Lewes Roberts, *The Merchants Mappe of Commerce* (London, 1638), 70.

*The Atlantic paradigm might seem unable to explain nineteenth-century European and U.S. imperial expansions, for in this century Europeans and Americans colonized Africa, the Middle East, Asia, and the Pacific. But the nineteenth-century U.S. and European colonization of the Pacific demonstrates that this paradigm can still do work for historians outside the Atlantic. According to Reed Ueda, certain archipelagos and islands have worked as "corridors" for the expansion of imperial projects. Hawaii played for the United States in the nineteenth-century Pacific the same role the Canary, Madeira, Azores, and Caribbean islands did for the Spanish and the Portuguese in the early modern period, namely, as a relay into new worlds of colonial institutions and their attendant multiculturalisms. Like the islands of the Atlantic, Hawaii became a relay for the expansion of pineapple and sugar plantations while witnessing the development of multiracial households and Creole cultures and cuisines. Was the early modern Atlantic experience used as an imperial model in any other setting outside Hawaii in the nineteenth and twentieth centuries?*

# Pushing the Atlantic Envelope: Interoceanic Perspectives on Atlantic History

## Reed Ueda

Any historical analysis that aims at understanding how the Atlantic World was created and "worked" in an interregional framework should include a perspective that shows the interactive societies of the Atlantic basin as forming a permeable and permeating structure rather than a contained and containing system. The interlinkage and interactivity of areas in the Atlantic basin that created an Atlantic World can thereby be seen as coexisting with the flow of forces between neighboring oceanic worlds. For historians who wish to study the Atlantic World in relation to global changes, it is helpful to envision the existence of an Atlantic periphery shaped by corridors that made the Atlantic region accessible, malleable, and extensive and that facilitated contact between Atlantic societies and societies in the Pacific Ocean and Indian Ocean regions. In this enlarged framework, the Atlantic World evolved and changed as its outer connections shifted and multiplied.

From a global vantage point, the Atlantic World can be visualized as an intensive regional structure with an extensive periphery that merged increasingly into a surrounding Pacific and Indian Ocean context in the course of the nineteenth century.[1] The building of transcontinental societies and economies appears from the perspective of the Atlantic core as centrifugal forces causing the disintegration of the Atlantic World. But these same processes can be seen, from the periphery, as extending the Atlantic World into interregional border spaces that facilitated the knitting together of societies of different oceanic regions in such a way as to precondition the globalization process of the late twentieth century.

Societies that had been integrated into North Atlantic and South Atlantic regional structures began to link with the societies of the Pacific world through the westward movement of population that accelerated in the nineteenth century. For example, westward expansion turned the United States into a continental corridor through which the Atlantic World connected with the Pacific rim, enabling its western coastal extremity to become an integral part of the Pacific region. By the twentieth century, the United States became a bi-oceanic transcontinental society, an Atlantic and a Pacific power. Thus, the building of transcontinental societies and economies—through railroads, domestic markets, and geographic mobility—may have ended the Atlantic World as it had existed from the sixteenth century to the nineteenth century, as suggested by J. R. McNeill's pithy remark: "The Portuguese caravel opened the Atlantic World, and the railroad closed it."[2] But in this interval, there was much occurring to suggest another dimension of change in which the periphery of the Atlantic World began to push outward into new zones of interaction with other regional peripheries.

The process of westward expansion in the United States and Canada brought not only natives of European ancestry from the eastern seaboard but also foreign-born settlers from Europe to the Pacific coastal regions of Anglophone North America. The Pacific coastal areas of Mexico, Ecuador, Colombia, Peru, and Chile also sprouted colonies of migrants from the Atlantic coasts of Latin America and from European countries on the Atlantic seaboard.[3]

Major archipelagos at geographically strategic locations in the Pacific basin played a key role in the development of interconnections between Atlantic and Indo-Pacific regions. The cultural and material forces of the Atlantic World flowed into the Pacific basin and from there into the eastern periphery of the Indian Ocean through a set of archipelagic links (map 1). The Philippines, the Aleutians, the Fiji Islands, the Hawaiian Islands, the Samoas, and French Polynesia were turned into interoceanic connecting points by the worldwide seaborne expansion of European imperial power. Island worlds of the North Atlantic near the European and African landmasses had once played a similar role in connecting the early modern economy and population of the Mediterranean region with an emerging set of colonies in the Atlantic basin. The Canaries, Azores, Madeiras, and eastern West Indies were corridors through which institutions, economic patterns, and people of the Mediterranean region began to pass into the Atlantic basin. According to Felipe Fernández-Armesto, the colonization of the Canaries by Spain "can therefore be seen as an episode in the long history of expansion."[4] Philip Curtin noted that this geographic shift was an evolutionary process as well: "The Atlantic islands in the fifteenth century thus came to be an intermediate step between the colonial institutions of the medieval Mediterranean and those of the Americas."[5]

As a location for the interaction of population, commerce, ecological factors, and diffusing cultural patterns, archipelagos were natural bridges between oceanic worlds. In an age when maritime travel reigned as the most efficient form of transport, archipelagos were highly accessible geographical sites for long-distance movers. Positioned on sea-lanes, they were small enough to be quickly settled and subjected to externally imposed cultural changes. Removed by the barrier of distance from other societies, they became stand-alone containers for the reciprocal exchange of inserted cultural modes and products and evolved quickly into local communities defined by Creole cultures and languages. Island worlds nurtured syncretic cultural complexes with the capacity to participate in interregional communication between societies in the Atlantic basin and the Pacific basin.

The central Pacific archipelago known by westerners first as the Sandwich Islands and then as the Hawaiian Islands, or simply Hawai'i (the current preferred spelling of Hawaii) offers a case study of how an island world functioned as an interoceanic corridor under modern conditions. In the nineteenth century, the Hawaiian Islands became part of the economic periphery of the Atlantic World. The sugar plantation and its labor

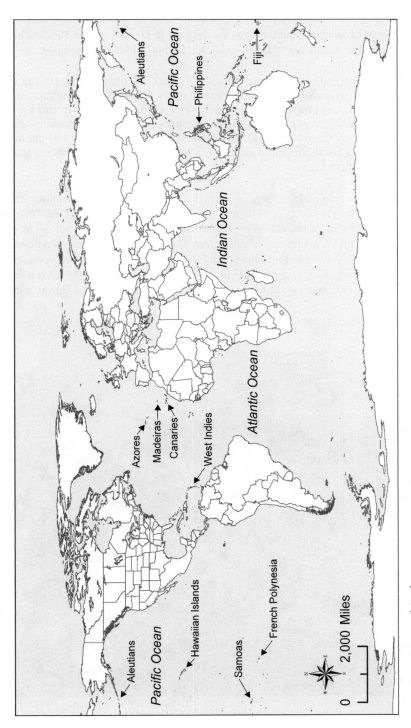

**Map 1** Major archipelagos.

system, a characteristic feature of the early modern Atlantic economy initially brought from the Mediterranean region, was established in Hawaii by the 1830s. Philip Curtin has charted the Atlantic-to-Pacific migration of this "plantation complex":

> [The] particular sugar revolution of the seventeenth century [in the eastern Caribbean islands] was only one among many. Each time the complex moved to a new place, it had brought on a new sugar revolution. The onward movement from Madeira to Brazil was a sugar revolution; the forward movement from the eastern Caribbean to Saint Domingue and Jamaica after 1700 was another; and still others lay in the future for Cuba, Mauritius, Natal, Peru, Hawaii, and Fiji— among others.[6]

Cattle ranching and whaling, which had developed in the Atlantic basin, also found a receptive site in Hawaii (fig. 1). Cattle ranches were established on the "big island" of Hawaii (the largest of the Hawaiian islands) and Maui, which also served as the Pacific home base of the New England whaling fleet. The products of commercial plantation agriculture, ranching, and whaling were crucial for integrating the Hawaiian economy with the Atlantic economy. Ninety percent of Hawaii's export total in 1878, 99 percent in 1899, and 98 percent in 1930 went to the United States. Sixty-seven percent of Hawaii's import total

**Figure 1**    Livestock grazing on a cattle ranch in Mau'i overlooking the Pacific Ocean.

in 1878, 78 percent in 1899, and 90 percent in 1930 came from the United States.[7] Trade and development pivoted on the interlinkage of structures of economic organization from the Atlantic region to Hawaii. The productive and commercial base of Hawaii, formed as offshoots of the Atlantic regional economy, turned these islands into an emergent central Pacific hub of transoceanic migration, ecological exchange, and transculturation.

The plantation, ranching, and whaling tripod brought settlers from New England who played a key role in the development of Hawaii's economic institutions. Hundreds of Protestant families, descended from or related to missionaries who began to arrive in 1820, formed an elite group of "malihini" (newcomers from the outside) implanted among the "kamaaina" ("people of the land," homegrown or native), and founded a commercial empire of sugar, pineapple, and coffee plantations.[8] The development of nineteenth-century Hawaii rested on an agricultural economy of scale controlled by a Creole oligarchy that paralleled the political economy of planter societies in the Atlantic basin.[9] James Dole came to Hawaii soon after graduating from Harvard and created a pineapple growing and processing business that evolved into the mammoth Dole Pineapple Company. The Parker Ranch, pioneered by John Palmer Parker of Newton, Massachusetts, who arrived on the "big island" of Hawaii in 1809 on a New England whaler, grew into one of the two largest cattle ranches on U.S. territory. In the decades before the Civil War, thousands of men from New England worked on the crews of the whaling fleets from New Bedford, New London, and Nantucket and made Lahaina in Maui their temporary home and base for their far-flung voyages to the northern Pacific and the edge of the Indian Ocean.

Successive waves of migration from a broad spectrum of societies in the Atlantic basin reshaped the ethnic and racial demography of the Hawaiian Islands from the nineteenth to the early twentieth century. Under the government of the Hawaiian monarchy and the successor U.S. territorial government that took over in 1898, immigrants from Portugal, Mexico, Germany, Scotland, Norway, Russia, Spain, and Puerto Rico were recruited to work in the plantations and ranches established by the first New England settlers and their descendants. From 1878 to 1887, 12,000 Portuguese immigrants arrived from the Azores and Madeira Islands. From 1906 to 1913, a second burst of immigration from these islands brought 13,000 more Portuguese newcomers. Six hundred Norwegians arrived in 1881; 1,400 immigrants from northwestern Germany came in the 1880s and 1890s; these were followed a little later by more than 2,000 Russians. The early years of the twentieth century brought 5,200 Puerto Ricans, 7,600 Spaniards, and smaller numbers of immigrants from Greece and Sweden. Large numbers of Scots migrated to Hawaii continuously from the nineteenth century; as a result, the 1980 U.S. Census enumerated 24,300 persons of Scottish ancestry in Hawaii. As a cumulative product of these flows, migrants from Atlantic settler societies and Europe constituted by 1910 a subpopulation of 44,000 persons, or approximately one-fifth of the entire Hawaiian Islands population.[10] They lived among a majority consisting of indigenous Hawaiians and Chinese, Japanese, Korean, and Filipino immigrants who came to work on the plantations.

Viewed from a worldwide perspective, Hawaii's peopling process is suggestive of how island societies, in the context of economic and technological change, played important roles in interlinking oceanic regions. Hawaii—the Pacific island world par excellence—was settled to a striking extent by peoples from other island worlds: first from the Atlantic (the Azores, the Madeiras, Britain, and Puerto Rico) and then from the Pacific (Japan and the Philippines, concurrent with the influx from Puerto Rico).

Island peoples proved to be widely available for participation in the mass-migratory movements spurred by the revolution in seagoing transportation and commerce.

Hawaii experienced a far-reaching environmental transformation as a result of the arrival of people, plants, animals, and microorganisms from the Atlantic region. This ecological encounter propagated epidemic diseases in the indigenous Hawaiian population, as it had among Native Americans in the sixteenth and seventeenth centuries. Like the latter, the indigenous population of Hawaii may have declined by 90 percent in the century after European arrival.[11] Hawaiian biodiversity was transformed by the importation of a host of plants and animals from the Americas (fig. 2). The examples that follow merely describe a few of the most visible imports. The "monkeypod" tree was brought from the forests of Central America, while the "kiawe" tree, or "mesquite," was acquired from South America; both species spread rapidly throughout the islands to become ubiquitous features of the landscape. The estimable Spanish horticulturalist Don Francisco de Paula Marin introduced many New World plants into Hawaiian terrain in the early nineteenth century.[12] Pineapple, coffee, papaya, and guava fruit were brought to Hawaii from the tropical areas of the Americas.[13] Horses and beef cattle proliferated as livestock ranching moved from the prairies of the Americas to the green upland pastures of Hawaii and Maui.

Situated at an interoceanic crossroads, the Hawaiian Islands became a fertile ground for transculturation between the worlds of the Atlantic and Pacific basins. In his study of the "colonial crucible" of Latin America, John Charles Chasteen provides a

**Figure 2** Cactus (first brought from Mexico) in front of a stand of Kiawe trees (introduced from South America).

description of transculturation as "the formation of new and distinctive" cultures, "fusions of two or more elements" in "kaleidoscopic combinations" that emerge gradually from a "give-and-take process."[14] "Imagine transculturation," Chasteen proposes, "as a thousand tiny confrontations and tacit negotiations taking place in people's daily lives, always within the force field of hierarchy and domination." As in colonial Latin America, transculturation in the Hawaiian Islands was embedded in a continuous process of contested interaction between indigenous people and newcomers.

The settlers from the Atlantic region brought new customs, styles, and artifacts that syncretized the local island culture. The Portuguese made "malasada" (fried dough) and "pao dulce" (sweet bread) into staples of local foodways. The Hawaiian ukulele, a kind of miniature guitar used in musical performance and dance, developed out of the "cavaquinho" brought by Portuguese immigrants (fig. 3). The cowboy subculture of Hawaiian cattle ranches was created by Spanish-Mexican "vaqueros" recruited to train locals who called them "Paniolos," a nickname that was a corruption of "espanole" or "Hispaniola." Missionaries, plantation owners, and ranch owners introduced elements of New England architectural style to the built environment of Hawaii. The cattle magnate John Palmer Parker built his ranch home in the "saltbox" style found in communities of coastal

**Figure 3** Portuguese immigrants. A woman holds the guitar-like musical instrument that evolved into the Hawaiian ukulele (from Eleanor C. Nordyke, *The Peopling of Hawai'i*, Second Edition. Honolulu: University of Hawai'i Press, 1989).

**Figure 4**   The Mokuaikaua Church of Kona on the 'Big Island' of Hawaii was built in the form of a New England Congregationalist church.

Massachusetts. The Reverend Asa Thurston worked with Hawaiian Christians to erect the Mokuaikaua Congregational Church in Kailua-Kona on the "big island" of Hawaii, designed to have the exterior and interior form of a classic Congregational church of a small New England town. The building materials, however, completely reflected the local Hawaiian environment (fig. 4). A visitor's guide to this historic site provides a vivid description of a construction that combined New England architecture with Hawaii's ecological assets:

> Someone has described the interior of the church as an ohia forest, for all the posts and beams are of a native Hawaiian tree species called ohia. . . . The pews, the pulpit, wooden screens and railings are constructed out of another indigenous tree known as koa, sometimes referred to as Hawaiian mahogany. The church walls are of lava rock cemented together by mortar made by mixing sand and lime. The lime came from burnt and crushed coral. Natives gathered the coral from the sea.

Perhaps the most pervasive daily aspect of transculturation was the "pidgin" English spoken by all who lived in Hawaii that developed from the social atmosphere of the labor gangs on the plantations. The Portuguese "luna," or overseer, played a key role in cobbling together "pidgin," which was first used in communications with laborers from China, Japan, Korea, the Philippines, and the societies of the Atlantic basin. A new local vernacular arose from the combination of a vocabulary of basic English words with terms drawn from the Hawaiian language, Portuguese, and other immigrant languages. It quickly became the everyday parlance of Hawaii.

Transculturation also reconfigured the public and civic culture of Hawaii to conform to a vision of Hawaii as a place to be civilized by Protestant Christianity and popular education. It was fitting that when James Michener wrote his best-selling novel *Hawaii*,[15] he was inspired by a stay in Walpole, New Hampshire, to frame the backdrop to his saga of Hawaii's New England missionaries.[16] New England had played a large role in creating the Pacific imaginary of Hawaii since the days when the first Congregationalist missionaries embarked from Boston on voyages to the Kona coast of the "big island" and the crews of whaling ships set sail from New Bedford for Lahaina, Maui.[17] Transplanted Yankee elites successfully proselytized the indigenous Hawaiian people, converting them into a Christian community. They also laid the modern foundations of Hawaiian education by fostering public school systems based on the common schools of Massachusetts and Connecticut and by sponsoring independent schools modeled on New England preparatory schools.

Settlers in Hawaii from the Atlantic region adapted to a new cultural and physical environment being created by the transculturative relationships among themselves and their Asian and Polynesian neighbors. The former became familiar with Hawaiian bark-cloth ("tapa") garments, Japanese farming implements, and Japanese footwear such as flip-flops ("zori") and platform shoes ("getta"). They grew accustomed to the presence of the mongoose, myna bird, bulbul bird, shama bird, ti plant, mango, and banyan tree—all imported from South Asia and ubiquitous in the everyday environment.[18] Newcomers from Atlantic communities encountered new faces of the built environment in the Buddhist and Shinto temples and graveyards, tong society lodge houses, Asian gardens, and Hawaiian cottages and sacred places of refuge. Their descendants in the twentieth century would see, within a few miles of downtown Honolulu, public statues of a Buddhist sage, the monarch Kamehameha I (who unified the Hawaiian Islands), and Indian independence leader Mohandas K. Gandhi, a hero to a prominent Hawaiian Indian merchant who sponsored its construction.

Over several generations, transculturative processes working at various levels of local life produced a trend toward cultural unification. For example, the diverse settler communities of Hawaii came to share a common diet and culinary style. At first, New Englanders, Europeans, and Latinos from the Atlantic World witnessed the new sights of Asian neighbors tending ducks, wet rice, soybeans, and "oriental" produce and Hawaiians farming taro and fishing with a spear and net. They found surprising, strange, and sometimes repugnant the food-preparation styles and dishes from the Pacific region, such as mashed taro root ("poi"), rice mounds ("musubi"), noodle soup ("saimin" and "udon"), soybean curd (tofu), dumplings ("manapua"), fish cakes ("kamaboko"), barbecue, curry, pickled cabbage ("kimchee"), pickled onion ("rakkyo"), and pickled radish ("takuan"). But through myriad experiences of sampling and sharing each other's food, the various communities of Hawaii would develop a common taste and culinary style called "local food." A breakfast would consist of American-style sunny-side-up eggs, Portuguese sausage ("chorizos"), and Chinese fried rice, while lunch might include "spam musubi" made from a rectangular mound of boiled Japanese rice topped by a slice of American Spam held in place by a wrapping of Japanese or Korean roasted, dried sea-weed. The popularization of these meals epitomized the cumulative, unifying effect of the continuous transculturation of Atlantic and Pacific life that diffused through the levels of everyday activities in the Hawaiian Islands. As recent historical studies have demonstrated, foodways and food production have revealed a great deal about the cultural and social history of ethnic interactions.[19]

The pervasiveness of transculturation in Hawaii also had an important demographic culmination in the form of widespread interracial marriage. Hawaii's cross-cultural pluralism fostered a tolerant atmosphere for racially mixed marriages. People of European ancestry who came to Hawaii from the United States, the other Americas, and Europe intermarried with indigenous Hawaiians and immigrants from Asia. In the 1920s, of marriages involving white males, 24 percent were interracial, and of marriages involving white females, 14 percent were interracial. By 1985, rates of inter-marriage had risen higher: 38 percent of marriages involving white males were interracial, as were 28 percent involving white females.[20] Substantially because of interracial marriages involving whites, the U.S. Census of 2000, which enumerated multiracial populations for the first time, revealed that Hawaii had by far the highest proportion of multiracial people of any state. The proportion of "the two or more races population" in Hawaii was 21.0 percent; while the next highest states were Alaska with 5.4 percent, California with 4.7 percent, and Oklahoma with 4.5 percent. (The national proportion of multiracial people was 2.4 percent.) These statistics bore out why Hawaii had been called the melting pot of races in the twentieth century.[21]

The pattern of modern Hawaiian history suggests that the "end of the Atlantic World" in the nineteenth century can be seen as the beginning of a new interoceanic world in which the Western Hemisphere came to share a greater interconnecting framework of collective life with East Asia and South Asia. Hawaii constituted an important facet of this complex world formed by a transregional, multicultural dynamic. As the Hawaiian Islands became a local site for the intermingling of forces from the Atlantic, Pacific, and Indian Ocean worlds, it grew into a platform for multiplying and intensifying interoceanic exchange processes, a geographic accelerator for new worldwide movements of trade, population, and capital.

As the Atlantic World extended its influences through economic, migratory, and ecological corridors that shaped a gradually integrating Pacific region in the nineteenth century, the Pacific World concurrently penetrated into the Atlantic through mass migration and trade. A major force in this Pacific-to-Atlantic movement was the vast movement of people who spread from the Pacific rim of Eurasia to the Pacific rim and Atlantic basin of North America and South America and to the core regions of the Caribbean. While most of the Chinese who emigrated overseas from the mid- to late nineteenth century moved to Southeast Asia, more than half a million Chinese immigrated to the Western Hemisphere—over 320,000 to the United States, 125,000 to Cuba, 100,000 to Peru, and 16,000 to British Guiana. Concurrently with the flow from China, laborers from India arrived in the Caribbean basin. About 200,000 Indians migrated to British Guiana, 100,000 to Trinidad, over 30,000 to Surinam and Guadaloupe each, and 20,000 to Jamaica. Shortly after the first waves of emigrants from China and India arrived in the Western Hemisphere, 300,000 Japanese immigrated to the United States from the turn of the nineteenth century to World War I. And, in the early decades of the twentieth century, 200,000 Japanese immigrated to Brazil, while Japanese immigrants settled in Canada and Peru in the tens of thousands. Creating an arc of migration from eastern Siberia to the Pacific rim of North America, over 50,000 Russians in the nineteenth century spread across Alaska to British Columbia and finally to Washington, Oregon, and California. After the turn of the century, 7,000 Indians and a few thousand Koreans immigrated to the United States. From World War I to the Great Depression, about 50,000 laborers from the Philippines immigrated to the Pacific coast of the United States.[22] By providing flows of labor to developing regions and networks of commercial activity to urban centers, trans-Pacific immigrants affected the economic development of the Atlantic World from its western periphery.

Immigrants from China, Japan, India, Korea, and the Philippines formed a significant source of manpower for rural and urban development. In the labor-short regions of the far western United States, they helped to build farms, factories, mines, and railroads. After the Civil War in the United States, rural districts and small towns of the South became an important destination for mobile Chinese. By the end of the nineteenth century, Asian immigrants were establishing themselves in the core areas of the Atlantic World. New York City's Chinatown became second in size in the United States only to San Francisco's. Concurrently, Chinese communities in Cuba expanded, and Indians formed sizable enclaves in Trinidad and Guiana. In the twentieth century, the Japanese population of São Paolo, Brazil, far surpassed the population of any Japanese local community in the far western United States or Canada and rose to over half a million.[23]

In these areas and others across the Americas where immigrants from China, Japan, and India settled, businesses run by these newcomers had a vital economic impact. Out of 12,700 Chinese in Cuba in 1899, almost 2,000 were merchants. In Peru, Chinese immigrants owned half the grocery stores in the city of Lima. Japanese immigrants became a primary factor in the commercial produce business of Los Angeles. In the state of São Paolo, Japanese immigrants in the decade before World War II ran enterprises that produced 30 percent of its agricultural output—which included 46 percent of cotton, 57 percent of silk, and 75 percent of tea produced—and concomitantly owned over a million acres of land. Indian immigrants became successful in British Guiana as commercial farmers and worked in various other business fields; the large Indian community of Trinidad produced one-third of the doctors and two-fifths of the lawyers in this island nation, controlling much of its professional business life.[24]

Finally, migrating peoples from Asia contributed to an international circulation of capital and commercial goods that connected the Pacific rim and the countries of the Atlantic World. In the late nineteenth century, Chinese fishermen of California's Monterey Bay region harvested abalone shells that they shipped to international markets in France, Germany, and China; they caught and processed squid that they sold to consumers in Hong Kong and China. Chinese merchants in San Francisco and Japanese merchants in Los Angeles brought to American markets enormous varieties of manufactured products from China and Japan, including processed food products, clothing, hardware, utensils, decorative objects, and other household items. An immense capital flow of remittances ran through Asian immigrant diasporic networks in Western Hemisphere countries to homelands in the Punjab of western India, the Pearl River delta of southern China, and the Ilocos district of the Philippines. In 1876 alone, Chinese immigrants in the United States sent $11 million in remittances to their families and villages in Guangdong province.[25]

An interoceanic perspective on Atlantic history from the nineteenth century reveals the intensifying involvement of societies in the Atlantic World in growing transregional patterns that reached beyond it to other regional worlds. Charting their historical development requires an understanding of how oceanic worlds flowed into each other, interacted with transcontinental societies, and created overlapping connective structures that preconfigured patterns of globalization in the twentieth century.

## Notes

1   K. N. Chaudhuri, *Asia before Europe: Economy and Civilization of the Indian Ocean from the Rise of Islam to 1750* (Cambridge, 1990); Sugata Bose, "Space and Time on the Indian Ocean Rim: Theory and History," in *Modernity and Culture: From the Mediterranean to the Indian Ocean*, ed. Leila Tarazi Fawaz and C. A. Bayly (New York, 2002); Walter A. McDougall, *Let the Sea Make a Noise: A History of the North Pacific from Magellan to MacArthur* (New York, 1993).

2   J. R. McNeill, "The End of the Old Atlantic World: America, Africa, Europe, 1770–1888," in *Atlantic American Societies: From Columbus Through Abolition, 1492–1888*, ed. Alan L. Karras and J. R. McNeill (London, 1992), 246.

3   Evelyn Hu-Dehart, "Latin America in Asia-Pacific Perspective," in *What Is in a Rim? Critical Perspectives on the Pacific Region Idea*, 2nd ed., ed. Arif Dirlik (Lanham, Md., 1998), 251–52.

4   Felipe Fernández-Armesto, *The Canary Islands after the Conquest: The Making of a Colonial Society in the Early Sixteenth Century* (Oxford, 1982), 1.

5   Philip D. Curtin, *The Rise and Fall of the Plantation Complex: Essays in Atlantic History*, 2nd ed. (Cambridge, 1998), 22.

6   Ibid., 73.

7   Andrew Lind, *An Island Community: Ecological Succession in Hawaii* (Chicago, 1938), table 2, 19.

8   Joseph R. Morgan, *Hawaii: A Geography* (Boulder, Colo., 1983), 141–57.

9   Lawrence H. Fuchs, *Hawaii Pono: A Social History* (New York, 1961), 21–22.

10   Eleanor C. Nordyke, *The Peopling of Hawai'i*, 2nd ed. (Honolulu, 1989), 42–52.

11   David Stannard, *Before the Horror: The Population of Hawai'i on the Eve of Western Contact* (Honolulu, 1989), 45–52.

12   Morgan, *Hawaii*, 152.

13   Gavan Daws, *The Illustrated Atlas of Hawaii* (Norfolk Island, Australia, 1970).

14   John Charles Chasteen, *Born in Blood and Fire: A Concise History of Latin America* (New York, 2001), 74.

15   James Michener, *Hawaii* (New York, 1959).

16   Christine Schultz, "One Perfect Summer Sunday," *Yankee Magazine*, August 1992, 123.

17   Hawaii as part of imaginative discourse is discussed by Rob Wilson, "Blue Hawaii: *Bamboo Ridge* as 'Critical Regionalism,'" in Dirlik, *What Is in a Rim?*

18   Robert J. Shallenbergen, *Hawaii's Birds* (Honolulu, 1984), 41–46, 83.

19   Donna Gabaccia, *We Are What We Eat: Ethnic Food and the Making of Americans* (Cambridge, Mass., 1998); Hasia Diner, *Hungering for America: Italian, Irish, and Jewish Foodways in the Age of Migration* (Cambridge, Mass., 2001); Rachel Laudan, *The Food of Paradise: Exploring Hawaii's Culinary Heritage* (Honolulu, 1996).

20   Nordyke, *The People of Hawai'i*, table 3-10, 222.

21   Nicholas A. Jones and Amy Symens Smith, *The Two or More Races Population: 2000* (Washington, D.C., 2001), 3; David Hollinger discusses the growth of mixed-raced populations and identities in *Post-Ethnic America: Beyond Multiculturalism* (New York, 1995), 41–43.

22   Hu-Dehart, "Latin America in Asia-Pacific Perspective," 253–72; Sowell, *Migrations and Cultures: A World View*, 125, 128–29, 215, 217, 334–42; Susan Wiley Hardwick, *Russian Refuge: Religion, Migration, and Settlement on the North American Pacific Rim* (Chicago, 1973). See also H. M. Lai, "Chinese"; Harry H. L. Kitano, "Japanese"; and Joan M. Jensen, "East Indians," in Stephan Thernstrom, ed., *Harvard Encyclopedia of American Ethnic Groups* (Cambridge, Mass., 1980).

23   James Loewen, *Mississippi Chinese: Between Black and White* (Cambridge, Mass., 1971); Lucy M. Cohen, *Chinese in the Post-Civil War South: A People without a History* (Baton Rouge, La., 1984); Xinyang Wang, *Surviving the City: The Chinese Immigrant Experience in New York City, 1890–1970* (Lanham, Md., 2001); John Kuo Wei Tchen, *New York before Chinatown: Orientalism and the Shaping of American Culture, 1776–1882* (Baltimore, 1999); Thomas Sowell, *Migrations and Cultures: A World View* (New York, 1996), 129.

24   Sowell, *Migrations and Cultures*, 126, 130, 217, 222–224, 336–337, 342; John Modell, *The Economics and Politics of Racial Accommodation: The Japanese of Los Angeles, 1900–1942* (Urbana, Ill., 1977); S. Frank Miyamoto, *Social Solidarity among the Japanese in Seattle* (1939; reprint, Seattle, 1981).

25   Lynn Pan, *The Encyclopedia of Chinese Overseas* (Cambridge, Mass., 1999); Rushni Rusomji-Kerns, Rajini Srikanth, and Leny Mendoza Strobel, eds., *Encounters: People of Asian Descent in the Americas* (Lanham, Md., 1999); Lane Ryo Hirabayashi, Akemi Kikumura-Yano, and James Hirabayashi, eds., *New Worlds, New Lives: Globalization and People of Japanese Descent in the Americas and from Latin America in Japan* (Stanford, Calif., 2002); Akemi Kikumura-Yano, ed., *Encyclopedia of Japanese Descendants in the Americas* (Walnut Creek, Calif., 2002); Sandy Lydon, *Chinese Gold: The Chinese in the Monterey Bay Region* (Capitola, Calif., 1985), 35, 57, 382; Sowell, *Migrations and Cultures*, 222.

# Part III

## *The Evolving Atlantic*

Unloading coffee in Brazil, ca. 1900. The Atlantic evolved in the nineteenth and twentieth centuries, yet continuities remained. Tropical products like coffee still connected the New World with Europe, even as goods that had once been luxuries became associated with mass consumption.

*In part 3, "The Evolving Atlantic," four historians demonstrate the relevance of the Atlantic paradigm to understanding the nineteenth and twentieth centuries while at the same time recognizing the changing nature of the Atlantic in the modern period. Atlanticists have confined their studies mostly to the period bounded roughly by 1500 and 1800. The American Revolution, Haitian independence, and the Latin American wars for independence typically signal the end of the Atlantic World, at least as it is formulated by most scholars and teachers. But if the world ever witnessed an "Atlantic Age," it was in the course of the long nineteenth century (from the end of the Napoleonic Wars to outset of the Great Depression). This was a period when tens of millions crossed the Atlantic to settle in the New World and many more returned back home. In absolute terms, such scale of movement and migration dwarfed the voluntary and forced migrations of the previous three centuries. José Moya shows that the nineteenth-century Atlantic was qualitatively different from that of the early modern period. The new Atlantic stemmed from unprecedented transformations in demographics (more births than deaths), politics (the breakdown of peasant communities, freedom of movement, citizenship, and nationalism), commerce (free trade), and technology (steam ships, railroads, telegraphy, and telephones). As these changes occurred, the former centers of the early modern Atlantic declined as the peripheries rose to become the sinews of vastly large, new trading circuits and economies of scale. According to Moya, this new Atlantic World ushered in "modernity" itself: cosmopolitanism at the most intimate and local scale, a thirst for novelty for its own sake, and a never-ending proliferation of ideologies seeking to understand the lived experience of change. Moya indicates that this new Atlantic World was relatively self-contained and thus distinct from today's global circulation of goods, peoples, and ideas. Yet why did the nineteenth-century participants often confuse their shared Atlantic experience with the globe itself?*

# Modernization, Modernity, and the Trans/formation of the Atlantic World in the Nineteenth Century

## José C. Moya

The Atlantic World is a relational concept. It refers not to a place, which is permanent (in terms of human, not geological, time), but to the sum of relations across the ocean. In this sense, it did not exist before 1492 (if we can exclude the Viking forays). It was "formed," not "transformed," after that date. We cannot say the same about 1770, 1800, or any other year. But, as the virgule in the title of this chapter implies, some of the changes during the nineteenth century were so drastic that they could be categorized as changes in kind rather than degree. The customary application of the concept only to the 1500–1800 period reflects a formalist perspective temporally bound by the formal political ties of European colonialism in the Americas.[1] In terms of social transatlantic connections in general, I would argue that the concept is applicable more to the late nineteenth and early twentieth century than to previous or later periods. The transatlantic circulation of goods, technologies, capital, ideas, and people (the only criteria that can give meaning to the notion of an Atlantic World) reached a magnitude then that dwarfed pre-1800 connections. And, in terms of human crossings and the density of personal connections, it surpassed the post-1930 period. This chapter examines these trans/formations by situating them in a transatlantic process of modernization, a process that eventually forged a sociocultural condition and worldview that can be accurately termed, as contemporaries did, "modernity."

The primary dictionary definition of "modern," "of or characteristic of the present," is useless for purposes of establishing some historical specificity insofar as it can refer to any time. The fifth definition, "of or relating to the period of history after the Middle Ages, from c. 1450 A.D. to the present day," sounds disarmingly quaint in its certitude but offers at least two heuristic leads. First, many of the transformations of the nineteenth century did indeed originate in the spurs of innovation of the late fifteenth and sixteenth centuries. Second, although one can always find antecedents, perhaps ad infinitum and ad nauseam, spurs of innovation and change do occur, and the "long" nineteenth century does resemble the "long" sixteenth in this respect.

In this sense, modernization is not simply a move toward the present but a process related to specific historical periods. It contains specific, recognizable elements and trends.

There were digressions and exceptions, particularly in Latin America during the aftermath of independence. But in general, economies in the Atlantic World of the nineteenth century moved from mercantilism to liberalism, toward an increasing division of labor (both internal and international), toward increasing commercialization and monetarization—not the other way around. The trends moved from agricultural to industrial, from rural to urban, from corporate to capitalist orders, from local isolation to global integration—not the other way around. Politically, no matter how erratic and incomplete, the tendency is equally clear: toward bigger and more powerful central government (in spite of the dominant liberal rhetoric), bureaucratization, secularization, legal equality, and mass participation. No matter how faulty democratic systems were, the franchise tended to expand, not contract; participation in secondary civic associations tended to grow, not decline.

Knee-jerk reactions against putative teleologies and metanarratives and the routine repetition of these objections have tended to obscure this. Teleology relates to the metaphysical study of ultimate causes and movement toward ultimate ends. To admit directionality in certain historical processes during specific periods is not at all teleologic. Neither is it a metanarrative, something that denotes a much more totalizing and grand tale. As the previous paragraph posits and this chapter illustrates, many of the nineteenth-century socioeconomic transformations displayed clear directionality.

One of the most momentous transformations of the nineteenth century offers a perfect example. Whether one views it as progress, as decline, or as neither, such a thing as demographic modernization—the transition from a system of high birthrates and death rates to one of low fertility and mortality—did take place in Europe during the long nineteenth century and is taking place in much of the world. This transition produced—as mortality fell faster than fertility—the first sustained population explosion in human history. Europe's population grew from 140 million in 1750 to 430 million in 1900, and its share of the world's inhabitants rose from 17 to 25 percent. This was not just a continuation of previous trends whose genealogy can be traced back in time.[2] It was an unprecedented phenomenon in the history and, apparently, prehistory, of *Homo sapiens*. Of course, there had been periods of population growth before. But growth had been slow (around 0.2 percent per year) and intermittent (with growth spurts rarely lasting more than two decades). The aptly named "demographic revolution" involved not only high growth rates (more than 1 percent per year in Europe during the nineteenth century) but also, for the first time in human history, continuous, unbroken expansion virtually unchecked by decimating plagues or—as long as the Pax Britannica endured—devastating wars.

The European demographic revolution fueled an unprecedented expansion in the second most elemental relation of the Atlantic World:[3] human crossings and connections. European migration to the Americas during the first three centuries of colonization had been less than massive. To begin with, the arrival of Europeans in the New World led not to demographic expansion but to the greatest demographic catastrophe in human history as almost nine-tenths of the native population succumbed to Old World diseases for which they had limited immunity. And newcomers did not make up for this loss. Less than a million Spaniards, three-quarters of a million Britons, and about half a million Portuguese entered the New World before the end of imperial rule.[4] Up to the middle of the nineteenth century, three times as many people had arrived in the Americas from Africa as from Europe.[5]

The European exodus to the Americas, however, would eventually be five times as large as the African one. Between the end of the Napoleonic Wars and the Great Depression (with a gap during World War I), 51 million Europeans migrated to the New World in the most massive transcontinental movement the world had ever witnessed. The global migrations of the past half century have finally surpassed that flow in absolute numbers, but they are far from matching it in relative terms (i.e., in relation to the planet's population then and now). If African slavery had been the characteristic transatlantic population flow of the eighteenth century, European peasant and proletarian free migration became the distinctive transatlantic movement of the nineteenth, particularly after its midpoint. Moreover, unlike African slavery, which was, despite some occasional returns, basically a one-way current, European migration included returns, back-and-forth crossings, and movements between the different nodes of the Western diaspora. These multidirectional movements multiplied primary social connections across the Atlantic World to an immensely higher degree than had been the case with Africa. Moreover, Africa's transatlantic connections withered after the middle of the nineteenth century with the end of the slave traffic and of the triangular trade that had connected Africa to the Caribbean, the northeast of Brazil, and Europe.

The massive European flow that replaced the African slave trade after the mid-1800s in transatlantic crossings was part of a wider process of modernization that included a series of other "revolutions."[6] The industrial one fueled the exodus in a variety of ways. During its early stages, it displaced more workers than it could employ. It promoted internal mobility and urbanization, which often served as a stepping-stone to overseas movement. It churned out an increasing variety of articles that generated a consumer culture of demands and desires, particularly among the young, the principal fount of transatlantic migrants. Contemporary popular theater in Europe abounded with characters who blamed the exodus on the younger generation's acquisitiveness and its cravings for factory-made shoes and garments instead of homespun espadrilles and blouses, for watches, guns, phonographs, bicycles, and other gadgets of the industrial age. Other products of the industrial revolution, such as cheap wood-pulp paper and the photograph, raised the emigration fever higher by carrying information and images of material success "across the pond."

The industrial revolution also made possible the international division of labor on which the commercial integration of the Atlantic World rested. It created direct demands for a variety of American raw materials: hides for machine belts and tallow for soap and lubricants from the huge feral cattle herds of the River Plate early in the century, cotton from the U.S. South, wool from Argentina (which had the largest sheep flock in the world by the 1880s) after the industrialization of woolen production in the mid-1800s, natural rubber from the Amazon after Charles Goodyear developed vulcanization around the same time, timber from Canada, and linseed from the pampas and the prairies. By promoting urbanization and the growth of a middle class, industrialization, along with the demographic revolution, expanded consumer demand for New World goods that were previously elite articles or grown by European peasants: Cuban sugar, Brazilian coffee, Virginian tobacco, Venezuelan and Ecuadorian cacao, and cereals, beef, and mutton from the temperate plains of Argentina, Uruguay, the United States and Canada. And the increased industrialization of North America and parts of South America created demand foci along the western shore of the Atlantic basin also. The principal British export to Argentina by the early twentieth century, for example, was not manufactured products but a raw material for industry: coal from Newcastle.

The trade of the industrial revolution rather than trade in general relied on and promoted a revolution in marine and land transportation that linked the Atlantic World ever closer. As long as specie and spices furnished the main articles of exchange, galleons, the sextant, and the marine chronometer sufficed. As heavy and bulky items with limited value per weight or mass (such as coal, iron, machinery, timber, rice, or wheat) became the main commodities of trade, advancements in the means of transporting them became a necessity, and the technological and innovative capacities that the industrial revolution unleashed made them possible. From the mid-1800s on, steamships increasingly replaced sailing vessels, the screw propeller supplanted the cumbersome paddle wheel, and iron (and later steel) hulls superseded wooden ones. These innovations in marine transportation were essential for both massive transatlantic trade and massive transatlantic migration.

The same is true of the "iron horse." Trains extended the pool of prospective emigrants from a few port areas into the European hinterland. Trains took them across the American continents. In both cases, railroads pushed the boundaries of the Atlantic World inland, making places like Chicago, Toronto, Warsaw, and Cordoba (Argentina) part of this world. Trains allowed the riverless Argentina pampas to become the second major exporter of cereals in the world, and most of that grain was shipped across the Atlantic. The importance and social savings of railroads were even higher in mountainous Mexico and the equally hilly coast of Brazil.[7]

The effects of liberalism were equally multifaceted. Although protective tariffs survived and at times even increased during the nineteenth century in various countries, mercantilist restraints tended overall to diminish, the abolition of the British Corn Laws in 1846 being an indicative signpost in the process. The impressive expansion of transatlantic commerce after the 1860s would not have been possible without a significant level of political commitment to free trade. Neither would the massive human exodus have been possible without a similar level of political commitment to freedom of movement. On the western shores of the Atlantic, liberalism provided the ideological fuel for the independence movements that ended the restrictions on entries that colonial gatekeepers had kept. On the other side, liberalism lifted the restrictions on exits in one European country after another in what Aristide Zolberg has called "The Exit Revolution."[8] By strengthening property rights, lifting restrictions, and promoting competition, liberalism stimulated the privatization of commons and the commercialization of agriculture in the Old World. This in turn encouraged transatlantic ties in two ways. It created a demand for New World fertilizers, such as Chilean nitrates and Peruvian guano, inserting almost single-handedly these countries into the Atlantic economy around the middle of the century, and it created greater opportunities and greater insecurity in the European countryside, elements that normally led—and in this case led—to increased population movement across the land and across the ocean.

Although, as stated in the opening paragraph, the concept of the Atlantic World has been mainly used for the 1500–1800 period, it was during the nineteenth-century demographic transition and economic shift from mercantile to industrial capitalism that this region dramatically increased its relative importance in the world. Demographically, Europe's and the Americas' proportion of the globe's population increased from

24 to 35 percent during the nineteenth century, while Asia's and Africa's proportions declined from 65 to 57 percent and from 11 to 8 percent, respectively. The economic shift was even more drastic. In 1800, Britain, France, and the United States together accounted for less than one-tenth of the world's manufacturing and China alone for one-third. By 1900, the share of the three North Atlantic countries had raised to almost one-half of the world's output, and China's had decreased to a mere 6 percent. As Bin Wong, Ken Pomeranz, Richard Von Glahn, and other historians of the "California School" have argued, the "Great Divergence" in economic development between the North Atlantic and the other advanced regions of the world (such as the Yangtze Valley in China and Gujarat in India) emerged not before 1800 but after.[9]

This transition from mercantile capitalism and colonial status to industrial capitalism and republican semidependency also shifted the social, economic, and political centers within the Atlantic World. On the eastern shores of this world, the Iberian kingdoms had played a hegemonic role during the first two centuries of its existence and an important one during the third; West Africa had supplied the bulk of the human westward flow.

In the nineteenth century, Africa's linkages with the New World increasingly weakened until they virtually disappeared. Portugal and Spain became only slightly less peripheral. In his 1776 *The Wealth of Nations*, Adam Smith already ranked Spain as the most "beggarly" country in Europe after Poland. Such evaluation reflected more than British Hispanophobia. By 1800, adult male literacy in Castille (10 to 15 percent) was thirty points lower than that of any other region in western and central Europe with the exception of Portugal.[10] In the next two decades, the Spanish Bourbons lost most of their Atlantic empire. By the mid-1800s, even in Cuba, the only remaining Spanish colony in the Americas along with Puerto Rico, the United States had replaced the official metropolis as the de facto economic power.

Britain, on the other hand, surfaced as the hegemonic power in the so-called economic imperialism, or neocolonialism, of the nineteenth-century Atlantic. The English rise in the Atlantic urban hierarchy reflects this process. As late as 1750, there were more cities with 10,000 inhabitants or more in Northern Italy (twenty-nine), southern Italy (twenty-five), and Spain (twenty-four) than in England and Wales (twenty-one).[11] A century later, the latter had already 123 such places. In 1890, it had 360. The proportion of the population living in cities went up from 34 to 80 percent between 1801 and 1911 as Britain became the most urban country in the world.[12] British urban dwellers became the most important exporters of manufactures and capital across the Atlantic and the most important consumers of the foodstuff and raw commodities that moved in the opposite direction. Indeed, the growth of the kingdom's port and industrial cities both derived from and fueled the new Atlantic liberal economy to a much greater degree than it had the old Atlantic mercantilist economy. Liverpool, in spite of its important role in the transatlantic slave trade, was still a minor city, surpassed in population by more than forty other urban centers in the continent, when the slave trade ended in 1807. In the following four decades, its population quintupled, and it became the sixth largest city in Europe and third largest in the Atlantic basin. Apparently, free trade (and Irish immigration) proved more advantageous than the slave trade and colonial monopolies.

The economic shifts on the western side of the Atlantic World were even more dramatic. Before 1800, the colonial success stories had been based on a combination of indigenous labor and precious metals or African slavery and tropical cash crops. The silver of Zacatecas and Potosi had turned Mexico and Peru into the shining stars in the firmament of a Spanish empire that spread from the Philippines to the Netherlands—the first empire over which the sun truly never set. The Spanish American viceroyalties had become a synonym of wealth in European languages, as when some characters in Mozart's 1790 opera *Cosi Fan Tutte* exclaim, "Ah, questo medico vale un Perú!" [Ah, this physician is worth a Peru!]. Sugar and slavery had turned Saint Domingue into one of the richest colonies in the world in the eighteenth century, worth many times more to the French than the great expanses of Quebec or Louisiana. Cuba's per capita gross domestic product had been 167 percent that of the United States in 1700 and still 112 percent in 1800.[13]

The nineteenth century drastically changed this situation. Prosperous Saint Domingue fractured its transatlantic connections as it became poor and isolated—although also less exploited—Haiti. Postindependence Mexico sank into political chaos and economic decline from which it recuperated only toward the end of the century. So did postindependence Peru, a country that was more urban in the eighteenth century than it would be in the nineteenth. The new economically booming and socially developing foci surfaced precisely in the most marginal and least successful corners of the European empires: temperate North and South America. The economic gap between Mexico and the United States is illustrative. For most of the colonial period, the former was actually significantly richer than the latter. By 1800, the per capita gross domestic product of the United States already doubled Mexico's. But the big chasm developed in the ensuing decades. By 1870, the United States had become seven times richer than its southern neighbor, a ratio that remains to this day.

Of the old colonial centers, only Cuba managed to retain—and even enhance—its prominent position in the Atlantic World during the nineteenth century. Indeed, although the island was one of the oldest colonies in the Americas and had been at the center of imperial trade since the beginning because of its strategic location, it developed a colonial plantation complex quite late. Before the middle of the eighteenth century it had been an entrepôt between the silver of New Spain and Spain, with a rural hinterland settled mainly by Spanish farmers and ranchers. The growth of sugar production and exports, particularly after the collapse of the sugar economy in Haiti during its revolution (1791–1804), shaped a peculiar form of capitalism during the nineteenth century. It combined the labor relations that had come to represent the polar opposites of backwardness and modernity in the political imaginary of the age: African slavery and European wage labor, with an intermediary form to boot, Chinese coolie labor.[14] The slave trade lasted longer in Cuba (until the mid-1860s) than anywhere else in the Americas.[15] Slavery itself (abolished in 1886) lasted longer than in any other country except Brazil, where it was abolished two years later. But after mid-century, Cuba also became the sixth largest receiver of European immigrants in the world and the largest employer of Cantonese coolies. Social relations of production thus seemed to combine those of the seventeenth-century Dutch East Indies (the originators of the Chinese coolie trade), eighteenth-century Saint Domingue, and nineteenth-century Uruguay.

Cuban hybrid capitalism is remarkable for the vitality of its quasi-modernity and the prominent place it gave the island within the Atlantic World. At the start of the nineteenth century, Cuba was already the most urban region in that world, surpassing the

Netherlands and England, and three times as urban as the colony's Iberian metropole.[16] By the end of the century, it was still the sixth most urban country on the planet.[17] The early introduction of the steam engine in 1794 and its wide use in sugar mills propelled the island into the forefront of the industrial revolution, albeit in an idiosyncratic way.[18] The technological innovations of the Atlantic World's nineteenth-century modernization reached the island amazingly early. Macadamized roads appeared in 1818, only two years after John McAdam himself had first built them in Bristol and a dozen years before they were built in the United States. The railway appeared in 1837, only a dozen years after its English debut, seven after its arrival in the United States, and a dozen before it would reach the imperial motherland.

Economic growth in temperate South America took off somewhat later than in temperate North America and even Cuba—after the middle of the century. But it was as dramatic. The River Plate area occupied by eastern Argentina, Uruguay, and southern Brazil had formed for much of the colonial period a backwater of the Iberian empires. By 1900, it had become the most developed region of Latin America. In 1800, Europeans were still using "worth a Peru" or "rich as Potosi" to convey great wealth. By 1900, these set phrases survived only in old books and had been replaced orally with "rich as an Argentine." Economic statistics support the expression. By the early 1900s, Argentina had become the eighth richest country in the world.

This leap rested precisely on the country's deep integration into the Atlantic economy: on the inflow of European capital, technology, manufactured goods, and labor and the outflow of the agropastoral bounty of the pampas. The country became the second most important receiver of European immigrants in the world after the United States. More Europeans arrived in Buenos Aires in just the three years preceding the outbreak of World War I (1.1 million) than had arrived in all of Spanish America during more than three centuries of colonial rule. As late as 1870, Argentina imported most of its cereals. By 1914, it had become the second largest exporter of grains in the world after the United States. Its foreign trade surpassed Canada's. It imported more goods per capita than any other country in the world with the exception of entrepôts like Belgium and the Netherlands.

Such integration would not have been possible in 1800, and a list of the obstacles can highlight, by contrast, the great transformations of the Atlantic World in the following century. In 1800, Europe had not yet accumulated enough surplus capital or surplus labor to usher in an age of global financial capitalism and mass migrations. That continent's mostly peasant and still relatively small population could not have supplied the farm laborers that the thinly populated temperate plains of the New World required for market production or a significant market for these plains' potential products. Even if they could have, mercantilist restrictions on the flow of people and goods on both sides of the Atlantic would have prevented it. Even if political restrictions had not existed, technological ones would have prevented it. Oxcarts and sailing vessels could not have taken millions of people and millions of tons of cereals, beef, and mutton from the hinterland to the port and then across the Atlantic. Without refrigerated ships, meat could have been transported only "on the hoof" or salted.

As the nineteenth century matured, the country steadily surmounted the previously mentioned obstacles. The invention of the repeating rifle and the telegraph and the organization of national armies after the middle of the century made possible the conquest of the last "Indian frontiers" in the Western Hemisphere (in the south in Argentina and Chile and in the west in the United States and to a lesser degree Brazil). Railroads facilitated their occupation, and wire fences facilitated the demarcation of property rights, selective breeding of animals, and the spread of commercial pastoral and crop production. The dramatic growth of the European population, its increasing urbanization, the emergence of consumer societies, industrialization, steamers, and the lifting of mercantilist restrictions on trade and migration overcame, as we noted before, many of the other obstacles to noncolonial Atlantic integration.

The socioeconomic shift that took place in the Western Hemisphere in general during the nineteenth century occurred also within countries. In the United States, the South, which until the 1830s had been the richest region of the country, ended up as the poorest, left behind by the exponential growth of the Northeast and Midwest. In Argentina, the once affluent Andean region, linked to the colonial silver economy of upper Peru, stagnated, while the Atlantic-oriented littoral became one of the ten richest regions in the world by 1900. In Brazil, the economic center moved from the old sugar-rich northeast to the diamonds and gold region of Minas Gerais in the eighteenth century and to the temperate south in the nineteenth.

The development of these regional gaps complicated racial inequality within the three countries. Most of the population of color (blacks in the United States and Brazil and mestizos in Argentina) resided in the once affluent colonial regions of plantations and mining. Their penury there had been caused not by economic scarcity but by politically sustained maldistribution. Chattel slavery and the semi–bondage labor arrangements of Andean Argentina had been, after all, legal practices instituted and upheld by the force of government. The abolition of slavery and coerced labor in the nineteenth century, by itself, might not have narrowed racial inequalities in a significant way even if the old colonial regions had retained their economic prosperity. A free market—even if it were truly free—might not have erased inequalities that had been originally produced and maintained not by market relations but by political power. Legal equality and the more open and competitive postabolition economic system might not have equalized the "playing field" when the starting points had previously been set so far apart by law and force. In the absence of any political rearrangement of the starting line, old inequalities were indeed preserved and reproduced by accumulated privilege, accumulated disadvantage, and unofficial discrimination. But the economic stagnation or decline of the old colonial regions worsened the situation by fusing problems of distribution and scarcity. In the colonial period, one could have characterized the nonwhite population in the three countries as poor people living in rich regions. The nineteenth century lifted the legal shackles that had kept them poor and/or enslaved but also turned them into poor people living in poor regions. Regional inequality became a structural reinforcer of racial inequality.

The relative lack of intraregional mobility further reinforced such inequality. Spontaneous migration depends on the cumulative development of social networks and social capital. Freed bonded laborers rarely migrate in large numbers during the generations immediately following emancipation. Before World War I, therefore, most of the population of color in Argentina, Brazil, and the United States remained in what had become the poorest regions of their respective countries. Meanwhile, European immigrants were heading directly toward the most dynamic regions precisely at a time when labor was scarce and wages and economic opportunities high. Blacks and mestizos moving to São Paulo, Chicago, or Buenos Aires mainly after World War I and the Great Depression became "the last arrivals"—in itself a disadvantage—and encountered less auspicious economic conditions. The link between regional and racial inequality was bolstered by divergent regional rates of urbanization during the nineteenth century. The population of color continued to be mainly rural, while European immigrants increasingly moved toward the New World cities that their presence helped expand.

Although the Western Hemisphere's integration into the Atlantic division of labor relied on the export of raw commodities, this stimulated sufficient activity in the secondary and tertiary sectors of the domestic economies to produce the fastest rate of urbanization in the world. In 1800, only one of the thirty-six cities in the world with over 100,000 inhabitants was in the Americas (Mexico City). By the time the liberal period of free migration and trade came to an end with the Great Depression, the Western Hemisphere contained 162 of the world's 678 cities with over 100,000 denizens. Its proportion of the globe's largest cities had thus gone up from 3 to 24 percent, the only continent to experience a proportional increase.[19] This growth also shifted the distribution of urban centers within the Western Hemisphere.

Before 1800, urban development in the Americas had concentrated in the Iberian domains (map 1). Those of the Spanish crown contained thirty-seven (or almost three-fourths) of the hemisphere's fifty largest cities around 1790; Brazil had seven, the

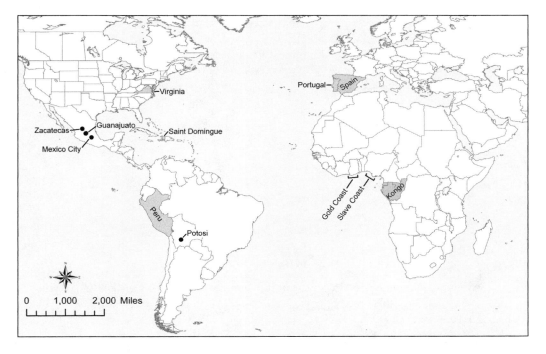

**Map 1**   Early modern centers of the Atlantic World.

United States five, and French Saint Domingue one. Nineteenth-century modernization and the mass arrival of Europeans that formed part of this process would change this dramatically. Already by the 1820s, New York had become the largest city in the hemisphere. By 1860, a 200-mile-long coastal strip in the northeastern United States contained the four largest cities in the New World (New York, Philadelphia, Brooklyn, and Baltimore). Saint Louis, Missouri, had by 1860 more than six times the population of San Luis Potosi, Mexico, which as late as the middle of the eighteenth century had been larger than any U.S. city. On the southern end of the hemisphere, Buenos Aires had been a minor town for most of the colonial period and still ranked sixth among Ibero-American cities as late as the mid-1800s. Four decades later, it had become the leading metropolis in Latin America.

Some of the old colonial cities that were able to reconfigure their Atlantic ties and received significant numbers of European immigrants, like Rio de Janeiro and Havana, were able to expand during the nineteenth century. But most of the expansion occurred in cities that had been unimportant in the colonial period or had not even existed (map 2). In one of the most spectacular urban leaps anywhere, São Paulo went from a town of about 20,000 inhabitants in 1870 to a city of over 600,000 half a century later, overtaking in the process all the once dominant cities of the northeastern plantation complex (Salvador, Recife, Olinda, Fortaleza, Sao Luis, and Belem). Buenos Aires's leap was, if anything, more spectacular: it moved up from nineteenth to third place among the cities of the

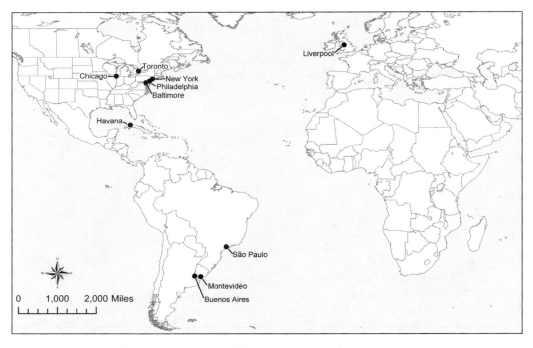

**Map 2**    Nineteenth-century centers of the Atlantic World.

Atlantic basin during roughly the same period. In the north, the most spectacular case rose—literally since the city invented the skyscraper—on the shores of Lake Michigan. Chicago went from a hamlet of 350 souls in 1830 to a town of 30,000 by the middle of the century to a metropolis of 2.2 million by 1910, when it stood as the second largest city in the hemisphere. Meanwhile, Charleston, South Carolina, which had ranked fourth among U.S. cities at the end of the eighteenth century, had dropped to twenty-second by the middle of the nineteenth and would drop to sixty-eighth by the end of the century.

Nineteenth-century modernization, thus, reversed the urban rank in the Western Hemisphere. Thirty-two, or 64 percent, of the cities that had ranked among the largest fifty in 1790 did not appear among the largest 100 in 1910. Inversely, seventy-nine of the largest 100 cities in 1910 were not among the largest fifty in 1790 either because they did not exist then or because they were just rural hamlets. This caused a dramatic regional change. In 1790, Latin America had contained forty-five, or 90 percent, of the New World's fifty largest cities and the United States only five. By 1910, Latin America had twenty-three of the New World's 100 largest cities and the United States seventy-two, with Canada holding the remaining five. Whether in South or North America, nineteenth-century urbanization was fueled by European immigration. By 1910, the largest eleven cities in the Americas and eighty-one of the largest 100 were cities of immigrants. And the five most urban countries (Uruguay, Cuba, Argentina, the United States, and Canada) were the ones with the highest proportion of immigrants in their populations.

Insofar as modernity, whatever its definition, is unfailingly situated in urban spaces, one can argue that the sites of the modern on the western side of the Atlantic World shifted during the nineteenth century from the colonial cores in Indo/mestizo- and Afro-America to Euro-America, the temperate ends of the hemisphere that had also been its socioeconomic margins, and to Cuba. Only the blinders of U.S.-centrism can obscure the fact that before 1776 the principal sites of modernity could be found not in Boston or Philadelphia but in places like Guanajuato and Salvador (in terms of the technology and market orientation of production) or Mexico City and Lima (in terms of books, theaters, architecture, music, and other cultural products).[20] And only the most equivocal definition of alternative modernities can conceal the evident relocation to places like New York, Chicago, Buenos Aires, Montevideo, and São Paulo that occurred during the nineteenth century.

Modernity shifted not only spatially but also in its internal content. Economically, it shifted—in the new nodes of modernity in the Americas—from growth to development, to use the distinction made by dependency theorists. The affluence of the old colonial centers had been based on natural endowments and the hyperexploitation of labor. This represented the most rudimentary form of economic growth: increase in output with some investment in productive infrastructure but no investment in social development. If anything, these regions had been misdeveloped. Their social structures became too unequal and vertical to provide a sound foundation for either nation building or a market economy. And the abrupt introduction of liberal capitalism in the nineteenth century often exacerbated these inequalities. In this regard, the colonial "failure" of marginal areas such as Canada, the Northeast and Midwest of the United States, the east of Argentina, the south of Brazil, and to a lesser degree Costa Rica, Chile, and parts of Cuba proved to be a blessing in disguise. Rather than misdeveloped by hyperexploitative colonial social relations, they were simply left less developed. The lack of dense indigenous populations and the limited importation of African slaves made these regions sparsely populated and increased the cost of labor and thus wages. Even Cuba, which like the United States and Brazil is a country with a dual heritage of plantation/slavery and European settlement, had some of the highest wages in the Western Hemisphere during the nineteenth century. Working-class wages in Argentina were eleven times higher than in Mexico. They were even higher in the United States and Canada.

Economic transformation on both sides of the ocean had an enormous impact on the sociocultural content and diffusion of modernity. The early modernity of the colonial period and the ancien régime was in most of the Atlantic World a veneer that covered a thin social slice. It is true that in places like the mining towns of the Mexican Bajío or the English midlands a protoindustrial proletariat had already appeared. It is also true that literacy had risen significantly in some, mainly Protestant, regions. But by the end of the eighteenth century, the population on both sides of the Atlantic was still made up by a mostly subsistence—and illiterate—peasantry with limited contact with broader material or cultural markets.[21] To be sure, generations of revisionist historians have modulated this tune. They have shown that rural societies in the ancien régime were not isolated and static. These finer brushstrokes have added details and nuance to the overall picture. They have not altered its contours. As Kinsley Davis noted half a century ago, cities may have existed since Sumerian times, but "urbanized societies, in which a high proportion of the population lives in cities, developed only in the nineteenth and twentieth centuries."[22] Before the late eighteenth century, modernity remained more project than reality, a mixture of ideas and ideals derived from Renaissance humanism and the Enlightenment that circulated among a small proportion of the Atlantic World's population. Its material and cultural goods—whether the sugar and cacao of the Americas, rococo paintings, the treatises of philosophes, or printed material in general—were still "luxury" rather than mass commodities.

The nineteenth century intensified modernity as an elite project and ideology. But the most momentous change lay elsewhere. That century massified modernity, turning it from ideology to a way of life. This can be detected even within high art. The transition to nonrepresentation in the plastic arts during the turn of the twentieth century was arguably the most conspicuous shift in Western art since the discovery of perspective during the Italian Renaissance. But this aesthetic revolution came alongside a social one.

As late as the 1880s, almost all plastic artists in Paris, the self-anointed capital of nineteenth-century Western culture, were—despite their cosmopolitan pretensions—either native Parisians or French provincials. A few decades later, they had become a truly cosmopolitan group nourished by continuing arrivals from throughout the Atlantic World: Picasso, Hugué, Miro, Gris, and Zuloaga from across the Pyrenees; Modigliani, Giacometti, De Chirico, Boccioni, and Klee from across the Alps; Max Beckman, Max Ernst, Franz Marc, Hans Hoffman, Emil Nolde, Lyonell Feinninger, Wilhelm Lehmbruck, and Georg Kolbe from across the Rhine; and Magritte, Mondrian, and Van Dongen from the Low Countries. From further east came the Czech Frank Kupka; the Norwegian Munch; the Rumanians Brancusi and Brouner; the Lithuanians Soutine and Lipchitz; and the Russians Chagal, Kandinsky, Natalia Goncharova, and Liubov Popova. From across the Atlantic came the Americans Man Ray, Alexander Calder,

Dulah Evans, and Edward Hopper; the Canadian Emily Carr; the Cubans Wilfredo Lam, Amelia Pelaez, and Mario Carreño; the Mexican Diego Rivera; the Uruguayan Torres-Garcia; the Argentines Xul Solar, Emilio Pettoruti, and Antonio Berni; and the Chilean Echaurren Matta.

These artists—and the much more numerous forgotten many whose works do not hang on the walls of major museums—turned what a few decades before had been a capital of Western art merely by self-proclamation into an actual one. In the process, cosmopolitanism evolved from posture to practice. The younger among these artists tended to study in the same places: the École des Beaux-Art first and the Academie Julian later. Whatever their age, they tended to live in the same neighborhoods: Montmartre first and Montparnasse later. Cosmopolitanism had indeed evolved from the ideological pose harking back to the universalist pretensions of the Enlightenment to the realm of the quotidian, of daily behaviors and encounters. Montmartre and Montparnasse had come to embody one of the distinguishing traits of the modern: the connection of the local and the global. And as the origins of their international bohemia indicate, the global at the time still meant the Atlantic World—or, rather, the foci of modernity within it.

Sociocultural changes at the mass level were even more significant in the transformation of modernity and of the Atlantic World. In 1800, three-quarters of adult males and a higher proportion of females in France, the standard-bearer of nineteenth-century cultural modernity, could not read or write. By the end of the century, literacy for both sexes was almost universal.[23] And so it was in most of the other nodes of modernity in the Atlantic World.[24] Primary schooling, which had been limited or nonexistent before the nineteenth century, became common and eventually massive and compulsory, drastically altering the lifestyle—or at least the use of time—of children and their parents.[25]

Mass literacy combined with technological innovation to create mass communication and to promote mass movement. Trains, steamers, macadamized roads, the omnibus, the electric tram, the subway, and later the automobile allowed the movement of goods, information, images, and people across the land and across the Atlantic to reach unprecedented levels. Carbon copies (1806); the telegraph (1844); the photograph (1840s); cheap, machine-made, wood-pulp paper (1850s); the mail system and typewriters (1860s); the telephone (1876); the linotype (1886, considered the most important advance in printing since the invention of movable type 400 years earlier); and the radio (1895) had a similar impact on the circulation of information. Reading became a mass activity. Internal migration and the great transatlantic exodus turned letter writing from an elite habit to a common practice. The postage stamp (introduced in England in 1840) became, according to the parliamentarian Enrico Ferri, "the most powerful immigration agent." European postal flows increased tenfold between 1876 and 1914.[26] Newspapers, magazines, and cheap novelettes became a mass business. Cheap wood-pulp paper and the linotype allowed common folks to become not simply consumers but also producers of printed matter. Immigrant societies (including those based on village ties), labor unions, socialist and anarchist groups, and a host of other popular associations printed millions of newspapers, magazines, and pamphlets that circulated throughout the new Atlantic World that their crossings had formed.

In the late nineteenth and early twentieth centuries, therefore, transatlantic linkages not only became denser than ever before but also delineated a geography that was more clearly demarcated than ever again. The area that these linkages defined became visible in anything from the geographical origins of painters in Paris to the shipping routes that carried linseed to make oil paint (from temperate South and North America to Europe) to the circulation of publications printed with linseed ink. Belle Epoque anarchists, for example, expressed their internationalist vision in hundreds of newspapers with universalist titles such as *Universal, Hijos del Mundo*, and *Dos Fraye Vort*. But the places where these newspapers were printed and the places where they were mailed or taken by wandering radicals show that that "universe" had boundaries. *Universal* was printed in Moscow and distributed throughout the Russian diaspora in France, England, Switzerland, and North and South America. The "Sons of the World" was printed by Spanish immigrants in Cuba and sent to Hispanophone coreligionists from Madrid to Montevideo. Jewish immigrants published newspapers titled *Dos Fraye Vort* (The Free World) in New York, Havana, Buenos Aires, Liverpool, Leeds, and London and remitted them throughout the Yiddish-speaking diaspora. That *Vort* was indeed wide. But it was Atlantic.

Anarchist Atlantic circles circulated more than printed paper. To begin with, those pages disseminated ideas, images, and practices. Indeed, anarchists often referred to their beliefs simply as "The Idea" or "The Ideal." By the early 1900s, the idea/l—and the practices associated with it, such as the formation of radical labor unions or "resistance societies," the general strike, theater, songs, bookstores, libraries, schools, newspapers, a visual iconography, and "direct action" or "propaganda by deed"—had spread among the working classes from Moscow to Montreal to Montevideo. The Russians Bakunin and Kropotkin were being read by millions from Saint Petersburg (the "Paris of the East") to Paris, from the "Paris of the South" (Buenos Aires) to that of the Caribbean (Havana). The naturalist plays of the Parisian Mirbeau, the Scandinavians Ibsen and Strindberg, and those of scores of working-class amateur authors of various (Atlantic) nationalities were being staged from the pampas to the prairies. The iconic image of the "Chicago Martyrs" (the eight anarchists imprisoned or executed after the 1886 Haymarket affair) circulated from Budapest to Buenos Aires and São Paulo to San Francisco.

As the bombs thrown by the "martyrs" in Chicago suggest, the transatlantic flow carried more than ideas, images, and material assistance. Seven of the "martyrs" had come from Germany. So had the alleged recipe writer, the fiery Johann Most and his explicitly titled pamphlet "The Science of Revolutionary Warfare: A manual of instruction in the use and preparation of Nitro-Glycerine, Dynamite, Gun Cotton, Fulminating Mercury, Bombs, Fuses, Poisons, etc, etc." Alexander Berkman, who attempted to kill steel magnate Henry Frick in 1892 to avenge the murder of eleven strikers, came from Russia. So did the person who bought the gun: Emma Goldman. So did Simon Radowisky, the teenager who assassinated Buenos Aires's chief of police in 1909 to avenge the victims of a police massacre. And the transatlantic current did not simply flow westward. Auguste Vaillant had just returned from the "Paris of the South," where he had converted to the "Ideal," when he hurled a bomb into the French Chamber of Deputies in Paris in 1892. Paulino Pallás, the Catalan typographer who, a year later, hurled two against General Martínez Campo in Barcelona had also just returned from Buenos Aires. Johann Most had found science's "best work" in its gift of "dynamite to the downtrodden millions of the globe." But that globe was far from global. The wandering dynamitards, as they were often called at the time, did wander far and wide. But they wandered within the Atlantic World.

The same was true of the other important internationalist labor movement of the period. In 1889, the Socialist Second International meeting in Paris called for a "universal protest" in demand of the eight-hour workday. The first of May of the next year, millions of workers took to the streets. This unprecedented level of coordination and mobilization from below was in itself a sign of the mass participation that came to characterize modernity for supporters and detractors alike. What in 1848 was little more than a slogan printed by a pair of German socialists in a manifesto seemed to have become a reality in 1890. Indeed, an exuberant Engels felt, as he witnessed 300,000 people marching through the streets of London, that the workers of the world had indeed united. But the streets through which this "great international army" marched demonstrated that it was an Atlantic World. They were located in Europe from Sweden in the north and Poland and Slovenia in the east to Portugal and across the ocean in six foci of the European Western diaspora: Chicago, New York, Havana, Buenos Aires, Rosario (Argentina), and Montevideo. Within a decade, May Day demonstrations had spread into the European eastern margins and into other regions of European settlement, such as Canada, southern Brazil, Chile, and Puerto Rico. After 1900, it spread to other Latin American countries. But by the outbreak of World War I, the universe of the "universal day of the workers" was still circumscribed by the Atlantic World and the European immigrant settlements in Australia and North Africa.

The universe of the Universal Postal Union, created in 1875 to unify the world's postal regulations, had similar boundaries. The union did facilitate a sine qua non of global integration, and the international circulation of mail skyrocketed. But of the fifty-two regions or countries that had joined before the end of the century, all but six were in the Atlantic World. The geographical spread of the railroad, that quintessential symbol of nineteenth-century modernity, reveals similar boundaries. All the first twenty countries to build railroads were in the Atlantic World. The "iron horse" reached a dozen Latin American countries (including landlocked and poor Paraguay and Bolivia) before it did Japan. The geography of the Atlantic had a greater impact in this technological diffusion than the relative economic development of the receiving region. The Atlantic World of the 1800s was obviously not self-contained. But its boundaries were real, not the a posteriori invention of a modernist metanarrative.

The contours of modernity and the Atlantic World around 1900 were set not only by the spread of machines but also by the transformation of ideas. Belle Epoque Atlantic modernity developed three novel traits that were either absent or relatively weak in previous versions of the concept. It was, to begin with, much more self-conscious. The term "modernism" had rarely if ever been used for a movement before 1800 or, for that matter, before the 1880s.[27] By the 1890s, it was being self-consciously used for what eventually became known as art nouveau in France, for the Catalan architectural trend associated with Antoni Gaudí, for the Spanish American literary movement associated with Ruben Dario, and, less self-consciously, for symbolist poets, any architecture that rejected historicism, postromantic writers, and neoromantic composers like Mahler, among others. In the next decades, it would be used as a self-defining label by groups as diverse as progressive French and Italian Catholics, Brazilian literati of the 1920s, and the architects (e.g., Le Corbusier, Mies Van der Rohe,

Walter Gropius, Richard Neutra, and Rudolph Schindler) of what also came to be known as the "International Style." International in this case meant in practice the "new" Atlantic World.

The diversity of trends encompassed by the same term illustrates the second novel—or accentuated—trait of post-1890 modernity: its polyphony. The following three decades probably produced more "isms"—from cubism to constructivism, symbolism to surrealism, and fauvism to futurism, just to use three letters of the alphabet—than the previous three centuries. At least in retrospect, modernity may have resembled a cohesive project during the sixteenth-century Renaissance or the eighteenth-century Enlightenment. But by 1900, the depiction of it as a unitary metanarrative of progress, instrumental rationality, scienticism, and a particular political project that has been produced by postcolonial, poststructuralist, and postmodernist critics is so reductionist that it does not even approach the level of caricature.

Belle Epoque modernity encompassed a dizzying array of voices that ranged from the hyperrational to the sensualist, from primitivism to futurism, from egoism to collectivism, from Marxian materialism to Kardesian spiritualism and theosophy. To use a musical simile, the contrast between the modernism of 1900 and that of 1800 could be equated to that between the formality and restraint of a Mozart symphony and the inclusive amorphousness of the Mahlerian versions of the genre or the tumultuous dissonance of Stravinsky's 1913 *Le sacre du printemps*, to many the piece that took music and ballet into the "modern age."

The contraposition of extremes in avant-garde ideology or art reflected the third novel—or augmented—trait of Belle Epoque modernity: its intrinsic need to challenge and exceed itself just to keep being, by definition, modern. At the time of the French Revolution—the birth date of modernity in some accounts—the term "avant-garde" was used only in military strategy. By the late nineteenth century, it was used almost exclusively for political radicalism, principally anarcho-communism—which actually represented the politics of antipolitics—and revolutionary socialism. In the following years, it came to include the artistic vanguard that often overlapped these political, or "antipolitical," movements.[28] The proliferation of the prefixes "neo" and "post" in the "ism" plethora further indicates modernity's compulsory movement toward the new. Indeed, in this continuous revisionism, in this relentless rush toward the edge, "postmodernism" became the only impossible "post." Perhaps, the definition of the term in the Catholic encyclopedia is not that off the mark: "Etymologically, *modernism* means an exaggerated love of what is modern, an infatuation for modern ideas, the abuse of what is modern."

That "abuse" had developed not during the sixteenth, seventeenth, and eighteenth centuries, as some have argued,[29] but during the next (and particularly toward its end), and by then it had a more defined geography than it would have in the future. Demarcating social spaces, particularly beyond the realm of face-to-face interactions, is as conceptually risky as fixing long chronologies. Space and time are continuums. Any demarcation or periodization is necessarily arbitrary. But some are less arbitrary than others. As historical periods go, the century-long Pax Britannica between the end of the Napoleonic Wars and the outbreak of World War I packs much more meaning than our traditional centuries, which are based purely on the putative birth of an obscure preacher in Palestine and our habit of counting by tens. This period witnessed the formation of industrial capitalism, nationalism, the demographic transition, avant-garde art, and the development of mass communication, mass culture, and mass movement—whether across the land or across the Atlantic. More Europeans, we should be reminded, came to the United States alone in just *three years* (3.2 million in 1905–1907) than had come to the entire Western Hemisphere in *three centuries* of colonial rule. Goods, technology, money, text, images, organizational practices, ideas, and ideals also crossed the Atlantic with a density and intensity that dwarfed that of the colonial past and probably surpassed that of the post–Great Depression period. Modern cosmopolitanism evolved from an ideological posture harking back to the universalist pretensions of the Enlightenment to actual behavior sustained by daily encounters, from concept to lived experience.

This century's meaning, moreover, concentrated spatially in the Atlantic World that it reconfigured. Almost all the markers of nineteenth-century modernity, from capitalism to cubism and from railroads to radicalism, emerged within and, before World War I, were circumscribed mainly by the Atlantic World. The circulation of humans and all sorts of material and cultural goods linked this world closer than ever, imparting it with more social meaning than most other large spatial constructs have. The Atlantic World, obviously, was far from hermetic. But its boundaries were more clearly demarcated in 1900 than they would be in 2000, when the circulation of goods, culture, and people had become a global phenomenon without any clear frontiers. Those boundaries are not simply heuristic constructions. They delineated then quite clearly a space where things were happening that were not happening—or happening with much less intensity—elsewhere.

Conceptually, we do not need to expand those boundaries beyond the Atlantic for the pre-1914 period just to make the obvious point that they were permeable. What we should do is actually define them more accurately. Africa may have faced the ocean, but its connections with this world had thinned after the mid-1800s and had shifted their axis later, north across the Mediterranean rather than west across the Atlantic. On the other hand, the notion that this was a *North* Atlantic World reflects little more than Anglo-American myopia. The Tropic of Cancer in this case was not only imaginary but also irrelevant. Both Havana, just south of that line, and Buenos Aires, south of the Tropic of Capricorn, were more modern and more closely tied to Atlantic circles during the nineteenth century than most cities in the United States and Canada.

## Notes

1   This formalist perspective is explicit in the title of Thomas Benjamin, Timothy Hall, and David Rutherford, eds., *The Atlantic World in the Age of Empire* (Boston, 2001). David Armitage refers to the "distinguished pedigree for identifying Atlantic history with 'early' modernity" in Armitage and Michael Braddick, eds., *The British Atlantic World, 1500–1800* (New York, 2002), 12. Elizabeth Mancke and Carole Shammas, eds., *The Creation of the British Atlantic World* (Baltimore, 2005), does not specify dates in the title but deals with the same period. Alison Games, *Migration and the Origins of the English Atlantic World* (Cambridge, Mass., 1999), does not specify dates either but deals with those who departed from London in a single year (1635). John J. McCusker, *Essays in the Economic History of the Atlantic World* (London, 1997), does not move beyond 1788 (or below the Equator),

indicating that the temporal (and spatial) connotations of the term "Atlantic World" had become so ingrained that that they did not need to be specified in titles.

2   Michael W. Flinn stressed the unprecedented nature of the European vital revolution in his aptly titled Chapter 6, "Breaking out of the System [of the *Ancien Régime*]," in *The European Demographic System, 1500–1820* (Baltimore, 1981). See also Michael Anderson, *Population Change in North-Western Europe, 1750–1850* (London, 1988).

3   The most elemental transatlantic connection—in the primary meaning of the word, not necessarily in the sense of "importance"—was the exchange on nonhuman living forms that altered the flora and fauna of both sides of the Atlantic and took place mainly during the sixteenth century.

4   Migrations from other European countries were much less significant. The largest of these, from western Germany to North America, never represented more than a fifth of the European stream to that destination. At any rate, James Horn and Philip D. Morgan have shown that only 1,042,000 Europeans in general reached the British domains in the mainland and the Caribbean before 1800 and that almost a quarter of these arrived to the United States after independence. "Settlers and Slaves: European and African Migration to Early Modern British America," in Mancke and Shammas, *The Creation of the British Atlantic World.*

5   Estimates of the African slave trade hover around 11 million, with 40 percent of these going to Brazil, 22 percent to the British colonies (three-fourths of them to the West Indies), 17 percent to the French West Indies, 17 percent to Spanish America (more than half of them to Cuba), and 4 percent to the Dutch colonies. Calculated from figures in Herbert S. Klein, *The Atlantic Slave Trade* (Cambridge, 1999), 210–11.

6   See Jose C. Moya, *Cousins and Strangers: Spanish Immigrants in Buenos Aires, 1850–1930* (Berkeley, Calif., 1998), chap. 1.

7   John H. Coatsworth, *Growth against Development: The Economic Impact of Railroads in Porfirian Mexico* (DeKalb, Ill., 1981); William R. Summerhill, *Order against Progress: Government, Foreign Investment, and Railroads in Brazil, 1854–1913* (Stanford, Calif., 2003).

8   "The Exit Revolution," in *Citizenship and Those Who Leave: The Politics of Emigration and Expatriation,* ed. Nancy L. Green and Francois Weil (Urbana, Ill., in press). Probably the first attempt to lift the restrictions on emigration characteristic of ancien régime Europe appeared in the new French constitution of September 1791. The first "natural and civil right" it guaranteed, listed before the rights of freedom of speech and of assembly, was the freedom "to move about, remain, and depart." That right to depart spread to the rest of Europe. John Torpey, "Leaving: A Comparative View," in Green and Weil, *Citizenship and Those Who Leave;* Moya, *Cousins and Strangers,* 20; Mervyn Matthews, *The Passport Society: Controlling Movement in Russia and USSR* (Boulder, Colo., 1993), 10–11.

9   Roy Bin Wong, *China Transformed: Historical Change and the Limits of European Experience* (Ithaca, N.Y., 1997); Kenneth Pomeranz, *The Great Divergence: China, Europe, and the Making of the Modern World Economy* (Princeton, N.J., 2000); Richard Von Glahn, *Fountain of Fortune: Money and Monetary Policy in China, 1000–1700* (Berkeley, Calif., 1996). For a contrary view that dates Europe's economic and technological advantage to 1500 and even before, see David S. Landes, *The Wealth and Poverty of Nations: Why Some Are so Rich and Some so Poor* (New York, 1998).

10  F. W. Grubb, "Growth of Literacy in Colonial America: Longitudinal Patterns, Economic Models, and the Direction of Future Research," *Social Science History* 14 (1990): 546–58.

11  Jan de Vries, *European Urbanization, 1500–1800* (Cambridge, 1984), 29.

12  C. M. Law, "The Growth of the Urban Population in England and Wales, 1801–1911," *Transactions of the Institute of British Geographers* 41 (1967): 125–43.

13  John H. Coatsworth and Alan M. Taylor, eds., *Latin America and the World Economy since 1800* (Cambridge, Mass., 1998), 26.

14 For the contradictions of these "archaic" and "modern" features of Cuban capitalism, see Dale Tomich, "World Slavery and Caribbean Capitalism: The Cuban Sugar Industry, 1760–1868," *Theory and Society* 20 (1991): 297–319.

15 David R. Murray, *Odious Commerce: Britain, Spain, and the Abolition of the Cuban Slave Trade* (Cambridge, 1980), 244.

16 Calculating the Cuban urban population in 1792 as those living in cities of over 10,000 inhabitants from data in Richard Morse, "Trends and Patterns of Latin American Urbanization, 1750–1920," *Comparative Studies in Society and History* 16 (1974): 439, produces a figure of 30 percent. The comparable figures given for 1800 in de Vries, *European Urbanization*, 39, are 29 percent for the Netherlands and 20 percent for England and Wales—the two highest rates in Europe and the second and third highest in the Atlantic world.

17 Calculated from data in Adna Weber, *The Growth of Cities in the Nineteenth Century* (New York, 1899), 136, 143–45.

18 Kenneth Pomeranz and Steven Topik, *The World That Trade Created: Society, Culture, and the World Economy, 1400–the Present* (Armonk, N.Y., 1999), 215, argue that industrial production may indeed have originated in Latin American sugar mills.

19 Homer Hoyt, "The Growth of Cities from 1800 to 1960," *Land Economics* 39 (1963): 167–73.

20 This argument informs Jorge Cañizares-Esguerra's award-winning *How to Write the History of the New World: Histories, Epistemologies, and Identities in the Eighteenth-Century Atlantic World* (Stanford, Calif., 2001). Its apparent iconoclasm reveals the pervasiveness of the blinders.

21 At the time of the French Revolution, rural inhabitants made up about 90 percent of the population in Europe, 92 percent in Mexico, and 95 percent in the United States. Jean-Luc Pinol, ed., *Histoire de l'Europe Urbain. Vol. II: De l'ancien régime à nos jours* (Paris, 2003), 26; the data for Mexico were calculated from data in ibid., 287–352, and Morse, "Latin America Urbanization." On literacy, see R. A. Houston, *Literacy in Early Modern Europe* (London, 2002), 141–62, and Mary Jo Maynes, *Schooling in Western Europe: A Social History* (Albany, N.Y., 1985), 14.

22 "The Origin and Growth of Urbanization in the World," *American Journal of Sociology* 60 (1955): 429. See also Eric Lampard, "Contemporary Urban Society: A Comparative View," *Journal of Contemporary History* 4 (1969): 3.

23 Maynes, *Schooling in Western Europe*, 14.

24 David Vincent, *The Rise of Mass Literacy: Reading and Writing in Modern Europe* (Cambridge, 2000), 9.

25 Ibid., 56–62.

26 Ibid., 4.

27 Tellingly, the official journal of the Modernist Studies Association, *Modernism/Modernity*, explicitly concentrates on post-1860 intellectual and artistic trends.

28 Miklós Szabolcsi, "Avant-Garde, Neo Avant-Garde, Modernism: Questions and Suggestions," *New Literary History* 3 (1971): 49–70.

29 Charles Piot, *Remotely Global: Village Modernity in West Africa* (Chicago, 1999), 179, defines modernity as "those everyday forms of culture, politics and economy associated with the rise of industrial capitalism in Europe of the sixteenth, seventeenth, and eighteenth centuries and disseminated globally by European imperial expansion."

*If the formation of independent nations in the New World usually finds historians turning inward to formulate nation-based narratives, Christopher Schmidt-Nowara uses the "age of revolution" as a departure point for his sweeping synthesis of slavery and emancipation in the nineteenth-century Atlantic. Schmidt-Nowara shows the continuities between the early modern Atlantic and the modern Atlantic: slavery, the slave trade, and the plantation system all persisted well into the nineteenth century. Indeed, modernity itself reenergized slavery in Cuba, Brazil, and the United States: the industrial revolution spurred demand for slave-grown cotton to turn into cloth and slave-grown sugar to provide calories for the working class. At the same time, slavery was challenged by new ideologies of individual liberty and the efforts of slaves themselves, for example, in slave revolts in St. Domingue (1791), Barbados (1816), and Jamaica (1831). In nineteenth-century Cuba, Schmidt-Nowara's focus, slaves did not successfully stage a massive revolt, but they did, in large numbers, join the war for independence that began in 1868. This put pressure on Madrid to begin the gradual emancipation of slaves, a process that culminated with full freedom in 1886. In what ways did these nineteenth-century dynamics differ from earlier emancipations that occurred, for example, in some northern U.S. states?*

# Continuity and Crisis: Cuban Slavery, Spanish Colonialism, and the Atlantic World in the Nineteenth Century

## Christopher Schmidt-Nowara

In 1879, the Brazilian representative in Madrid wrote to the Foreign Ministry in Rio de Janeiro about recent developments in one of Spain's two remaining American colonies: Cuba. Such reports were common in this period as both the Spanish and the Brazilian monarchies tried to control the process of slave emancipation. Throughout the 1870s and 1880s, Madrid reported back to Rio on emancipation laws, the likelihood of Spanish immigration to Brazil, and the impact of indentured Chinese workers on the Cuban economy. This particular report highlighted the gravest challenge facing the colonial government in Cuba: how to manage the abolition of slavery in the context of an anti-colonial uprising:

> Because General Martínez Campos 'Captain General of Cuba' decided that in the peace treaty with the Cuban insurgents there should be inserted a clause emancipating the slaves who fought in the rebel ranks, it was foreseeable that those 'slaves' who did not take up arms against Spain would demand the same. That is the only explanation for the slave insurrection in the district of Santiago, which today is in a state of siege.[1]

The Brazilian government's insistent fascination with emancipation laws, the outcomes of emancipation, and immigration, both Asian and European, in Spain's Caribbean colonies indicate not only the pressing nature of labor in Brazil but also that, in the nineteenth century, the interactions among different governments and slave societies shaped the destruction of Latin American slavery. Beginning in the late eighteenth century, the Atlantic World witnessed broadly based revolts against European colonial rule in the Americas and the consolidation of new nation-states. Slavery and the African slave trade always figured centrally in the revolutionary and nation-building process, not least because, as the previous report indicates, slaves themselves took up arms to fight for liberation, especially in Spanish America. Slavery was at times undermined by anticolonial and interimperial warfare (Haiti and most of Spanish America) and at other times strengthened (Brazil). To illustrate this process, this chapter explores the factors that influenced the history of slavery in Cuba from an Atlantic perspective (map 1).

**Map 1**    Nineteenth-century Atlantic.

Three issues central to this collection will receive scrutiny: first, the persistence of the characteristic economic, political, and cultural forces of the Atlantic World beyond the early modern period; second, different ways of conceptualizing the history of slavery and emancipation on an Atlantic scale; and, finally, whether "Atlantic history" is a sufficient container for comprehending this history or whether a more global focus is appropriate.

# SLAVERY, FREEDOM, AND LATE IBERIAN COLONIALISM

The Iberian empires relied heavily on the African slave trade. The sugar plantation—for example, in Santo Domingo in the sixteenth century, Cuba in the nineteenth, and Brazil throughout its colonial history—was decisive in shaping the volume and destination of the slave trade to the Americas. Nonetheless, the sugar plantation did not monopolize slave labor. Other agricultural products like coffee and tobacco relied on slaves. So too did mining, the core of the Spanish imperial economy in Peru and Mexico beginning in the sixteenth century and later in Brazil, where the discovery of gold in the province of Minas Gerais turned that region into a major slave-based economy. Beyond the export sector, skilled male slaves filled trades in cities like Havana and Rio de Janeiro, while enslaved women provisioned local markets throughout the colonies. Thus, while the demand for plantation labor was the major engine driving the transatlantic slave trade (to the colonies of rival powers as well), slave labor was to be found in every corner of the Iberian empires, though in varying degrees. Where plantation agriculture was most highly developed, as in Brazil and Cuba, the slave population was higher in absolute and relative numbers (table 1).[2] As these figures indicate, there were also large numbers of free blacks and mulattoes in the Iberian empires, composing almost half or even the majority of the population in some colonies, including the big plantation societies. This robust segment of the population demonstrates that even during the heyday of the slave trade and the wide use of slave labor, escape from enslavement was possible in the Iberian empires.

One of the most influential attempts to explain this equipoise between slavery and freedom is Frank Tannenbaum's *Slave and Citizen: The Negro in the Americas*, published in 1946. Tannenbaum, inspired by the Brazilian historian and sociologist Gilberto Freyre, posited essential differences between slavery in the Iberian and British empires. In the former, the colonizers had implanted medieval legal codes that granted important rights and protections for the enslaved. Moreover, the Catholic Church insisted on the equality of all, slave and free, before God. Thus, the peculiar institutions of the medieval Iberian monarchies, as they crossed the Atlantic Ocean, offered African slaves important prerogatives and avenues to freedom, such as the right of self-purchase (*coartación*), which checked the harshest impulses of New World slavery. In contrast, the British colonizers, in Tannenbaum's rendering, settled in the Caribbean and North America with little Old World exposure to slavery. Because of that void, they had to devise slave laws on an ad hoc basis as the plantation system took off in Barbados, the Chesapeake, and other colonies. British slave laws thus responded to the immediate interests of the planter class, completely divesting the enslaved of any protection or rights. In other words, unlike in the Iberian empires, the full brutality of plantation slavery went unchecked in the British, a system built to cut off the possibility of freedom.[3]

**Table 1**   **Population of Afro-Latin America, circa 1800, from *Afro-Latin America* by George Reid Andrews, copyright 2003 by Oxford University Press. Used by permission of Oxford University Press.**

| Country | Afro-Latin Americans | | | Whites | Mestizos | Indians | Total |
|---|---|---|---|---|---|---|---|
| | Free | Slaves | Subtotal | | | | |
| Brazil | 587,000 | 718,000 | 1,305,00 | 576,000 | | 61,000 | 1,942,000 |
| | 30 | 37 | 67 | 30 | | 3 | 100 |
| Mexico | 625,000 | 10,000 | 635,000 | 1,107,000 | 704,000 | 3,676,000 | 6,122,000 |
| | 10 | >1 | 10 | 18 | 12 | 60 | 100 |
| Venezuela | 440,000 | 112,000 | 552,000 | 185,000 | | 161,000 | 898,000 |
| | 49 | 12 | 61 | 21 | | 18 | 100 |
| Cuba | 114,000 | 212,000 | 326,000 | 274,000 | | | 600,000 |
| | 19 | 35 | 54 | 46 | | | 100 |
| Colombia | 245,000 | 61,000 | 306,000 | 203,000 | 122,000 | 156,000 | 787,000 |
| | 31 | 8 | 39 | 26 | 16 | 20 | 100 |
| Puerto Rico | 65,000 | 25,000 | 90,000 | 72,000 | | | 162,000 |
| | 40 | 15 | 56 | 44 | | | 100 |
| Peru | 41,000 | 40,000 | 81,000 | 136,000 | 244,000 | 771,000 | 1,232,000 |
| | 3 | 3 | 6 | 11 | 20 | 63 | 100 |
| Argentina | | | 69,000 | 70,000 | 6,000 | 42,000 | 187,000 |
| | | | 37 | 37 | 3 | 23 | 100 |
| Santo Domingo | 38,000 | 30,000 | 68,000 | 35,000 | | | 103,000 |
| | 37 | 29 | 66 | 34 | | | 100 |
| Panama | 37,000 | 4,000 | 41,000 | 9,000 | | 12,000 | 62,000 |
| | 60 | 6 | 66 | 15 | | 19 | 100 |
| Ecuador | 28,000 | 5,000 | 33,000 | 108,000 | | 288,000 | 429,000 |
| | 7 | 1 | 8 | 25 | | 67 | 100 |
| Chile | | | 31,000 | 281,000 | 34,000 | 37,000 | 383,000 |
| | | | 8 | 73 | 9 | 10 | 100 |
| Paraguay | 7,000 | 4,000 | 11,000 | 56,000 | | 30,000 | 97,000 |
| | 7 | 4 | 11 | 58 | | 31 | 100 |
| Costa Rica | | | 9,000 | 5,000 | 30,000 | 11,000 | 55,000 |
| | | | 16 | 9 | 55 | 20 | 100 |
| Uruguay | | | 7,000 | 23,000 | | | 30,000 |
| | | | 23 | 77 | | | 100 |

*Note:* Brazil totals incomplete; two captaincies (Mato Grosso and Pará) did not provide racial data. Ecuador figures show whites and mestizos combined. Colombia figures in italics indicate author's estimate. Empty cells represent "no data."

Tannenbaum's work was clearly an "Atlantic" history of slavery in the Iberian empires and postindependence Latin America, as it emphasized institutions and values that crossed the ocean in the process of conquest and colonization. Scholars of Latin American slavery continue to pursue his insights, exploring how service to the monarchy or the use of ecclesiastical institutions and religious culture gave slaves opportunities to pursue freedom or greater autonomy from their masters.[4] However, to understand more fully not only how some slaves escaped their bondage in Latin America but also how slavery as a whole was eventually destroyed, it is necessary to go beyond Tannenbaum's emphasis on the Iberian background to colonial Latin American slave societies.

On the one hand, Tannenbaum's treatment of the Old World has nothing to say about the African background to slavery and freedom in the Americas. To take one example, one of the largest slave rebellions in Brazilian history, in the city of Salvador da Bahia in 1835, was carried out by Muslim slaves, known in Brazil as Mâles, who began arriving via the slave trade in significant numbers earlier in the century. Their mode of organization was inspired by their experiences of religion and warfare in strife-torn regions of West Africa.[5] Less spectacular but far more common than armed uprising was maroonage. Historians have found that African-born slaves were more likely than Creoles to seek freedom through maroonage, flight from their masters. In some cases, flight was short term, a negotiating tactic used to make demands against masters. In others, however, the aim was escape from slavery and slave society altogether. Runaways formed communities outside the plantation belt, called *quilombos* or *mocambos* in Brazil and *palenques* in Spanish America, committed to preserving their independence and autonomy. Social and political organization in these rebel communities frequently drew on African precedents.[6]

On the other hand, Tannenbaum's thesis has received withering criticism over the decades for exaggerating the mild nature of Latin American slavery, especially from historians who work on the major plantation societies, such as Brazil and Cuba. While Tannenbaum portrayed Latin American slavery as practically contractual, studies of plantation societies call attention to the lethal nature of work there and the lengths to which planters and colonial officials went to preserve the slave regime against any challenge from the enslaved.[7] For example, in her study of emancipation in nineteenth-century Cuba, Rebecca Scott demonstrates that planters and the Spanish colonial state clung to slavery as the core of the plantation labor force until the bitter end. Although some slaves continued to purchase their freedom over the course of the century and others were manumitted by their owners, these were generally urban slaves, far removed from the plantation. As the author notes, "on the eve of final emancipation *coartación* affected only a tiny fraction of Cuba's slaves." Put another way, obtaining freedom and destroying slavery in Cuba—and elsewhere in Latin America—were hard-fought battles, not the inevitable prizes of beneficent slave laws.[8]

Thus, while following a version of Atlantic history that emphasizes the transplant of Old World institutions in the New, we can understand many aspects of the long-term structures of slavery and freedom in Latin America. From the beginnings of Spanish and Portuguese colonization of the Americas until the final destruction of slavery at the end of the nineteenth century, slaves continued to purchase their own freedom or that of loved ones, to complain to magistrates or ecclesiastical courts about abusive owners, or to run away, either temporarily or with the hope of escaping enslavement altogether in *quilombos* and *palenques*. Meanwhile, some owners continued manumitting slaves for a variety of motives. However, these routes to freedom originated and for the most part existed in colonial regimes committed to the African slave trade and persistence of slavery. In other words, slavery and freedom were part of the edifice of empire in the Atlantic

World. What happened to slavery and the expectations of freedom when the imperial edifice was shaken to its foundations?

To address this question, we need to combine our focus on the long history of slavery and colonialism with the conjuncture known to historians as the "age of revolution" and an approach to Atlantic history that emphasizes the interaction among different slave societies and political centers. By the later eighteenth century, old regime institutions and practices worked in tense coexistence with new ideologies that stressed individual liberty as the foundation of human society and revolutionary movements in the Americas and Europe that aimed at overthrowing the monarchies and empires that enabled the traditional avenues to freedom. Revolutionary movements for national independence and popular sovereignty in the Americas and Europe alike not only generated increasing ideological hostility toward slavery, across class and racial lines, but just as importantly also created political and military crises that permitted slaves and their allies to claim new spaces of freedom. In New World colonies rent by warfare, slaves could flee their masters, take up arms, and make increasing demands of revolutionary leaders to abolish slavery. None of the major European empires was immune from this process. In turn, the British, French, Spanish, and Portuguese monarchies not only fought among themselves but also had to combat, usually unsuccessfully, major insurrections against colonial rule. Slave regimes throughout the Americas were transformed: some strengthened, others forever weakened or destroyed.

## WAR, SLAVERY, AND REVOLUTION IN THE LATE EIGHTEENTH CENTURY

The first great revolutionary upheavals of the era, the American (1776), French (1789), and Haitian (1791) revolutions, demonstrated the centrality of slavery to the struggle over empire and nationhood. For example, in both the American and the Haitian revolutions, loyalist and patriot forces relied significantly on slave and colored militias. In British North America, Lord Dunmore created the Ethiopian Regiment, composed of slaves promised freedom for their service against colonial insurgents. In St. Domingue (Haiti), free colored planters raised their own force of slave troops to help them press their claims for political rights from the French metropolis. During the American Revolution, free people of color from St. Domingue served the French crown in the Battle of Savannah, while free colored troops based in Cuba helped the Spanish crown regain Florida from the British.[9]

The struggle for Florida had a longer history. A Spanish colony since the sixteenth century, Florida became a safe haven for slaves who fled neighboring British colonies during the eighteenth. Many of these runaways settled in the town of free blacks, Gracía Real de Santa Teresa de Mose, which abutted the city of St. Augustine, and distinguished themselves in battles against English invaders. In the nearby Caribbean colonies of Cuba and Puerto Rico, Spain had always relied on militias composed, separately, of free *pardos* (blacks) and *morenos* (mulattoes) (fig. 1).[10] During the eighteenth century, an era of heightened imperial competition and warfare, these militias took on greater importance in both offensive and defensive operations. The colonial regime also incorporated slaves into some of its units as it braced for combat with its British rival by expanding the armed forces.[11]

## SIGLO XVIII

Artillero de la dolación de Pto-Rico

Miliciano Moreno de Puerto Rico.

Miliciano de Caballería de Pto. Rico.

Miliciano de Infanteria de P. Rico.

Lit Boletin Pto-Rico

**Figure 1** Spanish Troops in Puerto Rico, including Black Militias. *Lealtad y heroismo de la isla de Puerto Rico* (Puerto Rico, 1897), 119. Courtesy Colleción Puertorriqueña, Universidad de Puerto Rico, Rio Piedras. These illustrations depict the units that repelled the British invasion of San Juan, Puerto Rico, in 1797. Earlier in the century, during the Seven Years' War, the British had successfully taken Havana, which they occupied for almost a year (1762–1763). That potentially catastrophic defeat prompted the Spanish monarchy to modernize its colonial defenses.

Although slave troops and black and mulatto militias fought in the American Revolution and although plantation discipline weakened during the war, planters eventually gained the upper hand after winning independence, strengthening the slave regime in the southern states, even as some northern states began abolishing slavery. In contrast, in St. Domingue, not only European colonial rule but also slavery was destroyed. The hundreds of thousands of slaves laboring on plantations played a central role in these victories, sending a far greater shock wave throughout the Atlantic World.[12]

By the late eighteenth century, the French colony of St. Domingue, on the western end of the island of Hispaniola, was the largest producer of cane sugar in the world. A small white population, divided between great planters and smaller property owners, shopkeepers, and professionals, ruled alongside a towering slave population, largely African born. There was also a significant population of people of color, many of whom had been freed by European fathers and some of whom were well prepared to take a leading position in the colony through education and the inheritance of wealth. Many free people of color were planters in their own right, though usually of coffee as opposed to sugar. Others filled positions in the colonial militia or the *maréchausée*, the gendarmerie dedicated to tracking down runaway slaves. They were accustomed to bearing arms, had served the French crown against the British, and identified strongly with the dominant colonial culture.

When revolution broke out in France in 1789, the *gens de coleur* saw the new regime as a potential ally against the "aristocrats of the skin" who sought to disbar them from the full enjoyment of their liberty through racial discrimination, which had grown more onerous since mid-century. They found numerous advocates in France but also had to confront the vexing question of slavery and an abolitionist society, the *Société des Amis des Noirs*, founded in 1788 and dedicated to the gradual abolition of colonial slavery. By the later eighteenth century, more and more enlightened Frenchmen had come to see New World slavery as a gross injustice. They also saw it as a powder keg ready to explode at any moment. Laurent Dubois has recounted how Louis Sebastien Mercier imagined awakening after centuries of slumber and encountering a monument dedicated to "The Avenger of the New World!" The Avenger was an "exterminating angel" who had led the slaves in victorious rebellion against European overlords throughout the Americas and brought slavery to an end.[13] These critics of slavery were not demanding rebellion and race war but, acutely aware of the violence bred by the slave trade, plantation labor, and racial discrimination, insisted that slavery be dismantled.

Thus, at the inception of the French Revolution, the questions of race, slavery, and citizenship were dramatically posed. When it became clear that the whites of St. Domingue and their French allies would enforce white supremacy, several free colored leaders, such as Vincent Ogé, returned to the colony and took up arms to force their claims. They were quickly defeated, horribly tortured, and executed, but new openings quickly presented themselves as both the colony and metropolis were divided. While the dominant groups fought among themselves, slaves in the northern part of the colony saw the opportunity to assert their own demands for freedom. Inspired by diverse African and European ideas of justice and freedom, a huge slave rebellion erupted in 1791 across the hinterland of the city of Le Cap and eventually spread to other parts of the colony.

As was the case with the American Revolution, rivals saw in this colonial unrest a chance to advance their own cause. Both the British and the Spanish fought to incorporate the rich colony into their own empires. The British dispatched thousands of troops to the Caribbean while Spain, from the adjoining colony of Santo Domingo, supported Toussaint Louverture, a well-educated former slave who, according to legend, was a reader of the Abbé Raynal, like Mercier a philosophe who had augured the violent destruction of New World slavery.

Ultimately, Toussaint defied his Spanish patrons. In 1793, he switched his allegiance from Spain to France in exchange for the legal abolition of slavery, ratified by the revolutionary government in France in 1794. For the next several years, he was the de facto governor of the colony, which he successfully defended for France against the Spanish and English. In 1802, France sought to restore slavery in its colonies. Although the French were successful in their other Caribbean colonies and able to capture Toussaint, other rebel generals, such as Henri Christophe and Jean-Jacques Dessalines, defeated a large European expedition and proclaimed the independence of the new nation, Haiti, in 1804.

By 1804, there were two independent nation-states in the Americas: the United States and Haiti. The fate of slavery was a crucial issue in the fight for independence and the consolidation of the new regimes. The United States reasserted the privileges of slave owners, though in the face of significant internal opposition. Haiti wiped out the colonial planter class and asserted the priority of slave emancipation. The wars of national liberation in the Americas always involved conflict over the survival of slavery, but the outcome was far from uniform. The same would hold true in the colonies of the Iberian monarchies a few years later.

## THE SPANISH AMERICAN REVOLUTIONS

If the French Revolution of 1789 and the ensuing struggle for dominance in different corners of the Atlantic opened the way for the destruction of slavery and colonialism in St. Domingue, it had a similar impact on Spain's American empire. Despite the efforts of planters and government officials, information about the Haitian Revolution circulated throughout the Atlantic World, inspiring would-be rebels against the established order. Moreover, events in Europe continued to exert important and unpredictable influence. When France invaded the Iberian Peninsula in 1808, the empires of Spain and Portugal suddenly found themselves thrown into profound crisis. The invasion had differing effects on slavery in the two empires. The Portuguese court embarked for Rio de Janeiro under British escort and remained there until 1822. With Rio as the new capital of the empire and the protection of British economic and naval power, Brazilian ports enjoyed greater freedom, urban and plantation slavery boomed, and political order reigned, at least in the short term.[14]

In contrast, a political vacuum opened in Spain and its overseas empire. The Spanish court fell captive to the French, and the country was submerged in a violent resistance to the occupying force between 1808 and 1814. Patriotic resisters gathered in the southern city of Cádiz to draft a constitution with the participation of deputies from the American colonies. In other words, in response to the crisis of invasion and war, the Spanish metropolis sought to reconstruct political legitimacy by replacing the toppled absolutist monarchy with a constitutional regime that incorporated the colonies as provinces with similar rights. As had happened with the French Revolution in 1789, slavery and the rights of people of color immediately presented themselves as complex and divisive issues. The language of the new constitution (1812) dubbed all inhabitants of the colonies as "Spaniards" but remained silent on slavery and barred free African-descended people from active citizenship unless they performed exceptional service to the nation. Thus, while seeking to break from the past by forging an empire based on constitutional rule, Spanish (and some American) framers nevertheless sought to prop up traditional forms of racial domination. The lessons of St. Domingue went unlearned; those who were denied freedom and equality as the old order was smashed would attempt to seize it when the opportunity presented itself.[15]

That opportunity came swiftly. The overthrow of the Bourbon monarchy led to an acute legitimation crisis in the colonies. Many patriots refused to recognize the authority of the new government or that of the French occupiers and rebelled against both, unintentionally shattering the colonial social order from the Río de la Plata in the south to Mexico in the north. We can see how the deep structures of slavery and freedom implanted during colonization interplayed with the revolutionary events of the era. The Cádiz government had emphasized the exclusionary aspects of Spanish rule in denying equality of rights to free people of color and defending the persistence of slavery. But on the ground in the Americas, loyalists and patriots alike benefited from the aspects of Spanish colonial slavery that endowed slaves and free people of color with military experience and expectations of freedom through various kinds of services. Moreover, the large free population, forged over centuries of colonialism by the multiple routes to freedom protected by slave laws and royal and ecclesiastical institutions, played an important role in the struggle over slavery and colonial rule. In other words, the long history of slavery in Spanish America had created populations willing and able to claim their freedom when given the chance, though for whom they would fight in doing so was not immediately clear.[16]

Both loyalist and patriotic forces mobilized slaves to fight on their sides during the protracted wars for independence. Loyalists could draw on old precedents by promising freedom in exchange for a term of military service. Such a compromise had existed throughout the colonial period and recognized the basic legitimacy of slavery as an institution while also honoring the mechanisms for acquiring freedom. Throughout the nineteenth century, from the first wars against Venezuelan patriots in 1809 to the final wars against Cuban patriots between 1868 and 1880 (more on this later), Spain was able to attract military recruits from the slave population, trading freedom for service to the king and nation, as it had done throughout the old regime. Patriot armies often tried to strike a similar bargain—many of their initial leaders were slave owners themselves, such as Simón Bolívar in Venezuela and Carlos Manuel de Céspedes in Cuba—yet found it harder to defend the persistence of slavery in the context of liberal and republican aspirations and the breakdown of traditional forms of order. As Peter Blanchard has observed, "The liberators' call for freedom with its associated slavery metaphor found favor at all levels of society, but it struck an especially resonant chord within the sector of the Spanish American population who in fact and by law were enslaved."[17]

Blanchard demonstrates that slaves from all corners of South America, where slavery was most widespread and where the battles were fiercest, flocked to patriot armies, using the language of national liberation to forward their demands for liberty. Free people of color also saw great promise in the revolutionary movements. For example, the Afro-Colombian population of Cartagena de Indias, long the major depot for the slave trade to Spanish America, enthusiastically supported the uprising against Spanish rule with the hope of achieving political equality under the new regime. Many were inspired by learning of the Haitian Revolution. Demands for equality and some vision of racial democracy pervaded revolutionary and postcolonial Spanish America as popular groups—slaves included—mobilized for independence and embraced liberal and republican ideologies. Under such conditions, efforts to formalize racial inequality as the Spanish colonial regime continued to do or to reinvigorate bonded labor were virtually impossible. Revolutionary leaders had to capitulate. Simón Bolívar, who led the struggle for independence in the viceroyalties of New Granada and Peru admitted, "It seems to me madness that a revolution for freedom expects to maintain slavery." With the important exception of Brazil, all Latin American states abolished slavery once they threw off colonial rule, though in most cases they compromised by granting freedom to slave combatants and passing gradual emancipation laws that extinguished slavery by mid-century.[18]

## CUBA AND THE SECOND SLAVERY

Cautious as many national states were, they nonetheless dealt fatal blows to slavery. As Robin Blackburn concludes, "Whatever the ultimate fate of the slaves left in Spanish America there was no question—barring foreign intervention or some dramatic domestic counter-revolution—of a new slave system arising in these lands, as manifestly was happening in the cotton states of North America." [19] This qualification is crucial because slavery could and did expand in the territories still ruled by Bourbons and Braganzas: Cuba, Puerto Rico, and Brazil. The first two remained Spanish colonies, and the last gained independence in 1822 yet under the leadership of a prince of the ruling Portuguese dynasty who pacted with colonial elites to ensure a relatively smooth and conservative transition to nationhood.

How could such a venerable institution survive the revolutionary maelstrom of the late eighteenth and early nineteenth centuries? Ironically, it was the very forces of modernity, on an Atlantic scale, that gave a lease on life to what Dale Tomich calls the "second slavery." [20] Tomich uses this category to characterize the conditions driving the resurgence of slavery in Cuba, Brazil, and the United States in the early to mid-nineteenth century when, despite the unleashing of antislavery movements on both sides of the Atlantic and slavery's destruction in large parts of the Americas, more slaves worked on New World plantations than ever before. The takeoff of industrial production in England created an escalating demand for the goods produced on American plantations, such as cotton in the United States, sugar in Cuba, and sugar and coffee in Brazil. Planters ruthlessly expanded the frontiers of exploitation, opening the Deep South in the United States, pushing eastward from Havana in Cuba and westward into the hinterlands of Rio de Janeiro and São Paulo in Brazil. Although using an old form of agricultural production, the slave plantation, they increasingly combined it with mechanized technology to increase productivity. They bought slaves from Africa when they could, especially in Cuba and Brazil, but also opened internal slave trades—for example, from the Brazilian northeast to the southeastern provinces and from the U.S. Upper South to the Deep South. Cuban planters looked beyond the Atlantic, trafficking in indentured workers from Yucatán within the Caribbean or grasping around the globe as they imported well over 100,000 Chinese contract laborers, many of whom they reduced to de facto enslavement on the plantations.[21]

Nonetheless, while market forces and the interests of states and local elites propped up—indeed rejuvenated—the slave trade and the plantation, the revolutionary conjuncture created a teeth-grinding friction between defenders and opponents of slavery. Cuba offers a complicated example of these institutional, political, and ideological tensions at work. Plantation slavery spread there in the later eighteenth century, advanced by imperial reforms carried out by the Bourbons and eventually by the destruction of its greatest competitor, St. Domingue. While revolution in its neighboring colony haunted planters and officials in Cuba, they were nonetheless optimistic about the prospects of maintaining social order within a slave-based economy. Francisco Arango y Parreño, a Creole planter and representative to the court in Madrid, for example, tried to have his cake and eat it too as he helped set the conditions for the Cuban plantation's takeoff. Well aware that he was proposing commitment to the slave trade and the plantation unprecedented in Spanish colonial history, Arango y Parreño argued that Cuba would avoid the turmoil of St. Domingue because of the suavity of Spanish slave laws and customs. Venerable colonial institutions would mitigate the worst extremes of rapid economic growth. Many Spaniards agreed with him. During the debates over the fate of slavery during the French occupation of Spain, some commentators held that the metropolis could safely maintain the institution in its American colonies because of the good treatment ensured by wise laws and customs. For example, one writer noted that slaves in the Americas frequently fled from British colonies to neighboring Spanish ones because there "they experience[d] greater humanity and consideration for their unfortunate condition." [22]

Cuban slave society, not surprisingly, did not develop as its defenders foresaw. Older practices and institutions that regulated relations among slaves, masters, and the colonial state did persist through the plantation revolution. *Coartación* and manumission continued, especially outside the plantation zone, as did maroonage, usually close to plantations. The colonial church sought to assert its authority over the slave population by enforcing rituals like marriage and baptism. Moreover, with the passing of a gradual emancipation law in 1870, the Moret Law, slaves and free people of color consistently used the law to defend their legal claims to freedom, indeed to such a degree that they hastened the final abolition of slavery in 1886.[23]

However, the forces that overthrew Haitian and Spanish American slavery earlier in the century also coalesced in Cuba, transforming the precarious balance between slavery and freedom in which Arango and others placed so much confidence. Even as planters and the state were collaborating in the construction of a plantation economy without precedent in the Spanish colonial empire, news of slavery's unmaking in other places circulated throughout Cuban society. The influence of the Haitian Revolution on

Cuban slave society has received close attention recently. Historians have always known that the destruction of slavery in a nearby colony preoccupied Cuban and Spanish elites throughout the century; new research gives some inkling of what they and other sectors of Cuban society knew and thought about Haiti. For example, there was considerable traffic between Cuba and the island of Hispaniola. Planters from St. Domingue and the Spanish colony of Santo Domingo fled to Cuba for safety. Spanish troops who fought in Hispaniola in the early days of the revolution returned to Cuba, as did black officers from St. Domingue, such as Jean-François (called Juan Francisco in Cuba and Spain), whom Spain had supported against the French until the peace of 1795. In 1812, Spanish officials uncovered the plan for a rebellion in Havana in the context of persistent slave uprisings around the island. The leader was José Antonio Aponte, a free black who was a militia officer and member of the Lucumí *cabildo*, a colonial social organization based on African ethnic affiliation. Investigators uncovered among his possessions a book of paintings that he would show to his coconspirators. Aponte's "libro de pinturas" included portraits of black and white revolutionary and royalist leaders, such as the Bourbon monarch Charles III, George Washington, Toussaint Louverture, Henri Christophe, Jean-François, and Dessalines (the book itself has never been recovered by historians, only descriptions in official documents).[24]

Although officials suppressed the Aponte rebellion and another widespread conspiracy in 1843 known as La Escalera, they were unable to stop the uprising of 1868 in the eastern end of the island for national liberation. Unlike the earlier Cuban rebellions, which were abolitionist in nature, the uprising led by Carlos Manuel de Céspedes was initially ambiguous concerning slavery, much like the leadership of separatist movements in other parts of Spanish America earlier in the century. Céspedes freed his own slaves in 1868 but shied away from definitive action against the institution as a whole. Nonetheless, the uprising altered the politics of slavery, intentionally and unintentionally.

As had occurred earlier in South America, the rebellion gave slaves new opportunities for freedom on the loyalist and patriotic sides, as both the Spanish and insurgent forces relied on slave troops. For the Spanish regime, the promise of freedom for military service did not represent a fundamental challenge to slavery—quite the opposite. Indeed, the colonial government, working with planters, was generally successful at delaying the final abolition of slavery. Even while the government combated the insurgency, it was able to keep slaves laboring on the sugar plantations of western Cuba.[25]

However, the metropolitan regime was less recalcitrant than it was during the Spanish American revolutions. While the Spanish government had countered the crisis set off by the French invasion in 1808 by reaffirming slavery and racial segregation in the colonies, after 1868 it moved to abolish slavery gradually, holding out in Cuba until 1886, and to contemplate the enfranchisement of the population of color. Not only the Cuban insurgency prodded Madrid, so too did significant abolitionist pressures in Europe. Since the early part of the century, the British government had sought the suppression of the Cuban slave trade, entering into several treaties with the Spanish government to that effect. Only in the 1860s, though, did Spain finally hold up its end of the bargain, setting the stage for the gradual abolition of slavery itself.[26]

Furthermore, for the first time, the government was met by an effective abolitionist movement in the metropolis, the Sociedad Abolicionista Española, founded by Antillean and Spanish liberals and republicans in Madrid in 1865.[27] The abolitionists insisted that slavery was cruel, destabilizing of the political order, and economically wasteful. The leading Spanish reformer, Rafael María de Labra, spoke to this latter point when he asserted that "free labor will always triumph [over slave labor] because it is less expensive, more conscientious, and more efficient." Moreover, in his view, the *immediate* abolition of slavery would resolve not only the question of labor but also the Cuban insurgency, which would lose support if the Spanish government acted decisively: "It is clear that slavery is the knot that holds together the current colonial regime. And that abolition is the door that opens onto liberty and democracy." What gave Labra and other abolitionists pause was the large percentage of Africans working on the great sugar plantations: "We are talking about a large group of men absolutely foreign by origin, by language, and by their customs. And not only foreign to Cuban society but to the habits and practices of the civilized world because they have been maintained in almost complete isolation from all culture and from everything that epitomizes the interests of modern society." [28] However, he concluded that Cuba's large urban slave population and the large free population of color would serve as stabilizing factors in the transition from slavery to freedom.

The abolitionists' juggling of questions of race, liberty, labor, and citizenship were decidedly reminiscent of the debates during the French and Haitian revolutions. And as in that case, so too in the colony itself were those issues heatedly contested, nowhere more so than among the supporters of the Cuban insurgency. For Cuban patriots, slavery became increasingly indefensible as slaves fled their masters in the zones controlled by the insurgents. The crisis of discipline caused by the uprising and the growing presence of runaway slaves in the insurgency finally moved the leadership to abolish slavery in the areas under its authority, generally in the eastern end of the island. Moreover, the support of free people of color, many of whom rose into the officer ranks, radicalized and broadened Cuban nationalist discourse. Ada Ferrer cites a rebel broadsheet used early in the insurgency to recruit slave troops to demonstrate the tensions created by the intersection of slave emancipation with nation building:

The blacks are the same as the whites.

The whites are not slaves nor do they work for the blacks.

Neither should the blacks be slaves nor should they work for the whites.

The Cubans want the blacks to be free.

The Spaniards want the blacks to continue being slaves.

The Cubans are fighting against the Spaniards.

The blacks who have any honor should go fight together with the Cubans.

The Spaniards want to kill the Cubans so that blacks can never be free.[29]

The wording of the broadsheet indicates that at the beginning of the fight for Cuban independence, the leadership, while holding out the promise of emancipation, drew a stark division between "blacks" and "Cubans," hedging on the question of citizenship and nationality. However, over the course of the struggle against both slavery and colonialism, people of color fought to overcome that division, demanding a postslavery and postcolonial nation in which all who fought for Cuba, regardless of color or class, were Cubans. In other words, over the latter part of the century, Cuban patriots came to fight not only for national liberation and slave abolition but also for a republic committed to racial democracy, a struggle that would persist beyond slave emancipation (1886) and liberation from Spain (1898).[30]

## CONCLUSION

Different approaches to conceptualizing Atlantic history help us comprehend the dynamics at work in Cuba and other parts of Latin America. Approaches that emphasize the implantation of Old World institutions and values in the New have continued relevance, as historians are more hesitant to argue that Cuba's plantation revolution carried all before it. Historians now draw attention to "the study of other social and cultural aspects of the lives of enslaved people, inside or outside the plantation."[31] Forms of organization and routes to freedom such as the African *cabildos*, *coartación*, military service, Catholic lay brotherhoods, maroonage, and manumission persisted in the shadow of the plantation. But those ideas of freedom and rights existed only in relationship to slavery; the freedom of some was predicated on the enslavement of the many. Emphasizing the continuity of colonial institutions does not explain when and how slavery and freedom came to be seen as irreconcilable conditions in Cuba and other parts of the New World or under what conditions people could effectively undermine a deeply entrenched institution.

To address these questions, one must register the protracted crisis in the Atlantic World initiated by revolutionary movements and imperial warfare beginning in the later eighteenth century. This shift of focus has implications for conceptualizing both the space and the time of Atlantic history. First, one must employ a different sense of the Atlantic World as a coherent space, one that is more multisided and interactive than the model that focuses on the implantation of Old World institutions and cultures in the New. Second, this move also implies overlapping temporal periodizations, putting the transformations of the eighteenth and nineteenth centuries in relationship to the deeper time of European colonization of the Americas. The intense movement of peoples, goods, and information; the major economic transformations; and the military conflicts within and among rival empires characteristic of the revolutionary era dramatically altered the politics of slavery, freedom, and colonialism throughout the Atlantic World. Here, the approaches of scholars like Robin Blackburn, Ira Berlin, Julius Scott, and Dale Tomich are indispensable. The era of anticolonial rebellions and interimperial warfare forever transformed New World slavery, especially in the aftermath of the Haitian Revolution. In Cuba, while political circumstances and market forces on an Atlantic scale facilitated slavery's spread in the nineteenth century, knowledge of the Haitian Revolution; the spread of republican, abolitionist, and nationalist ideologies; and anticolonial warfare directly challenged the institutions that defined the balance between slavery and freedom under the old regime. Moreover, as in other parts of Spanish America earlier in the century, the large free population and the habits of freedom forged over the long period of colonial rule provided the foundations of a vision of racial democracy, a social and political order in which freedom existed without slavery and without legally sanctioned racial discrimination.

Thus, the continuity, resurgence, and crisis of Cuban slavery in the nineteenth century show that the forces shaping the Atlantic World continued to coalesce beyond the early modern era and to define the expectations of the revolutionary age. I have concentrated on the destruction of that world to demonstrate its persistence. The breakup of the European empires, the consolidation of new nation-states, and the abolition of the slave trade and slavery destroyed or transformed the dominant political and economic structures that defined the Atlantic World since the first era of conquest and colonization. This process, initiated with the revolutions in North America, France, and St. Domingue, was uneven and protracted, in the case of Cuba persisting until the very end of the nineteenth century. José Moya argues convincingly in his chapter in this volume that the nineteenth and twentieth centuries were the era par excellence of Atlantic history, as the flow of people and goods increased dramatically, as did the extent of territory linked to the Atlantic economy. However, that stage of Atlantic history effectively opened with the destruction of an earlier one in which the slave trade and unfree labor figured centrally, for it was with the definitive over-throw of slavery in the second half of the nineteenth century that the mass migration of Europeans to the Americas began.

Finally, a comment on whether there is a global dimension to this Atlantic history. That Cuban and Spanish planters in the mid-nineteenth century looked halfway around the globe to recruit indentured Chinese workers in significant numbers indicates that these societies were not bound only by the confines of the Atlantic World. However, I do believe that Atlantic history is distinct from global history, even if there are approaches and themes—such as the tensions between colonies and metropolis, battles over the boundaries between free and unfree labor, and nationalism and citizenship—that are parallel in many circumstances. The struggles for and against slavery and for and against independence in Cuba resembled similar conjunctures of forces in other American colonies such as Haiti and Colombia: they took place in societies shaped by centuries of European colonization, the African slave trade, and relations with neighboring empires and nations. The contours of this world were thus defined by the complex interactions among Africa, Europe, and the Americas as subject populations sought to undo specific forms of economic, political, and racial domination forged between the sixteenth and nineteenth centuries.

## Notes

1    Oficio dated Madrid, 9 October 1879. Biblioteca Itamaraty, Missões Diplomáticas Brasileiras, Oficios, Madri, 1875–1880, 220/1/15.
2    George Reid Andrews, *Afro-Latin America, 1800–2000* (New York, 2004), 41.
3    Frank Tannenbaum, *Slave and Citizen: The Negro in the Americas* (New York, 1946).

4    For a recent ringing endorsement of Tannenbaum's continued importance, see Alejandro de la Fuente, "Slavery and Claims-Making in Cuba: The Tannenbaum Debate Revisited," *Law and History Review* 22 (2004): 339–69. See also the exchange occasioned by this article: María Elena Díaz, "Beyond Tannenbaum"; Christopher Schmidt-Nowara, "Still Continents (and an Island) with Two Histories?"; and Alejandro de la Fuente, "Slavery and the Law," *Law and History Review* 22 (2004): 371–87. Another work that draws explicitly on Tannenbaum's approach is Jane Landers, *Black Society in Spanish Florida* (Urbana, Ill., 1999). Other works that demonstrate the routes to freedom and autonomy enabled by the legal and religious institutions of Iberian colonialism include L. Virginia Gould, "Urban Slavery-Urban Freedom: The Manumission of Jacqueline Lemelle," in *More Than Chattel: Black Women and Slavery in the Americas*, ed. David Barry Gaspar and Darlene Clark Hine (Bloomington, Ind., 1996), 298–314, and María Elena Díaz, *The Virgin, the King, and the Royal Slaves of El Cobre: Negotiating Freedom in Colonial Cuba, 1670–1780* (Stanford, Calif., 2000).

5    João Jose Reis, *Slave Rebellion in Brazil: The Muslim Uprising of 1835 in Bahia*, trans. Arthur Brakel (Baltimore, 1993).

6    Stuart Schwartz, "Rethinking Palmares: Slave Resistance in Colonial Brazil," in *Slaves, Peasants, and Rebels: Reconsidering Brazilian Slavery* (Urbana, Ill., 1992), 103–36. An especially vigorous emphasis on the African background to slave life in the Americas is James Sweet, *Recreating Africa: Culture, Kinship, and Religion in the African-Portuguese World, 1441–1770* (Chapel Hill, N.C., 2003). An indispensable introduction to these questions is John Thornton, *Africa and Africans in the Making of the Atlantic World, 1400–1800*, 2nd ed. (Cambridge, 1998).

7    Schwartz, "Sugar Plantation Labor and Slave Life," in *Slaves, Peasants, and Rebels*, 39–64; Mary Karasch, *Slave Life in Rio de Janeiro, 1808–1850* (Princeton, N.J., 1987).

8    Rebecca J. Scott, *Slave Emancipation in Cuba* (Princeton, N.J., 1985), 14, 3–41. See also Laird Bergad, *Cuban Rural Society in the Nineteenth Century: The Social and Economic History of Monoculture in Matanzas* (Princeton, N.J., 1990).

9    Laurent Dubois, *Avengers of the New World: The Story of the Haitian Revolution* (Cambridge, Mass., 2004), chap. 3; Ira Berlin, *Generations of Captivity: A History of African-American Slaves* (Cambridge, Mass., 2003), chap. 3.

10    "Siglo XVIII," *1797. Lealtad y heroismo de la isla de Puerto Rico* (Puerto Rico, 1897), 119.

11    See Landers, *Black Society in Spanish Florida*, and Herbert S. Klein, "The Colored Militia of Cuba: 1568–1868," *Caribbean Studies* 6 (1966): 17–27.

12    The following discussion relies on Dubois, *Avengers of the New World;* Robin Blackburn, *The Overthrow of Colonial Slavery* (London, 1988), 161–264; C. L. R. James, *The Black Jacobins* (New York, 1963); and David Patrick Geggus, ed., *The Impact of the Haitian Revolution in the Atlantic World* (Columbia, S.C., 2001).

13    Dubois, *Avengers of the New World*, 57.

14    See Karasch, *Slave Life in Rio de Janeiro*.

15    Jaime Rodríguez O., *The Independence of Spanish America* (Cambridge, 1998); Josep M. Fradera, *Gobernar colonias* (Barcelona, 1999); Tamar Herzog, *Defining Nations: Immigrants and Citizens in Early Modern Spain and Spanish America* (New Haven, Conn., 2003).

16    A major new synthesis of this era is Andrews, *Afro-Latin America*, chaps. 1–3.

17    Peter Blanchard, "The Language of Liberation: Slave Voices in the Wars of Independence," *Hispanic American Historical Review* 82 (2002): 500.

18    Simón Bolívar, quoted in ibid., 514; Marixa Lasso, "Haiti as an Image of Popular Republicanism in Caribbean Colombia: Cartagena Province (1811–1828)," in Geggus, *The*

*Impact of the Haitian Revolution*, 176–90, and "Revisiting Independence Day: Afro-Colombian Politics and Creole Patriotic Narratives, Cartagena, 1809–1815," in *After Spanish Rule: Postcolonial Predicaments of the Americas*, ed. Mark Thurner and Andrés Guerrero (Durham, N.C., 2003), 223–47. See also Andrews, *Afro-Latin America*, chaps. 1 and 2, and Alejandro de la Fuente, "Mitos de 'democracia racial': Cuba, 1900–1912," in *Espacios, silencios y los sentidos de la libertad: Cuba entre 1878–1912*, ed. Fernando Martínez Heredia, Rebecca J. Scott, and Orlando F. García Martínez (Havana, 2001), 235–69. Finally, the work of Julius Scott has been fundamental in the study of the spread of knowledge of the Haitian Revolution. See "A Common Wind: Currents of Afro-American Communication in the Age of the Haitian Revolution" (Ph.D. diss., Duke University, 1986).

19   Blackburn, *The Overthrow of Colonial Slavery*, 375.

20   Dale Tomich, "The 'Second Slavery': Bonded Labor and the Transformation of the Nineteenth-Century World Economy," in *Through the Prism of Slavery: Labor, Capital, and World Economy* (Lanham, Md., 2004), 56–71.

21   See also Blackburn, *The Overthrow of Colonial Slavery*, 519–50, and Berlin, *Generations of Captivity*, chap. 4.

22   D. Isidro de Antillón, *Disertación sobre el origen de la esclavitud de los negros* (Valencia, 1820), 115–16 n.8. On Arango y Parreño and Cuban slavery, see Manuel Moreno Fraginals, *The Sugarmill*, trans. Cedric Belfrage (New York, 1978), and Dale Tomich, "The Wealth of Empire: Francisco Arango y Parreño, Political Economy, and the Second Slavery in Cuba," in *Interpreting Spanish Colonialism: Empires, Nations, and Legends*, ed. Christopher Schmidt-Nowara and John Nieto-Phillips (Albuquerque, N.M., 2005), 54–85.

23   See de la Fuente, "Slavery and Claims-Making"; Scott, *Slave Emancipation in Cuba;* and Verena Martínez-Alier, *Marriage, Class and Colour in Nineteenth-Century Cuba*, 2nd ed. (Ann Arbor, Mich., 1989).

24   Matt Childs, "'A Black French General Arrived to Conquer the Island': Images of the Haitian Revolution in Cuba's 1812 Aponte Rebellion," in Geggus, *The Impact of the Haitian Revolution*, 135–56; Jane Landers, "Spanish Atlantic Creoles and the Circulation of Abolitionary Ideology," paper presented to the NYU Atlantic History Workshop, New York, September 2003 (cited by permission of the author); Ada Ferrer, "Noticias de Haití en Cuba," *Revista de Indias* 63 (2003): 675–93.

25   On military service for Spain, see David Sartorius, "For an Ever-Faithful Cuba: Slaves in the Spanish Army during the Ten Years' War," in *Global Conversations: New Scholarship on the History of Black Peoples*, ed. Darlene Clark Hine et al. (in press) (cited by permission of the author).

26   David Murray, *Odious Commerce: Britain, Spain and the Abolition of the Cuban Slave Trade* (Cambridge, 1980).

27   Christopher Schmidt-Nowara, *Empire and Antislavery: Spain, Cuba, and Puerto Rico, 1833–1874* (Pittsburgh, 1999).

28   Rafael María de Labra, *La abolición y la Sociedad Abolicionista Española en 1873* (Madrid, 1874), 32, 34–35, 36.

29   Quoted in Ada Ferrer, *Insurgent Cuba: Race, Nation, and Revolution, 1868–1898* (Chapel Hill, N.C., 1999), 39.

30   See Ferrer, *Insurgent Cuba;* Karen Robert, "Slavery and Freedom in the Ten Years' War, Cuba, 1868–1878," *Slavery and Abolition* 13 (1992): 181–200; Aline Helg, *Our Rightful Share: The Afro-Cuban Struggle for Equality, 1886–1912* (Chapel Hill, N.C., 1994); Alejandro de la

Fuente, *A Nation for All: Race, Inequality, and Politics in Twentieth-Century Cuba* (Chapel Hill, N.C., 2001); and Rebecca J. Scott, "The Provincial Archive as a Place of Memory: The Role of Former Slaves in the Cuban War of Independence (1895–1898)," *History Workshop Journal* 58 (2004): 149–66.

31   Díaz, *The Virgin, the King, and the Royal Slaves of El Cobre*, 13.

*Jason Young looks backward chronologically in order to look forward. He uses close readings of texts written by three eighteenth-century former slaves to explore the origins and continued relevance of "double consciousness." In 1903, the great intellectual W. E. B. Du Bois coined this term to capture the "two-ness" felt by African Americans such as himself, the tensions of being at once "an American" and "a Negro." In the century since the term's invention, numerous scholars have used double consciousness to explain the conflicted identity of twentieth-century African Americans. Young's move is to show how double consciousness continues to have explanatory power today even as he explores the phenomenon's historical roots. The violence of slavery, he argues, led former slaves to experience varying degrees of double consciousness. To demonstrate this, Young analyzes narratives written by three former slaves: Olaudah Equiano, Ukawsaw Gronniosaw, and Jacobus Eliza Johannes Capitein. As these men made their way around the Atlantic, they fashioned identities that partook of African and European elements. Sometimes these disparate elements meshed comfortably, while at other times they created nearly unbearable tensions. Finally, Young brings all these strands together in an examination of a twentieth-century author whose life and writings resonate with these same themes. Novelist Caryl Phillips, born in St. Kitts, raised in England, and resident in the United States, can be understood only in light of the Atlantic perspective employed by Young. Clearly, there are important similarities between the double consciousness experienced by Phillips and his eighteenth-century counterparts; what are the most significant differences?*

# Black Identities in the Formation of the Atlantic World

## Jason Young

A critical treatment of the rise of the Atlantic World suggests that the dislocations commonly perceived as part of modern black life are in fact rooted in the premodern period and are historically linked to the dislocations that first attended the creation of the Atlantic World. In this chapter, I argue for the centrality of the Atlantic as an organizing principle in the construction of contemporary black identities. In addition to analyzing moments of historical significance, I focus on examples from contemporary black literature—especially the work of Caryl Phillips—to illustrate the persistent importance of the Atlantic in the formation of black life.

The fractured nature of black life and identity is generally perceived as a peculiarly modern phenomenon, the consequence of an intense struggle on the part of blacks, both in Africa and throughout the Americas and Europe, to resolve their own histories and cultures with modernity. The modern age is intimately linked with the idea that through scientific and technological innovations, "social institutions could be created that would make men happier and free them from cruelty, injustice, and despotism."[1] Agricultural technologies promised to end famine, empiricism would root out superstition, and medical advances would eliminate debilitating disease. Even more, advances in travel and communication would bring the world's peoples into closer contact, promising a more coherent and unified human experience. The modern age was to reflect a clear and final break from the world that preceded it. But these promises failed to materialize. Even as agricultural technologies developed, so did the number of the world's hungry; though medical innovations produced new cures for disease, some of the most dynamic technologies of the modern age were applied to the instruments of death and the machines of war. These contradictions had their most brutal effect, perhaps, in the colonial areas of Africa, Asia, and the Americas, where increased bureaucracy and rationalism contributed to the varied brutalities of the colonial world.

Rather than positing the modern age as an absolute break from the era that preceded it and instead of viewing modernity as an institution that might unite all of humankind into a more cohesive whole, Paul Gilroy, writing in *The Black Atlantic*, casts our gaze toward the fractures that constitute modern life: "the distinctiveness of the modern self might reside in its being a necessarily fractured or compound entity."[2] Indeed, the modern subject is enmeshed in a series of unavoidably complex configurations based on the peculiar alchemy of race, gender, sexuality, class, and geography that forever marks our bodies.

That gender, class, race, and sexual orientation have complicated questions related to citizenship and subjectivity should be of little surprise. To take but one example, the very definition of the modern subject is based on classical Greek notions of the citizen, a term that itself implies an exclusive civic membership designed to produce and reproduce privilege. The course of American jurisprudence and protest movements have been devoted, for the past few centuries, to expanding and extending the benefits and privileges of citizenship to an ever widening swath of the American populace: to the poor, blacks, women, and, more recently, homosexuals. Typically, the privileged classes have held tightly to the reins of power and prestige, for in every extension of the rights of franchise and property comes a concomitant loss of influence. So begin the increasingly adamant calls in recent years against the injustices of reverse racism.

For their part, Enlightenment humanists complicated the idea of the citizen-subject by idealizing human beings as rational and civilized, even as they imagined a foil embodied in the savage lurking somewhere out there.[3] In so doing, Enlightenment thought established rigorous distinctions between the dominant and the subordinate. These distinctions were subsequently authorized and legitimated, giving rise to notions of ethnicity, class, and gender as "natural" categories of difference.[4] In this sense, all rationality, literature, science, art, and even all thought are attached to the history, genius, and glory of "one race, one sex, a restricted set of class fractions within a few national cultures."[5]

While the fissures constitutive of modernity affect us all, they do not affect us all equally or uniformly, and they have particular significance for blacks. Much of the disruption that we perceive in the modern age stems from the inability of Enlightenment thinkers, plantation owners, and slave ship captains to resolve their reverence for an era of rationalism with the reliance on unspeakable brutality to achieve their ends. As such, the modern age came to be defined both by leisure and labor, by wealth and poverty, by freedom and slavery. As Toni Morrison suggests, "We should not be surprised that the Enlightenment could accommodate slavery. . . . The concept of freedom did not emerge in a vacuum. Nothing highlighted freedom—if it did not in fact create it—like slavery."[6] Some figure the violence of American slavery as anachronistic, arguing that plantation slavery constituted "a premodern residue" that disappeared once it was revealed to be fundamentally incompatible with Enlightenment rationality and capitalism.[7] In fact, the violence of the plantation not only is constitutive of the modern age but also is perhaps its most essential component part. This is true not only because enslaved Africans produced the raw materials from which the products of leisure and status were created but also because large-scale industrial production in the West took the operation of the slave plantation as one of its earliest examples and models.[8] Or, to make the point in a different way, the very idea of race, so crucial in the development of national identities in the mother country and in their extension in the colony, was based on notions of "racial difference inherited from the pre-modern era."[9]

Blacks, then, are the inheritors of a strange and ambiguous legacy, born of being both within and without the modern world. Gilroy highlights the fractured nature of life for blacks in the West who consistently find themselves between two worlds: one black, the other white. Gilroy writes, "The intellectual and cultural achievements of the black Atlantic populations exist partly inside and not always against the grand narrative of Enlightenment . . . [they] stand simultaneously both inside and outside the western culture which has been their peculiar step parent."[10] One thinks immediately here of jazz, the foundational principles, philosophy, and soul of which are deeply connected to African musical forms, even if articulated largely through European musical instruments.

But, unlike Gilroy, I am arguing that this double consciousness is not the result of modern anxieties. The dislocations commonly perceived as part of modern black life are in fact rooted in the premodern period. To relocate the idea of double consciousness in an earlier period is to rethink the role that race played in the development of the Atlantic World and to reestablish the roots of the contemporary malaise of race and racism. Typically, the cultural, linguistic, and religious negotiations and adaptations that blacks have made to whiteness have been figured as acculturation—a gradual process whereby blacks adopt new cultural practices and beliefs while rejecting previous cultural norms. Through religious conversion, language, dress, and diet, the African becomes English, French, or Dutch, even if only imperfectly so. Or these cultural anxieties are noted as a type of trendy duality such that blacks are celebrated for their multiracialism or multilingualism. In this case, blacks are described as cultural translators and important middlemen enabling communication between distinctly different cultures. The notion of double consciousness seeks to address a critical matter generally ignored by both of these approaches, namely, the utter violence constitutive of these dislocations and transitions.

Richard Wright, famed novelist and essayist, long argued that the cultures of Africa had little or no influence on the cultures of America's twentieth-century blacks. Indeed, no small number of Wright's contemporaries in academic circles were making similar arguments. Sociologist E. Franklin Frazier, for example, maintained,

> Probably never before in history has a people been so nearly completely stripped of its social heritage as the Negroes who were brought to America. Other conquered races have continued to worship their household gods within the intimate circle of their kinsmen. But American slavery destroyed household gods and dissolved the bonds of sympathy and affection between men of the same blood and household.[11]

For his part, Wright described the traditions of African Americans as bare, our memories hollow: "Negroes had never been allowed to catch the full spirit of Western civilization, they lived somehow in it but not of it. And when I brooded upon the cultural barrenness of black life, I wondered if clean, positive tenderness, love, honor, loyalty, and the capacity to remember were native with man."[12] Wright was encouraged to change his thinking, however, on a trip to Ghana, where he was astonished to find women performing "a sort of weaving, circular motion with their bodies, a kind of queer shuffling dance which expressed their joy in a quiet, physical manner." He continued,

> And then I remembered: I'd seen these same snakelike, veering dances before . . . where? Oh, God, yes; in America, in storefront churches, in Holy Roller Tabernacles, in God's Temples, in unpainted wooden prayer-meeting houses on the plantations of the Deep South. . . . And here I was seeing it all again. . . . How could that be?[13]

When Wright visited Africa, he had been confident that he would not be able to "walk into the African's cultural house and feel at home and know [his] way around."[14] He had long contended that black Americans, because of what we had undergone in the United States, "had been basically altered, that his consciousness had been filled with a new content. . . . Then, if that were true, how could I account for what I now saw? And what

I now saw was an exact duplicate of what I'd seen for so many long years in the United States."[15]

Despite the complexities that attend the relationships between the artistic and cultural production of Africans and that of their progeny and contemporaries in the New World, and notwithstanding the diversity and innovation that mark black aesthetic production on both sides of the Atlantic, one is still left with Richard Wright's dilemma and confusion—that despite being separated by time and distance, blacks are not only composed of their experiences in the New World but also constituted by the long arm of Africa, the reach of which extends even into the twenty-first century. Part of the anxiety of being black in the modern age, then, is the difficulty that one has with resolving this duality.

For his part, W. E. B. Du Bois figured this curious relationship as double consciousness, a set of internal sufferings that marked black life in the modern world. Du Bois wrote, "One ever feels his two-ness—an American, a Negro; two souls, two thoughts, two unreconciled strivings."[16] For Du Bois, these sufferings were particularly modern, arising from the "strange meaning of being black here in the dawning of the Twentieth Century. . . . [For] the problem of the twentieth century is the problem of the color line."[17]

Much of the force of Du Bois's notion of double consciousness rests in its dynamism and adaptability. Michelle Wright argues convincingly that Du Bois's reference to "the veil" that separates the black world from the white world operates variously in different situations. He symbolized the Mason-Dixon Line, the difference between the South's violent racism against the North's supposedly greater restraint, as well as the epiphanic moment when the black American first experiences exclusion and realizes his or her paradoxical status as an outsider from within.[18] Perhaps because of its malleability, the notion of double consciousness has informed the thinking and artistic production of black writers over the course of the twentieth century. Indeed, black writers have consistently addressed double consciousness as a central theme affecting the lives of African Americans. Ralph Ellison revisited the great difficulty of resolving the critical two-ness that marks modern black life in *The Invisible Man:*

> I am an invisible man. No, I am not a spook like those who haunted Edgar Allen Poe; nor am I one of your Hollywood-movie ectoplasms. I am a man of substance, of flesh and bone, fiber and liquids—and I might even be said to possess a mind. I am invisible, understand, simply because people refuse to see me . . . it is as though I have been surrounded by mirrors of hard, distorting glass. When they approach me they see only my surroundings, themselves, or figments of their imagination—indeed, everything and anything except me.[19]

Writing in 1967, twenty years after Ellison's novel first appeared, Frantz Fanon returned to the subject: "As long as the black man is among his own, he will have no occasion . . . to experience his being through others . . . the black man among his own in the twentieth century does not know at what moment his inferiority comes into being through the other."[20] But eventually, blacks come face-to-face with whiteness, bombarded by its mirrors of hard, distorting glass. For Fanon, the moment occurred as he walked down a street and met the gaze of young white girl: "Look, a Negro . . . Mama, see the Negro! I'm frightened."[21] This incident recalls another recounted by Du Bois:

> I remember well when the shadow swept across me. . . . In a wee wooden schoolhouse, something put it into the boys' and girls' heads to buy gorgeous visiting cards . . . and exchange. The exchange was merry, till one girl . . . refused my

card,—refused it peremptorily, with a glance. Then it dawned upon me with a certain suddenness that I was different from the others . . . shut out from their world by a vast veil.[22]

In the end, blacks must ever see themselves "through the revelation of the other world."[23] Or, as Fanon noted, "not only must the black man be black; he must be black in relation to the white man."[24] As the gaze of whiteness intruded on his body, Fanon felt "responsible . . . for my body, for my race, for my ancestors. . . . I discovered my blackness, my ethnic characteristics; and I was battered down by tom-toms, cannibalism, intellectual deficiency, fetishism, racial defects, slave-ships, and above all else . . . 'Sho' good eatin'."[25] Like Du Bois and Ellison, Fanon saw this dual existence as peculiar to the modern age, a direct result of colonial subjugation.[26]

But these negotiations had occurred long before African colonialism or the varied apartheid and segregation regimes to which blacks have been subjected in the nineteenth and twentieth centuries. Despite Du Bois's contention that double consciousness reflected modern tensions, and notwithstanding the forward-looking nature of his project (Du Bois was, in the end, quite prophetic in his declaration that the problem of the twentieth century was the problem of the color line), some indications suggest that Du Bois may have been looking backward in time as he figured his own conceptions of race and racism. Writing in *Notes on the State of Virginia*, Thomas Jefferson considered the presumably inherent differences between blacks and whites:

> Whether the black of the negro resides in the reticular membrane between the skin and the scarf-skin, or in the scarf-skin itself; whether it proceeds from the colour of the blood, the colour of the bile, or from some other secretion, the difference is fixed in nature, and is as real as if its seat and cause were better known to us. . . . Are not the fine mixtures of red and white, the expressions of every passion by greater or less suffusions of colour in the one, preferable to that eternal monotony, which reigns in the countenances, *that immovable veil of black* which covers all of the emotions of the other race?[27]

As Michelle Wright argues, Jefferson's usage transforms blackness from a color to a barrier, an "immovable veil." In effect, the intransigence of the veil, its utter inertia, "points to an unattainable humanity on the part of Negroes, even though they are part of the human family."[28] Du Bois was almost certainly familiar with Jefferson's symbolic use of the veil. Indeed, one finds the following passage in *The Souls of Black Folk:*

> Then it dawned upon me with a certain suddenness that I was different from the others; or like, mayhap, in heart and life and longing, but shut out from their world by a vast veil. I had thereafter no desire to tear down that veil, to creep through; I held all beyond it in common contempt, and lived above it in a region of blue sky and great wandering shadows.[29]

Despite his own contention that he floated above the veil, Du Bois assured his readers that he was in fact "bone of the bone and flesh of the flesh" of those blacks still constrained to live life behind the veil of race and racism.[30]

Like their counterparts in the twentieth century, writers of the eighteenth century struggled desperately to reconcile questions of race and racial difference. Black writers acknowledged their debt to their African ancestry even as they attempted to find a place for themselves in the West. In following this line of argument, I do not mean to collapse double consciousness into a flattened notion expansive enough to cover all the geographical and temporal differences under consideration. Black writers dealt variously with questions of race, identity, home, and belonging in different locales at different times. These differences will become evident in the treatment in this chapter. Still, the historical dynamics of slavery, the slave trade, and the varied systems of racism and violence to which they gave birth were as relevant to the writing of Du Bois, Ellison, Fanon, and Wright as they were to earlier writers.

Olaudah Equiano (fig. 1) made clear his double existence in the very title of his narrative, *The Interesting Narrative of the Life of Olaudah Equiano, or Gustavus Vassa, the African, Written by Himself.*[31] One notes the duality of his name, Equiano, or Gustavus Vassa, making clear both his identity as an African and his identification as an Englishman. In fact, though modern commenters tend to refer to him as Equiano, we would do well to remember that this goes against his own practice. Indeed, Equiano referred to himself, both in public and in private, as Gustavus Vassa.[32] If the name caused some disjunction, the appendage—"the African, written by Himself"—was no less startling for eighteenth-century readers. An African, by widespread European presumption, was not only illiterate but also largely uneducable. That this African had written, by his own hand, a narrative of his life immediately rendered him worthy of attention. The frontispiece of the first edition further emphasized the double consciousness so characteristic of the text. Equiano was figured in the image with his dark skin bound tightly in an Englishman's garb, with hair well managed and dressed.

The narrative begins with a description of Equiano's birthplace: of its customs and culture, dress, diet, marital customs, and dance. From this beginning, Equiano drew parallels between his own native culture and that of the Jews: "And here I cannot forbear suggesting what has long struck me very forcibly, namely, the strong analogy, which . . . appears to prevail in the manners and customs of my countrymen and those of the Jews."[33] The connections were, indeed, so strong that Equiano suggested "the one people might have sprung from the other . . . for we had our circumcision: we had also our sacrifices and burnt-offerings, our washings and purifications, on the same occasions as they had."[34] In this instance, Equiano wanted to make clear that his own countrymen were inheritors of that same humanity to which Europeans lay claim. Inferiority was no more a natural disposition to the African than it was to the European: "Let the polished and haughty European recollect that his ancestors were once like the Africans, uncivilized and even barbarous. Did nature make them inferior to their sons? And should they too have been made slaves?"[35]

Two years after his arrival in England, Equiano had learned to speak and comprehend the English language quite well. He longed to resemble Englishmen, to imbibe their spirit, and to imitate their manners. Equiano's mastery of the English language offered him a special avenue of resistance when he found himself being mistreated by whites. In one instance, after having learned that he had been sold to a Captain Doran, Equiano protested,

> I told him my master could not sell me to him, or anyone else. "Why," said
> [Doran], "did not your master buy you?" I confessed he did. But I have served
> him . . . and he has taken all my wages . . . besides this I have been baptized;
> and by the laws of the land no man has a right to sell me: and I added that I had
> heard a lawyer, and others at different times tell my master so. . . . Upon this
> Captain Doran said I talked too much English.[36]

**Figure 1**   Portrait of a Negro Man, Olaudah Equiano, 1780s (previously attributed to Joshua Reynolds), by English School (eighteenth century). Courtesy Royal Albert Memorial Museum, Exeter, Devon, United Kingdom.

On yet another occasion, Equiano—now free—found himself near Savannah, Georgia, when two white men accosted him with intent to kidnap him and sell him as a slave. Equiano warned his attackers, "Be still and keep off, for I had seen those tricks played upon other free blacks. . . . At this they paused a little, and one said to the other—it will not do; and the other answered that I talked too good English."[37]

To further his claims of English identity, Equiano learned to shave, to dress hair, and to read the Bible. Equiano's religious instruction gave him great pleasure when he realized that the laws and rules of his country were "written almost exactly" as in the Bible. Some mention should be made here of Equiano's varied negotiations with English identity. Indeed, Equiano's sense of double consciousness was both secular and spiritual. He admired much about English dress, diet, habit, and comportment, and he adopted these behaviors. But he also underwent a deep religious conversion that helped him in his varied engagements with British culture and identity. That Christianity resembled the ritual practices and principles of his youth implied that Christianity might offer an avenue and a vocabulary by which he could better understand his changing identity. This does not mean, however, that his religious conversion was calculated or inauthentic. Instead, the very deep reverence that many eighteenth-century black writers had for Christianity reveals their commitment to creating a spiritual identity that helped them make sense of the long journeys, geographical and otherwise, they made. And so, Equiano emphasized the similarities between his African ancestry and the British mores to which he was exposed. So successful was he, in fact, that he considered himself *"almost an Englishman."*[38]

Indeed, other eighteenth-century blacks proved themselves even more successful than Equiano in brokering the cultural and linguistic distances separating African and European identities. Briton Hammon, an eighteenth-century sailor and contemporary of Equiano, was captured by Spanish forces after having been shipwrecked and was subsequently imprisoned in Havana. Hammon eventually escaped his imprisonment and sought refuge aboard the *Beaver*, an English man-of-war docked at Havana. Hammon recalled,

> The next day the Spaniards came along side the Beaver, and demanded me again . . . but the Captain, who was a true Englishman, refus'd them, and said he could not answer it, to deliver up any Englishman under English Colours.[39]

Within the context of imperial competition, the British captain, *a true Englishman*, granted Hammon a protection born of national pride. But the relationship of blacks in eighteenth-century Britain to patriotism was necessarily complicated. Ignatius Sancho, born a captive aboard a slave ship and raised in England, lamented in 1779 the apparent decline of the empire:

> Ireland almost in as true a state of rebellion as America.—Admirals quarrelling in the West-Indies—and at home Admirals that do not choose to fight.—The British empire mouldering away in the West—annihilated in the North. . . . —For my part, it's nothing to me—as I am only a lodger—and hardly that.[40]

To be an Englishman, for Equiano and other black writers of the period, meant more than claiming allegiance to a particular national identity. Indeed, England connoted a racial, religious, and ethnic identity to which Equiano aspired. But he knew that the goal was ultimately unattainable. So Equiano suggested in one passage of his narrative,

> I was one day in a field belonging to a gentleman who had a black boy about my own size; this boy having observed me from his master's house, was *transported* at the sight of one of his own countrymen, and ran to meet me with the utmost haste. I, not knowing what he was about, turned a little out of his way at first, but to no purpose; he soon came close to me, and caught hold of me in his arms as if I had been his brother, though we had never seen each other before.[41]

That the boy was transported (presumably to Africa) and that he carried Equiano along with him in his embrace placed Equiano in a curious position. Although he had become well versed in matters of English dress, diet, language, and religion, he was still ever on the verge of being transported through the gaze of others back to Africa. It is in this sense that Equiano regarded himself as only *almost an Englishman*, though his efforts toward that goal persisted.

Such were the cultural and racial divisions of Equiano's life that he attempted on several occasions to cross the barrier that separated black from white. While in service aboard a ship set for Turkey, Equiano attempted to secure the freedom of a shipmate who was being pursued by a West Indian planter. He wrote, "My being known [by the planter] obliged me to use the following deception: I whitened my face, that they might not know me; and this had the desired effect."[42] This incident recalls an earlier moment when, after having first arrived in England, Equiano tried desperately, if naively, to rid himself of the most crucial barrier to his full integration into English society: "I therefore tried oftentimes myself if I could not by washing, make my face the same color as my little playmate, Mary, but it was all in vain; and I then began to be mortified at the difference in our complexions."[43] In this instance, Equiano drew clear connections between whiteness and beauty, marking a significant change from his earlier perceptions. Recalling perceptions of beauty in his homeland, Equiano wrote, "I remember while in Africa to have seen three negro children, who were tawny, and another quite white, who were universally regarded as deformed by myself and the natives in general, as far as related to their complexions."[44]

Eventually, however, Equiano became enamored with whiteness and, with all necessary apologetic decorum, remarked, "I also could not help remarking the particular slenderness of their women, which at first I did not like, and I thought them not so modest and shamefaced as the African women."[45] In this way, the very locus of sexual desire shifted in Equiano's mind from the presumably more modest and ample African women to white women. Mary, his young playmate, at a mere five or six years of age, symbolized both innocence and sexuality. On one occasion, when Equiano was preparing to set sail, little Mary cried so much at his departure that nothing could pacify her until his return: "It is ludicrous enough, that I began to fear I should be betrothed to this young lady"[46] That the idea of Equiano's betrothal to Mary seemed ludicrous stemmed both from her tender age and from her whiteness. Nor is it mere coincidence that Equiano's narrative ends with his marriage in 1792 to an Englishwomen, Susan Cullen, with whom he had two children, Anna Maria and Johanna. Equiano's double consciousness was born not of a gradual resignation or acculturation but rather of the very real violence and hatred visited on his life, history, customs, and body and from the subsequent wars that raged within him.

Like Equiano, Albert King, born Ukawsaw Gronniosaw, was captured as a slave in West Africa, in Gronniosaw's case between 1710 and 1714. Before being bought by a Dutch trader, Gronniosaw was held in the custody of an African king who governed a coastal town in present-day Nigeria. The king, fearing that Gronniosaw had been sent by his countrymen as a spy, sentenced the captive to die. On the morning of the scheduled execution, Gronniosaw was given a ritual bath, and all his gold jewelry and ornaments were ceremonially cleaned to prepare the captive for his transition to the land of the dead. In the end, Gronniosaw faced his expected demise with such courage that "it pleased God to melt the heart of the King," who decided to sell him to European traders as a slave rather than take his life.[47] When a Dutch trader arrived on the coast several days later, Gronniosaw begged to be bought, knowing full well that if he were not sold on the coast, he would surely die there. In the end, he was bought, and on being taken aboard ship, he was dispossessed of all his gold jewelry:

> When I left my dear mother I had a large quantity of gold about me, as is the custom of our country, it was made into rings, and they were linked into one another, and formed into a kind of chain, and so put round my neck, and arms and legs, and a large piece hanging at one ear in the shape of a pear. I found all this troublesome, and was glad when my master took it from me.[48]

When Gronniosaw's new master took his gold, he not only affected a material change in his new captive but indeed attempted to divest him of the cultural, social, and political (Gronniosaw had been a nobleman in his homeland) systems that combined to give the gold meaning. Indeed, the gold had enough meaning for Gronniosaw's African captors that they saw fit to polish and clean it as part of his death ritual. Later, Gronniosaw was washed by his Dutch captors and "clothed in the Dutch or English manner."[49] Although Gronniosaw was washed by both his African and his European captors, the meanings attached to that washing differed in each case. While Gronniosaw's washing when in African captivity connoted a ritual cleansing, the latter suggested the presumed inherent dirtiness of Africans. Gronniosaw donned not only European-styled dress when he was clothed in the *Dutch or English manner* but also the cultures of the West that now enslaved him. Not long after having assumed English dress, Gronniosaw adopted English presumptions and prejudices regarding Africa, including a persistent conflation of blackness with evil and references to the Devil as a black man who lives in Hell.[50]

If Equiano perceived *English* as a racial and cultural identity, Gronniosaw thought of the same as a moral and ethical identity. He wrote,

> I had for a great while entertained a desire to come to England.—I imagined that all of the inhabitants of this island were holy; [that] the people must be all righteous. . . . I had a vast inclination to visit England, and wished continually that it would please providence to make a clear way for me to see this island. I entertained a notion that if I could get to England I should never more experience either cruelty or ingratitude, so that I was very desirous to get among Christians.[51]

Similarly, eighteenth-century poet Phyllis Wheatley also perceived her enslavement at the hands of Europeans as evidence of the workings of a Divine Hand in her life. In one of her best-known poems, "On Being Brought from Africa to America," Wheatley wrote,

> 'Twas Mercy brought me from my Pagan land,
> Taught my benighted soul to understand
> That there's a God, that there's a Savior too:
> Once I redemption neither sought nor knew.
> Some view our sable race with scornful eye,
> "Their color is a diabolic die."
> Remember, Christians, Negros, black as Cain,
> May be refin'd, and join th' angelic train.[52]

As with many black writers of the eighteenth century, Wheatley emphasized the malleability of black customs, comportment, religion, and behavior. Even the sons and daughters of a so-called Pagan land could become so refined as to warrant acceptance on the angelic train.

For his part, Gronniosaw's lofty hopes for English morality and decorum were dashed when, on arrival, he was "astonished . . . to hear the inhabitants of that place curse and swear, and be otherwise profane. I expected to find nothing but goodness, gentleness, and meekness in the Christian land, and I suffered great perplexity of mind at seeing so much wickedness."[53] After having been robbed and cheated of his money on various occasions, Gronniosaw finally realized that he "had got amongst a bad people, who defrauded [him] of [his] money and watch." All his promised happiness being blasted, Gronniosaw "could scarcely believe it possible that the place where so many eminent Christians had lived and preached could abound with so much wickedness and deceit. [He] thought it worse than Sodom."[54] He then began to "entertain a very different idea of the inhabitants of England than what [he] had figured to [him]self before [he] came among them."[55] Gronniosaw's great disappointment reflects not only his opinion of the British but also his opinion of himself. He had negotiated the cultures of Africa and Europe in his own life. He had been relieved of his gold and the noble status that it implied; he had been washed and then dressed in the English manner and had adopted Christianity. In effect, he had attempted a resolution of double consciousness in his own life. But if England was less than the moral and ethical refuge that he had anticipated, if it could not divest him completely of his stains and sins, if it could not erase Africa, then his varied conversions might have been for naught. He was, in the end, still African and European, clean and dirty, black and white.

Much like Gronniosaw, Jacobus Eliza Johannes Capitein was also deeply concerned with issues of European ethics and morals, particularly the question of the moral right of Christians to hold other Christians in bondage. Born in 1717 in the central region of present-day Ghana, Capitein was sold at eight years of age to Arnold Steenhart, a Dutch sea captain who, in turn, gave the young slave as a gift to Jacobus van Goch, a pastor in the Dutch mission at Elmina. When Van Goch left Africa for the Netherlands in 1728, he took Capitein with him. On arrival in the Netherlands, Capitein became effectively a free man, slavery being illegal in the country.

Capitein's formal education was eventually entrusted to Johan Philip Manger, a Reformed minister who afforded the newly freed youngster a formal education in the classics and the ministry.[56] On completing his education and being baptized, Capitein (the moniker had been given him on arrival in the Netherlands) assumed his first three names, "Jacobus Eliza Johann," in honor of his benefactors. Interestingly, we know little of his African name, though some sources indicate that he was known as Asar.[57] Capitein entered the University of Leiden and, with the economic support of various philanthropic, religious, and commercial organizations, defended in 1742 the thesis by which he is known today. His project, *A Political-theological dissertation examining the Question: is slavery compatible with Christian freedom or not?* argued that because the freedom promised in the Gospels was spiritual and not physical, slavery was, indeed, compatible with Christianity.[58] In effect, Capitein, a former slave, offered theological support for the system that had enslaved him.

As a newly ordained minister, Capitein returned to Guinea as an employee of the Dutch West India Company (DWIC) to lead the spiritual welfare of its Elmina post.

Capitein's attempts to reintegrate himself into the African society that he had left were beset with difficulties. Theologically, Capitein distanced himself from the Africans he encountered, at least in part because he found no fault with a faith that promised spiritual freedom to blacks in the next world but enslaved them in this one. Personally, he was born an African but was formed and educated in Europe. He perceived his would-be countrymen as heathens and had, as part of his early education, written a treatise to that effect. Capitein authored "On the Calling of the Heathen," which made clear Capitein's conviction that heathens needed to be called from the error of their unbelief.[59] Professionally, Capitein was torn by the better interests of his congregants on the one hand with those of his benefactors—principally the DWIC and those burghers who had funded his education—on the other. Indeed, in translating the Ten Commandments into Fante, Capitein excluded that portion of the Fourth Commandment that extended rest to servants and slaves on the Sabbath. While this interpretation favored the agents of the DWIC who paid Capitein, it angered church leaders in the Netherlands, not to mention the African servants and slaves who worked at the DWIC post.[60] Throughout Capitein's professional career, one notes his strict obeisance to the agents of slavery, both religious and commercial. In effect, many of his actions, both personal and professional, were constrained by the Europeans whose livelihoods were based on the extension of slavery.[61]

This is revealed most clearly when Capitein wrote church leaders of the difficulty that he was having integrating into African society. He proposed a marriage to a young local woman and hoped that church leaders would grant him a blessing for the union. In a 1743 letter, Capitein explained that he hoped the union would help him "win the trust and confidence of the black people here in Elmina, because they would then see that although I differ from them in lifestyle and religion, I am not alienated from them."[62] Unfortunately, church leaders refused to endorse the marriage on grounds that the girl was a heathen and that as her intended, Capitein was ill-suited to instruct her. They held that the would-be bride should be sent to the Netherlands for a full and proper instruction, to which her parents objected. The matter was finally resolved when church leaders, without forewarning Capitein, sent Antonia Ginderdros from the Netherlands to marry the minister. They were wed a short time after her arrival.[63] Perhaps most telling of the distance that separated Capitein from the Africans of his homeland is the fact that though he died in Elmina, there is no marker signifying his grave. Indeed, a central aspect of the religious lives of eighteenth-century Africans living along the Gold Coast concerned the proper treatment, burial, and remembrance of the dead. Burial grounds were regarded as sacred sites because the dead were thought to play a large role in the lives of the living and it was to the dead to which one looked for help in times of need. Part of the crisis of the transatlantic slave trade resided in the fact that it forever separated the ancestors from their progeny, thus leaving the living without proper guidance.[64] That Capitein was not afforded a proper burial in his homeland suggests something of the cultural chasm that separated him from his would-be converts. Still, Capitein has been immortalized in verse. The following lines were written by his friend, Brandijn Rijser:

> Observer, contemplate this African: his skin is black
> But his soul is white, since Jesus himself prays for him.

He will teach the Africans faith, hope and charity;
With him, the Africans, once whitened, will always honor the Lamb.[65]

This poem, along with Capitein's death, illustrates the duality that marked his life: of the various strivings between homeland and foreign soil, between his so-called black skin and white soul.

From the varied strivings of eighteenth-century black writers, we turn our attention now to a consideration of these matters in the work of a twentieth-century writer whose corpus is directed toward the connections between the modern and the premodern with which we are now concerned. Essayist and novelist Caryl Phillips, whose works address the cultural and racial disjunctions of the modern black subject, also looks to the world of seventeenth- and eighteenth-century race and slavery as a way of addressing contemporary concerns regarding identity. Writing in *The European Tribe*, Phillips recounts his own intellectual genealogy via a trip he made from Oxford to Los Angeles. While browsing in a bookstore, Phillips came across Ralph Ellison's *Invisible Man:* "I had already discovered what it meant to be invisible in America," he later recalled, and purchased the book along with Richard Wright's *Native Son*.[66]

Although Phillips grew up during the 1970s, he has much in common with twentieth-century black writers of an earlier generation whose forays into race and racism informed his own feelings of angst. Ellison's protagonist in *Invisible Man* had written—in the passage cited previously—of being surrounded by "mirrors of hard, distorting glass. When they approach me they see only my surroundings, themselves, or figments of their imagination—indeed, everything and anything except me."[67] So Phillips writes of his own experiences in England: "She still looks askance at 'strangers' as they alone reinforce a sense of self. Ultimately, the one certainty for Europe is that she knows a 'nigger' when she sees one: she should—they were a figment of her imagination, a product of her creative mind."[68] Much as Du Bois and Fanon were arrested by the gaze of young whites, so Phillips recalls his own experience after a swimming pool opened near his home in London. He visited the pool only to find himself ensnared in the gaze of a young white girl: "I heard a small girl's voice cry, 'Mummy, that man's dirtying the water.'" The girl's mother reassured the child, "Be quiet, Shelley. He's just a darkie."[69] In this way, Phillips's own early formation resembles that of other twentieth-century writers: an eerie feeling of invisibility, the violent intrusion of a white girl's glare.

Even as Phillips draws his creative and intellectual legacy to black writers of the twentieth century, he understands full well that the disruptions and dislocations experienced by blacks in modern life emerge from a premodern past. Writing in *The Atlantic Sound*, Phillips considers the life and letters of Philip Quaque (1741–1816), an African-born missionary who, ordained as the first non-European priest in the Anglican Church in 1765, returned to his homeland in 1766 to serve both as a missionary to his own people and as the official chaplain of Cape Coast Castle. Much like Capitein, Quaque returned to Africa after eleven years of religious education in Europe only to find his reintegration into his former homeland fraught with difficulties. The language that he spoke as a child now grated on his ears as a "vile jargon" as Quaque lost not only his ear for the language of his youth but also his native tongue, requiring a translator to speak to would-be African converts. Although Quaque twice married local African women while working at Cape Coast, he was, like Capitein, never successful in bridging the gaps that now separated him from the people of his homeland. He remained ever in limbo between the European slavers for whom he worked and the Africans to whom he ministered. Perhaps his own personal purgatory is best revealed in the fact that his personal quarters at Cape Coast were located directly above the slave dungeons within which thousands of Africans awaited transport to the Americas.[70]

It is, perhaps, Quaque's life that Phillips has in mind when he writes in *Higher Ground* of an African collaborator in the slave trade who, like Quaque, was set adrift between two cultural worlds: one African, the other European. Phillips's nameless slaver and translator had forgotten many of the customs and rituals of his countrymen, detested their native language, and developed a disgust for the boiled rice and stewed yam that constituted their staple fare.[71] Working under the auspices of Mr. Price, a European slave trader, the nameless translator was well aware of his own isolation. While on a slaving foray into the interior, the translator was beset by the collective gaze of an African village:

> They stare back at my clothes and Price's person with similar disdain. It is moments such as these that I loathe. Marooned between them, knowing that neither fully trusts me, that neither wants to be close to me, neither recognizes my smell or my posture, it is only in such situations that the magnitude of my fall strikes me.[72]

Caryl Phillips had reasoned of Philip Quaque that at some point he must have "made peace with a version of himself" that was ultimately at odds with his African compatriots.[73] So Phillips's own nameless translator in *Higher Ground* constructed a peace for himself born of pragmatism and a deep sense of duty. In response to the collective gaze of the African village, the translator remarks, "Why do they seem intent on blaming me? . . . I merely survive, and if survival is a crime then I am guilty. I have no material goods, no fine hut to dwell in, nobody to wait on me. . . . I merely oil the wheels" of their own collaboration.[74] Indeed, once the translator arrives on the coast, he busies himself with the duties of slaving:

> My task is now simple: to help arrange the shackling of one man to another. . . .
> I must listen and act, and listen and report, and point out those who might destroy the imagined harmony of our commercial household. My first day's work is always the most trying as I begin to prise the fit from the weak, the liar from the honest man, the pregnant from the bloated. . . . This sorting takes many days but there is no relief for it is eventually replaced by the agony of waiting for the ship to arrive, and being forced to listen to their low moaning, and enduring the awful wind-borne stench.[75]

Eventually, their moaning becomes his own as the translator is eventually betrayed by his European associates, finding himself in the hold of a slave ship, chained to those he had first manacled. He was beaten by his fellow captives until darkness brought an end to their blows. Eventually, they simply let him be and resumed their mournful, aspirant dirges: "In this dungeon the musicians and holy men begin to sing, to feed the spirit with songs of hope . . . here is darkness, sickness, waiting, men, dying, and song; but I have long since forgotten the words to their songs."[76] Like Richard Wright, however, the translator recognized the foreign to be ever so familiar: "This is the same choral chant that I would listen to when I was the man next to Price, the same hitherto baffling rebellious music that now makes a common sense."[77] Ultimately, the translator's greatest success depended on his finally deciphering the language of his own people.

While the story of the nameless translator ends on the West Coast of Africa, Phillips's most ambitious travels through the resonant histories of the Atlantic World are found in the novel *Cambridge*, a whirlwind tour of the Atlantic rim through his protagonist, an enslaved African named Olumide whose experiences in the Carolinas, England, and the West Indies leave him enmeshed in a world of contradiction and complexity. Like Equiano, Olumide's movements from the interior of West Africa to the world of plantation slavery are marked by a series of passages, each one bringing him into closer proximity to the lives, languages, and cultures of the slavers. After arriving in the Carolinas, Olumide was met by "one of my own tint, clad in their liver" who informed him that he was not to remain in America long but was instead to travel to England, "the original home of the white man," to serve massa.[78] He was subsequently washed and clothed in the English manner, much like Equiano and Gronniosaw, and was instructed in the rudiments of the English language. While en route to London, Olumide was afforded the aid of a crewman who instructed him in the "gentlemanly art of dressing hair (although with my wool he quickly retired)."[79] Perhaps most important, Olumide was given, by force, a new name. The ship's captain adopted for Olumide the new moniker "Thomas" and attended its application with a "flurry of cuffs" so that, by degrees, Olumide was made to submit and become known as "Black Tom."

Soon after having been beaten, Black Tom began to observe the manner of his master, to imitate it. Like Equiano and Gronniosaw, Black Tom "earnestly wished to imbibe the spirit and imitate the manners of Christian men."[80] He held England in the highest regard and thought London "the most enviable capital in the world."[81] After but a brief time, Black Tom's ancestry came to signify in his mind all manner of savagery and incivility; indeed, "Africa only spoke to me of a barbarity I had fortunately fled."[82] With mastery of language and some education in Christianity, Black Tom's "uncivilized African demeanor began to fall from my person."[83] Soon enough, Black Tom required a new designation and appealed to his master to be renamed David Henderson. Having agreed with the new name and the new status that it reflected, David's master "ordered a new livery" for his servant, now born again. Having acquired the English language, livery, and religion, David Henderson's transformation was near complete. His marriage to his master's maidservant Anna, a sturdy Englishwoman, finalized the transition. Notably, David's master had deemed Anna "unworthy of fleshy exploration," preferring instead the company of Mahogany Nell, a black maidservant, who was frequently called to the master's bed. The master derived great comfort from these encounters, "for they were frequent and . . . brutal in their lengthy pleasure."[84] Although the powers of coercion and violence constitutive of racism affected both men and women, they were experienced differently with regard to gender, a matter to which Phillips is sensitive. For black women, the specter of sexual violence differentiated their experiences when compared not only to black men but also to white women. Indeed, Anna and Nell have much in common; they are both poor maidservants whose lives are determined, at least to some degree, by the master of the household. But Mahogany Nell's subjection to serial rape derives, in part, from being an African. This is not to suggest that English women or men were not subject to sexual violence. Instead, I am arguing that sexual crimes perpetrated against English men and women violated certain ethical standards that were presumed not to apply to black women.

David traveled throughout England with his wife as a missionary and considered himself "an Englishman, albeit a little smudgy of complexion!" The couple preached the gospel to all those who would hear and collected donations from all who would give to finance a larger missionary effort in Africa.[85] But the people of England were not fully prepared to accept David (not to mention his marriage to a white bride) on his terms. For, in fact, he was not quite an Englishmen, a matter that David addresses at length:

> We who are kidnapped from the coast of Africa, and bartered on the shores of America, occupy a superior and free status in England, although an unsatisfactory reluctance to invoke the just English law permits the outward appearance of slavery to be enacted by some persons. This creates in the minds of many true Englishmen a confusion as to the proper standing of black people in their presence.[86]

Indeed, some not only were unable to view David as an Englishman but also had some difficulty in seeing him as a man. On one occasion, David was accosted by an Englishman who "felt certain that he had seen something black in the form of a man lay hands upon a white woman. . . . That I was not only a man, but was indeed a part of that host of men created in the name of the Lord was new education for this fool of weak intellect."[87]

In the end, his plans to establish a mission school in West Africa failed miserably. His wife and child fell sick and died in succession, but not before David had exhausted nearly all his money attempting to restore their health. Eventually, he gathered some funds and set out to establish the mission alone but was instead robbed en route to Africa, confined in chains, thrown into the belly of a ship, and sent, once again, across Atlantic waters to serve as a slave in the West Indies. David's shock was pronounced when he realized that he, "a virtual Englishman, was to be treated as base African cargo."[88] Again David Henderson was to be given a new name. This time his West Indian owner named him Cambridge. In the end, Cambridge struck out against his new master and was subsequently hanged without ceremony.

Caryl Phillips's work reflects the crucial connections between twentieth-century articulations of racial angst and anxiety with their eighteenth-century counterparts. Notably, Phillips's reconstructions of black life during the seventeenth and eighteenth centuries direct our attention not only toward the past but also toward the development of these same issues in the present day. Indeed, as Phillips's corpus so ably demonstrates, we simply cannot understand Ellison's invisibility or Du Bois's two-ness without making critical reassessments of premodern notions of racial construction. Double consciousness developed as a means to deal with the terrible violence of slavery and the slave trade, and in reading these narratives, we must address the vexed negotiations that blacks in the West have made without rendering them simply acculturated and/or assimilated. Instead, this reading of double consciousness allows us to view better the multiple negotiations with power that black writers have been constrained to make over the past few centuries. In so doing, it sheds additional light on contemporary treatments of fractured black identities that were also formed in the crucible of violence.

## Notes

1   Stuart Hall et al., eds., *Modernity: An Introduction to Modern Societies* (Cambridge, Mass., 1996), 37.

2   Paul Gilroy, *The Black Atlantic: Modernity and Double Consciousness* (Cambridge, Mass., 1993), 46.

3   Sylvia Wynter, "Beyond Miranda's Meanings: Un/silencing the 'Demonic Ground' of Caliban's 'Woman,'" in *Out of the Kumbla: Caribbean Women and Literature*, ed. Carole Boyce Davies and Elaine Savory Fido (Trenton, N.J., 1990), 358.

4   Ibid., 359; V. Y. Mudimbe, *The Invention of Africa: Gnosis, Philosophy, and the Order of Knowledge* (Bloomington, Ind., 1988), 64.

5   Ibid.

6   Toni Morrison, *Playing in the Dark: Whiteness and the Literary Imagination* (New York, 1992), 38.

7   Gilroy, *Black Atlantic*, 49.

8   See, for example, Eric Williams's classic study *Capitalism and Slavery* (1944; reprint, Chapel Hill, N.C., 1994), esp. chaps. 4 and 5.

9   Gilroy, *Black Atlantic*, 49; see also Mudimbe, *Invention*, 6–16, 107–8.

10  Gilroy, *Black Atlantic*, 49.

11  E. Franklin Frazier, *The Negro Family in the United States* (Chicago, 1939), 21.

12  Richard Wright, *Black Boy (American Hunger): A Record of Childhood and Youth* (1944; reprint, New York, 1991), 37.

13  Richard Wright, *Black Power: A Record of Reactions in a Land of Pathos* (Westport, Conn., 1954), 56–57.

14  Ibid., 57.

15  Ibid., 57, 66, 265–67

16  W. E. B. Du Bois, *The Souls of Black Folk* (1903; reprint, New York, 1989), 5.

17  Ibid., 1.

18  Michelle Wright, *Becoming Black: Creating Identity in the African Diaspora* (Durham, N.C., 2004), 84.

19  Ralph Ellison, *Invisible Man* (1947; reprint, New York, 1990), 3.

20  Frantz Fanon, *Black Skin, White Masks* (New York, 1967), 109, 110.

21  Ibid., 111–13.

22  Du Bois, *Souls*, 4.

23  Ibid., 5.

24  Fanon, *Black Skin*, 110, 112.

25  Ibid.

26  Ibid., 17.

27  Thomas Jefferson, *Notes on the State of Virginia* (1787; reprint, Chapel Hill, N.C., 1955), 138, emphasis added.

28  Wright, *Becoming Black*, 57, 61, 62.

29  Du Bois, *Souls*, 4.

30  Ibid., 2.

31  Some fascinating questions have recently been raised regarding the veracity of Equiano's account, especially concerning his claims of African birth. See Vincent Caretta, "Olaudah Equiano or Gustavus Vassa? New Light on an Eighteenth-Century Question of Identity," *Slavery and Abolition* 20 (1999): 96–105. Regarding my concerns, I am pursuing the tensions between the manner in which people perceived themselves privately and portrayed themselves publicly. In this sense, the ultimate veracity of Equiano's account, though an interesting avenue of investigation, is not my principal concern.

32  Olaudah Equiano, *The Interesting Narrative of the Life of Olaudah Equiano, or Gustavus Vassa, the African* (1789; reprint, New York, 1995), xvii.

33  Ibid., 32–43.

34  Ibid., 44.

35  Ibid., 45.

36  Ibid., 93–94.

37  Ibid., 159.

38  Ibid., 77, 92.

39  Briton Hammon, *A Narrative of the Uncommon Sufferings and Surprising Deliverance of Briton Hammon, a Negro Man*, in *Black Writers in Britain, 1760–1890*, ed. Paul Edwards and David Dabydeen (Edinburgh, 1991), 11.

40  Paul Edwards and Polly Rewt, eds., *The Letters of Ignatius Sancho* (Edinburgh, 1994), 186.

41  Equiano, *Interesting Narrative*, 85.

42  Ibid., 180.

43  Ibid., 69.

44  Ibid., 38.

45  Ibid., 68.

46  Ibid.

47  James Albert Ukawsaw Gronniosaw, *A Narrative of the Most Remarkable Particulars in the Life of James Albert Ukawsaw Gronniosaw, an African Prince, Related by Himself* (1779; reprint, London, 1840), 7.

48  Ibid., 8.

49  Ibid.

50  Ibid., 9.

51  Ibid., 14, 16.

52  Phyllis Wheatley, *Poems on Various Subjects, Religious and Moral* (Boston, 1773), 18.

53  Gronniosaw, *Narrative*, 16.

54  Ibid., 16–17.

55  Ibid., 18.

56  Grant Parker, *The Agony of Asar* (Princeton, N.J., 2001), 7–8.

57  Ibid., 8–10.

58  Kwesi Kwaa Prah, *Jacobus Eliza Johannes: A Critical Study of an Eighteenth Century African* (Trenton, N.J., 1992), 37–42; Parker, *Agony of Asar*, 7–17, 104.

59  Parker, *Agony of Asar*, 10.

60  Prah, *Jacobus Eliza Johannes*, 50.

61  Ibid., 48.

62  Ibid., 47.

63  Parker, *Agony of Asar*, 14–16.

64  Michael Gomez, *Exchanging Our Country Marks: The Transformation of African Identities in the Colonial and Antebellum South* (Chapel Hill, N.C., 1998), 112.

65  Quoted in Parker, *Agony of Asar*, 49.

66  Caryl Phillips, *The European Tribe* (Boston, 1987), 7.

67  Ellison, *Invisible Man*, 3.

68  Phillips, *European Tribe*, 121.

69  Ibid., 126.

70  Caryl Phillips, *The Atlantic Sound* (New York, 2000), 176.

71  Caryl Phillips, *Higher Ground* (New York, 1995), 39.

72  Ibid., 22.

73  Phillips, *Atlantic Sound*, 180.

74  Phillips, *Higher Ground*, 24.

75  Ibid., 57.
76  Ibid., 59.
77  Ibid., 60.
78  Caryl Phillips, *Cambridge* (London, 1991), 139.
79  Ibid., 140.
80  Ibid., 143.
81  Ibid., 141.
82  Ibid., 143.
83  Ibid., 144.
84  Ibid., 141.
85  Ibid., 147.
86  Ibid.
87  Ibid., 150.
88  Ibid., 156.

*Studying either early modern or contemporary Ireland as part of the larger Atlantic World readily makes sense. Ideologies and institutions first tried in Ireland were brought by the English into the New World. Moreover, in the wake of the Irish famines, millions left Ireland in the nineteenth century for the United States, and ever since they have remained committed to the politics of both Ireland and Northern Ireland. But can one study Ireland as part of a larger contemporary Catholic Atlantic? Patrick F. McDevitt answers this question in the affirmative by exploring the impact that liberation theology, a quintessentially Latin American cultural product, has had on the Church of Ireland. According to McDevitt, the Irish Church emerged transformed out of its missionary encounter with Latin America in the second half of the twentieth century. Irish priests brought back from Latin America a novel, less hierarchical idea of church organization, one in which lay involvement was encouraged. To the traditional emphasis on "orthodoxy" (the study of theological canon), the Church began to emphasize "orthopraxis" (the living experience of Christ in the poor). Following in the footsteps of Latin American liberation theologians, the Irish Church created new institutions and practices to service the poor. Even television, first introduced in Ireland by the Church, was colored by the pastoral concerns of the newly discovered Latin American theology. Seen from the perspective of discrete cultural exchanges, the Atlantic paradigm remains a viable analytical category for the twentieth century. But can McDevitt's insights be applied to other forms of cultural exchange, such as the impact of Latin American literature and popular music on Europe?*

# Ireland, Latin America, and an Atlantic Liberation Theology

## Patrick F. McDevitt

Both as an institution and as represented by individual clergy, the Roman Catholic Church has exerted a profound influence on the development of the Atlantic World from the earliest days of transatlantic contact. The year after Columbus's first voyage, Pope Alexander VI divided all "undiscovered" lands of the New World between the Spanish and the Portuguese. Catholic priests accompanied many early voyages and blessed the conquerors and their endeavors. Others, most famously Bishop Bartolomé de Las Casas, protested European treatment of the Amerindians and questioned the moral and ethical basis of Spanish exploitation after contact quickly turned to conquest.[1] On the whole, by frequently providing theological justification for conquest, exploitation, and oppression, the Catholic Church has been a major legitimating power in Latin America from the first moments of European expansion. Far from being confined to the early modern period, this influence continues to the present.

Even though the Church frequently sided with the powerful against the weak, the progressive tradition of Las Casas was not extinguished, and segments of the Church dedicated to improving the lot of the poor remained. In the 1960s, as the Church was undergoing a period of self-reflection and institutional change, a theology that stressed action, social justice, and special attention to the interests of the poor was born in Latin America and came to be known as "liberation theology." As a result of interaction between developments in Europe—most important, the reform-oriented Second Vatican Council (hereafter Vatican II)—and the local conditions in Latin America and the Third World, progressive elements within the Latin American Church aligned themselves on the side of the poor, oppressed, and disempowered and against powerful people and institutions that, they argued, fostered conditions of poverty and deprivation.[2] This "popular church," as it has come to be known, criticized both reactionary governments as well as traditionalists within the Church hierarchy for propping up the status quo. For instance, an Irish priest writing from Peru in 1964 argued that the decline of the traditional Church among the peasants of Latin America was a problem of the Church's own making. He wrote, "It must be admitted that the Church is not without blame for the present situation. We do not reap because we did not sow. The apparent indifference about social problems on the part of some bishops in the past and the failure to fight for justice will make sad reading when the history of this continent is written."[3]

Liberation theology may have been a product of Latin America, but its influence was felt far beyond the continent. From Latin American seeds, theologies of liberation that addressed the oppression of other groups—including women, Africans, African Americans, and Asians—grew around the world.[4] The focus of this chapter will be the ways in which liberation theology was received by progressive elements in the Irish Catholic Church. The popular church and its implications for the world beyond Latin America caught the attention of many in the Irish Church and subsequently were the focus of numerous books, pamphlets, documentaries, and conferences in Ireland. Even as overall wealth and standards of living rose in the 1970s, poverty and inequality remained hallmarks of Irish society. Among the many Irish who were dismayed by this, there formed a receptive audience to the ideals of liberation theology. Thus was created a truly Atlantic liberation theology.

## IRELAND AND LATIN AMERICA

Ireland has had a long-standing religious relationship with Latin America through the many Irish missionaries who have worked there for over four centuries. For example, more than two dozen Irish Jesuits were stationed in Latin America between the late sixteenth and late eighteenth centuries. Fr. Thomas Field of Limerick entered the Society of Jesus in 1577 and spent ten years in Brazil before moving to Paraguay, where he established a province of the Society in 1587.[5] These early pioneers were followed by other religious orders, including orders that in the twentieth century would come to be known for their progressive approach, especially the Maryknolls, Jesuits, Columbans, and Capuchins.

Transatlantic contact between Ireland and Latin America was not solely ecclesiastical in nature. For centuries, Irish people have gone to Latin America as merchants, emigrants, and soldiers. *The Southern Cross* of Buenos Aires, an Irish newspaper, was founded in 1875. Irishmen played key roles in the founding and development of the navies of Argentina, Brazil, Chile, Ecuador, and Uruguay. The O'Higgins family was among the most powerful in Chile in the eighteenth and nineteenth centuries, and Don Bernardo O'Higgins was a key figure in Chile's struggle for independence. An Irishwoman named Elisa Lynch was, for a short time, the most powerful woman in Paraguay while she was the mistress of President Francisco Solano Lopez and de facto first lady. Hundreds of Irishmen fought with Bolivar, including his aide-de-camp, an Irishman named Charles Chamberlain. Likewise, Kerryman Arthur Sandes commanded the First Venezuelan Rifles and eventually became of the governor of Cuenca province in Ecuador. Arguably, parallels between the history of Ireland and that of many Latin American countries have created a natural affinity based on the shared histories of being largely agrarian, former colonial states, economically dependent on larger countries, subject to endemic political violence, and dominated by conservative Catholicism.[6]

Historically, the long-standing Irish missionary drive was focused largely on saving souls. In 1958, Pope John XXIII asked religious orders and individual hierarchies in the First World to increase the number of priests they sent to Latin America. In 1960, he wrote specifically to the Irish bishops asking them to allow and encourage Irish diocesan priests to serve in Latin America with the Columban fathers, an Irish missionary order headquartered in Navan, County Meath. These drives to increase the number of

First World priests in the Third World were often as much about fighting the two great bogeymen of Cold War Ireland, communists and Protestants, as they were about what would come to be known as liberation theology. Fr. Thomas Walsh, an Irish priest writing from Athlone, County Westmeath in 1966, argued that it was absolutely essential for Irish priests to go to Latin America because the "Communists have already launched their crusade to capture Latin America, sending millions of dollars yearly in order to win these people over to Communism. They are sending thousands of youths of promise and ability every year for training in leadership in universities behind the Iron Curtain. . . . It is well to note also that the Protestant Churches are not inactive in this religious crisis in Latin America."[7]

Fr. Walsh most likely did not envision so many Irish priests and religious choosing to ally themselves with socialists across Latin America.[8] Even so, in response to the developments of Vatican II and the growth of social justice activism, this mission evolved into one centered on humanitarian ends and political engagement. In the wake of the August 1968 Latin American Bishops Council meeting in Medellín, when the basic tenets of liberation theology were articulated and supported despite strong minority opposition within the conference, a sea change in the lives of foreign missionaries began to occur.[9] In 1971, the Irish Missionary Union reported that more than a third of Irish missions were engaged in full-time development work aimed at improving living standards of the people they served.[10] Richard Keelan, an Irish missionary, argued in 1977 that it was the Church's duty to work for the development of the mass of the population who are poor and that this mission inevitably means conflict with reactionary forces. Keelan wrote,

> The foreign missionary must be trained for that conflict. His training must be for the world in which he has to work: looking back at the years of my own training in the seminary, I see . . . now that we were trained for another order of thing that was even then passing. As a result of such training too many of us foreign missionaries today who want to come to grips with the causes of oppression do not have the background or expertise in human sciences such as economics or sociology to do so. But some at least of the missionaries who come after us will have it.[11]

One might wonder why a region as Catholic as Latin America would need missionaries in the first place. In short, there was a severe shortage of locally born priests. In many countries, such as Guatemala, Nicaragua, Honduras, and Venezuela, to name only a few, there was a very high percentage of foreign-born priests.[12] Furthermore, indigenous priests were often concentrated in cities and at schools that catered to the wealthiest segments of society, leaving few to minister to the many. The relative shortage of priests left those who worked with the poor often overwhelmed and completely occupied with ritual events such as marriages, funerals, and baptisms. Fr. Michael Crowley of the Cork diocese wrote to an Irish Catholic publication from Pueblo Nuevo de Colan, Peru, in 1964. In the diocese of Piura, which had an estimated population of 1 million, there were twelve parishes without any priests whatsoever, and most parishes were understaffed. Accordingly, actual pastoral contact ranged from superficial to nonexistent.[13]

By the middle of the twentieth century, there were growing fears in the Vatican that Latin America's masses could follow the European example and be lost to the Church.

In order to combat this potentiality, Pope Pius XII, in his 1957 encyclical *Fidei Donum* (Gift of Faith), for the first time permitted diocesan priests (as opposed to priests belonging to religious orders) to be placed with missionary congregations in the Third World. As a result, an increasing number of European, including Irish, priests went to Latin America to work with the poorest congregations, which were commonly avoided by those indigenous priests who saw the priesthood as a means of upward mobility.

One such diocesan effort was the Cork Mission to Peru, which was founded in 1961 when Bishop Lucey of Cork responded to a request from Cardinal Cushing of Boston (whose diocese had helped fund the construction of churches in Cork) to send priests to Peru with the Missionary Society of St. James. After three years in the rural provinces, the Cork mission moved to the shantytowns of Trujillo, where churches were built and parishes staffed thanks to the contributions of the parishioners of Cork. The mission was staffed by priests who went for a limited time and then returned home, often bringing with them lessons learned from the Peruvian popular church.[14]

The "option for the poor" is an essential part of liberation theology. The first step toward making a genuine option for the poor was to increase one's contact with them, which is exactly what thousands of religious did, including many priests, brothers, and sisters from Ireland. The less rigid hierarchy and general ethos of the popular church in Latin America was particularly attractive to religious sisters, who were able to engage in more direct pastoral work there than had previously been available to them. In Africa and Asia, running schools and hospitals was still the predominant female missionary activity.[15] In contrast, in light of the severe shortage of priests in dioceses that served the poor, female religious Latin America had unprecedented opportunities to engage directly in pastoral work, such as discussing the Gospels and helping parishioners use their faith to confront the problems they faced in everyday life.

Sharing the conditions of the poor is not, of course, the same as being poor. Adopting the living standards of the people to whom they ministered, whether in Ireland or abroad, taught priests object lessons about their own relative affluence, but it was not the same as actually being poor. In Latin America, this might mean living in spartan conditions with limited modern conveniences; at home, it might mean giving up the car and housekeeper that were traditional perquisites of being a priest in Ireland. First World priests and others had, by dint of their nationality and connections to religious orders, the option of leaving any time they wanted. The poor do not generally have this option. Nonetheless, working with and on behalf of the poor was a dangerous activity. Fr. Peter Lemass, writing home while working as a missionary in Bolivia in 1985, attested that "practically every country of Latin America has its stories of Christian martyrdom over the past twenty years. In Salvador the largest group of murdered people are the catechists. The Bible is a seditious publication there. . . . People who speak out for human rights, or live with the poor are labeled Marxists, and either imprisoned, disappear or are killed."[16]

The essence of liberation theology as it developed in the 1960s was its emphasis on action and the belief that the world was not meant to be as it existed. In other words, the world was thought to be out of sync with the divine plan. For believers, the most striking evidence of this disjuncture was the unremitting poverty in which millions lived. According to the liberation theologians of the 1960s, this poverty and deprivation were the result of institutionalized selfishness, greed, and hence sin. Therefore, they held that the job of Christians was to work to change the political, economic, and social systems that foster inequality and deprivation. It was not enough for the Church to preach the gospel; rather, it must actively involve itself with bringing about change which will end injustice.[17]

Building on Vatican II, liberation theologians saw the Church as having a twofold mission in the world: to spread the message of salvation, but, equally important, "there is the temporal mission of the Church in the world which involves the creation of a better world. As such the temporal mission of the Church should be seen not as some 'additional' or 'extra' role for the Church; rather it is something that is derived intrinsically from the religious mission of the Church."[18] On the whole, the traditional subjects of Catholic theology, such as debates over the transubstantiation of the Eucharist or the hypostatic union in Christ, were absent from the theology of liberation, which instead focused on the Christological questions of how Christian teachings should be enacted in the world. This desertion of the traditional realms of theology, however, led to opposition and criticism and charges of being communists. Lemass commented on this different focus and its consequences: "Latin American theologians seem to be more concerned with orthopraxis than with orthodoxy, and so are accused of engaging in Marxism."[19]

Not surprisingly, since liberation theology was frequently derided by critics as little more than a front for Marxism, it consequently engendered fierce opposition from the right.[20] However, liberation theology generally sought a political position opposed to both liberal individualism and communist collectivism and rather emphasized the primacy of human dignity or, in other words, human rights.[21] Marxist social analysis certainly contributed a great deal to liberation theology's understanding of the world, but liberation theologians steered clear of "Marxist social theory with its materialism, determinism and atheism, i.e., Marxism as such."[22] To be sure, while explicit Marxism may or may not have been embraced, Marxist-inspired dependency theory, which holds that Third World poverty is a structural component of a world capitalist system that enriches the First World while impoverishing the Third, undergirded all liberation theology.[23] Even so, the influential Irish theologian Fr. Dermot A. Lane argued that the Church should be against all absolutes, left or right. He wrote that the "Christian faith must be as adamant in its protest against every left-wing political system which tries to promise heaven on earth as it is of every right-wing political group which tries to give absolute value to the established order. Neither socialism nor capitalism may be regarded as adequate programmes in themselves for the ultimate transformation of man and the world that belongs to Christian faith in the world."[24]

## BRINGING LIBERATION HOME TO IRELAND

Irish missionaries and religious who went abroad did more than simply help those who were less fortunate and minister to underserved flocks; they also went to learn about how the Church might be transformed from one that resided among the elites of society to one that served the needs of the entire communion. Innovative administrative and liturgical developments were brought home and implemented in parishes around Ireland, from the creation of "neighborhood groups" in imitation of the Latin American "base Christian communities" to the establishment of social outreach programs. The poor, of course, did not live only in the Third World. Back home in Ireland, efforts were made by priests and lay groups to increase contact between people of different classes and to facilitate a dialogue so that they could grasp their commonalities and work together to create a more just society. One such program introduced affluent teenagers and inner-city working-class families to one another in an effort to dispel myths of ignorance and mutual misperceptions.[25] As modest as these steps seem in comparison to the revolutionary change being attempted in Latin America, they were still significant attempts at movement in a Church known for its unchanging character.

It was certainly not preordained that Ireland would be as welcoming as it was to a theology favoring the socialist regimes of Latin America, and certainly not every priest or parish in Ireland embraced the liberalizing trend. As the most conservative of the European churches, the Irish Catholic Church fought against the "godless communism" of the Soviet Union. In preconciliar days, the main preoccupations of the Church in Ireland were defensive—warding off trends, actions, and thoughts that were deemed subversive to the Catholic status quo, including most of the modern world, save capitalism. Much of that mind-set remained in Ireland through the 1960s and 1970s; at the highest levels, the Irish Church retained its conservative character. The archbishop of Dublin, John Charles McQuaid, was described by one biographer as the "ruler of Catholic Ireland" and dominated the Irish Church for more than three decades before his retirement in 1971.[26] Still, it had long been a point of pride for the Irish that the country sent so many priests and religious to the missions. When those people returned to Ireland with plans and schemes to invigorate the Irish Church, there was a reservoir of goodwill and respect on which they could draw.[27]

The changing missionary culture had a ripple effect on the Church in Ireland as missionaries visited home on leave and on fund-raising trips and corresponded with home congregations and colleagues. One of the key elements in liberation theology was a reversal of the top-down hierarchy of the traditional Church and the encouragement of lay participation. It was this sort of endeavor rather than any explicitly revolutionary ideal that influenced the Irish Church. Just as the Latin American bishops had taken the spirit of Vatican II as the impetus to rethink their own pastoral mission in light of local conditions, so did many Irish priests take the example of Latin America to rethink how they organized their parishes. Likewise, returning missionaries used the model of the popular Church they had witnessed in Latin America to invigorate an Irish Church that was strong on ritual observance but somewhat weaker on actively living the gospel. Irish Jesuit Fr. Michael O'Sullivan organized the first conference in Ireland on liberation theology in 1976, about which he stated, "We saw in Latin America how to be a Church relevant to reality, to have an option for the poor and a thrust for social justice."[28]

For example, Fr. Christy Mangan had for sixteen years been secretary to Archbishop John Charles McQuaid before spending three years in the early 1970s with the Columban fathers in Chile. On returning to Ireland and taking over a parish in the seaside Dublin suburb of Dun Laoghaire, he encouraged the creation of "neighborhood groups" in imitation of the base Christian communities of Latin America. Some groups simply trained catechists for the parish, while others aimed to be something broader. They offered forums where people who might not otherwise converse freely with one another, because of class differences for example, could meet to discuss not religion per se but rather their lives and communities. These groups also took over much of the running of the parish that normally would have been in the care of the parish priest, thus freeing him to attend to more pastoral and spiritual matters while simultaneously lessening the traditional opacity of the workings of the Church.[29] These efforts were emblematic of many parishes around the country where priests who had had contact with the Church in Latin America sought to import changes into Ireland, a reverse mission if you will.

Tony Brown, a member of the Irish Commission for Justice and Peace, a Catholic body, argued that there was an intimate connection between working for justice in Ireland and the rest of the world while recognizing that poverty and lack of opportunity were relative concepts. Brown wrote, "Justice is an indivisible concept and we must be true to its imperatives whether we are considering the situation in Ireland—North or South—or in the developing countries of the Third World. Our mission must be to the whole world. The issues arising in looking at justice at home are the same as those involved in international justice, even though the scale may be different."[30] Many of the same problems that missionaries had encountered in Latin America—such as the acceptance of exploitation as either natural or caused by the victims of poverty—were also experienced by kindred spirits in Ireland. One of the difficulties for progressive Irish priests was trying to translate the spirit of liberation theology, the necessity of which was strikingly obvious to First World visitors to the slums and shantytowns of the Third World, to the Ireland of the 1970s and 1980s. Fr. John McCormack, for example, who served as the curate in the Cathedral of Christ the King, Mullingar, argued in 1966 that choosing the "option for the poor" was not just something that was to be done in the Third World. Rather, for McCormack, "when the Bible speaks of the poor it includes all who are deprived in one way or another—those who have no money, the sick, the illiterate, the unfortunate, the timid, those who are persecuted, those without influence in the world."[31]

Likewise, the Irish theologian Dermot A. Lane wrote that there was an "underlying harmony and unity" that "exists between liberation and salvation, progress and evangelization, and the historical struggle for justice and the kingdom of God." Lane contended that central to this dual mission (of liberation and salvation) was "development education." For Lane—and for the trustees of Trócaire (the development agency of the Catholic Church in Ireland) and the Irish Commission for Justice and Peace who supported him—it was essential that development education "deals with *world development* and not just the development of the third world." He continued, "Without such a unified approach there is always the possibility that development in one part of the world may give rise to underdevelopment in another part of the world."[32] Similarly, Fr. Frank Purcell, an Australian Columban father writing in the highly influential Irish Catholic journal *The Furrow*, argued, "It seems to me that it is not enough for the Church and her missionaries to work against world poverty and injustice in the Third World alone. Some of the principal obstacles to the full liberation of men through Christ are to be found, not in the developing countries themselves, but in the very countries from which missionaries have set out."[33] This was one of the challenges that many progressives in the Irish Church faced: how to reach a population that was itself just emerging from widespread poverty and was still substantially poorer than its European neighbors.

Bishop Cahal B. Daly, bishop of Down and Conor, urged Irish Catholics to fight the apathetic impulse to do nothing in the face of poverty. Daly reasoned that the biblical statement that the poor will always be here should not be taken out of context to mean that one should not work to alleviate poverty or that the poor should fatalistically accept their lot. According to the bishop, "The clear message of the Gospels is that in the Palestine of the time of Jesus many people were poor while a few were rich; but that Jesus identified himself with the poor and called upon his disciples to do the same."[34] Expounding on themes that are central to liberation theology, Daly acknowledged the specificity of the local historical example while maintaining the absolute primacy of human dignity based on the absence of material destitution. While recognizing that poverty is a relative measure that changes from place to place and from time to time, he still noted that even in Ireland there were people who were absolutely poor in the sense that they did not have sufficient food to eat, fuel to keep warm, appropriate accommodation, or educational opportunities. All these things, he argued, conspired to deny them their basic human dignity.

Daly contended that focusing on the poor was a natural position for the Irish Church to take. In fact, "the Church in Ireland has historically been a Church of the poor rather than a Church of the rich."[35] For Daly and other progressive bishops in the Irish hierarchy, choosing the option for the poor was not simply the theologically correct path to follow but a necessary one if the Irish Church was not going to suffer the same fate as other European churches and lose the allegiance of most of the working classes. "The credibility of the Church will increasingly depend in the future on her relevance to the problems of poverty and on the clarity and courage of her proclamation of social justice and her effectiveness in working for a more just society."[36]

Perhaps the most high-profile interaction between the ideals of liberation theology and Ireland is to be found in the long-running television documentary series Radharc (the term is Irish for "view" or "perspective"). Ironically, Radharc, which became something of a megaphone for progressive Catholic views, grew out of an initiative of Archbishop McQuaid, frequently considered to be among the staunchest conservative and antireform clerics at Vatican II. The archbishop decided in the late 1950s, several years before there was local television in Ireland, that when the new media did arrive, the Church ought to have priests who were knowledgeable about television production. He therefore sent a small number of young priests, beginning with Frs. Joseph Dunn and Desmond Forristal, to the United States and England to learn the trade. This small investment was followed by the purchase of cameras and sound equipment and the injunction that they should create short films dealing with religious issues in their spare time. What developed was an independent, self-financing film company comprised largely of priests but including some lay workers who filled the need of the nascent Irish Television Service RTÉ (Radio Telefís Éireann) for inexpensive and local programs.

Radharc's purview was religious programming, but they forged their own model by addressing religious questions through investigative reporting about individuals of interest. This personalized approach gave a human face to what were essentially didactic programs. The show quickly found an audience and remained a staple of Irish television for more than two decades. Their concentration on local events was soon superseded by many trips abroad. Beginning with the inaugural overseas film, a study of Irish chaplaincies for Irish immigrants in England, Radharc films were heavily weighted in the direction of social welfare and social justice. England was soon followed by Africa, Latin America, and Asia. Over the course of the next twenty-five years, Radharc covered issues that bore directly on liberation theology and the direction of the Church. In thirty documentaries made in Latin America and the Caribbean, the filmmakers of Radharc brought figures such as Archbishop Camara, Archbishop Romero, Fidel Castro, and Jean-Bertrand Aristide to Irish television screens. They addressed human rights abuses and the dirty war in Argentina, U.S. policy in support of right-wing authoritarian regimes, and the rise of the Sandinistas in Nicaragua.[37] Hence, the Irish public was consistently exposed to some of the most radical and cutting-edge issues in the Catholic Church, brought to them by trusted faces with Irish accents.

Typical of the open-minded and progressive worldview embodied in the Radharc mission is an article that Fr. Peter Lemass, one of the main interviewers for the series, wrote for *The Furrow* about a trip to Cuba that resulted in two Radharc programs.[38] Like many Irish adherents of liberation theology, Lemass saw Castro's Marxist interpretation of Third World problems as largely accurate. Lemass called the book Castro wrote when president of the nonaligned countries movement as "an impressive document, the best statement I have seen of the problems of the Third World."[39] In fact, all things considered, Lemass concluded that "the poor are certainly better off since the Revolution in Cuba."[40] While recognizing that communist Cuba enforced indefensible limitations on speech and political dissent and deploring the official atheism of the regime, Lemass also commented on the successes of the revolution: the relative lack of absolute poverty and illiteracy, the best health care for the common person and the lowest infant mortality rate in Latin America, and the greater independence of women in Cuban society. Part of the blame for the sad state of the Church in Cuba was placed firmly at the feet of the Church itself for refusing to reconcile itself with Castro's imperfect regime. He commented that priests in Cuba hoped for some relaxation of the Vatican's unbending opposition to Marxist regimes: "These men regret that so often the Catholic Church is so negative when she speaks about Marxism, without giving any credit for the generosity and self-sacrifice of many Marxists, or recognizing the real advances that a Marxist country like Cuba has made."[41] He even included Castro's claim of admiration for Jesus: "In my opinion Christ was a great revolutionary . . . he condemned the rich, the merchants and the Pharisees with very strong words. He washed the feet of his disciples. What worthier example can one find?"[42]

Tellingly, Lemass compared the shortcomings of the Castro regime with those of traditional Church institutions. In discussing the lack of freedom of the press, he lamented that in the papers "there is no space for disagreement, no room for criticism. It is like working as a priest in a diocese where all the official statements are of growth and development, yet you can see around you many human problems. To speak out would be spitting against the wind. In many ways Marxism reminds me of the Church. The reaction to criticism is one of hurt surprise. 'Can't you see the size of the problem? So how can you say these things? Better roll up your sleeves and help us.'"[43] In the end, Lemass hoped that the atheistic nature of Castro's revolution, which he blamed on the Church's failure to engage the regime, would serve as an object lesson for future dealings in Nicaragua where the Sandinistas hoped to create a socialism that was based equally on Marx and the Gospels. "If the Church had been more perceptive, and more sympathetic to the worthier aims of the Revolution, then the Cuban brand of Marxism could have been Christian."[44]

As noted previously, Radharc did not limit itself to Latin America and pursued similar stories in Africa, Asia, and the Pacific. Given the near-universal presence of Irish missionaries, there was almost always a local angle that could be used to get at larger, more global issues. Their cameras also were turned critically on problems at home, including, among others, the plight of young offenders in Irish prisons, homeless people in Dublin, the Irish seminary system, the religious life of Irish prostitutes, the finances of parishes, Northern Ireland, gender in the Church, drug abuse, alcoholism, inner-city life in Dublin, divorce, and unemployment. It is important to remember that at any point these priest-filmmakers could have been silenced with a simple order. They had taken a vow of obedience, and if their bishop had ordered them to cease, their only alternative would have been to leave the priesthood. Liberation theology and a desire to remake the Church in a more egalitarian mode was a prominent yet minority opinion within the Church as a whole. So, the absence of a such an order is indicative of an acceptance of multiple viewpoints in the Irish Church despite a continuing reputation for monolithic conservatism.

One thing that could not be done, of course, was to directly question the Irish hierarchy. However, the implied applicability of many of the foreign reforms was certainly not lost on the Irish public. One reviewer of a film about a meeting of Brazilian bishops titled "The Men are Dangerous" concluded by saying, "I think it would not be overstating the matter one whit to say that Radharc went to Brazil to show us Ireland."[45] Nor was Radharc alone in using references to Latin America to criticize Ireland. In 1965, Fr. Dermot Carthy, a Columban father writing from Peru, stated that "the Latin Americans are not yet hostile to the Church. They have a great amount of goodwill but little else. It is tragic to see this goodwill being frittered away on building hilltop crosses and on wayside chapels and on endurance-test processions."[46] Those familiar with the preconciliar Irish Church recognize the implied criticism of Ireland in that remark since building hilltop crosses and wayside chapels and participating in long processions were quintessential activities of Irish Catholics in the 1950s.

The most infamous Church–state clash in postwar Irish history was the conflict in 1951 over the Mother and Child Scheme advocated by the minister of health, Dr. Noel Browne. The scheme would have provided for free universal healthcare for mothers and children up to sixteen years of age but was roundly denounced by the Irish bishops and consequently withdrawn by the interparty government led by Taoiseach John A. Costello. The scheme quickly became a shorthand way of pointing out both the conservative nature of Irish Catholicism and the undue influence that the hierarchy exerted in Irish politics and society.[47] It is also seen as indicative of just how out of step Ireland was with the rest of western Europe that was by that time embracing the welfare state. In the two and a half decades that followed the Mother and Child controversy, Ireland has adopted a standard European-style, welfare-state model and has produced numerous groups that have organized to lobby the government to limit the gap between the rich and poor in Ireland. This lobbying has often taken as its basis the social justice rhetoric of liberation theology.[48]

While there is not the same historical connection between Ireland and Latin America as there is between Ireland and the United States or the United Kingdom, the Irish people have taken a deep and prolonged interest in the region, not least because of the widespread contact engendered by missionaries. Irish nongovernmental organizations have been especially active in Latin America, as has Trócaire, whose annual Lenten fund-raising drive is as much of an institution as the Salvation Army bell ringers in the

United States at Christmastime. Richard Quinn, a Holy Ghost father, argued that the good work of Irish missionaries need not be carried out by missionaries at all. In an article titled "Time for an Irish Peace Corps?" Quinn contended that "as development workers are welcome, Irish development workers will be welcome. Their motivation will be less suspect than that of their colleagues from expansionist trading nations, or from those with a colonial past."[49] The long reign of the conservative Pope John Paul II, a stern opponent of socialism in all its forms and defender of conservative Catholic social teachings, had the effect of limiting the effectiveness of the progressive wing of the Church in Ireland, but it did not lessen Ireland's interest in and concern for the Third World and social justice in general, which is in some ways the intellectual and spiritual offspring of the Latin American theology of liberation. These exchanges of ideas and individuals are as important for understanding the culture of the Atlantic World in the past forty years as earlier exchanges are for the early modern period. They are also a key way in which an increasingly affluent Irish society made sense of its changing position in Europe and the world.

Fr. Niall O'Brien, a Columban father who had spent nearly four decades in the Philippines working with poor sugarcane workers, died in 2004. O'Brien became an internationally known figure when he was jailed along with eight others by the Marcos regime on trumped-up murder charges in the 1980s. He received a hero's welcome when he was released from jail and spent his time in Ireland writing about the plight of the poor and how liberation theology offered a road map for improving the world.[50] Ordained in 1963 and sent to the Philippines the following year, O'Brien came to symbolize the extraordinary efforts of Irish religious abroad who have dedicated their lives to teaching the social aspects of the Gospels and helping the world's poor. Although the Irish Church at the end of millennium has been severely shaken by abuse scandals and falling attendance, the good works carried out in the name of liberation theology remain a bright spot for Irish Catholics, as illustrated by the national mourning of O'Brien's death.

In conclusion, the effect of liberation theology on Ireland has been as mixed as its effect in Latin America. Catholic conservatives, whether clerical or lay, did not simply hand over the keys of the churches to radical critics who wished to remake the Church in their own images. However, neither has liberation theology been just a passing fad, as was widely predicted in the years of its infancy. Consistent with its goal of engaging the outside world, liberation theology and those inspired by it have continued to challenge the affluent of the First and Third Worlds to confront the crippling poverty and inequity that remain so prevalent today.[51]

## Notes

1    Juan Friede and Benjamin Keen, eds., *Bartolome De Las Casas in History: Toward an Understanding of the Man and His Work* (DeKalb, Ill., 1971).

2    Gustavo Gutiérrez, *A Theology of Liberation: History, Politics, and Salvation*, rev. ed., trans. Caridad Inda and John Eagleson (Maryknoll, N.Y., 1999); Leonardo Boff and Clodovis Boff, *Introducing Liberation Theology* (Maryknoll, N.Y., 1987); Phillip Berryman, *Liberation Theology: Essential Facts about the Revolutionary Movement in Latin America and Beyond* (Philadelphia, 1987).

3    Michael Crowley, "Writing from Pueblo Nuevo de Colan, Piura, Peru," *The Furrow* 15, no. 6 (June 1964): 414.

4    Alfred T. Hennelly, S.J., *Liberation Theologies: The Global Pursuit of Justice* (Mystic, Conn., 1995); Paul Surlis, "Medellin: Ten Years Later," *The Furrow* 29, no. 10 (November 1978): 689–94.

5    Peadar Kirby, *Ireland and Latin America: Links and Lessons* (Blackrock, 1992), 81–82.

6    For the story of Elisa Lynch, see Sian Rees, *The Shadows of Elisa Lynch: How a Nineteenth Century Irish Courtesan Became the Most Powerful Woman in Paraguay* (London, 2003). See also Kirby, *Ireland and Latin America*, for a general historical account of connections between Ireland and Latin America.

7    Thomas Walsh, "Writing from Tobberclair, Athlone, Co. Westmeath," *The Furrow* 17, no. 3 (March 1966): 198–99.

8    For a generally sympathetic account of Fidel Castro's Cuba by an Irish priest, see Peter Lemass, "Fidel Castro's Cuba," *The Furrow* 36, no. 6 (June 1985): 365–75.

9    In Spanish, the Council is called the *Consejo Episcopal Latinoamericano* and is often referred to by its acronym, CELAM.

10   Frank Purcell, "Missionaries and the Problem of World Justice," *The Furrow* 23, no. 4 (April 1972): 206.

11   Richard Keelan, "On Being a Foreign Missionary," *The Furrow* 28, no. 9 (September 1977): 574.

12   Berryman, *Liberation Theology*, 11–12.

13   Michael Crowley, "Writing from Pueblo Nuevo de Colan," 413.

14   Kirby, *Ireland and Latin America*, 139–41.

15   Ibid., 137–38.

16   Peter Lemass, "Liberation Theology," *The Furrow* 36, no. 1 (January 1985): 22–23.

17   Dermot Lane, ed., *Ireland, Liberation and Theology* (Maryknoll, N.Y., 1977), 9–13.

18   Dermot A. Lane, "Faith and Politics," *The Furrow* 24, no. 6 (June 1973): 329–30.

19   Peter Lemass, "Theology for Lay People," *The Furrow* 37, no. 6 (June 1986): 400.

20   For a discussion of the relationship between Marxism and liberation theology, see Edward A. Lynch, *Religion and Politics in Latin America: Liberation Theology and Christian Democracy* (New York, 1991), 3–34, and Michael Novack, *Will It Liberate? Questions about Liberation Theology* (New York, 1986), 13–32, 165–70.

21   Dermot Keogh, *Church and Politics in Latin America* (New York, 1990), 18.

22   William Cosgrave, *Liberation Theology* (Dublin, 1987), 11.

23   The most influential work on dependency theory was André Gunder Frank, *Capitalism and Underdevelopment in Latin America: Historical Studies of Chile and Brazil* (New York, 1967).

24   Lane, "Faith and Politics," 335.

25   Paul Lavelle and Peter Lemass, eds., *The Urban Plunge: Meeting the Challenge of a Divided City* (Dublin, 1988).

26   John Feeney, *John Charles McQuaid: The Man and the Mask* (Dublin, 1974); John Cooney, *John Charles McQuaid: Ruler of Catholic Ireland* (Dublin, 1999).

27   Louise Fuller, *Irish Catholicism since 1950: The Undoing of a Culture* (Dublin, 2002), 213–25.

28   Kirby, *Ireland and Latin America*, 143.

29   Fr. Mangan's story was told on the television series Radharc in the episode "Return Ticket to Chile" (originally aired October 12, 1982 on RTÉ).

30   Tony Brown "Working for Justice," *The Furrow* 29, no. 10 (October 1978): 618–19.

31   John McCormack, "The Church of the Poor," *The Furrow* 17, no. 4 (April 1966): 213.

32  Dermot A. Lane, "Education for World Development," *The Furrow* 29, no. 10 (November 1978): 709–10.

33  Frank Purcell, "Missionaries and the Problem of World Justice," *The Furrow* 23, no. 4 (April 1972): 206.

34  Cahal B. Daly, "The Poor You Have Always With You . . . ," *The Furrow* 36, no. 2 (February 1985): 71.

35  Ibid., 73.

36  Ibid.

37  For a comprehensive insider account, see Radharc cofounder Joseph Dunn's three books on the subject: *No Tigers in Africa: Recollections and Reflections on 25 Years of Radharc* (Blackrock, 1986), *No Lions in the Hierarchy: An Anthology of Sorts* (Blackrock, 1994), and *No Vipers in the Vatican: A Second Anthology of Sorts* (Blackrock, 1996).

38  Lemass, "Fidel Castro's Cuba," 365–75. The two programs that came out of this trip were titled "Here There Is No Christmas: Church and Revolution in Cuba Conflict" (first aired February 2, 1986) and "Cuba—Land of Hope and Glory: Achievements and Problems" (March 6, 1986).

39  Lemass, "Fidel Castro's Cuba," 366.

40  Ibid., 370.

41  Ibid.

42  Ibid., 366.

43  Ibid., 372.

44  Ibid., 374.

45  Tom O'Dea, quoted in Dunn, *No Tigers in Africa*, 68.

46  Dermot Carthy, "Writing from Parroquia Nuestra Senora Del Rosario, Tahauntinsuyo, Peru," *The Furrow* 16, no. 3 (March 1965): 169.

47  Fuller, *Irish Catholicism*, xiiii, 74–78, 85, 231.

48  See Sean Healy and Brigid Reynolds, "Christian Critique of Economic Policy and Practice," in *Religion and Politics in Ireland at the Turn of the Millennium*, ed. James P. Mackey and Enda McDonagh (Blackrock, 2003), 185–97.

49  Richard Quinn, "Time for an Irish Peace Corps?" *The Furrow* 25, no. 10 (October 1974): 551.

50  Niall O'Brien, *Revolution from the Heart* (New York, 1987), and *Island of Tears, Island of Hope: Living the Gospel in a Revolutionary Situation* (Maryknoll, N.Y., 1993).

51  For tremendous examples of mature liberation theology in action, see Paul Farmer, *Pathologies of Power: Health, Human Rights, and the New War on the Poor* (Berkeley, Calif., 2005), and Tracy Kidder, *Mountains beyond Mountains: Healing the World: The Quest of Dr. Paul Farmer* (New York, 2003).

# INDEX

## A

Abdala, Gaudar ben, 155
abolition, 129, 211, 212, 213
Adair, James, 70
Adelman, Jeremy, 61
Africa, 2, 12, 53, 119, 129–44, 181,
    195, 224, 227, 229–31
  historiography of, 12, 131–32
  images of, 1, 228
  slavery in, 140–43
African Americans, xviii, 130, 139,
    186, 204, 228
  religion of, 12, 39–40
African diasporas, 3, 38, 129–44
Ahmad, Mulay, 158
alcohol, 68, 105
Algiers, 155
Alibamon Mingo, 67, 68
Ambar, Malik, 136
American Indian Movement, xxiv
American Revolution, xx, 204, 206
Amsterdam, 40
anarchists, 192–93
Annales School, 5, 112
Antinomian Controversy, 30
Arabs, 79, 80, 86, 114, 116
archipelagos, 162, 164–66
Argentina, 185–86, 195, 247
  blacks in, 139, 202
Arkansas, 123–24
Armitage, David, 7, 113, 151, 152
Aron, Stephen, 61
Ashkenazic Jews, 40
Asia, 93, 94, 97, 102–3, 111–24
  immigrants from, 172–73, 184, 210
  missionaries in, xix, 13–16
Atlantic Ocean, ix–x, 77–87
Atlantic paradigm, 2, 3, 163, 178
  and global history, xvii–xxi, 13–16, 93–94,
    111–13, 163–64, 195, 214
  definition of, xxiii
  shortcomings of, x, 92, 110, 112–13, 128,
    129–32, 149

Atlantic World, 3, 61–62, 149, 163, 179–95,
    199–201, 238, 240
  hybridity in, 61, 221
  in early modern period, 3–19, 21–34, 39–56
  in modern period, 179–95, 199–214, 239–48
  nation-based, ix, xxiv, 2, 34, 38, 39, 56
  trade in, 3, 149, 185–86
Austen, Ralph, 134
Axtell, James, 11
Aztecs, 23–24

## B

Bailyn, Bernard, 112
Barbados, 40–41, 43, 44, 198, 201
Beckert, Sven, 120
Bengal, 104, 120–22
Bentley, Jerry, 113
Bianco, André, 85
Bienville, Jean Baptist le Moyne de, 63–67, 69, 70
Black Atlantic, xx, xxiv, 39, 128, 139, 219–34
"Black Legend," 157
Blanchard, Peter, 208–9
Bolívar, Simón, 208, 209
Bond, Edward L., 22
borderlands, 61–62
Boxer, Charles, 3
Braddick, Michael, 154, 156, 157
Braudel, Fernand, 132, 133, 150–51, 152, 157
Brazil, 95, 103, 173, 186, 188, 207, 209
  blacks in, 202
  rice in, 119, 123
  slavery in, 201, 203, 209
  sugar in, 104
brazilwood, 104
British Atlantic, 21, 35, 41–50, 149–59, 224–29
British Empire, 104, 120, 149–59, 226
Brown, Peter, 13
Buddhism, 98–99
Buenos Aires, 185, 188–89, 195, 240
  Afro-Argentines in, 139
burial, 44–45, 51, 230
Burma, 111, 124
Bynum, Caroline Walker, 26